Supply Chain Strategies

Supply Chain Strategies

Customer-driven and customer-focused

Tony Hines

ELSEVIER
BUTTERWORTH
HEINEMANN

AMSTERDAM • BOSTON • HEIDELBERG • LONDON • NEW YORK • OXFORD
PARIS • SAN DIEGO • SAN FRANCISCO • SINGAPORE • SYDNEY • TOKYO

Butterworth-Heinemann is an imprint of Elsevier
Linacre House, Jordan Hill, Oxford OX2 8DP, UK
30 Corporate Drive, Suite 400, Burlington, MA 01803, USA

First edition 2004
Reprinted 2006

British Library Cataloguing in Publication Data
A catalogue record for this book is available from the British Library

Library of Congress Cataloging-in-Publication Data
A catalog record for this book is available from the Library of Congress

ISBN–13: 978-0-7506-5551-4
ISBN–10: 0-7506-5551-8

For information on all Butterworth-Heinemann publications
visit our website at books.elsevier.com

Printed and bound in *The Netherlands*

06 07 08 09 10 10 9 8 7 6 5 4 3 2

Contents

Dedication

I would like to dedicate this book to my parents for all their help, support and encouragement in my formative years. Particularly in memory of my Mother, who taught me to listen, think and respond, in that order, an approach that has served me well in life.

Finally, I would like to thank Janice for all her support, encouragement and forbearance in allowing me to pursue this work in her time.

Preface

This book is essentially about supply chain strategies and strategic management of supply chains. It differs from most recent books on the topic because it turns the focus away from purely operational aspects of supply towards strategies that focus upon the customers, their requirements and supply chain imperatives. There has been much discussion about terminology in the literature. Should it be a chain or is it a network? Is it a supply chain or is it a demand chain? Nevertheless, the title is correct in the sense that managers, academics and students have begun to understand conceptually the subject matter of the text in terms of supply chains. It makes sense therefore not to introduce a new terminology. The book is about supply chains, which are customer-focused and customer-driven. It is essentially a strategic and market-driven approach to the study of this topic rather than an operational, purchasing or supply-based view. Nevertheless, it recognizes that the origins have come from an eclectic set of underpinning disciplines with a major contribution from the purchasing and operations management literature. Whilst these contributions are important, their focus and concerns were in many respects different from the major concerns of this text, which primarily focus on how supply chains can be organized effectively and efficiently to satisfy the market and customer demand.

> The successful organization of the future will be customer-focused not product or technology focused, supported by a marketing information competence that links the voice of the customer to all the firm's value-delivery processes. (Webster, 1997)

All organizations have a supply chain. Whether or not the organization manufactures or supplies goods and services there is a supply chain. This is a route that these goods and services take to their market. There are many debates as to whether or not the terms 'supply chain' or 'supply networks' better describe the approach and this is debated in the text along with a variety of other alternatives. Nevertheless, this text has chosen the language in common usage by managers, which is 'supply chains'. The value of the text is its focus on the customer as a driver and focal point for all activities within the supply chain, a point that is sometimes omitted from many academic papers, practitioner articles and books that purport to be about some aspect of supply chain management. This book redresses the imbalance of these internally focused approaches and opens up the debate about what it means in contemporary organizations throughout the world to manage their supply chains and to formulate supply chain strategies. This book is not focused in a single discipline. It acknowledges that in business different perspectives are required but that ultimately it is the customer that determines the future of all business activity within an economic system.

Reference

Webster, F. E. (1997). The future role of marketing in the organization. In Lehman, D. R. and Jocz, K. E. (eds), *Reflections on the Future of Marketing*. Cambridge MA: Marketing Science Institute.

Chapter 1

Globalization – global markets and global supply strategies

LEARNING OUTCOMES

After reading this chapter you should:

- be aware of the impact that globalization is having upon world consumption and production;
- know that not everybody agrees that globalization is of benefit to all people in the world economy;
- be able to define globalization as a phenomenon and recognize the key drivers of change in the global economy;
- be aware of the political and regulatory environments in which organizations operate and their impact upon supply chain strategies;
- know the risks involved in sourcing and procuring suppliers and supplies from different parts of the globe;
- know the impact of new technologies and innovation, and how these developments impact upon supply chain strategies.

Introduction

The aim of this text is to develop a different approach to the study of organizational supply chains by shifting the terrain from the usual field of purchasing/operations towards a more strategic approach focusing upon customer-driven and customer-focused strategies for managing supply chains. Taking a strategic approach involves direction setting, establishing an agenda for change and allocating resources effectively whilst simultaneously utilizing resources efficiently. To achieve these strategic objectives it is essential that organizations focus their supply chain activities to satisfy customers. Managers need to think differently about what they do and the purpose of the organization and organizational networks in satisfying demand through effective (strategic) and efficient (operational) supply chain structures, relationships and strategies. Operational thinking is pervasive in most organizations. Indeed this should come as no surprise since most managers are promoted to positions demanding strategic thinking and strategic skill from positions demanding different, important operational thinking and skill sets. In such circumstances the tendency is often to retain operational thinking without recognizing the shift required in their new roles to think strategically. The ability to think strategically and translate that thinking into operational activities likely to work in practice is an important competence for strategic development to be successful. Those managers who can successfully make the transition from operational to strategic thinkers are a very powerful force for their organization.

The shift in focus from operational to strategic is illustrated as follows:

From: Operational focus	To: Strategic focus
Immediate time frames	Medium to longer term time horizons
Concrete	Conceptual
Action/activities/doing	Think, reflect and learn before any action taken
Reactive/problem-solving 'fire-fighting'	Proactive/identify future opportunities
Routine 'day-to-day'	Future development and change programmes
Production/service processes	Viewing the total supply chain from the customer's perspective
Viewing supply as a production problem	Viewing supply as a customer issue – a market problem
Resource utilization – efficiency focus	Resource (including competence) development, planning and acquisition – effectiveness focus
Operational efficiency	Strategic effectiveness
'Hands-on' approach	'Hands-off' approach
'Feet on the ground'	'Hellicopter view' or 'view from the bridge'

Schonberger (1990) was one of the first to recognize that building a chain of customers was perhaps more important conceptually than thinking in terms of operational supply chains. The idea of turning attention towards a customer focus turns supply push perspectives into demand-led strategy. More recently Pratt (2001), a former Chairman of the Chartered Institute of Marketing, stated in his 'Platform' p. 5 'Marketing Business'.

Supply chain management is perceived to be the province of the purchasing profession, the logistics department or the IT function, but it's about time that marketers woke up to the fact that they may be looking down the wrong end of the telescope.

In many respects this is an important statement since it recognizes that supply chain management is not a functional activity. Not wishing to alienate any particular group of professional managers interested in supply chain strategies it is perhaps important to emphasize that supply chain management is an organizational and trans-organizational responsibility. It should not be viewed as a function or a functional activity belonging to any particular professional discipline.

The major business challenges for organizations developing supply chain strategies include developing capabilities to manage: *value, volume volatility, velocity, variety, variability, visibility* and *virtuality*. In order to do so, organizations need to look at the ways in which they interact with customers at every level and view these challenges from a customer perspective. Customers expect value and suppliers need to anticipate and identify what customers value in order to supply a bundle of goods and services that equate with value in order to exchange money for products. Value in exchange, use and over time may be important to the customer. This is the value challenge. Customers nowadays are seldom prepared to purchase quantities suppliers would like to supply, at a time determined by the supplier, in standard form, with non-standard performance a highly probable outcome. This perhaps best describes a hitherto mass-production era. Today's customer is more demanding in every sense. Meeting the demands of customers when required by ensuring that capacity can be increased when demand is high and lowered when demand is lowered without incurring excessive or unnecessary cost is the volume volatility challenge. Velocity is recognition that speed of response has become an important competitive advantage in many commercial contexts. Variety is a recognition that customer requirements vary and suppliers need to be capable of customizing products and services as a consequence. Variety is also what drives customers by introducing new products and services; by being able to anticipate customer demand. Variability is the challenge of management control in ensuring that goods and services satisfy quality criteria and deliver the required standard for customer satisfaction. Visibility is a core capability for managing the total supply chain from source to consumer. Visibility or transparency ensures that parties within the total supply chain know what the current pipeline looks like. Information and communication technology has allowed organizations to view frequently status reports on sourcing, procurement, production, logistics and customer demand ensuring that there are no blockages, unnecessary inventories or unplanned cost build up. Integration of systems, policies and procedures across organizational boundaries between organizations working together within a supply chain to satisfy the customer has been the catalyst for visibility whilst technology provided the means. 'Virtuality' has allowed organizations to replace inventory with information through the creation of digital supply chains supported by ICT. Organizations need to focus their attention on customers by creating capabilities that deliver market-driven supply chain strategies.

Supply chain strategies must be responsive to customer requirements and in that sense organizations need to develop sustainable strategies, offering service to the customer, with speedy responses, suited to the customer, at a standard quality supported by systems, structures and relationships that deliver customer satisfaction.

From: Business challenges – seven V's that customers want	To: Supply chain strategies – seven S's that deliver organizational strategies
Value – offer customers value for money based on their preferences. Value not simply in exchange but through time and use	*Sustainability* – must offer customers' consistent value. For example, based on their preferences for time, place, cost, flexibility, dependability and quality. Must identify order qualifiers and order winners and compete managing complexity
Volume volatility – customers want to postpone their own supplies until they have a 'best forecast' of demand or accurate demand based on actual sales data. This may mean adjusting order quantities on a regular basis. They are no longer prepared to place standard order volumes in many sectors because their own market demand is volatile	*Service* – the ability to deliver different quantities of goods through managing capacity not simply operationally but strategically (no longer sufficient to rely on economies of scale). Develop capabilities to manage capacity flexibly to deliver products and services to customers when they are required in the quantities demanded, e.g. from mass production to mass customization (from n to 1)
Velocity – speed of change and speed of response (demand conditions, market structures, production technology, supplier capabilities)	*Speedy response* – developing responsive capabilities to deliver goods and services when they are required, e.g. efficient consumer response, quick response
Variety – ability to customize the product/service offer (move from economies of scale to economies of scope or to 'economies of value to customer')	*Suited to customer requirements* – developing flexibility capabilities – e.g. agile, lean supply chains, innovations and new product developments
Variability – ability to reduce variabiity and offer standard quality	*Standards* – developing supply chain strategies to assure customer quality standards are met effectively and co-operate within supply chains to compete across supply chains

Visibility – enabling all parts of a supply chain to be transparent and avoid blockages, 'iceberg' inventories and hidden costs; keeping the customer informed

Systems focused on customer satisfaction – re-design business processes and develop enabling strategies for all relevant parties including customers to view supply chain information relevant to them (e.g. collaborative, co-operative rather than competitive strategies)

Virtuality – an ability to coordinate intangible and tangible assets within the supply chain facilitated by information and communication technologies gives customers confidence and ensures dependability

Structures and relationships – for example, develop digital supply chain strategies to replace unnecessary inventory movements by moving and exchanging information instead of goods

Supply chain strategy – a definition

The supply chain encompasses all activities associated with the flow and transformation of goods (products and services) from initial design stage through the early raw materials stage, and on to the end user. Additionally, associated information and cash flows form part of supply chain activities. Supply chain strategies are required to manage the integration of these activities through improved supply chain relationships, to achieve a competitive or co-operative advantage. Integrating the supply chain requires an organization to synchronize not only its own activities but also the activities of external organizations that either supply inputs to or receive outputs from the organization. In grocery retail supply chains they use the term 'from seed to store', in textile and apparel supply chains the term 'from concept to consumer' and in heavy industry and manufacturing industry 'from mother earth to mother earth' illustrating the full cycle from extraction, conversion, through to customers, consumption and recycling. This is illustrated in Figure 1.1.

Competition and co-operation are uneasy partners within all economic systems. Political attitudes of regional, national and international communities determine how co-operation and competition are regulated. Laws enforce the regulatory frameworks and trade agreements made between organizations in different nation states. Different organizations in the same country, region or internationally enter contractual obligations centred on the supply and demand for goods and services. These contractual obligations bring with them responsibilities to uphold agreements without recourse to legal remedy and yet legal remedy must be available when one or other of the parties to it do not honour agreements. Laws govern economic behaviour and attitudes within nation states and internationally. However, legal compliance should be a last resort and most business and organizational dealings

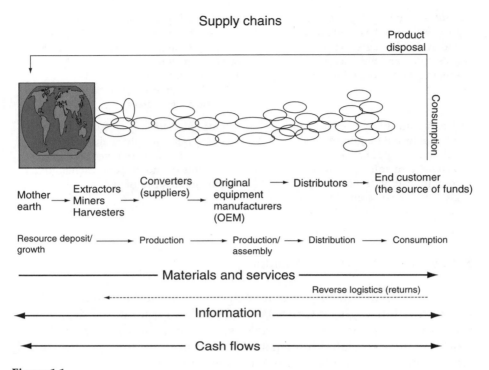

Figure 1.1

on a day-to-day basis rely on agreement and co-operation between the parties within the relationship. Competition and co-operation are discussed in this text in the context of different supply chain strategies, structures and relationships. Competitive forces are at work in private and public service organizations and consequently differently configured supply chain strategies are required within the same organization and across organizational boundaries.

This text aims to convince the reader that context is important in the supply chain strategy decisions. There is no such thing as either a universal supply chain strategy or an industry-wide supply chain, but there are rather different types of supply chain structures, strategies and relationships all of which must aim to satisfy the ultimate customer.

This chapter explains some of the forces at work in the organizational environment that have a major impact changing the ways in which businesses conduct their activities. Perhaps the biggest influencing factors in recent years have been the velocity of change in market conditions, the rapid development of information and communication technologies (ICT) and globalization. This chapter will explore each of these factors and examine their impact upon organizational supply chain strategies.

Globalization

The term 'globalization' has been coined to represent the ways in which markets have converged throughout the world and the ways in which production poles have shifted geographically to satisfy global consumers. It is a trend. It is not saying that we have arrived at the destination yet. It is saying that in this world economic system there are identifiable influences and trends that are developing new and emerging patterns of economic behaviour that can be clustered under one theme, hence, globalization. Other writers have defined it in different ways. Beynon and Dunkerley (2000, p. 3) claim that globalization is a defining feature of human society at the start of the twenty-first century. Mattelart (2000, p. 97) states that globalization has a hegemonic role in organizing and decoding meaning of the world. Schirato and Webb (2003, p. 1) define it as power relationships, practices and technologies that characterize and shape the contemporary world. The convergence trends identified in markets, products, consumer behaviour and society encapsulate the concept of globalization as used within the context of this text.

It is important to recognize that convergence is one part of the equation and that divergence and anti-global forces represent the other part. Almost 20 per cent of the world population lives in poverty. This is defined by the World Bank as people living on less than US $1 per day. Supporters of globalization are believers: they stress the benefits, they are optimistic and they see globalization as the culmination of revolutionary structural change. Sceptics view globalization as evolutionary change, continuing the trend of colonial expansion that was at its height between 1870 and 1914. They are more pessimistic than the protagonists.

International trade is nothing new. We have engaged in international trade since mankind has been able to walk even before the development of nation states, as we now know them. The 'Silk Road' from east to west is an early example of a supply route transporting products from where they were made in China to the markets of Europe where they were sold. Although the term 'supply chain strategy' had not yet been coined, those ancient traders following their trade routes to market were engaged in market-led supply chain strategies.

Commercial revolution – the rise of national and international organizations

In the nineteenth century both in the USA and in Europe industrial development took place on an unprecedented scale. The first industrial nation was Britain. The history books record how the first industrial revolution witnessed human migration from the countryside to newly developed towns and cities built around newly developed industries conducted in factories. Thus domestic production moved out of the homes and into factories where products could be manufactured in volume to achieve economies of scale in production. As this new economic order began to take shape the businesses that developed became larger, employed larger numbers of people and eventually became national rather than merely local businesses. These businesses transformed the ways in which people lived their lives, earned their livelihoods and consumed goods. As markets developed so too did transport and communication systems to ensure that the product from these factories could be sold, earn profits for the owners and wages for the workers. This economic cycle also created consumers who would spend their earnings. These businesses have created new centres of population (towns and cities), transport links between production centres and their markets developed nationally with roads, canals and later railways to ensure that goods could easily be transported to their market. In every respect these were market-led developments.

Later many national organizations expanded their sphere of reference to engage in international trade. Similarly as international trade develops so too does the infrastructure to oil the wheels of commerce. Sea links, rail links, road links and air links have developed to support the growth of international trade. Ideas of what constitutes an industry, a market and competition constantly change as a consequence of these shifts in boundaries. Today in many markets boundaries appear to be less important whilst in others they are very important and present real barriers to trade. Recent innovations in ICT have enabled many organizations to shift their spheres of operation yet again. This time they are not physical infrastructural developments like roads and railways but they are electronic links, partly physical, fibre-optic cables, satellite communication systems transmitting information between different parties and partly waves and signals in the 'ether'. The digital economy dealing in information and financial exchange is contributing to economic growth and development of trade alongside the physical economy moving tangible goods to markets.

The changing business environment

Many commentators and journalists to describe anything remotely international glibly use the word 'global'. It has become a byword for protest at world summits and World Trade Organization (WTO) meetings (witness Seattle, Cancun, Doha), a mantra of the anti-global protest groups that consider anything global to be associated with capitalist expansion and that is considered to be undesirable. In economic terms there are observable examples of unstoppable forces at work that are changing people's lives in a variety of ways. There are indeed large corporations that span the world trading across international borders and having annual revenues higher than many nation states.

Transformations in the world economy and the shift in power, people, capital and other resources have been taking place since ancient times. It is a contemporary phenomenon in the sense that the transformations are faster, more visible and affect more people in the world population than ever before. Visibility in particular is an important driver through electronic media, television, telecommunications and the Internet relay pictures, words and events instantly from what were once remote world locations into the homes of many people globally. Political, economic, social and technological landscapes are continuously changing the nature and structure of international organizations, national economies, interactions and exchanges. The patterns of development observed vary enormously and there are great paradoxes. For example, it is estimated that more than 400 million people use the Internet regularly but over half the world population has never seen or used a telephone. Uneven developments through time, space and place mean that global phenomena will be observed and experienced differently. In Ohmae's (1994) triad countries and his borderless world there will be economies bounded by the borders of North America, Western Europe and the Japan/Pacific Rim basin that may have developed quickly with consumer markets that have developed homogenized tastes and preferences. However, there are economies in South America, sub-Saharan Africa and other parts of the globe that are drained by debt and poverty with populations that are diverse in their needs. Patterns of employment, economic well-being, poverty and wealth are very different across the globe. There are large regional groups that have developed in the latter part of the twentieth century to protect the interests of those countries within the group: significantly the European Union (EU) and the North American Free Trade Association (NAFTA). Those countries excluded from what some observers refer to as the 'Rich man's clubs' scramble for position to enter because they feel that their interests would be better served from inside. Looking East or South we may view globalization very differently from those facing North or West.

Velocity of change

Global capital markets are predicted to grow in value from $20 trillion in 2000 to $200 trillion by 2010, a multiple of ten times in 10 years (Means and Schneider, 2000). To demonstrate the velocity of the expected change it is worth noting that during the last 20 years of the twentieth century global capital markets grew from $2 trillion in 1980 to $20 trillion by 2000. The start of the first decade in the twenty-first century is witnessing an unleashing doubling in the speed of change. The e-revolution is transforming the ways in which business-to-business (B2B) and business-to-consumer (B2C) markets are interacting. The e-business revolution has arrived. Much publicity has surrounded the dot.com collapse in 2000 but this is a blip on the economic landscape. It is not just or simply the technological impacts that are leading to long-term market change but a series of changes that have developed during the last decades of the twentieth century. These factors influencing conditions are: globalization and global economic shifts on an unprecedented scale; organizational restructuring; ICT; a growing recognition that differentiation strategies and not simply cost-based strategies are required to survive and thrive in the twenty-first century; and finally, the rise in consumerism with more fickle buying behaviour. The more 'savvy' consumers and businesses in the start of the new century are migrating to e-business, digital shopping, telephone commerce, e-retail and e-finance. The choice is not simply between traditional and e-business strategies but rather they are complementary and should not necessarily be seen as separate. Business is the same in many ways as it has always been. Markets are identified or created in which buyers and sellers exchange information, goods, services and money. What is different is the ways in which markets are structured and how organizations conduct transactions and relationships. Production, distribution and consumption have limitless boundaries across the globe and the digital economy has changed the patterns of economic activity. Consumers have more choice, are likely to be less loyal, are not prepared to accept second best and have become more sophisticated in their tastes and their approach to buying and consuming goods and services.

Global companies want to achieve market dominance by developing powerful brands that transcend local domestic markets and change the nature of hitherto local competitive markets. Global organizations satisfy customers by understanding better their needs and serving them locally. These organizations exploit global markets by producing or procuring products in low-cost countries and distributing them in markets that can sustain higher prices. Consumers in these markets recognize value and benefit from lower prices for high-quality goods and services. Consider your own consumption habits and how prices have fallen for a range of products and services during the past few years. An economy ticket of British Airways from London to San Francisco cost around £700 in 1985; today you could buy a ticket for around half that. However, in real terms after taking the falling value of money over the period it is probably nearer to a quarter of the price it was

then. In 1980 a VHS video recorder cost around £600; today you could buy one for around one-sixth of the price and it would have more features and be technologically superior. Many more consumer products purchased in the 1980s would have been manufactured and assembled in Europe than would be the case today. There has been a shift in manufacturing industry from the western world to the lesser-developed countries (LDCs) located mainly in the Far East. If you were to examine labels on your food, beverages, TV sets, video recorders, cameras, telephones, computers, clothing and footwear, you would probably find in many cases a multitude of countries around the globe had been involved in their production. Levi jeans from China with zips from Japan, studs from India, Nike sports shoes from China or India, branded shirts from Bangladesh, Vietnam or Cambodia, curtain fabrics from South Korea, Taiwan or China, Sony computers and cameras made in China and so on. One example of this shift in production is the establishment and development of the Sri Lanka's clothing industry. Prior to 1977 the major export earner was tea. In 1977 Sri Lanka began to produce clothes for UK and US markets mainly from an almost zero base. In 2001 exports from clothing accounted for 52.7 per cent of Sri Lanka's exports and tea represented 14.1 per cent. These shifts in production have caused structural changes in the make-up of Western economies. Many heavy engineering and manufacturing jobs have disappeared as the economies in the West have become more dependent on services as a proportion of their gross domestic product (GDP). Automobile manufacture, shipbuilding, textiles and electronics are key industries in Japan, South Korea and China. In 1950 these countries were newly industrializing countries reliant on agriculture for their main sources of income and these contemporary prominent industries either did not exist or were in an embryonic state.

Global trends

Today we witness further global shifts in service industries. It is not simply manufacturing jobs under threat. If you telephone American Express to check details on your credit card you may be transferred to a call centre in India and not to someone in Brighton in the UK (which is the address on the payment slip) as you might think. Similarly you may purchase property and have your conveyancing carried out by a local solicitor or so you think but trained legal staff in India accessing information through the Internet may conduct the work. If you purchase a computer and decide to ring the helpline for assistance in setting it up, you may find that your expert helper is located not in the UK but perhaps once again in India. According to Deloitte Consulting

2 million jobs could move to India from the West by 2008. The world's top 100 financial institutions could save costs of $138 billion in the next 5 years by moving operations offshore. Thirty per cent of these operators already have some offshore operations and this is expected to rise to 75 per cent in 5 years. Amicus state that 200 000 British jobs will be lost as operators move offshore by 2008 in back-office functions and call centres. India has 1.5 million graduates who speak English according to the Confederation of Indian Industry.

Political uncertainties carry associated risks for suppliers locked into global markets and global supply networks. Since 11 September 2001 these risks have increased for all parties. There is paradoxically an increasing interdependence in the global economy and the rich world depends on the poor world to sustain western consumer lifestyles while the LDCs depend on orders and business involvement with the DCs to sustain employment, maintain and improve the quality of life of the LDC population. With over 6 billion people in the globe our lives are intertwined whether we realize it or not. However, one thing has become clear that in the industrial or post-modern world governments of all political persuasion in all countries are less able to engineer economic success than they would like to admit. The record of the last 50 years or more speaks for itself. Most governments meddle – they have consistently introduced regulatory controls even in what we regard as developed freer societies and intervention distorts markets sometimes in desirable ways and sometimes in unplanned ways.

Ethical considerations have become more of a concern in consuming marketplaces. The social conscience of conspicuous consumption sometimes pricks the skin and the economic guilt complex of western society is exposed. Seattle and Cancun bear witness to Naomi Klein's (2000) 'No Logo' thesis. There is also the concern of the impact that commercial activities are having on the global environment. Deforestation is but one consequence of economic activity, scarred landscapes from drilling for oil and other geological mining activities are amongst others. Changes to weather patterns and natural river flows have all been disturbed by individual and private industrial activities, national interest is both perpetrator and protector and yet there is the paradox of the individual without a voice being subsumed by private interests while governments are incapable either individually or collectively of looking after the majority interest. The collective good is often in the hands of wealthy or just politically powerful individuals and organizations. Democratic interests may not be fully represented.

Regulation and deregulation of markets can alter patterns of demand, production and consumption. For example, the demise of the multi-fibre agreement (MFA) in textiles in 2005 sees a quota-free world in textiles and apparel, which will again lead to global shifts in production as buyers seek to lower costs and sellers, seek to supply at the desired cost. Exchange rates also determine the balance of trade for many locked in global competition.

Yergin and Stanislaw (1998, p. 13) noted a world trend towards deregulation, privatization of nationally owned assets and freer markets. They describe it as the 'greatest sale in history' whereby governments dispose of business assets worth trillions of dollars privatizing steel plants, airlines, telecommunications, utilities, railways, hotels and to their list one could add healthcare and education. Once sacrosanct publicly owned assets are released in a market free for all. The phenomenon can be observed across the world in the former Soviet Union, Eastern Europe, China, Western Europe, Asia, Latin America, Africa and the United States. This observed trend has major implications for procurement and other supply chain strategies as new global suppliers replace traditional suppliers of labour, materials, goods and services, since the new management teams will seek to achieve cost savings and efficiency gains.

International trading organizations tend to fall into one of four categories identified by Keegan and Green (2002, p. 16):

- *Ethnocentric* – The home country is viewed as superior and the organization sees similarities between the home country and other countries. Management activities are centralized, and standard products and services are supplied to markets seen as similar to the home market.
- *Regiocentric* – The organization sees both similarities and differences in a world region (e.g. North America, Europe, Southeast Asia). It adopts either an ethnocentric or polycentric approach in doing so. Products and services therefore may be either standardized extensions or locally adapted depending on whether they adopt an ethnocentric or polycentric approach.
- *Polycentric* – Views each host country as different. Many differences require products and services to be locally adapted. Markets are viewed as different; essentially, new products for each new market.
- *Geocentric* – takes a worldview seeing both similarities and differences in the home and host countries. This is an integrated world approach synthesizing the ethnocentric and polycentric attitudes. Products and services will be sourced locally and globally, and they will be distributed to global markets (locally and globally).

Social change is endemic throughout the globe; it is simply the rate of change that differs and the base from which the country is starting. There is a trend of rising expectation. People generally want to be able to buy and consume more but this is relative. Those on average daily incomes below $0.20 cents cannot consume as much as those on more than $100 per day. Some argue that markets are becoming similar, well some are. Perhaps in Western Europe and the USA there are similarities but for all those similarities there are differences as wave after wave of failed retail global expansion demonstrates.

The political and legal regulatory framework

Probably the most important structural influence is the political and legal regulatory frameworks that impact upon organizational activities. The 'Bretton Woods Agreement' in 1944 signalled the new order of regulation with two major financial institutions established: the International Monetary Fund (IMF) and the International Bank for Reconstruction and Development (IBRD) later renamed the World Bank. These institutions were to underpin the post-World War economies and oil the wheels of commerce and industry in international markets. In 1947 the General Agreement on Tariffs and Trade (GATT) was established with the purpose of removing trade barriers and various types of trade discrimination. In principle if not always in practice the GATT was intended to promote freer trade between the countries subscribing to it and liberalize markets opening up new markets to newly developing countries by removing trading barriers. It developed mechanisms for dealing with the many trade disputes that broke out during the course of its life although it had no compliance mechanisms relying largely on self-governance between the parties in dispute to reach agreement. Following the Uruguay Round of talks in 1994 agreement was reached to replace GATT with the WTO taking over its role from 1 January 1995. It is based in Geneva and provides a forum for trade negotiations and to act as mediator between the 141 member states. There have been a number of recent major disputes between member states. In 1995 the US government wanted to impose 100 per cent tariff duties on Japanese cars imported to the US in retaliation for the Japanese refusing to take US merchandise. The US argued that the Japanese refusal to allow US imports were responsible for around one-third of the trade deficit between 1990 and 1994. Further recent trade wars have nearly erupted between Europe and the USA over the EU's quota policy and refusals to accept certain country's banana exports into Europe as a consequence. For example, Britain until recently still imported most of its bananas from former colonies in Caribbean countries excluding the former US territories access to UK and EU markets. The USA threatened to refuse entry to EU exports and some industries particularly EU textile exports were seriously disrupted.

WTO regulations in practice

The EU is about to retaliate against the US by imposing import duties of 30 per cent and in some cases by 100 per cent on a range of US exports after the WTO authorized its retaliation against US steel import tariffs and tariff subsidies. If these are not scrapped by the US the EU will impose the duties by 15 December 2003.

Source: Drapers Record (2003), p. 2, 15 November 2003.

In 1999 world trade exceeded $5.9 trillion. According to the IMF intra-regional trading accounts for the largest world trade flows. In 1998 intraregional exports in Europe and Central Eurasia (the largest intra-regional amount) was worth $1176 billion. Imports from Asia and Oceania stood at $242 billion and exports to that region at $215 billion. The trade flows in 1999 between industrialized countries was around $3.8 trillion (exports) and $3.76 trillion (imports). Developing countries exported $1.74 trillion and imported $1.98 trillion. Trade growth in developing countries is accelerating. Nevertheless, two-thirds of world exports are still accounted for by the developed world. The top 10 exporting and importing countries are listed in Table 1.1.

Table 1.1

	Top 10 exporters			Top 10 importers	
Rank	Country	1999 (US$ billions)	Rank	Country	1999 (US$ billions)
1	USA	765.3	1	USA	1013.3
2	Germany	517.8	2	Germany	465.9
3	Japan	448.6	3	UK	319.2
4	P.R. China	323.5	4	France	298.0
5	France	295.7	5	Japan	278.2
6	UK	262.1	6	The Netherlands	212.4
7	Canada	243.3	7	Canada	211.6
8	Italy	217.0	8	Italy	204.7
9	The Netherlands	182.3	9	P.R. China	163.3
10	South Korea	146.5	10	Hong Kong	154.7

Source: IMF/World Bank.

Country risk

Doing business with particular countries around the globe carries a particular risk. Dun and Bradstreet assess and rank country risk indicators and produce tables that indicate the levels of risk across seven categories with seven being highest risk and one lowest. Table 1.2 illustrates a comparative cross-border risk assessment conducted in October 2003. The list from top to bottom also has some element of ranking within the categories 1–7. In making the assessment political risk, commercial risk, macroeconomic risk and external risk are categories of assessment. Each is explained briefly:

- *Political risk*. The internal and external security situation, policy, competency, fostering and enabling of the business environment.
- *Commercial risk*. The sanctity of contract, judicial competence, regulatory transparency and degree of systemic corruption that affect commercial transactions are assessed.
- *Macroeconomic risk*. Inflation, balance of payments, money supply growth and indicators that determine the country's ability to deliver sustainable growth.
- *External risk*. The current account balance, capital flows, foreign exchange reserves, size of external debt and all such factors determining the country's ability to attract foreign exchange and investment.

Regional trading blocs

In the twentieth century the most important preferential trading agreement was the British Commonwealth preference system. The UK, Canada, Australia, New Zealand, India and other former British colonies had preferential trading arrangements covering all classes of goods and services. The UK ended this arrangement when it entered into the European Economic Community (EEC). The decision to do so taken in 1972 became more important in the 1990s and beyond as the European Union began to achieve greater integration of trading policies and practices across the union. The majority of UK exports and imports are conducted in intraregional trade within the EU.

The reality of global markets

The nature of supply chains in most industries is global. Supplies are sourced from a variety of locations throughout the world to make a product that is demanded by consumers who may also be located globally.

Table 1.2

Low risk 1	2	3	4	5	6	High risk 7
Luxembourg	Kuwait	Bahrain	Brazil	Cote d'voire	Argentina	Afghanistan
Australia	Malta	Israel	Kenya	Gabon	Azerbaijan	Congo DR (Zaire)
Austria	Singapore	South Korea	Panama	Guatemala	Cambodia	Iraq
Canada	Spain	Mexico	Peru	Iran	Ecuador	Zimbabwe
Denmark	Chile	Oman	Philippines	Romania	Honduras	
Finland	Greece	Saudi Arabia	Uganda	Syria	Nepal	
France	Hong Kong SAR	China	Dom. Republic	Kazakhstan	Venezuela	
Ireland	Italy	Estonia	Lebanon	Libya	Yemen	
The Netherlands	Japan	Jordan	Bulgaria	Pakistan	Nigeria	
Norway	Mauritius	Poland	Colombia	PNG	Paraguay	
Sweden	Portugal	Costa Rica	Croatia	Turkey	Russian Federation	
Switzerland	Qatar	Czech Republic	El Salvador	Zambia	Sudan	
UK	Botswana	Egypt	Ghana	Bangladesh	Ukraine	
US	Slovenia	Lithuania	Jamaica	Bolivia	Kyrgyz Republic	
Belgium	Taiwan	Malaysia	Mozambique	Cameroon	Macedonia	
Germany	Tunisia	India	Tanzania	Indonesia	Nicaragua	
Iceland	Cyprus	Latvia	Uruguay	Sri Lanka	Albania	
New Zealand	Hungary	Namibia	Vietnam	Algeria	Angola	
UAE	Morocco	Senegal		Ethiopia	Belarus	
	South Africa	Slovakia		Fiji	Bosnia and Herz.	
	Trinidad and Tobago	Thailand		Malawi	Cuba	
					Georgia	
					Myanmar	
					Serbia and Mont.	
					Sierra Leone	
					Tajikistan	
					Turkemenistan	
					Uzbekistan	

Source: www.dnb-solutions.com/uk/ft (October 2003).

Production, distribution and consumption are a global phenomenon. There are of course great variations in developed and lesser-developed economies. In the automobile industry we can observe the global car (Table 1.3). For example, the Ford Escort was manufactured in Halewood near Liverpool in the UK and in Saarlouis in Germany. However, if you examined the product assembly more closely you would have soon realized that this vehicle contained sub-assemblies from many different parts of the world.

Table 1.3

Ford Escort – a world car

Country	Sub-assemblies
UK	Carburettor, clutch, ignition, exhaust, fuel pump
Germany	Pistons, front discs, speedometer, fuel tank, spindles
Belgium	Seat pads
Sweden	Hose clamps, cylinder bolt
The Netherlands	Paint, hardware
Canada	Glass, radio
Spain	Wiring harness, battery
Japan	Starter motor
Norway	Exhaust flanges, tyres
Austria	Radiator, heater hoses
Denmark	Fan belt
Switzerland	Speedometer, gears
Italy	Cylinder head, defroster grills
USA	EGR valves, wheel nuts, hydraulic tappet

The first global industry?

Historically the textiles and clothing industries have played a prominent role in the process of economic development. In the eighteenth century the textiles and clothing industries led the Industrial Revolution in Europe and more recently were crucial to the success of export-led growth in the dynamic newly industrializing economies of East Asia. Globally the textiles and clothing industries are large employers of labour with 13 million directly employed in textiles and a further 10 million in clothing manufacture. However, as Dicken (1998, p. 284) remarks these figures are likely to grossly underestimate the actual numbers of people involved who are not recorded in any official statistics or estimates. In 1998 the figures for employment in the clothing industry alone were estimated at 10.7 million which was a substantial increase on previous estimates (OETH, 2000, p. 10). The increase was attributed to more accurate statistics from the Peoples Republic of China. Between 1995 and 1999 EU employment in clothing fell by 9.1 per cent. Globally 14.2 per cent of all employment is accounted for by textiles and clothing manufacture. In the EU 7.5 per cent is the comparable figure for employment in textiles and clothing. World production in textiles was valued at US $485 billion and clothing at US $335 billion in 1998. Asia is the largest exporter of clothes and Western Europe the largest importer. This is indicative of global production and consumption trends. The textiles and clothing industries were the first manufacturing industries to take on a global dimension and are the most widely dispersed industries across the developed and developing world.

The world's largest companies

Table 1.4 shows the top 40 world corporations by revenue in 2001. It is interesting that the number one position is held by a US retailer and that only one British company appears in the top 40 although Royal Dutch Shell which is Anglo-Dutch is in as well. The list is dominated by the US and Japanese corporations. The largest British retail organization, Tesco, is ranked 114 in the world and Marks and Spencer is ranked 439. Carrefour France is the largest European retailer ranked 37. Corporations located in oil, automobiles, electronics, telecommunications and financial services are the industrial sectors that dominate the top 40 list.

Global businesses develop powerful information systems that provide their owner(s) with vast databases that they can mine to identify market trends and utilize for targeted promotional activity. New product innovation and creativity to leverage both the brand and the vast arrays of information that these global brand owners have at their disposal require them to think in new ways about their business and the competition they face. Owning assets is no longer as important as owning customers. This belief is evidenced by recent trends to restructure organizations and to outsource many of the functional and traditional activities previously regarded as essential to the well-being of the organization. Efficient and effective supply chains are required to manage customer demand and brand operations. Customer relationship management (CRM) is supported through e-commerce. Back-office support activities are more focused on satisfying customers and fulfilment of the marketing promise is critical to the organization's future. Organizations are focused on value creation rather than merely short-term profitability. Creating value streams is important as markets and marketing processes; supplier networks and operations throughout the

Table 1.4

		The world's largest corporations			Revenues	
Rank 2001	Rank 2000		Country		$ Millions	% Change from 2000
1	2	Wal-Mart Stores	US		219 812	13.7
2	1	Exxon Mobil	US		191 581	−8.9
3	3	General Motors	US		177 260	−4
4	7	BP	Britain		174 218	17.7
5	4	Ford Motor	US		162 412	−10.1
6	16	Enron	US		138 718	37.6
7	5	Daimlerchrysler	Germany		136 897	−8.8
8	6	Royal Dutch Shell Group	NET/Britain		135 211	−9.3
9	8	General Electric	US		125 913	−3
10	10	Toyota Motor	Japan		120 814	−0.5
11	12	Citigroup	US		112 022	0.2
12	9	Mitsubishi	Japan		105 813	−16.4
13	11	Mitsui	Japan		101 205	−14.2
14	60	Chevrontexaco	US		99 699	107.4
15	14	Total Fina ELF	France		94 311	−10.9
16	15	Nippon Telegraph & Telephone	Japan		93 424	−9.5
17	13	Itochu	Japan		91 176	−16.9
18	25	Allianz	Germany		85 929	21
19	19	IBM	US		85 866	−2.9
20	24	ING Group	The Netherlands		82 999	16.6
21	21	Volkswagen	Germany		79 287	0.6
22	23	Siemens	Germany		77 358	3.3
23	18	Siumitomo	Japan		77 140	−15.4
24	34	Philip Morris	US		72 944	15.3
25	20	Marubeni	Japan		71 756	−15.9
26	32	Verizon Comms	US		67 190	3.8
27	29	Deutche Bank	Germany		66 839	−0.4
28	27	E.ON	Germany		66 453	−2.9
29	33	US Postal Services	US		65 834	2
30	17	AXA	France		65 579	−24.8
31	38	Credit Suisse	Switzerland		64 204	8.2
32	22	Hitachi	Japan		63 931	−16
33	28	Nippon Life Insurance	Japan		63 827	−6.2
34	65	American International	US		62 402	35.7
35	37	Carrefour	France		62 224	3.9
36	382	American Electrical Power	US		61 257	347.3
37	30	Sony	Japan		60 608	−8.4
38	58	Royal Ahold	The Netherlands		59 633	23
39	53	Duke Energy	US		59 503	20.7
40	31	AT&T	US		59 142	−10.4

Source: Fortune, 22 July 2002.

globe become integrated through e-linkages in a complex chain moving parts, products and information around the network in order to meet customer demand. Different strategies are required to pursue this goal as time and distance shrink (Cairncross, 1998). Internet strategies present opportunities to integrate complex supply chains from concept design to store to consumer. Markets and market opportunity may be both local and global. Organizations will be managing networks to leverage brand values and this can be achieved using global communication systems from anywhere in the world.

Figure 1.1 illustrates the environmental influences acting upon an organizational value chain. The diagram represents production of goods and services in the centre and some key-stage activities that create value for the customer, consumer and producer. In essence this value chain is a supply chain moving and transforming inputs into finished goods and services that are bundled to add value for the customer. Time, place and space determine value since outputs are required by customers in a particular market (space or place) and at a particular time. Time, place and space affect value and prices. For example, it is important that perishable food products reach their markets while still in good condition if suppliers are to achieve the agreed price. In moving perishable products to market it is essential that they reach the places where the customers are located within the time the product is in saleable condition. It is not simply produce that is perishable but other outputs such as market information is perishable. A buyer will be prepared to pay higher prices for information that is timely when it is history it may be worth less. Organizations operate within a larger environment and changes occurring in that environment affect what happens inside the organization. The larger economic system into which organizations are locked may experience changes to interest rates, exchange rates and other economic conditions that impact upon how a single organization is able to act and react. The economic environment will determine the rate of change in the technological environment. Innovations occur when forces create conditions that make them necessary or desirable. Both these factors influence value creation within an organization. Changes in societal values lead to change in the political and legal environments that in turn impinge upon and control the activities of single organizations.

The importance of manufacturing industry

Many commentators refer to a post-industrial society in reference to the UK. However, it is salutary to realize that 15 of the top 25 largest corporations (see Table 1.4) in the world are involved in heavy engineering and manufacturing in diverse areas: automobiles, computer hardware, power turbines and consumer electronics. Six in supply energy, three are in financial services and one Wal-Mart is the world's largest retailer. Only two can claim to be British, BP and Royal Dutch Shell, in which the latter is partly British.

Manufacturing accounts for less than one-fifth of the UK economy providing 14 per cent of total employment but 64 per cent of exports and creates wealth and spending power that feeds service industries. There were on average 820 insolvencies each week in manufacturing in 2002 the highest in 10 years and output saw its largest fall since 1991. It is often stated that the UK is a creative nation and ideas are the source of wealth. However it is important to recognize that the USA filed 30 450 patents in 2001, Japan 19 845, Germany 21 308 and the UK just 4853. The conversion rate of ideas into commercial products in the UK is also poor by international comparison. The tax system, rising infrastructure costs, higher insurance costs and planning regulations all impact upon investment ability. In 2002 many high-profile companies ceased to manufacture in the UK. Dyson moved its manufacture of vacuum cleaners to Malaysia, Dr Martens to China, Black & Decker to the Czech Republic, a total of 350 000 jobs in all moved offshore. In the same year many retailers were sourcing more supplies from overseas than from the UK with an impact upon local manufacturing. Dyson[1] said it was not simply a matter of low labour cost in their case since transport cost and duty more than offset the savings. The decision was taken because vital manufacturing infrastructure and support was available on a scale not seen in Britain for 30–40 years. According to Dyson, China with its mantra of employment over profit will be the workshop of the world by 2010 and UK industry will not be able to compete on cost, quality or reliability. Stripped of manufacturing clients service industries too will suffer and many skills will disappear as cost-efficient service industries in places like India develop further. India is already a magnet for software developers, call centres and online accountants. The multiplier effect will impact upon the UK Balance of Payments and tax revenues to support an ageing population. It will compromise industrial strength, innovation and military capabilities.

If one considers that these changes occur in an environmental system that is global then organizations may be influenced by changes taking place in parts of the world that they may not be fully aware of. For example, take the example of a local purchase of mange tout peas from Tesco in the UK one may track the supply of this produce back to Southern Africa maybe Zimbabwe where conditions are such that political instability may threaten supplies. The labour market is such that farm workers may earn as little as 50 pence per day for their hard toil and be subjected to compliance and regulation from the supermarket buyers from the UK who aim to satisfy consumer demand for the product by ensuring compliance standards and attractive pricing and presentation. Compliance may take the form of checking for insects, washing and ensuring that only standard sized peas enter the food chain for the supermarket. Once packaged a 100-gram packet may sell for between 75 pence and £1 equivalent to the pay for one or two days' labour by the farmhand in Africa. Thus people in different lands throughout the globe are interconnected in ways that they might not consider or think about. A dinner party in Chelsea or Kensington may have produce from various parts of the globe and will have touched many peoples' lives in one way or another on its journey to the table. Every day consumers make decisions to purchase products and services in their country, which will impact in some way on someone in a remote part of the globe that they may not even be able to point to on a map. Impacts are both positive and negative in their effect. These statements simply serve to confirm the interconnectedness of market-driven supply chains spanning the globe. Figure 1.2 locates the supply chain within an economic system which shapes other influencing factors that include: technological change and innovation; legal, quasi-legal and regulatory factors; political and socio-cultural factors.

Gereffi (1994, p. 97) drew a distinction between two types of driver that were production-driven and buyer-driven chains. In producer chains trans-national corporations (TNCs) or other large enterprises played a central role in controlling backward and forward linkages. The administrative headquarters controlled the supplies in these

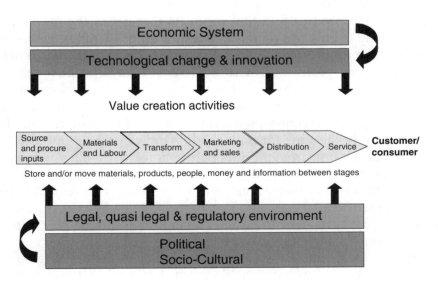

Figure 1.2

chains. In buyer chains it is large retailers, brand named merchandis-ers and trading companies that play the pivotal role setting up decen-tralized production networks as in the example of Tesco and mange tout peas. More and more so in western markets it is the market that drives the supply chain and this is the raison d'être for this book. One could argue as Gereffi and others did that producer-driven chains existed in capital- and technology-intensive industries such as auto-mobiles, electronics, computers and aerospace. However, one could also argue that these industries are also ultimately subject to the mar-kets they serve. Business history is littered with a kaleidoscope of examples of failed products that were essentially producer-driven and in some cases technically superior to products that they were competing with and that the market determined a success. This is why it is essential to consider supply chain strategies from the cus-tomer perspective. Organizations need to adopt a customer-focused view of how their supply chain strategies are structured and how relationships and customer interactions are managed for the benefit of the customer. By focusing upon the customer's needs the supply chain becomes market-driven rather than producer determined. Organizations locked together in customer-focused supply chains must search for efficiencies to drive cost down and to add value for the customers they serve.

New technologies and innovation

It is well known that being first to market can determine the lifetime income for the product and that products that get to the marketplace on time may earn on average between 7 and 10 times in revenue streams that products which are late achieve. Being late may generate cost rather than profit and there have been classic product develop-ment errors in many industries. For example, the late development of a particular aircraft was estimated to have cost the developers more than twice the expected revenue stream for the aircraft in its market lifetime. It is not simply the time for new product developments but also time compression in procurement and production cycles. This is why we have seen many organizations thinning their supply base to work more closely with fewer organizations with the capability to respond faster. Replenishment lead times not just first-order lead-times need to be responsive. Systems need to be able to communicate accurate response data between the buyer and supplier.

Consider the example of colouring processes in textiles. Digital sup-ply chain technologies have enabled sampling process times to be cut or even eliminated on some products. There are essentially three areas where technical experts in colour can maximize impact with retailers and become suppliers of first choice. These areas are:

1. Colour creation
2. Colour communication
3. Colour control

By managing this aspect of the supply chain effectively and efficiently the retailers concerned can achieve the following benefits:

- Save time in sampling processes and production.
- Time = money.
- The retailer can also become more responsive to changes in consumer behaviour because they have a reliable supplier and they can be confident of accurate response not simply quick response.
- Suppliers who can communicate error-free colour data that their dyers and colouring houses can use to create a perfect production match to the design colour will be the one's who benefit. Again saving time and cost.
- Finally, consistency through the application of standards for matches, and wash and wear performance are a pre-requisite of accurate response systems.

Some of the biggest changes have occurred in Information and Communication Technologies (ICT) using open platform technologies. Companies no longer need to buy into proprietorial legacy systems but may use standard platforms of technology to build systems integration that meets standard requirements to exchange their documents, sounds, pictures and spreadsheets. These developments have revolutionized businesses and made the world even more of a global marketplace. e-Business although in its infancy is maturing fast. The crash of 1999–2000 was but a blip on the evolution chronology.

So how have new developments in ICT helped and what are these supply chain processes that organizations seem to have become obsessed with managing and why are they important? ICT developments have given firms the opportunity to integrate systems that can be applied to manage the whole organization's processes and to link with their suppliers and customers. This integration as it is referred to enables time compression, error-free data transmission opportunities, waste avoidance, cost efficiencies and opportunities for value enhancement and value adding activities for the customer. Flows of information, goods and money can be managed seamlessly and processes become transparent. This visibility enhances the service suppliers and customers can expect and achieve.

Conclusions

The nature of supply chains in most industries is that they may be both global and local. Supplies are sourced from a variety of locations throughout the world to make a product that is demanded by consumers who may also be located globally. Markets are both local and global. Commercial, industrial and organizational contexts determine the shape of national, inter-regional, intraregional and international supply chains. Production, distribution and consumption are a global phenomenon. There are of course great variations in developed and lesser-developed economies. Economic change is rapid and market conditions are shaped by demographics, psychographics (lifestyles, attitudes and values) and geographics. Nevertheless, it is important to recognize that some supply chains remain local for political, social and economic reasons. Local markets may be supplied globally and locally, just locally or just globally. Nevertheless, there is evidence to suggest that as world trade grows so to do the opportunities to source, procure, produce and consume more globally. Byrom and Medway (2003) identified a unique manifestation of this in a remote small local island community engaging in global trading activities as a consequence of using Internet technologies. Residents in the Pitcairn Islands (a remote island in the South Pacific), descendents of the 'HMS Bounty' crew, had developed a number of new products for Internet tourists. Items could be ordered and delivered anywhere in the world. Fulfilment and delivery times leave something to be desired since they use the mail ship that passes by every 6 months to carry merchandise to the markets where demand is. Thus the death of distance is not quite upon us and geography still has meaning even in the virtual world of commerce. Nevertheless, global enterprise and local production and innovation have been fuelled by technological innovation in web-based e-commerce.

In reality a variety of supply chain decisions are conditioned by their environmental conditions, economics, politics, social, cultural and technological factors. These factors influence the decisions taken by organizations and not necessarily in equal measure or in rational logic. However, the most important influence should be the customer. Any supply chains raison d'être must be to serve the customer and the final consumer.

Globalization as a phenomenon is itself a consequence of competitive pressures that have led producers towards an endless search for ways to lower production costs first through efficiency measures often internal to a single organization or network of organizations locked in a continuous supply chain. Second, the search for lower cost sources of supply shifts production and organizations controlling production to offshore locations throughout the globe where conditions are more favourable than in the home market where the products will be sold and consumed. Often these global shifts have a devastating impact upon domestic markets where production jobs are lost, investment declines and the trade balance worsens. Investment declines not simply as a consequence of production erosion but also in relative terms for those organizations that remain locked into industrial decline because investors and governments are unwilling to take the financial and political risks that investment in the future requires. This reduction in investment is a consequence of perceived increasing uncertainties.

Economies of scale are often an important factor in determining the success of retailing organizations since they are able to extract additional value from their suppliers owing to their size and market power position and secure further economic efficiencies through economies in distribution of the merchandise to consumers. Being large when markets are saturated in domestic economies requires retailers to develop beyond their own geographical boundaries. For the very large retailing groups it is a matter of who can get to the future first and who can dominate market share. These large retail groups have enormous purchasing power and are able to extract economies of scale from their operations and economies of scope from their existing and developing supply chains. Change is not only identified through economic shifts but also through cultural and social transformation that has been hastened by rapid communication and transportation infrastructures. Consumer behaviour has changed as markets have converged. Consumer behaviour patterns are changed not simply by consumers themselves but by the professional purchasing and procurement officers of retailing groups who exert enormous influence over consumer choice. For example, professional retail buyers make decisions about what merchandise and brands to purchase or replenish and these decisions can limit consumer choice as well as expand it. Adopting an integrated marketing approach is a necessary condition to achieving consumer satisfaction. Supply chain structures, strategies and processes are interdependent upon and a corollary of consumer demand patterns identified through market intelligence and marketing information. Supply chains are in effect the corollary of demand chains.

Figure 1.3 presents a conceptual model of factors influencing customer-focused supply chain strategies. The conceptual model illustrates key influences that shape the conditions in which customer-focused supply chain strategies are formed. Environmental conditions (PESTEEL) influence the conditions that impact upon the increasing trend to globalize and determine levels of investment and investment opportunities that

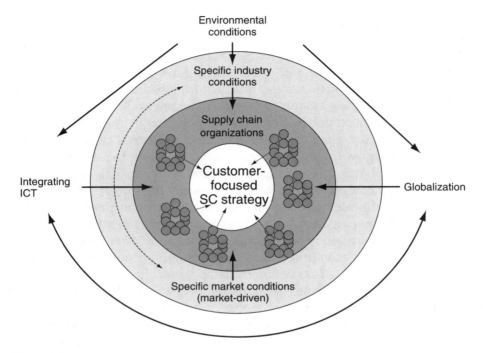

Figure 1.3

in turn determine the velocity of change in developing integrating ICT and the propensity to innovate. However, globalization and integrating ICT have an impact on each other in determining the velocity of change and the desire for change. These three influential factors shape the conditions in which all industries and organizations operate. They also influence the market conditions that prevail at any point in time. It is market conditions that drive markets and determine exchange values through supply and demand. Market conditions are also influenced by environmental conditions (e.g. political and legal regulatory frameworks). In the model the market conditions on the supply side drives supply chain organizations towards particular supply chain strategic choices, e.g. supplier selection, procurement, inventory policies. Supply chain organizations are influenced by all the factors both directly in the firm's immediate that is their microenvironment and directly or indirectly through changes occurring in the macroenvironment. Supply chain organizations must develop supply chain strategies that use resources efficiently and effectively to satisfy their end customer by having customer-focused supply chain strategies.

The next chapter examines strategic concepts and the notion of customer-focused supply chain strategies further.

Discussion Questions

1. Explain the term globalization.
2. Discuss the implications of globalization for organizations designing and developing their supply chain strategies.
3. Identify the key drivers of change that affect supply chain strategy.
4. 'Any supply chain strategy involves risk'. Discuss.
5. Discuss the importance of regional trading blocs in developing supply chain strategies.
6. Discuss the influences of technology and innovation on global supply chains.
7. Explain what is meant by supply chain strategy.
8. Discuss how organizations are often pushed into supply chain strategies through operational activities.
9. Explain the importance of manufacturing industry in a post-industrial society.
10. 'Global markets need global supplies'. Discuss.

Note

[1] James Dyson's comments are taken from In my opinion 'Leading the way to a new economic miracle – Unless we take steps now, China with its mantra work over profit, will be the workshop of the world', RSA Journal, June 2003.

References

Beynon, J. and Dunkerley, D. (2000). *The Reader*. London: Athlone Press.

Byrom, J. and Medway, D. (2003). Cyber solutions to remote problems: online trading in British overseas territories – a review and research agenda. *European Retail and Distribution Conference Proceedings*, Paris.

Cairncross, F. (1998). *The Death of Distance*. London: Orion Business Books.

Dicken, P. (1998). *Global Shift*. London: Paul Chapman Publishing.

Fortune (2002). *Fortune Magazine*, July.

Gereffi, G. (1994). The organization of buyer-driven global commodity chains: how US retailers shape overseas production networks. In *Commodity Chains and Global Capitalism* (Gereffi, G. and Korzeniewicz, M., eds). Westport, CT: Greenwood Press, pp. 95–122.

Keegan, W. J. and Green, M. C. (2002). *Global Marketing*, 3rd edn. Englewood Cliffs, NJ: Prentice-Hall.

Klein, N. (2000). *No Logo*. London: Flamingo/Harper Collins.

Mattelart, A. (2000). *Networking the World, 1794–2000* (trans. Liz Carey Librecht and James A. Cohen). Minneapolis, MN: University of Minnesota Press.

Means, G. and Schneider, D. (2000). *Meta-Capitalism – The e-Business Revolution and the Design of 21st Century Companies and Markets*. New York: John Wiley & Sons.

OETH (2000). *Key Trends in 2000*. Paris: OETH.

Ohmae, K. (1994). *The Borderless World – Power and Strategy in the Global Marketplace*. London: Harper Collins.

Pratt, J. (2001). Platform, *Marketing Business*. Cookham: Chartered Institute of Marketing.

Schirato, T. and Webb, J. (2003). *Understanding Globalization*. London: Sage.

Schonberger, R. J. (1990). *Building a Chain of Customers*. New York: Free Press.

Webster, F. E. (1997). The future role of marketing in the organization. In *Reflections on the Future of Marketing* (Lehman, D. R. and Jocz, K. E., eds). Cambridge, MA: Marketing Science Institute.

Yergin, D. and Stanislaw, J. (1998). *The Commanding Heights*. New York: Simon & Schuster.

Chapter 2

Strategic concepts and the customer-focused, market-driven supply chain

LEARNING OUTCOMES

After reading this chapter you should:

- know and understand differences between strategic planning and strategic management, descriptive and prescriptive approaches and different levels of strategy discussed in the literature;
- know that strategy is both process and content and that levels determine the context;
- be aware that realized strategies are consequences of both planned and unplanned (emergent) strategic processes;
- know different definitions of strategy and be able to define strategy in context;
- be aware of a number of different strategic conceptual frameworks and different approaches to strategic planning and strategic management;
- know and understand why supply chain strategies are important to most modern businesses.

This chapter examines a number of important strategic concepts. It begins by examining traditional approaches to planning and strategic management. Definitions of strategy are offered and different levels of strategy are explored. Strategic thinking and learning are discussed within the context of developing competence and capabilities before establishing the importance of setting strategic objectives. In turn, setting strategic objectives requires resources being applied to implement chosen strategies and appropriate performance measures developed to evaluate strategic performance. Finally, the importance of customer-focused supply chain strategies and the concept of strategic fit are discussed within this broad framework of strategic development.

Strategy

Supply chain strategies are pivotal to the success of most contemporary business organizations and they may be equally important for not-for-profit organizations too. Organizational decisions relating to the design and structure of supply chains determine supply chain strategies and are an important recurring theme throughout this text. It is important to recognize that supply chain strategies exist whether or not they are planned. In other words all organizations *de facto* have a strategy. An organization making an operational decision to procure materials may not be conscious of determining a supply chain strategy but that decision taken *ex-ante* may have longer-term consequences both for the purchaser and supplier. For example, *ex-post* it may have determined the lead times, costs and quality involved in production or service provision over a long time period. Essentially what appeared to be an operational decision has become a strategic decision, albeit an unconscious one in the example. The chance meeting in the early years of the twentieth century between Mr Marks and Mr Dewhirst set in train one of the longest lasting supply chain relationships in history for both Dewhirst, the clothing manufacturer, and Marks and Spencer, the retailer. What was essentially a 'one-off' meeting for Marks to acquire shirts for his new penny bazaar in Leeds led to a strategic supply decision. This is not to say that all strategic decisions are serendipitous, many are planned. This book can only really help with the latter type of strategic decision. If you require help with the other type of unforeseen event then you might consider a clairvoyant.

Strategic planning or strategic management?

Strategic planning is an activity that all organizations undertake. How they set about this task may differ as has been acknowledged by many commentators (de Wit and Meyer, 1998; Mintzberg, 1994; Porter, 1980). Strategic planning conceptually involves knowledge of where the organizations fit into its macro- and microenvironment to establish the position of the organization and setting objectives for where the organization would like to be at some future time period, usually 3–5 years from now and creating a plan that will deliver organizational objectives. Marketing, operations and resources (assets, people and money) are critical to achieving any strategy. A firm must attract customers, it must deliver products and services and to do so will need to have resources in place and utilize them effectively. The organizational supply chain is a bridge between customers and operations that deliver and fulfil the customer promise. Planning is important but managing the plan is equally important. Therefore, both strategic planning and strategic management are required if managers want to move the organization to their desired destination, metaphorically speaking.

Defining strategy

Strategy comes from the Greek word '*strategos*' meaning 'general' but in its modern usage in the strategic literature it has been used in different ways. Strategy in contemporary general usage refers to a plan of how to get to a chosen position. In economic terms it is the means (how) to achieving the ends (objectives). Historically, writers have referred to strategies discussing means and ends (Andrews et al., 1965; Chandler, 1962). Hofer and Schendel (1978, p. 5) refer to this as a broad definition of strategy. The narrower definition focuses purely on the means to achieving the end result.

Descriptive and prescriptive approaches to strategy

Historically, the strategy literature tends to fall into two distinct categories – descriptive and prescriptive. Descriptive approaches report observations of organizational strategy and they may attempt to explain. Prescriptive approaches make statements of what strategy ought to be, whereas in essence descriptive approaches focus on what has been. Practising managers and consultants often adopt the prescriptive approach in a planning context. Academics and practising managers may describe actual strategy observing patterns from the past behaviours of the firm.

Mintzberg (1997) offers a number of definitions using five Ps:

- *Plan* – looking forward is the traditional definition of strategy (prescriptive);
- *Pattern* – looking back at consistency of behaviours over time (descriptive);
- *Position* – looks in at products and markets;

- *Perspective* – looks out, fundamental way of doing things, a theory of the business;
- *Ploy* – manoeuvre (to attack, to defend).

Strategy as planning and positioning is the traditional definition of strategy. If you were to ask most practising managers what strategy is, they would probably reply that it is a plan offering the prescriptive definition. However, if you were to ask them to explain their organizational strategy, they may respond by describing past events and patterns of behaviour, offering a descriptive definition. It is important to recognize that realized strategies are not always deliberate and intended strategies are not always realized. When a strategy is realized, but was not intended, it is referred to as an emergent strategy. For example, an organization may pursue a series of opportunistic strategies that can be recognized as forming a particular pattern of activities converging over time. Real strategies are neither purely planned nor purely emergent. Realized strategies are a combination of both deliberate and emergent strategies. Figure 2.1 illustrates realized strategy as a combination of planned and emergent strategies. It shows that some planned strategies fail and are never realized.

Strategies are sometimes viewed as directional, focusing effort, giving definition and meaning or establishing a consistent planned approach to

Figure 2.1

Source: Adapted from Mintzberg et al. (1998).

business organization. Each of these different perspectives has associated advantages and disadvantages.

Strategy as	Advantage	Disadvantage
Direction	Plan a course through the environment	Setting a pre-determined course without knowledge of the environment in advance is perilous
Focus of effort	Promotes co-ordination of effort	Groupthink results
Defining the organization	Provides meaning	Meaning becomes too simplistic and rich complexity is lost
Providing consistency	Reduces ambiguity provides a theory of business	Distorts reality

Source: Adapted from Mintzberg et al. (1998).

So what exactly is strategy?

There are a number of common areas of agreement about what strategy is and they are listed as:

- Strategy concerns both the organization and its environment;
- Strategy is complex;
- Strategy affects the overall welfare of the organization;
- Strategy is both content and process;
- Strategy is not purely deliberate;
- Strategy exists on different levels;
- Strategy involves different thought processes (conceptual and analytical).

Hart (1991, p. 121) states that high-performance firms have to balance conflicting approaches to strategy simultaneously:

- Planned and incremental;
- Directive and participative;
- Controlled and empowered;
- Visionary and detailed.

According to Mintzberg et al. (1998) design, planning and positioning have dominated the strategic literature and the bias has been reflected in practice. This is stated in part as justification for examining a number of different non-rational and non-prescriptive approaches within the text 'Strategy Safari'.

In this text descriptive and prescriptive approaches will be adopted as appropriate to the context and the realized consequences of strategic evaluation, choice, implementation and control are viewed as the result of management decisions, which may have been planned and/or emergent. Strategic evaluation and choice are associated with risk and uncertainty. One flawed assumption of many strategic planning processes is that *a priori* decisions capture all critical information relevant to the decision in advance of the implementation time period. Information is always partial. It is just a matter of degree. Assumptions are just that. Strategies are human management decisions made on partial information in advance of the actual time period, with assumptions about conditions, interactions, attitudes, behaviours, actions and reactions in the environments the firm operates in. Managers interpret information and make assumptions based on their knowledge, experience, advice and learning from their own mistakes and the mistakes of others. Strategic planning relies on forecasting future environmental conditions ahead of the time period in which the plan will be implemented. Strategic management is the process of managing the organization's strategic position in the time period in which the plan is implemented.

It could be argued that developing supply chain strategies is a planning process and implementing and controlling supply chain strategies is a management process. Whichever stance is taken one thing is certain – both are needed to consciously strategically manage an organization.

Levels of strategy

It is important to recognize that strategy may be formulated at different levels of the organizational structure. Corporate level strategy is determined for the whole corporation. Take a firm that has several different divisions, it may develop strategies for the whole organization and each of the different divisions may be strategic business units (SBUs) each with their own strategy. In such instances the SBU strategies must be congruent and fit with the overall corporate objectives and corporate strategy.

Corporate strategy

Corporate strategy is concerned with questions such as: 'What type of businesses should the organization be in?', 'Which markets should the firm pursue?', 'What purchasing and supply chain strategies should be implemented throughout the corporation?', 'What infrastructure needs to be developed to support the whole of the organization to achieve its goals?'. Decisions about diversification and primary structures for the organization together with the contributions that the organization's portfolio of businesses should make to the whole are all corporate level strategy issues.

Business strategy

Business level strategy focuses attention on what the SBUs need to do to achieve their business level objectives within the corporate whole. Questions such as: 'How can the SBU compete in a particular market?', 'What products and services should be offered?', 'Where to locate SBUs?', 'How can the SBU finance its operations in line with overall corporate policies?', 'What supply chain structures are needed to achieve the SBU's strategic objectives?'.

Operational strategy

Operational strategies tend to focus on products and markets and how best to achieve business objectives set by at corporate level and SBU level. Managing capacity, where to locate facilities, managing technologies, people and values may all form part of operational strategy. Operations strategy sets broad policies and develops plans for effective use of organizational resources that best support the firm's long-term competitive strategy. Operational strategies need to be integrated with corporate strategy. Decisions may relate to the design of facilities, processes and the infrastructure required to support processes. Many supply chain strategies fall into this category although they could also be at business or corporate level.

Competitive strategies

Supply chain strategies are most definitely competitive strategies. In competitive markets customers drive markets and markets drive organizational behaviour. Customers make purchasing decisions for a variety of reasons such as cost or service attributes relating to a purchase. Firms need to position themselves to meet the customer's demands. As a consequence, a number of key operational competitive dimensions determine the competitive position in the marketplace. These may include:

- *Cost* – keeping the cost of products or services low allows the firm to offer the customer better value for money through competitive pricing. Focus on this attribute will be particularly important when the firm is in competition with low-price competitors. Low cost alone may not be sufficient to attract and keep customers and the firm may need to compete on other dimensions too. Furthermore, being the lowest cost provider may not be sustainable over time. It is important to acknowledge that there is always only one lowest cost operator in the marketplace, any marketplace. Competing with that lowest cost supplier may or may not be feasible given the firm's size and capabilities. Product markets that compete on price alone are effectively commodity markets where the customer cannot distinguish between the products available from competing firms. Competition is often fierce and profit realization relies on high volumes being achieved.
- *Quality and reliability* – there are two aspects of quality: first, product/service quality and second, process quality. Continuously improving quality and reliability of the products and services offered may be important in the market being served. The organizational objective must be to specify product/service quality at the appropriate level acceptable to the particular market. Overspecification may add cost but not necessarily value from the customer's perspective. The second aspect of process quality is particularly important for all firms competing in the market because no customer wants products with defects. Process quality determines the reliability of the product/service and its reliability. Error-free products are the result of 'zero-defect' processes. Techniques and tools such as statistical process control (SPC), sigma six, are part of this total quality management (TQM) to deliver reliability. Quality kite marks such as ISO9000/9001 are badges that signify that the organization has appropriate quality processes to a particular standard in place.
- *Speed of delivery* – the speed at which a product/service can be delivered may determine a competitive advantage in some markets. For example, security or emergency services that offered a response on site within 10 minutes of the alarm being raised would be preferable to a service offering a response within 1 hour. In retailing, Inditex, the Spanish retailing group behind the Zara fashion brand, have built their success and reputation on being able to get merchandise from design concept to retail store within 3 weeks.
- *Delivery reliability* – delivering on time or ahead of time may help the organization to establish delivery reliability, which may be critical to

secure repeat business. Failure to deliver on time may result in loss of existing contracts and exclusion from future contract negotiations, bidding or tendering.

- *Flexibility* – the ability of a firm to change processes or products. For example, the firm may need to develop and/or introduce new products quickly for its customers. Innovation, design, access to and capabilities in managing new technologies and changing processes may all be part of being strategically flexible.
- *Responsiveness* – the ability to cope with changes in demand. For example, retail stores may offer promotions to customers that stimulate higher than normal demand for a product or range and suppliers will need to be able to respond to this change. Capacity planning and being able to adjust upwards and downwards to changes in demand patterns as and when required is a capability required for longevity of an organization.

In addition to the organization's reputation, its brand, service and technical abilities will affect its capability to compete effectively.

Strategies to co-operate through strategic partnerships and alliances are also necessary and may form part of an organization's competitive strategy. Recently the word *co-opetition* was coined to describe this type of strategy.

These different levels of strategy overlap and strategic decisions may or may not be exclusive to a particular level. Strategic decisions will be taken at corporate, business or operational levels depending upon how the organization is structured and how its managers interact with each other.

Strategy or strategies?

It is also important to understand that organizations may not simply pursue a single strategy but that multiple objectives may require multiple strategies. These multiple strategies may need to be pursued simultaneously in parallel with each other. It is critical that managers do not attempt to implement conflicting strategies. These are strategies that work against each other to the detriment of the organizational unit pursuing the strategies. In this context the focus of the effort should be co-ordinated if the strategies are to be coherent and congruent with each other.

For example, an SBU may decide to pursue a global sourcing strategy and simultaneously pursue strategies to dominate a particular local market. These two strategies are not necessarily in conflict. However, if the corporate strategy had set an objective of where the organization should possibly source locally to serve local markets, then the SBU strategy may conflict with corporate level strategy. It is important for managers to reconcile such conflict to minimize the effects of conflicting strategies. The consequences may be real or perceived. By this statement it is clear that real effects are tangible such as difficulties in implementing global sourcing when resources including the firm's infrastructure make it difficult to pursue and the effect may result in disruption to product flows and increasing cost. Perceived consequences may be intangible (feelings, attitudes and behaviours of customers towards the organization as a consequence of the particular strategy) such as customers making choices to avoid the organization's merchandise as a consequence of its global sourcing policy. The real effects may not materialize immediately. For example, an organization may not be aware that consumers have collectively decided to avoid its products especially if it is a new market. There will be no past history to compare current performance against. It may lead the organization to conclude wrongly that other reasons were the cause of the problem. Perceptions may ultimately lead to real consequences such as a fall in revenue, increased operating cost or insufficient profit.

Strategic thinking, systems and learning

Schon (1971) created the notion of business firms as learning systems evolving in relation to their changing environment. Rapid inventive transformations of the firm happened as innovation occurred. Classical firms were built around products. Clothing is an example. Clothing manufacturers required people who understood design, fabric properties, dye processes, cutting and sewing operations. Professional managers competent in sourcing, purchasing, production, logistics, marketing and finance complete the firm. The firm is an intermediate link that interacts with its suppliers and the ultimate consumer. Since the 1940s there have been many turning points with transitional themes as summarized in Table 2.1.

Table 2.1 Examples of transitional shifts adapted from Schon (1971)

From	*To*
Static product line	Product innovation
Single product line	Product diversity
Product-based	Process-based
Firms as bounded systems	Firms with blurred boundaries within the supply chain

In the 1950s firms began to think of innovation as commonplace and an integral part of the firm, whereas previously entrepreneurs established firms around their inventions. Research and growth were seen as important elements of the firm's system. Consumers used technologies developed in the Second World War in peacetime to deliver new products in demand. Simultaneously firms developed improvements to technological and marketing systems to deliver their new products to customers. There was a general broadening of the industrial base and by the 1960s clothing became fashion, shoes became footwear. Different technologies were employed to develop new products from new materials. Traditional industries were invaded by science-based industries throughout the latter part of the twentieth century. Textiles, shoes, paper, graphics have been transformed through invasion by chemical, petrochemical, electronics and ICT. Well-defined products with well-defined technologies were no longer the norm.

Strategic thinking science or art?

The notion that strategic thinking is scientific in approach comes from the planning school approaches to strategy. However, in common with most epistemological development this is only part of the story. Strategy is also a creative process and as such maybe strategy formulation is more of an art than a science. Figure 2.2 illustrates these two different

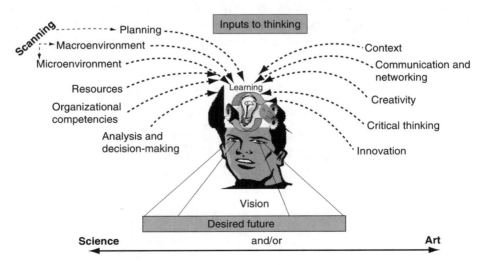

Figure 2.2

approaches and demonstrates that strategic thinking is conducted systematically and creatively. Strategic thinking is both science and art. One side of the brain deals with the rational approaches to formulating strategy and the other side deals with creative and serendipitous approaches to strategy. Learning comes from a variety of sources including experience, reading, observing, doing and thinking. The problem with many practising managers charged with strategic responsibility in many organizations is that they spend too much of their time doing, observing and experiencing and too little of their time thinking and reflecting upon experiences, observations and practices.

Static or dynamic environments

Figure 2.3 depicts a simple four-box model abstracting four different types of environment in which organizations may sit. These environments are polar opposites and you may argue that the world is not so simple. Nevertheless, it gives a framework from which to identify some basic factors influencing firm behaviour and to further analyse conditions and consequences. In the figure, environments are classified as stable or dynamic. Stable environments may be complex or simple. Simple stable environments are predictable. Demand for a product or service in this type of environment would be relatively constant with little variation. Another dimension to stable environments are those that can be classified as more complex: they are more difficult to handle but there is still little change over time which allows the organization to predict demand with some accuracy. For example, a seasonal business may have complexities in terms of products offered but peak periods and trough periods will occur with regularity. Stable environments are easier to manage. Dynamic environments pose a challenge

Typology of environments

	Stable	Dynamic
Complex	Difficult to handle but little change over time	Very uncertain, constant change High risk
Simple	Predictable	Fast moving but reasonably predictable

Figure 2.3

for managers. Dynamic environments may also be classified as dynamic or simple. Simple environments are fast moving but they are reasonably easy to predict. For example, many grocery retailers would operate in a fast moving environment but the demand for certain staple foods, soap powder and detergents may be reasonably well predicted. However, by contrast fashion retailing is both complex and dynamic. Complex because customer demand is fickle and fashions change between the time the retailer orders and supplies goods to the customer. The risks are greater in the latter type of business. Of course we have assumed that businesses operate distinctly in one of the four types of environment for means of illustration. In reality, a single business may have product ranges or services that span all four types making the supply chain challenges a complex conundrum.

Traditionally the areas that the supply chain spans cut across different disciplinary areas of academic study (marketing, operations, human resource management, finance, economics). However, there is a clear case for adopting a Gestalt approach to the study of these areas within supply chains. Managing organizational supply chains is key to the success of most contemporary complex organizations. Organizations need to be both efficient and effective in how they manage and fulfil their customer requirements. Efficiency requires the organization to make best use of resources (doing things right) and effectively is about doing the right things. Organizations need policies, procedures and systems to deliver effectively. These three factors need to be sufficiently flexible to respond to the customer if they are to be effective.

The strategic planning process is illustrated in Figure 2.4. It shows that organizations must scan their environment before setting strategic objectives and developing a plan. Environmental scanning entails an

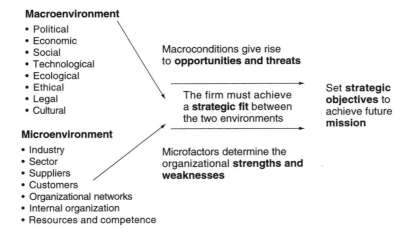

Figure 2.4

examination of the macro- and microenvironments in which the organization operates. The macroenvironmental scan examines political factors, economic factors, social changes occurring, cultural shifts, changes in technology that are impacting on businesses and market structures, ecological influences, ethical dimensions of conducting business and legal considerations. Developing a good knowledge and understanding of these macro-conditions and their consequences is essential.

In addition to understanding the macroenvironment managers need to understand their immediate environment. First, it is important to know the rules of the industry the firm operates in and business models that lead to success in the industry. Knowledge of the organization's position within the industry is required in order to identify particular strengths or weaknesses. Strengths can be developed and harnessed to pursue the particular strategy the firm decides. Weaknesses may be minimized and developing or buying in new competencies needed to move the business in its desired direction may close gaps.

One useful conceptual model to understand the strategic nature of industry competitiveness was developed by Porter (1980). The model shown in Figure 2.5 depicts five forces that are present in the organization's immediate industrial or sectoral environment.

The forces identified recognize the power balance between suppliers and buyers in a particular industry. If there are many suppliers and few buyers the power resides with the buyers. Conversely, if there are

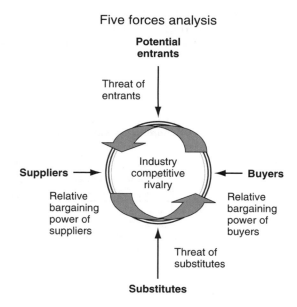

Figure 2.5

many buyers and few suppliers the power resides with the suppliers. In many respects this simplifies the buyer–seller relationship in one dimension and it will become clearer later in the text that buyer–supplier relationships are more complex than this simple model suggests. Nevertheless, understanding the nature of power in the relationship is important. The vertical line depicts the effect of new entrants to an industry and how that can change the nature of competitive rivalry. For example, in retailing the entry to the UK market by Wal-Mart was achieved through takeover of an existing retailer ASDA. The new entrant happened to be the largest retail business in the world with long established suppliers and market strategies based on low price and volume. The new entrant was able to capture market share immediately through takeover and influenced the way in which other retail competitors behaved towards it. Tesco, currently the largest retailer in the UK, responded by cutting prices on many lines. The retail sector has also seen consolidations through merger and takeover in a scramble for existing players in the market to become ever larger to compete effectively. Other new entrants have also had an impact in other sectors; for example, Zara's entry to the UK high street has revolutionized the way in which many of the long established fashion retailers think and operate their businesses, particularly how they manage their supply chains. Organizations that offer substitute products or services will also change the nature of competitive rivalry in an industry. For example, the development of the Internet and electronic mail has had an impact on how the postal and telecommunication industries operate. How competitors in the industry respond to each other as a consequence of these forces is itself a further factor influencing competitive rivalry.

In applying the five forces model it is important to define the industry or sector that is the focus for the analysis. This may be more difficult than it at first appears. There are of course standard industrial classification (SIC) codes that one could use. However, these have their limitations since the competition may exist outside the traditional classification. Take, for example, a designer womenswear retail store. You may decide to define the competitive rivalry by market or product. In examining the competitive rivalry do you compare all womenswear retailers since they may offer competitive products some of which will be designer-wear, some may be haute couture and others may be mass-market retailers? Do you include or exclude department stores? Whatever your decision in drawing such comparisons it will impact upon the subsequent analysis. It is also important to recognize different applications in terms of B2B and B2C markets. Figure 2.6 provides an illustration for B2C using designer-wear retailers as the focus of competitive rivalry and gives examples of the

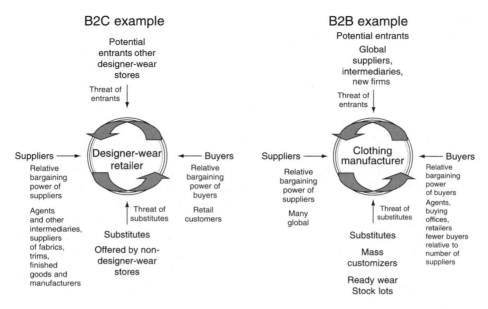

Figure 2.6

influences on that market. Alongside this is an illustration of the model applied to B2B markets using clothing manufacturers as the focus of analysis.

Another useful conceptual model examining the environmental influences related to supply chains was developed by Saunders (1997, p. 55). Figure 2.7 shows how the firm and its competitors are influenced primarily by conditions prevailing in supply markets and customer markets. In this respect it is similar to the five forces model horizontal line

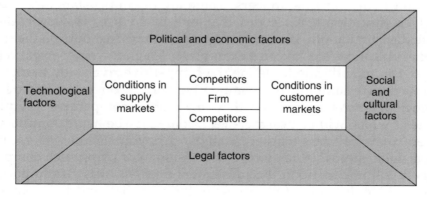

Figure 2.7
Source: Adapted from Saunders (1997, p. 55)

considering the relative bargaining power of suppliers and buyers. However, it is different in recognizing other conditions that may influence the firm and its competitors apart from the relative bargaining power. The model then shows how wider influences in the macroenvironment are influencing market conditions and the behaviour of the firm and its competitors. In this respect the model integrates the macro- and microenvironmental factors influencing the organization.

Most of these conceptual models appear to assume that the influences are unidirectional impacting upon the organization. The reality is that firms interact with their environment and as a consequence they too influence to a greater or lesser extent the environmental conditions. For example, large organizations may well apply greater pressure on government to implement particular policies, pass particular laws, maintain monetary and economic policy and so on. Smaller firms may act collectively to achieve greater influence over their environment.

Conditions in the organization's macroenvironment may lead to the identification of particular opportunities or particular threats facing the firm. An organization will only be able to maximize opportunities and minimize threats if it is able to exploit the opportunities or repel the threats identified. Their ability to do so will depend upon their capabilities. Organizational capability is dependent upon resources that the firm is able to deploy and how effectively and efficiently those resources can be applied.

Until recently, structuralists maintained a dominant view in strategy and in the development of strategic knowledge explaining superior performance through structural features such as barriers to entry, substitute products, industry structures and the nature of competition (Ansoff, 1965; Porter, 1980, 1985). A different view was held by Selznick (1957) and Penrose (1959), who were early movers towards a resource-based view of strategy. More recently, Wernefelt (1984), Prahalad and Hamel (1990) and Barney (1991) have suggested that skills and capabilities are more significant in determining strategic success rather than a myopic focus upon the external competitive environment. Collis and Montgomery (1995) suggested that focus on both the competitive environment and the organizational capabilities was necessary in examining the organization's performance in its competitive environments. In essence, the range of views expressed simply acknowledge the different emphases. The *'outside in'* approach is essentially structuralist and focuses attention on the environmental impact upon the organization's strategy. Whereas the *'inside out'* approach recognizes that firm's need to be capable of taking advantage of the opportunities identified from the outside. To create successful supply chain strategies the firm needs to be able to understand both aspects. In effect this is strategy as perspective.

Competence and capability

Christopher (1996, p. 71) comments that one of the most profound changes is the recognition that even the largest business organizations will have only relatively few competencies in which they can be said to have a real distinction. This recognition has resulted in a focus upon core business and a trend to outsourcing everything else. The growth of outsourcing has placed increasing emphasis on managing relations between partners in the organizational network. Although the language of 'core competence' is recent, the concept of specialization on which it is based can be traced back to Adam Smith in 1776 and the theory of comparative advantage expounded by David Ricardo in the economics literature in the nineteenth century.[1] Furthermore, a number of different commentators have used different terms such as *firm resources, organizational capabilities* and *core competencies* interchangeably. See Table 2.2 for a summary of usage of terms.

Definitions of core competence

Definitions of core competence are somewhat tautological. Resources are called strengths and a firm's strengths are regarded as strategic resources (Nanda, 1996, p. 100). Selznick (1957) was first to introduce the concept of a distinctive competence but he never defined it. Andrews (1971, p. 46) later stated that a distinctive competence was something a firm did well. In similar vein Hofer and Schendel (1978, p. 25) refer to resources that will

Table 2.2

Terminology	*Reference*
Distinctive competence	Andrews (1971)
	Hofer and Schendel (1978)
	Selznick (1957)
Strategic firm resources	Barney (1986a)
	Barney (1986b)
Invisible assets	Itami (1987)
Strategic firm-specific assets	Dierdickx and Cool (1989)
Core competencies	Dosi et al. (1991)
	Prahalad and Hamel (1990)
Corporate culture	Cremer (1989)
Corporate capabilities	Nohria and Eccles (1991)
Organizational capabilities	Baldwin and Clark (1991)
Dynamic capabilities	Teece et al. (1997)

achieve the firm's goals or objectives. Dosi et al. (1991) take the definition a step further by stating that they are differentiated skills, complementary assets, organizational routines and capabilities that achieve a firm's competitive capacities in a particular business. This latter definition appears to move towards a position of acknowledging contextual influences. Prahalad and Hamel's (1990) definition was more narrowly focused towards human resources. Later Prahalad and Hamel (1994) widen the scope of their definition referring to bundles of skills. Barney (1986a,b) uses the term 'strategic firm resources' to mean the same as a 'distinctive competence' or a 'core competence'.

Whatever their chosen terminology is the focus for most of these authorities is the same. They are adopting a similar stance examining the key strengths the firm has or is capable of building to achieve its strategic goals. They may all be classified as taking a resource-based view of the organization. Organizations either develop competencies internally or they buy-in the competencies they require. Mergers or acquisitions often have a primary aim of purchasing particular markets (e.g. a means of achieving a market entry strategy such as Wal-Mart's purchase of Asda UK to get immediate market share), purchasing particular technologies (e.g. Glaxo's acquisition of Smith-Kline Beecham to acquire biotechnologies) and purchasing 'know-how' or knowledge through acquisition. Collaborative arrangements may achieve similar ends without the responsibilities and risks of ownership.

Prahalad and Hamel (1994, p. 219) define a core competence as follows:

A core competence is a bundle of skills and technologies that enables a company to provide a particular benefit to customers.

Examples given of a core competence by Prahalad and Hamel (1994, p. 219) include *'pocketability'* at Sony, *on time delivery* at Federal Express, *logistics* at Wal-Mart leading to choice, availability and value for customers. To this list one could add *supply chain management* per se as a core competence. It is not simply an aspect of managing the supply chain such as on time delivery that is a core competence in many contemporary organizations, but if one considers an organization like Amazon.com the ways in which it sources and procures product, stores and moves product from the various suppliers and onto the customer by bundling different skills and e-business technologies to deliver products faster and at lower cost than many of its competitors, is a good example of supply chain management per se as a core competence for that organization.

Core competencies are skills or capabilities that make an organization unique. The key question is what share of the future markets will these competencies enable the organization to capture. The identification of core competence gaps can help an organization recognize (a) where it wants to be; (b) which competencies it should build; and (c) how they should be built. This recognition will lead to the strategies that the organization will pursue. Core competencies represent intellectual capital. Questions arise such as what is core and what is non-core, how long does it take to build the competencies and how many such competencies are necessary to compete effectively. In answer to the first part a core competence is a source of competitive advantage. In Porter's terms there are only two sources of competitive advantage: cost and differentiation (Porter, 1985). Pursuing this line of argument it would appear that a core competence must either give a cost advantage or differentiate the organization from its competitors. Restructuring the organization and downsizing may be one way to achieve competitive advantage by becoming smaller and lowering costs. Re-engineering processes and continuous improvement are another route to competitive advantage by being better, i.e. more efficient and hence lower cost. Or re-inventing industries and regenerating strategies to alter the rules of engagement are another source of competitive advantage to become different. Prahalad and Hamel (1990) make clear that competitive advantage itself is not a core competence and that a core competence is a critical success factor (CSF) but that not all CSFs are core competencies. It can take 5–10 years to build core competencies and it is unlikely that any organization will have more than fifteen core competencies and the range will usually be between five and fifteen (Prahalad and Hamel, 1994, p. 224). Finally, for a competence to be core it must satisfy three criteria: (i) it must make a disproportionate contribution to customer perceived value; (ii) it must be competitively unique, i.e. not unique to the firm as such but must in some way differentiate the firm's offering in a unique way; and (iii) it must be extendible meaning that the competence may be applied to new product areas or to new market developments and not just to existing product groups or existing markets. Core competencies will therefore enhance customer value or reduce cost.

Prahalad and Hamel (1994, p. 224) discuss the idea of non-core and core in relation to competence in detail. They argue that it doesn't matter whether or not the term used is competence or capability and recognize that firms competing on their capabilities is not a novel or new idea in itself. It is further suggested that simply to list all the competencies a firm has is not very useful in terms of assisting managers since equal attention cannot be given to all these items. Focus needs to be upon competencies that are at the centre of what the firm does rather than at the periphery. In other words it is *core* to what they do. For any competence to be regarded as a core competence it must pass three tests:

1. *Customer value*: The competence must contribute to customer perceived value disproportionately and deliver fundamental customer benefits.

2. *Competitor differentiation*: In order to be regarded as a core competence the capability must be competitively unique. Thus a competence that resides in all firms in an industry is not unique and cannot therefore be regarded as core unless the individual firm has a competence level that is substantially superior. It is notable that Prahalad and Hamel (1994, p. 227) continue their argument about core and non-core by referring to underdeveloped competencies ubiquitous within an industry.

3. *Extendibility*: Core competencies are the gateways to tomorrow's markets according to Prahalad and Hamel (1994, p. 227). Managers must abstract away from a particular product configuration in which the competence is embedded and imagine how it can be applied to new product arenas.

Learning and organizational capability

According to Prahalad and Hamel (1994) core capabilities and competencies differentiate a company from its competitors leading to a competitive advantage. Organizational learning has been defined as the capability of an organization to adapt to its environment (Hedberg, 1981). Garvin (1993) identified organizational learning as a capability required by all firms.

The model in Figure 2.8 is a conceptualization involving three learning loops that develop a firm's capabilities and core capabilities in relation to managing supply chains beginning with resources, routine operations, work practices and taking account of external environmental conditions

Figure 2.8 Learning to develop capabilities

and mission. Resources at the firm's disposal determine supply chain structure. Mission and management actions can affect resources and determine supply chain strategy. Relationships link both supply chain strategy and structure, and connect the firm with its internal and external operating environment.

The first loop creates routine practices using resources. The second loop combines work practices and organizational routines determined by management action and interaction. Relationships are an important focus for learning in the context of the supply chain in this second loop. The third gives meaning to capabilities in the context of the competitive environment and mission. Management intervention aims to provide direction to learning processes (Argyris, 1991). Core capabilities are components of organizational context, radical learning means learning how to do radically new things (bottom loop), which are important in radically new ways implying activity in the top loop (Argyris and Schon, 1978).

Individual competence and organizational capability may be improved through learning. Organizations are able to build strengths and minimize weaknesses through learning. Learning how to learn and how to manage learning inside the organization is critical to improving strategic performance (Argyris, 1996).

Example of learning loops in action

An organization may decide to assign workers to their daily tasks or routines, allocate materials to a production line and decide on the number of lines and which equipment to use for the day's activities. These are everyday occurrences in a factory setting; they are routines and located in the first loop at the bottom. Management intervention may occur in the second learning loop to make adjustments to the size of the workforce, the number of machines, to train the workforce or to change processes to improve capabilities and performance. Work experience (learning curve effect) and individual/team learning may improve individual and team performance in the second loop. The third learning loop is market-facing and market-driven. The third loop also contains learning from daily routines in the first loop, an evaluation of capabilities in the second loop and the influences upon organizational context from the marketplace and from the corporate mission. The final loop leads to strategic management interventions. The nature of the competitive environment and market conditions balanced with organizational capabilities that exist may influence the organization to decide to move production from one location to another, to invest in new plant or divest of existing plant to achieve its corporate or SBU strategic objectives.

Developing strategic objectives

In developing strategic plans after scanning the macro- and microenvironments the managers will need to identify opportunities and threats to determine possible future directions. These opportunities and threats need to be balanced against the organization's current and potential competencies and capability to implement a particular strategic plan. Managers will want to set objectives or planned outcomes that should be a consequence of pursuing a particular strategic direction. Objectives need to be measurable so that managers can assess progress towards their goals. It may be trite to state that objectives need to be 'SMART' but SMART they should be, i.e.:

- **S**pecific (the stated objective should be as precise as it can be);
- **M**easurable (need to be able to identify and measure actual achievements against the plan);
- **A**chievable (given resources at the firm's disposal);
- **R**elevant (does this objective fit the firm's purpose/mission);
- **T**imed (specific dates by which progress can be measured).

For example, the statement of a particular objective to satisfy the criteria might read: to achieve a 5 per cent increase in share of the UK mobile phone market measured in retail values rather than volumes by 2006.

There is often an assumption that setting objectives is a scientific process. Systematic it may be, scientific it is not. Setting objectives is a subjective process involving human judgement and as such involves all the human frailties that exist in individuals and in collective decision-making processes. Evaluations may be made subject to specific *a priori* criteria laid down by a management team to give a feeling of objectivity to the final decisions taken. Nevertheless, ultimately it requires judgement to set objectives, human judgement. The appropriateness of the strategic objectives set by the management team are a manifestation of their knowledge, experience and understanding, hence their managerial competence.

Committing resources to a plan and 'opportunity cost'

Once the managers responsible collectively develop specific strategic objectives for the organization they will need to evaluate a number of strategic options and make choices to commit resources to the plan. In economic terms the resources are referred to as factors of production: land, labour, capital and entrepreneurial effort. There is an opportunity cost of applying resources to a particular plan – the opportunity cost being the alternative plans that could have been implemented using the same resources.

Once strategic objectives have been agreed and strategic choices evaluated the detailed plan is formulated. Strategic plans have operational implications. For example, if the strategic objective is to lower cost of bought-in materials by a specific and measurable percentage over a 5-year timeframe, managers may choose to source products from countries where the quality of product is similar to an existing supplied item, but the cost of producing the items is lower because of the economic conditions prevailing in the country of supply. Making this choice may impact upon the firm's operations. For example, the firm may need to plan more carefully to take account of longer delivery times or longer production lead times than those achieved by local suppliers. The firm may also need to forecast the impact of exchange rate fluctuations upon prices agreed with suppliers, which may be in a foreign currency. Furthermore, changes in economic conditions in the country of manufacture such as inflation, unemployment and interest rates will inevitably impact upon the supplier's cost base either favourably or unfavourably. Political stability in the source country where the supplier operates may introduce further dimensions of risk and uncertainty, which impact upon operations.

Figure 2.9 illustrates the strategic management processes. Once the plan has been formulated, it is implemented and there needs to be some management control. The latter are interventions by managers to keep the plan on course to achieve the strategic objectives.

Figure 2.10 illustrates the strategic planning processes with feedback loops that demonstrate how control is affected. Control is achieved by measuring the planned outcomes against the actual performance during a particular planning period. Strategic plans covering say a 5-year period may be divided into operational time periods, e.g. a financial

Figure 2.9

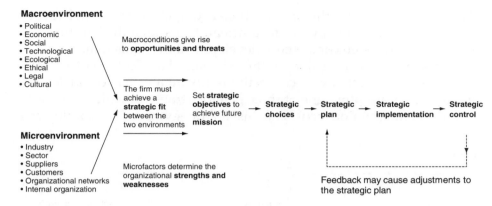

Figure 2.10

year. Performance indicators may be set for each operational time period that give an indication of how the organization is performing against its strategic objectives.

Finally, Figure 2.11 demonstrates that strategic control may not simply make adjustments to the plan alone. Strategic control may be exercised by re-examining the effectiveness of implementation. It may require a re-think of the strategic choices that the management of the organization have made or it may require the organization to re-visit the strategic objectives that were originally set. Changes may need to be made to any or all of these matters. In the process of exercising strategic control it may

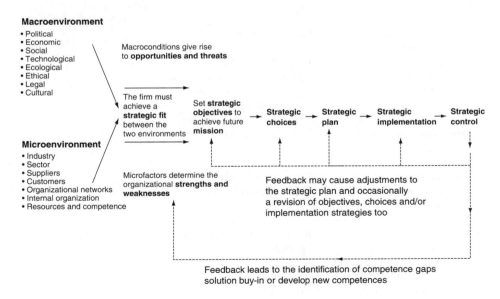

Figure 2.11

also become clear that the organizational competencies to implement a particular chosen strategy are insufficient. Gaps identified in this way may be filled through competence development or acquisition.

It was mentioned earlier in this chapter that Porter (1980, 1985) recognized two sources of competitive advantage that could lead to organizations adopting one of three generic strategies which are lowest cost, differentiation or focus. A focused strategy may also employ cost

Table 2.3

Strategic option	Customer values	Communicated to the customer through
Cost leader Reduce cost base – through efficiency and productivity measures	*Low prices above all else*	*Price and price promotions*
Lean purchasing	Efficiency	
Lean production (LP)	Efficiency	
Learning curve effect	Efficiency	
Experience	Productivity improvements	
Economies of scale	Productivity improvements	
Specialist knowledge, skills, systems, technologies that lower cost	Productivity improvements	
Differentiation	*Reputation*	*Branding and brand values and levels of service*
Quality of product and/or service	Quality over price	
Reliability	Reliability over price	
Flexibility (e.g. agile production)	Ability to switch later in the purchase cycle more important than price alone – postponement	
Responsiveness – speed in response, processes, deliveries	Time above price	
Dependability	Depend on fulfilment	
Value for money (not just cost)	Value above pure price	
Focus Niche – a small but easily identifiable target market	*Specific needs being satisfied* Specialization	*Service attention*
Customer requirements	Customization	
Local, regional, national, international markets	Coverage	

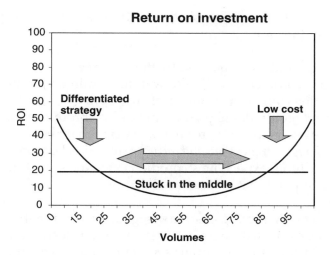

Figure 2.12

or differentiation as its main strategy. Table 2.3 illustrates the three strategic options and the likely supply chain focuses required by the customer and how the strategy might be communicated.

Figure 2.12 illustrates that high returns on investment may be achieved through either a differentiation strategy or through means of a low-cost strategy. Low-cost strategies rely on high volumes and low unit profitability which when combined, achieve higher than normal returns on investment. A differentiated strategy returns higher than normal returns on lower volumes. Porter (1980) stated that firms that tried to pursue a mixed strategy of low cost and differentiation get 'stuck in the middle'.

Supply chain strategies and strategic fit

Supply chain strategies are conducted under the umbrella of the corporate strategy of the organization. Competitive strategies are market-focused. Strategic fit has to be achieved between the supply chain strategies and the competitive strategies adopted by the organization. To achieve the strategic fit the organization has to:

(a) *Understand the customer* by being customer-focused and recognizing the key requirements in each target segment they serve.
(b) *Understand the nature and structure of their own supply chains* and how they respond under changing conditions in the market and the micro- and macroenvironment.

Market variables determine six key attributes of any supply chain structure and they are:

1. *Volume* – quantities demanded by the customer.
2. *Time* – the customer is willing to wait for fulfilment of the order.
3. *Variety* – determines the number of suppliers.
4. *Service level* required – high, medium or low product availability.
5. *Price* – how sensitive the product is to price changes.
6. *Rate of change, innovation and new product development* – customers buying fashion expect new products, whereas customers buying standard apparel that is functional do not.

The purpose of identifying customer segments is to identify similarities between groups of customers in order that their needs can be satisfied efficiently. Customers in different segments may have similar needs to other segments but most times the differences will be greater than the similarities observed. Where similarities are observed the supply chain structures and strategies may be similar and economies may be achieved by sharing costs across the target segments. Where differences are identified there is less room to develop standard services across the target groups and the costs of supply chains may be higher as a consequence. However, it is not simply about cost (but cost is important), it is about responsive supply chains. These are supply chains that are able to meet the challenges placed upon them by high-velocity changes in demand.

Chopra and Meindl (2001, p. 29) draw a distinction between demand uncertainty created by the customer in the market and implied demand uncertainty. The latter is the demand uncertainty implied by the supply chain itself and how it is structured to deal with attributes valued by the customer. For example, the customers need for a larger range to select from implies that there will be a greater variance in demand. Similarly if delivery lead times reduce, this implies that demand uncertainty increases because there is less time to react to a change in delivery times experienced. If variety is reduced this implies a decrease in uncertainty as demand for products become more aggregated and hence more certain. Retailers often say that increases in customer service levels are a one-way street meaning they cannot reduce them, there is no turning back. As customer service levels increase and products are more readily available there is an implied risk owing to surges in demand. Retailers often exacerbate the condition by offering promotions in-store across product categories. Stores offering short lead times and high variety have a higher level of implied demand uncertainty than do those with longer lead times and low variety. The paradox appears to be that the better you become at attempting to meet customer demand, the higher the risk through the uncertainty of implied demand. A further example is the textile apparel supply chain. Downstream at the apparel manufacturer high variety and fast responsive supply chains carry greater implied demand uncertainty than do the textile fabric mills, where customers place orders months in advance of the time it is required for apparel manufacture. Forecasting is easier when demand is more certain. The environment is far more stable. Mark-downs are high for products with high implied demand uncertainty (e.g. fashion items).

Fashionable clothing has the following attributes: high variety, small volumes, fast lead times in production and delivery, and changes offering new design and innovations are done quickly rendering old fashion obsolete. As a consequence there is high implied demand uncertainty. If retailers were able to make a perfect forecast or, better still, not rely on forecast at all but act upon actual demand information, a situation whereby there was either excess inventory or excess demand that could not be fulfilled would never arise. Inventory would be scheduled to arrive in time to meet customer demand. Synchronization of these processes would be achieved more effectively thus increasing profitability. Figure 2.12 illustrates the importance of accurate forecasting. In practice what happens in many retail supply chains is that commitments are made well in advance of the selling season, and volumes and other critical decision variables such as colour, size, styles and categories are based on forecast demand. Value can be lost in season if forecasts are inaccurate and inevitably they are, sometimes by very large percentages. Risks at the retail end of the supply chain are very high which is why fashion margins are set relatively high to cover the risks involved. If stocks do not move as expected hard decisions are taken quickly to mark-down aggressively to move inventories through the retail supply chain. Inevitably this lowers overall profitability but it does attempt to avoid the risk of being stuck with inventories incurring holding costs.

If demand is greater than expected sales can be lost by not having sufficient product to sell (Figure 2.13). This may be equally disturbing for retailers who have invested heavily in promoting merchandise and sales. In effect they will have spent money generating demand which they cannot fill but a competitor might. In effect they have subsidized the competition. Retailers would like to act on real demand and this means they need to have responsive suppliers. A responsive supplier in this context means one who is able to make and deliver quickly to meet demand. This allows a retailer to postpone production until they are sure of demand, thus avoiding risk whilst simultaneously not losing customers by not being able to meet excess demand. Wastage is eliminated in the supply chain, stock-holding risks (mark-downs, obsolescence) are removed and customer demand is met efficiently.

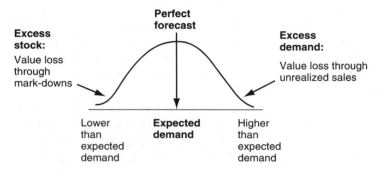

Figure 2.13

Fisher (1997) identified that implied demand uncertainty is correlated to other characteristics of demand as shown in Figure 2.14.

The spectrum of arrangements might include low implied demand uncertainty for functional items through to high implied demand uncertainty owing to fashion. Goods and service with high implied uncertainty are often new with little direct competition, and as a result the profit margins are higher than those with lower implied risk. Forecasting is more accurate when demand patterns are more certain. Increasing implied demand uncertainty creates difficulties in matching supply and demand. A stock-out or overstock situation is likely as in the case of fashionable clothing. Overstocks lead to mark-downs or lost income through under-stocking, e.g. retail promotions.

Understanding the customer is only the first step to designing strategic fit. Meeting demand is the next step. The question is how responsive is the supply chain to the customer's demand? Supply chains have many different characteristics but all supply chains have two important attributes: cost and service. In this respect we can equate service with

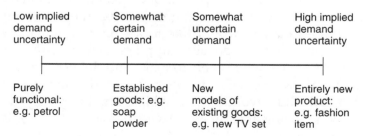

Figure 2.14

responsiveness rather than a narrower definition of service level availability. Supply chain responsiveness is a measure of ability to:

- respond to volume changes in demand;
- compress lead times (quick response or QR);
- deal with variety of products;
- build and deliver innovative new products quickly (QR);
- achieve a high service level.

Supply chains displaying more of these characteristics are said to be more responsive. However, there is a trade-off between responsiveness and cost. For example, capacity may need to increase to deal with larger volumes and more variety, and hence this will incur higher cost. Every strategic decision to improve responsiveness will increase cost. Figure 2.15 illustrates that high levels of responsiveness are dependent upon increasing cost. The responsiveness cost frontier represents a spectrum of strategic choice. Supply chain efficiency is therefore measured as a cost of producing and delivering goods and service to the customer. Increases in cost lower efficiency but they will increase responsiveness. A supply chain can be highly efficient or highly responsive – it cannot be both in this model. For each increase in responsiveness there is a decrease in efficiency.

Putting responsive and efficient supply chains as a trade-off recognizes that different levels of responsiveness have associated cost implications. A highly efficient organization may be less responsive. Take the case of a textile mill: it has time to plan production to ensure that volumes achieve economies of scale and the customers have been accustomed to waiting, so speed of response has been less important for large volume operators. At the other end of the spectrum the QR apparel manufacturer employed to get replenishment items into fashion retail stores in 2 or 3 weeks is under a time pressure and efficiency in terms of cost and economies of scale is less important to the retail customer than ensuring that they do not miss the selling period. Figure 2.16 illustrates the concept of strategic fit further for an organization focused upon efficiency. It illustrates how each of the

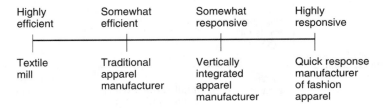

Figure 2.15

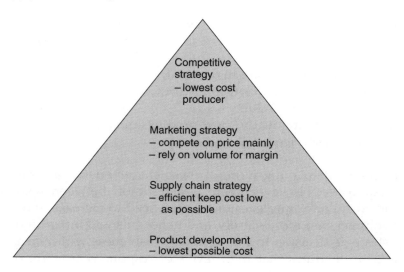

Figure 2.16

functional strategies fit with the organization's overall competitive strategy. Having the right supply chain strategy must be strongly associated with the organization's competitive strategy. The supply chain strategy cannot be planned or implemented independent of the corporate strategy.

Understanding what the customer needs and designing supply chain strategies that can meet their needs is what customer-focused supply chains are all about. Figure 2.17 illustrates the trade-off involved.

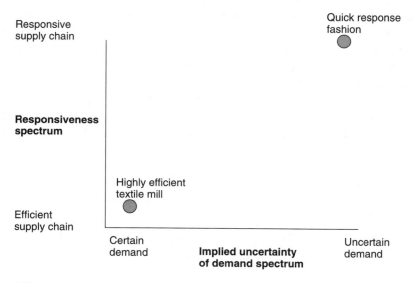

Figure 2.17

In the two examples both achieve a strategic fit in terms of their competitive strategy. The large textile mill competitive strategy is to have large volume orders to gain economies of scale to minimize operational costs and offer customers best prices. Because the mill can be reasonably certain regarding the implied demand it is more focused on achieving efficiencies which are valued by its customers rather than responsiveness which would cost more and which the customers may value less than the price paid. In the case of the QR fashion manufacturer speed of response is highly valued by the retail customer so that they do not miss the season sales. Price is less important and therefore supply efficiency is not as important as ensuring timely supply. There will be a strategic fit between the corporate and supply chain strategies in this case because the organizational competitive advantage is built around speed of response and so too is the supply chain strategy. Fisher (1997) identified a comparison of different strategies based on whether the organizational primary aim was to be efficient or responsive. Table 2.4 summarizes the different approaches discussed.

Table 2.4

	Efficient supply chain	*Responsive supply chain*
Primary goal	Supply at lowest cost	Quick response (QR)
Product design strategy	Maximize performance at lowest cost	Create modularity to share materials, components, parts to allow postponement and product differentiation
Pricing strategy	Lower margins, higher volume, price is the prime customer-driver	Higher margins as price relatively less important to the customer
Manufacturing strategy	Lower cost through high plant utilization	Maintain capacity to meet unexpected demand
Inventory strategy	Minimize inventories to lower cost	Maintain buffer inventories to meet unexpected demand
Lead time	Reduce but not at the expense of cost increases	Uncompromisingly lower lead times even if it means incurring higher costs
Supplier strategy	Select suppliers on the basis of cost and quality	Speed, flexibility, quality and dependability are the most valued characteristics of a supplier
Transport strategy	Choose lowest cost mode of transport	Choose fastest means of delivery depending on need regardless of cost

Source: Adapted from Fisher (1997).

Synchronizing the supply chain to meet customer demand

The value proposition put to the customer should be congruent with the needs identified in the market segment. It is important to recognize that within organizations there may be scope to have different supply chain strategies focused upon different groups of customers. In other words there may not be a single supply chain strategy for the whole organization. Rather there may be a number of different supply chain strategies that fit strategically with the corporate strategy and the different competitive strategies being pursued in different market segments.

There are two clear elements to any market offer and they are:

1. *Visible elements* – choice presented to the customer (the store, the catalogue, the website, the sales people and the merchandise) and delivery;
2. *Invisible elements* – the back-office, the factory, the supply chain.

Production of goods and services is largely hidden from the customer in most situations unless, e.g. the Chef cooks a meal at your table and presents the food in front of your eyes, you would never know what goes on behind the scenes in most restaurants. You only see the finished article, food delivered to your table. The panic to get the right vegetables, fish and other ingredients to prepare the food, the stand-in Chef owing to illness, the earlier fire in the kitchen, the fact that two staff are off tonight, the fact that the cooker is playing up – you are blind to. The ambience is calm and relaxing in the restaurant itself and this is the only part you see.

Synchronizing production and supply chain activities with customer choice is the key to successful fulfilment. Meeting the customer need becomes the focus for restaurant staff in the example. The fact that there are labour shortages and supply chain issues is something they need to sort out to deliver the menu they have offered. It is an example of a highly responsive supply chain.

Summary

It has been noted that strategy is both content and process. Many of the frameworks are in effect process models of how to form and formulate strategy. These processes allow the content of strategy to develop. For example, the strategic planning framework begins with environmental scanning and analysis that determine opportunities and threats, and organizational strengths and weaknesses. From this analysis content for vision, mission, purpose and strategic objectives are set and determine strategic choices, having evaluated a range of options, means to the desired ends. Visions are translated into a detailed plan, process and content, which is implemented (process) and then controlled (process).

These strategic processes are similar at different levels of strategy. It is content and context of strategy that is different at different levels of strategy. In the supply chain system context, for supply chain strategies to develop, the development process may be intentional, deliberate and planned. The realized supply chain strategies may be the result of planning and/or a consequence of unintended, non-deliberate, emergent influences. Past strategies may be described identifying both the planned and emergent strategies realized by an organization. Future strategies are planned and offer prescriptions to achieve a desired future objective. Management interventions occur as a consequence of recognition that an emergent strategy is desirable or not desirable. Management effort might be increased to shape the desired emergent strategy or to dampen and curtail an undesirable emergent strategy. Management interventions also shape the strategic plans, the intended strategies chosen to deliver the strategic objectives.

This chapter began by discussing approaches to strategy as descriptive or prescriptive. Differences between strategic planning and strategic management were noted from the literature. Strategic concepts were also linked to discussions of supply chain strategies. A number of different definitions and statements of what strategy is according to various commentators over time were offered. It was recognized that in reality realized strategies might be planned or emergent and that some planned strategies are never realized. A number of important strategic conceptual frameworks and planning models were also introduced. The next chapter will focus upon the emergence of supply chain management and the need for supply chain strategies. These strategies must be customer-focused and market-driven. The final part of the chapter explained the need to develop supply chain strategies that fit with the organization's competitive strategy.

Discussion Questions

1. Define strategy.
2. Discuss the difference between strategic planning and strategic management.
3. Explain what you understand to be the differences between descriptive and prescriptive strategies.
4. Identify different levels of strategy and give examples of each type of strategy.

5. 'Strategic thinking is required to develop strategy'. Do you agree?
6. 'Competence and capabilities are important for an organization to develop appropriate supply chain strategies'. Discuss.
7. Explain why organizational learning is important to achieve strategic objectives.
8. Explain why it is important to develop supply chain strategies that take account of 'strategic fit'.
9. 'Committing resources to supply chain strategies has an opportunity cost'. Discuss.
10. 'Synchronizing supply chain activities is an important part of any supply chain strategy'. Discuss.

Note

[1] Adam Smith published the Wealth of Nations in 1776 and within the work described in great detail the benefits of specialization in relation to the production of pins. The essence of the argument was that through specializing in a particular skill each worker could become more productive in that aspect of work. As a consequence of specializing in a particular skill or a few skills each worker's contribution to the total production process becomes more effective and a firm is able to produce more in a given time. David Ricardo referred to 'comparative advantage' and although this concept was discussed at the macroeconomic level comparing countries it has great similarity with the arguments presented at the microeconomic level when drawing comparisons between firms. A comparative advantage is said to arise when a particular country is able to concentrate its efforts or resources on those activities in which the country has a comparative advantage. A core competence is a skill which a firm has that distinguishes it from its competitors. By focusing upon its core competencies a firm can achieve a competitive advantage. Therefore, historically economists were concerned with specialization to achieve a comparative advantage at a macroeconomic level, whereas today managerial economists have focused upon core competencies to achieve a competitive advantage at the firm level.

References

Andrews, K., Learned, E., Christensen, C. R. and Guth, W. (1965). *Business Policy Text and Cases*. Holmwood, IL: Irwin.

Andrews, K. R. (1971). *The Concept of Corporate Strategy*. Holmewood, IL: Dow Jones Irwin.

Ansoff, I. (1965). *Corporate Strategy*. London: Penguin.

Argyris, C. (1991). Teaching smart people how to learn. *Harvard Business Review*, **69** (3), 99–109.

Argyris, C. (1996). Prologue: toward a comprehensive theory of management. In *Organizational Learning and Competitive Advantage* (Moingeon, B. and Edmondson, A., eds). London: Sage.

Argyris, C. and Schon, D. (1978). *Organisational Learning*. London: Addison Wesley.

Baldwin, C. Y. and Clark, K. B. (1991). Capabilities and capital investment: new perspectives on capital budgeting. Harvard Business School Working Paper No. 92-004.

Barney, J. B. (1986a). Types of competition and the theory of strategy: towards an integrative framework. *Academy of Management Review*, **11**, 791–800.

Barney, J. B. (1986b). Strategic factor markets: expectation, luck and business strategy. *Management Science*, **32** (10), 1231–513.

Barney, J. B. (1991). Firm resources and sustained competitive advantage. *Journal of Management*, **17** (1), 99–120.

Chandler, A. D., Jr. (1962). *Strategy and Structure: Chapters in the History of the Industrial Enterprise*. Boston: MIT Press.

Chopra, S. and Meindl, P. (2001). Supply Chain Management – Strategy, Planning and Operation. Upper Saddle River, NJ: Prentice-Hall.

Christopher, M. G. (1996). *Marketing Logistics*. Oxford: Butterworth-Heinemann.

Collis, D. and Montgomery, C. (1995). Competing on resources: strategy in the 1990s. *Harvard Business Review*, July–August. Boston, MA: Harvard Business Press, pp. 118–28.

Cremer, J. (1989). Common knowledge and the coordination of economic activities. In *The Firm as a Nexus of Treaties* (Aoki, M., Gustafson, B. and Williamson, O. E., eds). London: Sage.

de Wit, B. and Meyer, R. (1998). *Strategy – Process, Content, Context*. London: Thompson Learning.

Dierdickx, I. and Cool, K. (1989). Asset stock accumulation and sustainability of competitive advantage. *Management Science*, **35** (12), 1504–11.

Dosi, G., Teece, D. J. and Winter, S. G. (1991). Towards a theory of corporate coherence. In *Technology and the Enterprise in a Historical Perspective* (Dosi, G., Giametti, R. and Toninelli, P. A., eds). Oxford: Oxford University Press.

Fisher, M. L. (1997). What is the right supply chain for your product? *Harvard Business Review* (March–April), pp. 83–93.

Garvin, D. A. (1993). Building a learning organization. *Harvard Business Review*, January–February, Boston: HBR Press, pp. 78–91.

Hart, S. (1991). Internationality and autonomy. I. Strategy – Making process: modes< archetypes and firm performance. *Advanced Strategic Management*, **7**, 97–121.

Hedberg, B. (1981). How organizations learn and unlearn. In *Handbook of Organization Design*, Vol. 1, *Adapting Organizations to their Environments*, (Nyrom, P. C. and Starbuck, W. H., eds). Oxford: Oxford University Press.

Hofer, C. and Schendel, D. (1978). *Strategy Formulation: Analytical Concepts*. Minnesota: West Publishing.

Itami, H. (1987). *Mobilizing Invisible Assets*. Cambridge, MA: Harvard University Press.

Mintzberg, H. (1994). The fall and rise of strategic planning. *Harvard Business Review*, January/February, pp. 107–14.

Mintzberg, H. (1997). The strategy concept 1: five P's for strategy. *California Management Review*, **30** (1), June, 11–24.

Mintzberg, H., Ahlstrand, B. and Lampel, J. (1998). *Strategy Safari – A Guided Tour Through the Wilds of Strategic Management*. London: Prentice-Hall Europe.

Nanda, A. (1996). Resources, capabilities and competencies. In *Organizational Learning and Competitive Advantage* (Moingeon, B. and Edmondson, A., eds). London: Sage, pp. 121–38.

Nohria, N. and Eccles, R. G. (1991). Corporate capability. Harvard Business School Working Paper No. 92-038.

Penrose, E. T. (1959). *The Theory and Growth of the Firm*. New York: Wiley.

Porter, M. E. (1980). *Competitive Strategy – Techniques for Analyzing Industries and Competitors*. New York: Free Press.

Porter, M. E. (1985). *Competitive Advantage: Creating and Sustaining Superior Performance*. New York: Free Press.

Prahalad, C. K. and Hamel, G. (1990). The core competencies of the corporation. *Harvard Business Review*. Boston, MA: HBR Press.

Prahalad, C. K. and Hamel, G. (1994). *Competing for the Future*. Boston, MA: Harvard Business School Press.

Saunders, M. (1997). *Strategic Purchasing and Supply Chain Management*, 2nd edn, London: Pitman.

Schon, D. A. (1971). *Beyond the Stable State*. London: Maurice Temple Smith Ltd.

Selznick, P. (1957). *Leadership in Administration*. New York: Harper and Row.

Teece, D. J., Pisano, G. and Shuen, A., et al. (1997). Dynamic capabilities and strategic management. *Strategic Management Journal*, **18**, 46–59.

Wernefelt, B. (1984). A resource based view of the firm. *Strategic Management Journal*, **5**, 171–80.

Chapter 3

The emergence of supply chain management and supply chain strategy as a critical success factor for organizations

The purpose of this chapter is to discuss the emergence of supply chain management, the underlying concepts and its development as an important influence upon successful strategies and operations. The chapter begins with a discussion of historical developments generally and in organizational management that have created the necessary conditions for the emergence of supply chains as an important focus for managers. It then moves on to address contemporary issues that occupy the mind space of practising managers. Empirical examples demonstrate the importance of the supply chain phenomena in creating successful strategies, structures and relationships that enhance organizational value. Finally, future directions are considered before outlining a new research agenda for this developing and important aspect of business management.

Introduction

Supply chain management was a phrase first coined in the early 1980s to describe the range of activities co-ordinated by an organization to procure and manage supplies (Oliver and Webber, 1982). Initially the term referred to an internal focus bounded by a single organization and how they sourced and procured supplies, managed their internal inventory and moved goods onto their customers (Harland, 1995; Macbeth and Ferguson, 1990). The original focus was later extended to examine not simply the internal management of the chain. It was recognized that this was inadequate and that the reality in managing supplies meant that supply chains extended beyond the purchasing organization and into their suppliers and their supplier's supplier (Christopher, 1992). It is recognized that there may be tiers of suppliers. Additionally it is recognized that the organization may have a customer who has other customers where their supplies are incorporated into other products or bundled in a particular way to provide a different product.

You may ask yourself the question why is managing a supply chain seen as important. First, customers have so much choice nowadays from an enormous field of competitors that delays in supply mean delays for the customers who probably are not willing to wait when they can obtain the same or similar substitute product elsewhere. Second, perhaps when you realize that the average retailer's balance sheet has inventories worth over 50 per cent of the total value of assets it brings the issue into focus. Third, the average manufacturing company spends over 50 per cent of every sale on raw material, components and maintenance repair operations (MRO) purchases, then it becomes crystal clear why managing the supply chain is so significant. In this context managing the supply chain is a CSF for most organizations (Barney, 1999; de Wit and Meyer, 1998; Leidecker and Bruno, 1984).

Historical developments

Organizations historically structured themselves into functions: purchasing, production, distribution, marketing, accounting. These functions managed discrete parts of the organization. In a business environment where organizations were in competition with one another it was important to control the internal organization in order to compete. As business networks have developed and become more complex the boundaries of organizations have become less discrete and somewhat blurred (Barney, 1999). Some commentators have gone so far as to suggest that this blurring of boundaries may mean that it is not organizations that are in competition any more but rather supply chains (Christopher, 1996). Functional structures have become historical straightjackets rather than practical. As a consequence 'functional silos' restrict intra-organizational and inter-organizational developments necessary to compete in the modern business environment (Slack et al., 2001).

Metaphorical descriptors – pipelines, chains and networks

It is interesting to examine developments both in the management literature and in practice. Much of the concern with supply chains developed from the purchasing and operations management literature throughout the 1980s and 1990s which have their roots in earlier organizational and management literatures relating to marketing, purchasing supply and economics disciplines. Metaphors have always been adopted to describe these organizational structures. In practice journals in the apparel sector throughout the 1970s and 1980s the term 'pipeline' was used to discuss the flows of raw materials through manufacturing processes and onto the final customer (Hunter, 1990; Hunter et al., 1993). The term 'supply chain' first appeared in a US Outlook article (Oliver and Webber, 1982). In the 1990s 'supply networks' became fashionable (Christopher, 1996). However, it doesn't help students or researchers in this area that commentators develop new terms frequently even though they are essentially referring to the concept of managing supply chains. For example, 'commodity chains' have been used to describe global production networks (Gereffi, 1994). The next two sections provide a discussion of the focus of analysis and the major themes that have emerged from the literature.

Levels of analysis

Early work referencing supply chain structures focused on internal operations from the point of entry into the firm until it exited to the customer (Macbeth and Ferguson, 1990). Indeed Oliver and Webber (1982) were referring to the integration of internal business functions and the flow of materials and information coming into and going out of the business when they originally coined the phrase. This particular definition equates closely to the traditional materials management perspective (Houlihan, 1984; Jones and Riley, 1985; Stevens, 1989). As Harland (1995) recognized the term 'supply chain management' has had different meanings for different writers. Many early studies and some later studies (Burt, 1984; Campbell, 1985; Hakansson et al., 1976; Heide and Miner, 1992; Lamming, 1993) have focused upon the dyadic aspect between a supplier (manufacturer or distributor) and a buyer (retailer or distributor). In supply chain terms these are only two links of the chain.

Themes in the literature

A number of themes may be observed from a study of the eclectic literature referring to supply chains. Figure 3.1 illustrates the developments that have taken place in what we have come to regard as supply chain management literature. Themes emerged as the focus and emphasis within the literature changed to reflect the practical concerns of managers at the time. The diagram illustrates the separate development of the different literature bases underpinning and discussing what we now regard as supply chain management concepts. The literature developed from tactical and operational concerns to address the strategic issues. Contemporary literature has synthesized different ideas from the underpinning disciplines into first supply chain management and later supply chain strategy. This section discusses some of those important themes.

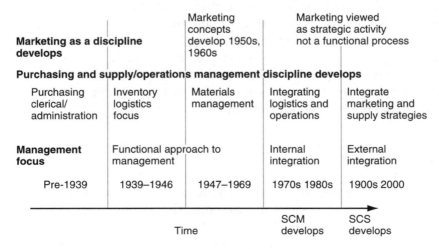

Figure 3.1

Transaction costs

Themes emerge from the literature often reflecting the contextual concerns of the time. For example, *transaction costs* were of prime concern from 1937 with active research conducted in the 1940s and 1950s and the main discipline through which the studies were conducted was economics (Coase, 1937; Heckert and Miner, 1940). There have been a few later studies on this theme such as Williamson (1979), Ellram (1994) and Hobbs (1996). A main focus of transaction cost analysis has been concerned with 'power'. Power is important in the transaction process since it determines the negotiation which is often based on price alone. Within this theme power is seen as important within the exchange process between two or more parties. In retail buyer–supplier transactions power has moved from suppliers in the 1940s, 1950s to the retailers in the 1960s, 1970s, 1980s, 1990s, 2000s with increasing concentration of retail buying in the hands of a few large retail organizations in most sectors including food and fashion.

Manufacturing supply chains and efforts to lower inventory costs

Since the First World War and more particularly after the Second World War *manufacturing management* and *industrial management* provided the context and the focus for research examining aspects of what we now recognize as supply chain management. For example, Forrester (1961) examined the 'bullwhip' effect of managing inventories and recognized that the further up the supply chain from the end customer one examines inventories it will be subject to amplified swings of over- and undersupply as a consequence of errors in the demand forecast. Research into the dynamics of supply chains and modelling the effect of changes to teach managers about the consequences have been a major theme since Forrester first examined the 'bullwhip' effect in the 1960s when systems thinking became popularized in management. The temporal dimension is important since simultaneously throughout the 1960s and 1970s interest was growing as computer power developed in mathematical programming applying optimization-modelling techniques to supply chain inventories. Since then many studies have concentrated on simulation and pipeline modelling (Fisher et al., 1994; Fransoo and Wouters, 2000; Goodwin and Franklin, 1994; Shapiro, 2001). Ellram (1991) on the other hand examined vertical integration suggesting that organizations that owned their supply chains were much more likely to be able to manage them effectively.

This tradition has been maintained through the works of different researchers: Lamming (1993) examining innovation strategies and lean supply in the automobile sector; Ford (1990) and much of the work of the Industrial Marketing and Purchasing Group examining a variety of supply chain interactions across different industrial settings; Hines

(1994) examining world-class suppliers; Hines and Rich (1994) and Slack et al. (2001) examining continuous improvement. The work examining value streams and value stream mapping conducted by Hines et al. (2000) builds on previous studies conducted into LP and agile manufacturing. Investigations into a number of specific techniques such as LP, Just-in-Time (JiT), world-class manufacturing (WCM) and TQM continue in this tradition. Harrison and Storey (1996, p. 63) classify these several operational supply chain concepts as new wave manufacturing (NWM). One could add to this list QR originally developed through pipeline management projects in the US textile industry conducted by Kurt Salmon Associates and others (Hunter, 1990; Hunter et al., 1992; Hunter and Valentino, 1995). QR is viewed as a derivative method of JiT by some commentators. Harrison and van Hoek (2002, p. 160) view QR as an application of JiT and lean thinking whereby customer demand is satisfied by producers and suppliers reacting quickly when demand is known rather than making for stock. Others view QR as a 'management paradigm and a methodology' (Lowson et al., 1999).

Time compression and responsiveness

Most of the emphasis in QR was focused upon 'pipeline' modelling to reduce time throughout the supply chain (KSA, 1987). However, in practice much of the controllable element was dyadic between the organization initiating demand and their immediate supplier (Iyer and Bergen, 1997). In some respects it could be argued that the success of QR might be dependent upon a number of dyadic relationships that are co-ordinated effectively. Questions arise over who can effectively co-ordinate and who is allowed to? Take the example of a large clothing retailer who contracts the manufacture of own label fashion. The retailers often co-ordinate all suppliers including the textile mills supplying fabrics to the manufacturer, the trim suppliers, production schedules and quality of the converter (contract clothing manufacturer) and logistics services to move goods between each one and deliver to the final destination. Each supplier in the chain has a dyadic relationship with the retail co-ordinator.

Time compression reduces costs by making each process cycle shorter. Shorter lead times in procurement, manufacturing, replenishment, customer purchasing and consumption result in faster throughput times in the supply chain system. Figure 3.2 illustrates the supply chain process cycles.

Efficient consumer response (ECR) is an extension of QR; it was developed as part of a grocery industry analysis conducted by Kurt Salmon Associates in the USA (KSA, 1993). This work was conducted a few years after they had done their work in the textile industry on QR. ECR's purpose being to integrate supply chain management with demand management to create smooth flows of product through the supply chain to satisfy consumer demand efficiently (at lowest cost).

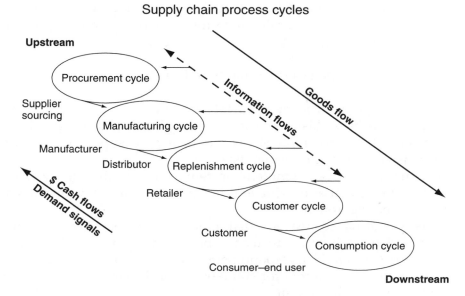

Figure 3.2

The four pillars of ECR are: store assortment, promotion, replenishment and new product introductions. The focus of ECR is between the retail organization and its suppliers whereas the focus for QR is on manufacturing capability and efficiency to deliver promptly.

Guiding principles of ECR were defined by KSA (1993) as:

1. Constantly focus on providing better value to the grocery consumer: better product, better quality, better assortment, better in-stock service, better convenience with lower cost throughout the total chain.
2. ECR must be driven by business leaders determined to achieve choice to profit by replacing the old paradigms of win/lose trading relationships with win–win, mutually profitable business alliances.
3. Accurate timely information must be used to support effective marketing, production and logistics decisions. Information must flow externally between partners through electronic data interchange (EDI) using UCS standards and will informally affect the most productive and efficient use of information in computer-based systems.
4. Product must flow with maximization of value-adding processes from the end of production/packaging to the consumer's basket so as to ensure the right product is available at the right time.
5. A common consistent performance measurement and reward system must be used to focus on the effectiveness of the total system. Better value through reduced costs, lower inventories and

better asset utilization. Clear identification of the potential rewards (increased revenue and profit) and promotion of equitable sharing of those rewards.

Clear supply chain themes emerging from ECR are:

1. Better value and efficiency in the total supply chain;
2. Profitable business alliances are key to managing the total supply chain;
3. High-quality information is needed to ensure supply chains are responsive to customer demands;
4. Bottlenecks must be identified and removed from the supply chain and activities that add value and lower cost for the consumer must be pursued vigorously;
5. Better performance measures that indicate effectiveness of the whole supply chain rather than focusing upon elements of it must be used if the total system is to respond better to market demand and better measurement is required for equitable reward sharing by those that added value to the system.

A number of important benefits were identified in the dry goods grocery segment in the US when ECR was proposed. They were:

1. $10 billion saving in the segment;
2. If ECR was extended to other retail segments this would increase to $30 billion with 41 per cent less inventory in the supply chain. This extension across segments is what happened when QR was introduced to the general merchandise segment;
3. Consumers are the primary beneficiary of ECR.

Definition of supply chain strategy

A new definition of supply chain strategy can be gleaned from ECR philosophy:

Supply chain strategies require a total systems view of the linkages in the chain that work together efficiently to create customer satisfaction at the end point of delivery to the consumer. As a consequence costs must be lowered throughout the chain by driving out unnecessary costs and focusing attention on adding value. Throughput efficiency must be increased, bottlenecks removed and performance measurement must focus on total systems efficiency and equitable reward distribution to those in the supply chain adding value. The supply chain system must be responsive to customer requirements.

The four 'pillars' of ECR

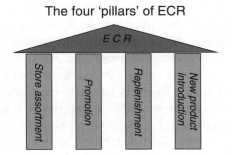

Figure 3.3
Source: Adapted from KSA.

ECR strategies focus on four key areas which are:

1. *Efficient assortment* – Optimizing store assortment and space allocation to increase inventory turnover and category sales per square foot.
2. *Efficient promotion* – Reducing the non-value-adding cost of trade and consumer promotion.
3. *Efficient replenishment* – Streamlining the distribution of goods from the production line to the retail shelf.
4. *Efficient new product introductions* – Cutting the cost of developing and introducing new products.

By being efficient in these four key areas retailers are able to satisfy their customers through ECR (Figure 3.3). ECR strategies and concepts have since migrated to other industry sectors partly through consultants who peddle key ideas across different industrial and commercial sectors.

Category management

The customer marketing research we conducted . . . marked a turning point into us becoming a market-led company. We were determined to follow the customer – so the business would go wherever the customer took us, and we would never try to shoehorn the customer into what we wanted to offer. We stopped following the competition and followed the customer.
> Terry Leahy, CEO, Tesco Plc quoted in *The Sunday Times*
> Business Section, p. 3, 16 November 2003

One important change in the way retailers have organized their businesses to become much more customer-focused is through use of category management. Essentially this technique puts products together in different ways that reflect the ways that customers buy products rather than simply grouping products by brand and/or within ranges. In this sense category management focuses on customer buying habits. It is heavily reliant on having accurate and reliable information about customers in order to make category decisions. For example, Wal-Mart in the US gleaned information about their customer buying habits in relation to the correlation of sales of nappies and beer on Friday evenings and as a consequence grouped the products together as a category, which improved sales further. The best practice principles of category management are illustrated in Figure 3.4.

In order to manage categories effectively and improve volumes and profitability retailers need to be able to combine different pieces of information together to obtain an informed view of consumer behaviour patterns. Figure 3.5 illustrates the information needed for category decisions.

Accurate scan data is required from every store noting what has sold. Previously retail organizations relied on warehouse shipment data to record sales but this is only a measure of what has been shipped to store and not what has been sold. Scan data does measure accurately consumer demand. Store level sales history based on scan data must be

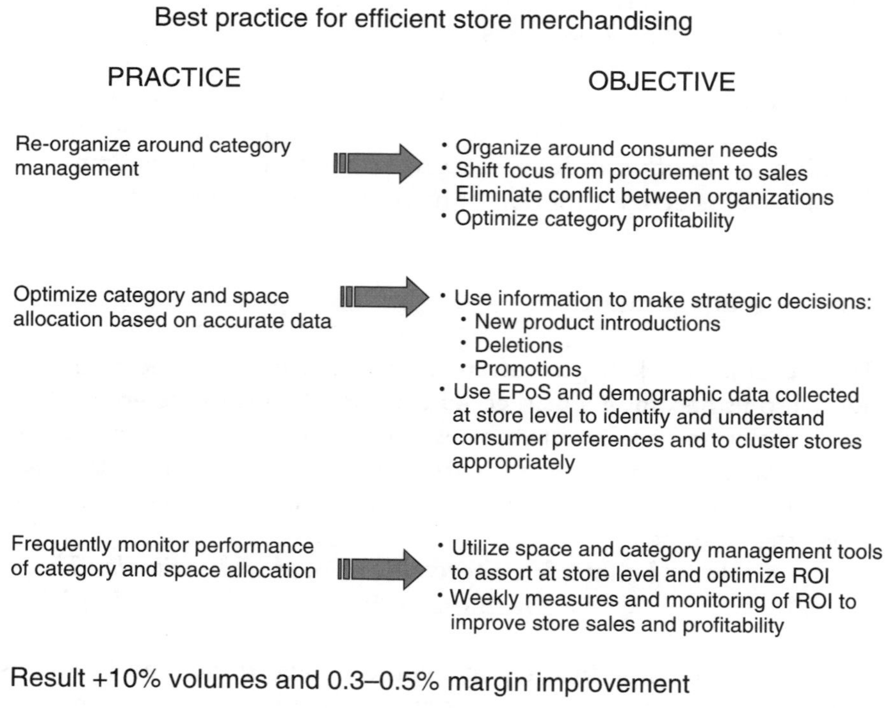

Best practice for efficient store merchandising

PRACTICE	OBJECTIVE
Re-organize around category management	• Organize around consumer needs • Shift focus from procurement to sales • Eliminate conflict between organizations • Optimize category profitability

Optimize category and space allocation based on accurate data	• Use information to make strategic decisions:
	  • New product introductions
	  • Deletions
	  • Promotions
	• Use EPoS and demographic data collected at store level to identify and understand consumer preferences and to cluster stores appropriately

Frequently monitor performance of category and space allocation	• Utilize space and category management tools to assort at store level and optimize ROI • Weekly measures and monitoring of ROI to improve store sales and profitability

Result +10% volumes and 0.3–0.5% margin improvement

Figure 3.4

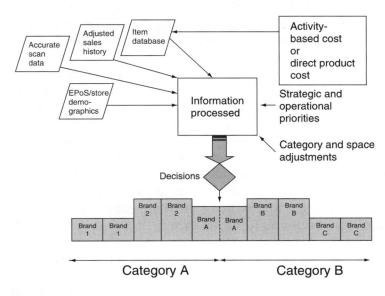

Figure 3.5

adjusted to take account of seasons and promotions to discern the under-lying sales pattern which can be used for allocating space. This par-ticular algorithm has been most difficult for retailers to solve. Another important factor to account for is demographic data for the store area. If stores do not stock a particular product, is it because it does not sell, would not sell or because stores have never tried it and their customers simply go elsewhere to satisfy their requirements? It may be that customers who go elsewhere also buy all other goods elsewhere and if the store was to hold that item not only would it attract sales for that product but for several other products too which may be product unrelated. The item database needs to store information on case sizes, weight, case quantities, dimensions, other physical attributes as well as cost and price. Ability to continuously update this data is essential as prices, costs and other data change. These variables too will inform the space allocation decision. Activity-based cost (ABC) or direct prod-uct profitability (DPP) cost data must also inform decisions. Typically in addition to cost of merchandise there are rafts of other cost. Costs maybe indirect (overheads for light, heat, administration, etc.) for each SKU and direct costs of handling, storage and movement of goods, which are specific to the category.

Better performance measurement using ABC, activity-based manage-ment (ABM), total cost of ownership (TCO) and DPP accounting methods are pre-requisites for category management decisions. More accuracy in measuring performance can improve the quality of space allocation decision-making. Traditional accounting measures have focused at product level. New measures must focus on the customer. The concepts are illustrated in Figure 3.6.

Many retailers are beginning to use palm top computers to view category data and inform their decision-making as they walk the store. Space allocation is tactical, operational and strategic. At a tactical level space can be adjusted for seasons, promotions and local events. At operational level space may be allocated according to availability of merchandise. Managers may also experiment and capture real-time data on which to base future decisions. At a strategic level decisions will be taken to deliver customer satisfaction which will impact sales volumes, profitability and return on investment (ROI).

Key drivers of sales margin gains are:

- Store specific categories (local variations given EpoS/demographics) and space allocation;
- Timely space adjustment for uptrending and downtrending categories;
- Effective transitions to seasonal categories;
- Emphasis on high volume or high margin items;
- Improved pricing strategies to enhance ROI;
- Space for broader assortment within category or to develop new category.

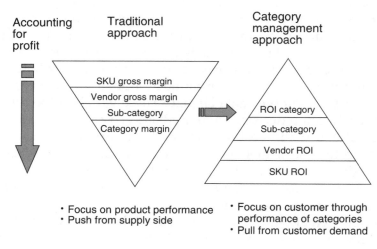

Category management requires new performance measures

Figure 3.6

Integration

Stevens (1989) recognized the importance of moving from functional silos towards an integrated supply chain. Figure 3.7 identifies the four stages that illustrate how an organization moves from being functional to integrated and in so doing offering improving customer service levels. Moving from the first-stage baseline organization to functionally integrated combines areas of common interest focused upon serving the customer better. Functions integrate at this stage. The third stage is developing internal integration. It is recognized that at each stage material flows become smoother and inventory holding becomes less. The final stage is integration between the organization's internal supply chain and its suppliers and customers. Flows of materials are optimized at this stage and blockages are removed from the supply chain system. Integration removes cost and time, and adds value for the customer as a consequence.

Managing upstream and downstream relationships with suppliers and customers allows superior customer value to be delivered at a lower total supply chain cost (Christopher, 1992). It is argued that by integrating the supply chain, total supply chain costs are lowered. This is important because it is critical to recognize that supply chains compete against each other not organizations. If a firm is part of an inefficient supply chain that is fragmented not integrated, that is inefficient rather than efficient and not delivering customer service as effectively

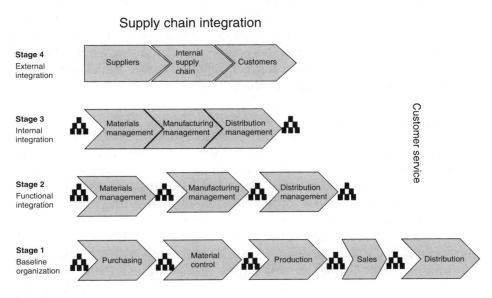

Figure 3.7

as alternative supply chains then the customer will migrate to the integrated, efficient and more effective supply chain. Customers buy products and services that meet their requirements. For example, a consumer shopping for fashion on a Saturday afternoon may want to make a purchase from their favourite store to wear something out that evening. If the store does not have stock available, in the right style, colour and size then the purchase cannot be made from that store. The retail store is the end of a supply chain that interfaces with the consumer. It is not simply the retailer that loses out, their customer has and their suppliers have. More importantly another retail store (a substitute) may benefit if they can supply an alternative item and their supply chain benefits not just the retailer.

Recent concerns with ethical trading and environmental issues

More recently sourcing and purchasing research has shown some interest in the ethics of buying products from low-cost offshore destinations where there is an impact upon the indigenous environment and community that may be considered detrimental (Green et al., 1998). For example, the well-publicized allegations against companies like Nike and GAP for the use of under-age labour in their supplier factories in Indonesia and Bangladesh. Concerns with damage to the environment with pesticides used to protect cotton crops. Excessive pollution caused by dyeing plants not complying with industry-wide standards on treatment of waste product. There have been countries where the local population is deprived of the nutritional value by exporting food products such as bananas. The issue of food miles has been raised whereby produce that could be supplied by a local farming community has been sourced from countries that may be many miles from the markets in which they are sold. There is a double concern regarding the impact of such decisions on the farming community that could supply the goods in the markets where they are sold and the concern that the transport pollution causes which is not fully costed nor paid for by those importing the goods.

Strategic perspectives

More recently the focus has shifted from what one may describe as operations management towards a strategic management perspective (Macbeth and Ferguson, 1990). Alliances and partnerships have provided the central focus for large-scale studies into supply chain strategies that have been adopted by some of the leading world organizations in major industrial sectors automobiles, aerospace, electronics, textiles, retailing and supporting service industries (Berry et al., 1994; Burt et al., 2003; Hines et al., 2000; Kanter, 1994; KSA, 1993, 1997; Lamming, 1993). Strategic capabilities are examined by Croom and Batchelor (1997), still following the traditions of manufacturing management. Themes in the mainstream strategy literature such as core competence (Prahalad and Hamel, 1990), capabilities (Stalk et al., 1992) and competing through time advantages (Stalk, 1988) have developed in parallel with research themes into supply chain strategies.

Supply chain structures and relationships

The term 'supply chain' conjures up an image of a linear structure with a chain and links between suppliers and buyers at each link (i.e. dyads). Indeed it is often represented in this way pictorially. However, the reality is much more complex. It has been recognized that the structure is more akin to a network structure between a number of suppliers and a number of buyers (Christopher, 1992). It has also been recognized that the supply chain may be hierarchical with first tier, second tier, third tier suppliers and so on. In other words the structures between one organization and a supplier may be further complicated by an array of arrangements at each tier point.

In the 1980s and early 1990s there was a great deal of interest in why Japanese firms were so successful. Much of the success was attributed to the total quality approaches and continuous improvement (Kaizen) philosophy based on the works of Deming and Juran. Deming's (1986) fourth point of his fourteen points on quality advocates that organizations work more closely with fewer suppliers. This is a practice that has been adopted by many retailing organizations throughout the 1990s following practices adopted by automobile manufacturers a decade earlier.

The literature on relationships in the supply chain discusses the traditional 'arms length' approach of purchasing in which adversarial relationships are a common feature on one pole and the 'partnership' approach which often adopts the analogy of marriage at the other pole. Often the focus of these studies examines the relationships existing between firms rather than the key business relationships within a supply chain context. Examples of the first category focusing on firm relationships would be Kanter's (1994) examination of strategic collaboration, Porter's (1980) value chain approach, Axelrod's (1984) evolution of relationships, Ford and Farmer (1986) on make or buy decisions and Chao and Scheuing's (1992) study of purchasing relationships. The work of Carlisle and Parker (1989) represented a turning point in recognizing that supply chain relationships and purchasing negotiations went beyond the adversarial discussions focused on price alone. Ellram (1991) recognized that these relationships could be much more complex and introduced the concept of networks to explain the types of relationships existing between suppliers and buyers to deliver products and services to the end customer. Around the same time a number of researchers were examining Japanese supply chain practices in the automobile industry discussed earlier. Womack et al. (1990) introduced the notion of tiers of suppliers as did Lamming (1993), together with the 'lean supply' concept; Sako (1990) suggested that companies adopting a partnership approach performed better than those that did not. However not all analysts agree, Hogarth-Scott (1999) questioned the value of supplier–buyer relationships in retailing stating that suppliers may have become hostages to fortune in this unbalanced power relationship.

An interesting alternative perspective that runs counter to much of the relationship literature is offered by Cousins (2002) who identifies three key propositions. First, partnership relationships do not exist. Rather there is a range of collaborating relationships and they are all competitive. Second, organizations do not trust each other but rather they manage risk based on business objectives. Third and importantly, the relationship itself is a process not an entity and as such focuses on definable outcomes, e.g. cost reduction through value engineering or joint product development and problem solving. The relationship observed will have been defined by the definable outcomes. This point of view is supported by Cox (1997), who argued that the collaborative approach was not necessarily more effective than a competitive strategy in the supply chain.

Empirical evidence

What differentiates much of the early work in the purchasing and supply literature from the later work examining contemporary supply chain issues are the shifts in focus that have occurred. Table 3.1 illustrates the timeline dimension. These issues are highlighted further through the empirical discussion that follows.

A capability to manage supply chains can prove to be a core competence for an organization. There are numerous examples of business success and failure being dependent upon supply chain capabilities. Amazon.com is a relatively new e-retailing organization whose very survival and growth has been built around technical and organizational developments related to managing the virtual store and fulfilling customer orders. One important aspect of their development has been their ability to build relationships with organizations external to Amazon who already possessed capability to fulfil their promotional promises.

Why quick response (QR)?

QR is an approach to supply chain management based on the concepts of reducing inventory holding cost, postponing the commitment of

Table 3.1

	Analytic focus
From (pre-1990)	*To (post-1990 to present)*
Predominantly internal focus	Predominantly external (dyadic, chain, network)
Operations	Strategies
Exchange/transactional focus	Relationship/structure focus
Functional processes	Integration
Cost efficiency (inputs/outputs)	Value-added (outputs–inputs)
Physical processes	Financial, informational and virtual processes
Product quality (only major concern)	Service quality and total quality approaches
Simple (e.g. dyadic structures and relationships)	Complex structures, e.g. networks
Traditional linear supply chains	Digital supply chains
Inventory management	Information and customer service

Source: Purchasing and supply chain literature, 1930s to present day.

resources in manufacture until a clearer picture of demand is known and having flexible manufacturing systems (FMSs) that are able to respond. QR techniques were pioneered in the textile industry during the 1980s. In 1986 Kurt Salmon Associates (KSA), a major US consultancy, were employed by the 'Crafted with Pride Council', a joint textile industry body, to examine US apparel and textile supply chains. They went about the task by process mapping activities in the pipeline and discovered it took 66 weeks total time for all manufacturing operations to be completed and for the processes to move raw materials through production and into the retail stores. However, the total time taken in actual production processes (spinning, weaving, wet processing, cutting, sewing, assembly, packaging and distribution to retailers) took only 11 weeks. This meant that 55 weeks were wasted in inventory delays mostly in the warehouse waiting for the next operation to call them out. This wasted time cost the US Textile and Apparel pipeline $25 billion according to KSA (1987). This was around 20 per cent of the total industry turnover and it was a cost that had been simply passed on to the consumer until faced with competitive pressure from overseas imports.

Another major success in applying QR principles during the 1980s to manage their supply chain was the Italian Fashion Knitwear Retailer, Benetton. It is not simply QR but the network of suppliers that is important to provide flexibility for Benetton as orchestrator of processes. More recently the company has transformed its organization to develop larger retail formats and exercise more control over its supply chain through vertical integration (Camuffo et al., 2001, pp. 46–52). The company has recently established ten 'production poles' outside Italy and they are either wholly owned as in the case of Spain, Portugal, Tunisia, Hungary, Croatia or a 50 per cent joint venture in the likes of South Korea, Egypt and India.

It is interesting that Benetton is similar in size of turnover $1.8 billion to Zara, the Spanish fashion retailer, which is often credited with bringing products to market quickly. Zara too is heavily vertically integrated with in-house production in 23 production centres supported by a network of outsourced production suppliers in smaller firms in Spain and Portugal close to its home base in Northwest Spain. This is in stark contrast to the majority of their competitors (Top Shop – Arcadia, GAP, H&M, Next, M&S, BhS) who mainly outsource production.

Since 1993 Giordino, a US fashion retailer, developed successful QR techniques that today are practised by other retailers such as GAP and The Limited. In the UK retailers like Marks and Spencer and Arcadia have also adopted QR principles for some of their more fashionable lines.

QR is a 'pull system' and relies on consumer demand information being used by all parties in the supply chain. As a consequence much of the early concerns were focused on the use of EDI and compatibility between retailers' and various suppliers' systems (Hunter, 1990; KSA, 1987). It is a system that demands close co-operation between parties in a supply chain. A major concern for fashion retailers is that they do not really know whether consumers will like this season's fashion until they see it and try it in store. It is not like many fast moving consumer goods (FMCG) categories such as detergent. Soap powder demand is much more predictable and does not have the complexities of a fashion item. Soap powder is bulk material, packaged in various sizes and promoted, for example, through coupons offering two for the price of one (buy one get one free). Fashion apparel may have five style variations, ten colours, ten size variations and fashion is perishable. Thus one simple garment may have 500 variables ($5 \times 10 \times 10$) to account for in the decision processes that the retailer makes. It is further complicated by the lack of standard sizing which often means that consumers purchase different size garments from different retailers. For example, a consumer buying size 12 at M&S may need to purchase size 14 at Next.

Returns (consumers returning to store a garment previously purchased) are also more of a problem with fashion. Goods are returned because they don't fit properly. This may be due to sizing problems or it may be due to a whim. For example, the consumer just did not like it when they tried it on again at home or their partner didn't like it. No one looks at soap powder and says 'I don't like the packaging on that let's take it back to the store'. So what's all this got to do with QR? Well if bulk manufacturing and all the associated costs can be postponed until consumer demand is known rather than simply forecast there is less likelihood of wasting resources. Historically, retail buyers would have relied on forecasting fashion demand well in advance of the season and be committed to orders perhaps 18 months in advance of the selling season (i.e. six seasons ahead). Forecasting is, however, notoriously inaccurate in fashion. Forecast inaccuracy is also expensive. Supposing your gross margin is 50 per cent and you over-forecast on just a single line by 50 per cent effectively you have no margin and should you need to reduce prices further to shift the stock then you will be incurring cost. This is why QR is so attractive for fashion retailing. QR means a retailer is able to lower risk by trying a product in a small quantity. If the garment sells they need to be able to replenish the items quickly to maintain availability of product and hence provide customer service.

What's different at Zara?

Table 3.2 illustrates some key differences between traditional apparel retailers and the Zara business model.

Table 3.2

Characteristics	Traditional Apparel Retailing Business Model	Zara Apparel Retailing Business Model
Supply strategy	Efficiency driven, large volumes planned at lowest total cost	Responsive to customer demand. Smaller volumes in response to customer demand identified by store data
Manufacturing operations	Outsourced to a number of different supplying contractors based on best prices (often globally). Do not own their supply chain but need to try and control it through standardized systems, policies and procedures. Larger organizations are able to exert pressure.	Backward vertical integration enables Zara to manage closely the different supply chain operations from design through to store. Zara own much of their supply chain. What they do not own is closely controlled and relatively local in Spain, Portugal and Morocco with short lead times.
Lead times	Long lead times 12–16 weeks fabric, 6–10 weeks apparel production, 2–3 weeks shipping times	Short lead times 8–10 days on some lines, most within 15 days including store shipment.

Table 3.2 (Continued)

Characteristics	Traditional Apparel Retailing Business Model	Zara Apparel Retailing Business Model
Demand based on	Forecasts well in advance of the selling season	Forecast much closer to season and heavily influenced by real time demand data transmitted from stores
Replenishment	Inventory levels trigger automatic replenishment orders from suppliers at pre-agreed contract prices	No replenishment – when it's gone, it's gone and move onto the next hot fashion
Designs	Based on trend forecasts 18–24 months in advance of selling seasons	Based on current catwalk shows. Digital photography and ICT used to transmit visual data back to in-house design team to sample and cost. 'Knock-off's as they are called in the trade for obvious reasons.
Fabrics (Textile chain)	Various fabrics produced to specification by Textile Mills 12–16 weeks lead times, production has to be booked well in advance. Fabrics colour dyed to specification well in advance of sale season.	Mainly standard 'greige' fabrics piece dyed to seasonal colours in demand. Hence colouring is postponed until demand is known.

Zara's business model is substantially different from that of traditional apparel retailers. It has been able to achieve a competitive advantage through exploiting these differences. In particular its ability to get fashionable product to stores quickly has meant that it has captured current customer demand effectively. The company has not invested heavily in originality of design but is fast at copying and capturing current fashionable design trends from international catwalk shows using the latest digital technologies. Vertical integration also gives the organization control of upstream processes such as manufacturing and dyeing processes. Furthermore, vertical integration has meant that the conversion processes can be better synchronized to customer demand through visibility of transactional data at the production units. Zara store managers use palm top computers to gather and transmit store data back to their central headquarters in Spain. Close geographical proximity of production units also helps plan and control production processes and logistics to reduce lead times, particularly transportation. The use of standard fabrics and piece dyeing technology has also ensured that production is not held up by the textile mills desire for efficiency. Finally, the fact that Zara stores did not adopt the replenishment concept that most large apparel retailers engaged in meant that they freed up time from having to manage the complexity of replenishing stocks and focused upon getting new products in store more frequently. The benefits from this simple change have been enormous. Firstly, new products drive footfall through stores, as fashion conscious consumers are attracted to visit more frequently. Secondly, the risks from holding stock that customers may not purchase are significantly reduced when quantities are lowered and store orders are made closer to the selling season. Thirdly, consumers are educated into knowing that if they see something they like they better buy it now because there is no replenishment and consequently unlike many retailers that replenish lines at the end of a season only to find that the customer will now only buy stock if it is marked down, Zara avoids significant markdown costs. The strategies have improved cash flow, profitability and sales turnover performances.

Some of the problems being able to apply the principles of QR reside in the textile areas of the supply chain. Textile production has two main sources: agriculture and chemicals. Each source has its own time cycle. Natural fibres such as wool or cotton take the best part of a year to develop. Man-made fibres can be made more quickly but production needs to be booked into the textile mills well in advance of the apparel manufacturing cycle. These cycles inevitably have consequences for retail purchasing and replenishment cycles. Many of the most successful QR practitioners are able to shorten these cycles by using 'greige' fabric that can be died late in the process. This allows them to achieve the flexibility they require to respond quickly to consumer demand information.

Figure 3.8 illustrates the traditional concept of supply *vis-à-vis* QR supply or fast fashion that retail organizations refer to (e.g. Zara). The QR is achieved by utilizing 'greige' cloth or stock fabrics as previously explained. The longest part of the fashion supply chain is taken up in design, sampling, fabric sourcing and procurement. In the figure three cycles are illustrated: the textile fabric cycle, clothing manufacturing cycle and the retail cycle to move the product to market and the customer. The shortest part of the supply chain are the manufacturing and retailing. If retailers can eliminate time and risk by producing closer to the selling period they can predict demand better and avoid overstocks and understocks. Zara are renowned for this and have been able to achieve success mainly by being vertically integrated and responsive to customer requirements. It is easier to apply QR techniques to 'commodity fashion' where consumers expect some fashion content but perhaps fabrics do not need to be innovative or the same as those

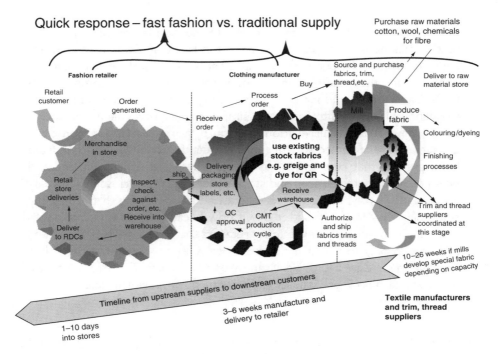

Figure 3.8

on the catwalk, it is the look that is most important since the fashion is relatively cheap and almost immediately disposable. Young fashion is fast fashion. Commodity fashion is almost a contradiction in terms, an oxymoron. Fashion suggests difference and commodity suggests similarity. Strategies underpinning fashion exploit difference whereas strategies underpinning commodities are based on price alone. Fashion based on fabric differences is more difficult to translate into QR. Fabric mills need lead times longer than the complete cycle for what passes for fast fashion. This is their challenge to produce economically and quickly in smaller quantities than they are used to supplying.

Fast fashion at Cecil Gee

Mos. Bros. started as a men's wear brand focusing on formal wear. Historically, many men have hired suits for occasions from Mos. Bros. (e.g. weddings, funerals and dinner suits). Cecil Gee (tailoring) is one of the more contemporary fashion brands the company owns. In the first half of 2003 sales were up by 10 per cent and stock flows from warehouse into store had been cut from 10 days to 48 hours. Overall the company report total lead times reduced from 7–9 weeks to 2 weeks. The company is placing smaller initial orders with suppliers and wants suppliers to be more flexible to change colours and/or fabrics for the second or third orders. The benefit to Cecil Gee is they are able to reduce their risk by lowering the risk of uncertain demand patterns and providing the retailer with flexibility to react quicker to trends. Mos. Bros. Finance Director, Richard Murray, said that the company held £2.3 million of suit fabric in 2002, a figure that had reduced to £500 000 in 2003. Supply chain improvements have contributed to an improved margin of 50 per cent in the first half of 2003. The company is committed to regional variations in product with stock being responsive to local market requirements.

Source: Adapted from an article in *The Sunday Times*, 1 November 2003.

Mass customization

In recent years a number of retailers and suppliers have experimented with 'mass customization'. These experiments have usually involved the production of relatively simple garments with customizations being limited but attractive enough to individual consumers for them to be willing to pay a premium over and above volume factory production prices. Two areas of focus have pre-occupied those advocating the approach. First, the development of camera technology that has been employed to take more body measurements than simply waist, leg, chest and collar sizes. These camera measurements have the advantage of being digitally accurate and digitally storable on smart-card technology. Measurements can be instantly transferred to simple CAD/CAM (computer-aided design and computer-aided manufacturing) equipment for customized production. Designs can also be customized (no. of pockets, buttons, zips, styles, colours) from previously stored images or may be taken from designs presented by the customer. The second area of focus has been quick dyeing techniques that allow fabrics to be coloured to a chosen design pattern at the point of sale. I have seen examples of prototype production equipment in development in the US, UK and South Korea. The equipment is mainly used presently for simple garments (T-shirts, simple dresses and shorts). It is both retail organizations and suppliers of clothing and textile products who see the potential benefits that these improving technologies have to offer. One major US supplier said they could foresee the day that every large store had a customization unit contained within it for certain clothing lines.[1] Levis has also had a widely publicized experiment with customizing jeans. Consumer benefits are clear if they can have a smart card that holds their personal data that retailers can use when they supply them with a garment they can be sure it will fit them. From a retailer's point of view the advantage is the consumer is more likely to be satisfied and as a consequence returns will be minimized and inventories will be lower if they are able to customize products in store. Mass customization may not simply offer the quickest response of all but it may offer an accurate response lowering the risks for both consumers and retailers. Key success factors in the fashion industry are often cited as responsiveness and flexibility. This has a specific meaning in a supply chain context. Flexibility means being able to adjust production quantities, styles, sizes and colours in line with the market demand. Responsiveness is being able to adjust the whole supply chain to the needs of the market.

e-Business strategies, fulfilment and digital supply chains

Various commentators using terminologies that shape contemporary views on the topic describe contemporary supply chains differently. The adjectives applied include: flexible, responsive, agile, lean, value-adding networks and value streams. Supply chains are more than the term suggests. They are value-creation mechanisms for customers. They are not simply 'supply'-focused nor are they necessarily 'chains'. Supply chains are dynamic, efficient, effective response networks delivering customer requirements flexibly and on time. These high-performance networks consist of customers, suppliers and information travelling through organizational 'arterial systems'. These arterial systems cut across functional, organizational and geographical boundaries. Supply chain strategies, structures and relationships are highly complex. Configurations will differ within organizations and between organizations.

Supply chain efficiency is critical to customer satisfaction. For example, retailers and their e-tailing operations are dependent on fulfilling the marketing promise. This is achieved through successful supply chain strategies and operations that are integrated and capable of delivering. Systems integration and effective use of ICT is a key requirement. This might take the form of e-procurement, e-design collaboration, order tracking and delivery systems using satellite technology for logistical operations and so on.

What distinguishes the traditional supply chain approach from a contemporary view is the capability for customers to self-design products/services at a price they find acceptable. Collaboration is not simply between a supplier and buyer but it may be possible through digital supply chains to collaborate with the ultimate consumer. This e-enabler may offer scope for those retail organizations and suppliers such as Levi to transform experiments on customizing products into a mainstream commercial strategy. The storage of expensive items that no one wants to buy is not necessary in a 'digital supply chain'. Information, time compression, responsiveness and the flexibility to switch production and delivery routing may all be achieved through the application of 'digital supply chain management'.

Benefits of supplier and customer collaboration are illustrated in Figure 3.9. Collaboration may include a number of benefits to supply chain parties and could include:

- Shared sales forecasts and production data;
- Shared infrastructure;
- Freight bundling;
- Rapid product development;
- Compressed supply chain cycle times;
- Supply chain benefits;
- Real-time connectivity;
- e-Marketplace infrastructure to provide many-to-one-to-many connectivity across the entire supply chain;
- Visibility across the entire supply chain;
- Real-time communication creates a parallel supply chain;
- Responsiveness;
- Reduced time to detect demand, commit, produce and fulfil.

New collaborative supply chain activities span the entire continuum from the start to the end point of the supply chain. They allow organizations to design, source, plan and analyse supply chain strategies and operations collaboratively. Supply chain benefits of successful collaboration are illustrated in Figure 3.10.

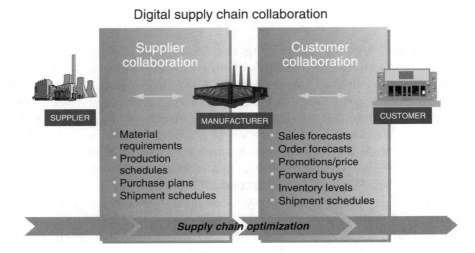

Figure 3.9

Successful collaboration may lead to..........

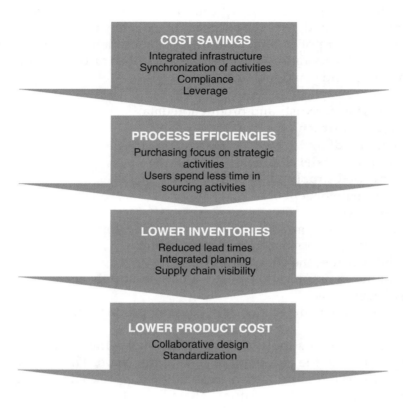

Figure 3.10

Conclusions

This chapter began by exploring the roots of and developments in supply chain management. Supply chain issues, strategies and operations were observable before the term itself was coined in the early 1980s. Practising managers and academics in management and engineering disciplines had concerned themselves with efficiency of operations and how to get the best out of a given set of resource inputs. As indeed had economists such as Coase, Heckert and Miner and later Williamson concerned themselves with transaction costs and wider societal cost issues and Penrose who had examined alternative theories to explaining firm behaviours rather than simply focusing upon the single objective of profit maximization which previous economists had done. Later writers have pursued these interests further in the context of managing supply chains (e.g. Ellram, Hobbs). These early practitioners and writers had a contribution to make in shaping thoughts and concepts that have developed and remained an important part of wider business management and more narrowly focused supply chain operations and strategies. There are clearly identifiable trends and developments that are observable in the literature from the concerns of early management and manufacturing writers examining ways to lower inventory costs and yet still fulfil the operational requirements to produce goods as and when required by the customer. Early manufacturing operations were structured to build stock in advance of the sales period and in some industries the time taken to build inventories might be half a year or more. So it is not difficult to see why managers would be keen to reduce time taken in these processes and to lower their risks in holding stock for long periods before a selling period. A great deal of time and effort of practising managers and academics has been given to these activities and indeed still is with simulation and modelling techniques to search for better supply chain structures, strategies and operations that remove waste, unnecessary movement and bottlenecks from the supply chain system. Lean supply and lean manufacturing systems together with world-class manufacturing, and continuous improvement concepts (Kaizen), are all examples of developments that have been born out of these concerns. The techniques and tools of 'New Wave Manufacturing' like QR and ECR too have developed from these concerns. The latter has its roots also located in marketing and concern with customer focus rather than simply technical or operational improvements to increase efficiency.

Integration was viewed as important from an operational perspective since it allowed firms to standardize operational procedures between different parts of the same organization and later between organizations comprising the supply chain. Modular manufacturing too was an opportunity for firms to standardize components and sub-assemblies within product building. For example, modern automobiles have standard parts that are interchangeable between different models made by the same manufacturer. This lowers inventory and lowers costs of manufacturing and procurement associated with those parts because they are common to cars across the brand range. Variability is limited. Previously firms would have held many different parts unique to a single model. Toyota's system of modular manufacturing changed the way automobile manufacturers designed and built vehicles.

Integration also meant that it became easier to create visibility between different parts of the organization and between organizations by investing in computer systems that could exchange data in standard formats using standard platform (e.g. I2 technologies, PeopleSoft, SAP, Oracle). Just a few years ago access to these technologies and standard platforms required a large capital investment but recent developments including widespread use of Microsoft Office and growing Internet usage have allowed smaller organizations and individuals to engage in the exchange of documents using standard formats and standard platforms for a much more modest investment. Furthermore many software companies have created links between legacy hardware and software systems and more specialized modern software to further allow many large organizations to gain utility from their high investment costs, which would otherwise be obsolete. Merant is one such company that has been successful in creating bridging software products to integrate systems.

Recent supply chain concerns have focused upon wider environmental issues including ethical and ecological concerns. It is envisaged that these ethical and ecological issues will become even more important in the next few years as consumers, politicians, national and international interests are given a higher priority by all concerned. Ethical sourcing and procurement is already high on the agenda of many organizations. Consumer and political pressure groups such as 'Behind the label' which has been influential in exposing sweatshops in the garment industry and 'Greenpeace' who have been influential in a number of areas such as greenhouse gas emissions, ozone depletion, genetically modified foods and wild animal protection. 'Friends of the Earth' are another highly visible and influential pressure group. Greening the supply chain and being more energy efficient has been a focus for government policy in the UK and this trend is likely to continue and get stronger. It is, therefore, essential for organizations to have sustainable supply chain strategies and to design supply chain strategies that lower risk form environmental, ethical and ecological pressure groups.

Strategic perspectives lift the study of supply chains above purely technical and operational concerns towards customer-focused concerns. Supply chain strategies focus on satisfying customer requirements. Operational management literature began to address the customer seriously during the 1980s influenced by the Kaizen philosophy for continuous improvement developed in Japanese manufacturing led by Toyota. The customer that literature addressed was referred to as the internal customer. Terms like 'your next factory operation is your next customer' and 'the next department/section is your customer' became commonplace in factories implementing Kaizen. There was also a literature addressing external customers that had been developed over 50 years in the marketing discipline, which had largely been ignored by operational managers whose prime concern was efficiency. Towards the end of the 1980s and throughout the 1990s this literature began to converge and the issues being addressed in relation to customer demand were mirrored in much of the purchasing, supply and operations disciplines. Being responsive to the customer became a prime concern in a fiercely competitive global environment. Synthesizing the issues, concepts and processes involved is in part one of the aims of this text. Being customer-focused requires organizations to consider how best to address the needs of the customer. The customer in this sense is the end customer in the supply chain although it is accepted that there are indeed internal customers at stages in the chain. Members engaging, interacting and exchanging goods, services, information and value throughout a supply chain do so to satisfy some end customer. Economists have always been concerned with means and ends in the context of supply chain strategies the end objective is to satisfy the customer and the means are the strategies, operations and tactics employed to do so. Strategic imperatives are how resources are employed and deployed to achieve those ends and in meeting organizational objectives, which might include profit, ROI and other financial measures for profit-motivated firms or service, value and benefits for non-profit-motivated organizations.

The next chapter turns the spotlight on what it means to have supply chains that are market-driven and customer-focused.

Discussion Questions

1. Several management disciplines converge to create the catalyst for the development of theoretical frameworks used in supply chain management. Discuss.
2. Explain why supply chain management is now seen as a critical success factor for contemporary organizations in different organizational contexts.
3. Cost and customer service are two critical issues that have historically been viewed as conflicting objectives requiring 'trade-offs'. Explain why in contemporary organizations the two may be viewed as compatible.
4. Select one major theme from the 'empirical evidence' and for an organization of your choice explain why it is important and how it influences their supply chain relationships and/or strategies.
5. Quick response was seen as a way of protecting domestic manufacturers from international competitors. Do you agree?
6. How successful was QR as a means of achieving competitive advantage in the 1980s US Apparel and Textile Supply Chain?
7. 'Fast Fashion' in many respects is the daughter of QR but what's different about it than simply the name change?
8. ECR differs from QR – can you explain the key differences?
9. Discuss the importance of collaborative supply chain strategies and explain the possible benefits.
10. Explain why logistics fulfilment is critical to supply chain strategy.

Note

[1] Interview conducted with board members at the VF corporation in North Carolina, USA, May 2000.

References

Axelrod, R. (1984). *The Evolution of Co-operation*. London: Penguin.

Barney, J. B. (1999). How a firm's capabilities affect boundary decisions. *Sloan Management Review*, Spring. Boston, MA: MIT Press.

Berry, D., Towill, D. R. and Wadsley, N. (1994). Supply chain management in the electronics industry. *International Journal of Physical Distribution and Logistics Management*, **24** (10), 20–32.

Burt, D. N. (1984). *Proactive Procurement*. Englewood Cliffs: Prentice-Hall.

Burt, D. N., Dobler, D. W. and Starling, S. L. (2003). *World Class Supply Management – The Key to Supply Chain Management, 7th edn*. Boston, MA: McGraw-Hill Irwin.

Campbell, N. C. G. (1985). An interaction approach to organizational buying behaviour. *Journal of Business Research*, **13**, 35–48 (reprinted in: Ford, D. 1990, *Understanding Business Markets – Interaction, Relationships, Networks*. London: Academic Press).

Camuffo, A., Romano, P. and Vinelli, A. (2001). Back to the future: benetton transforms its global network. *MIT Sloan Management Review*. Boston: MIT Press, pp. 46–52.

Carlisle, J. A. and Parker, R. C. (1989). *Beyond Negotiation: Customer–Supplier Relationships*. Chichester: Wiley.

Chao, C. N. and Scheuing, E. (1992). An examination of the relationships between levels of purchasing responsibilities and roles of those in purchasing decision making. *First PSERG Conference*, Glasgow.

Christopher, M. G. (1992). *Logistics and Supply Chain Management – Strategies for Reducing Costs and Improving Services*. London: Financial Times/Pitman Publishing.

Christopher, M. G. (1996). *Marketing Logistics*. Oxford: Butterworth-Heinemann.

Coase, R. H. (1937). The nature of the firm. *Economica*, **V**, 386–405.

Cousins, P. D. (2002). A conceptual model for managing long term inter-organizational relationships. *European Journal of Purchasing and Supply Management*, **8** (2), 71–82.

Cox, A. (1997). *Business Success: A Way of Thinking about Strategy, Critical Supply Chain Assets and Operational Best Practice*. Lincolnshire: Earlsgate Press.

Croom, S. and Batchelor, J. (1997). The development of strategic capabilities – an interaction view. *Integrated Manufacturing Systems (UK)*, **8** (5), 299–313.

Deming, W. E. (1986). *Out of the Crisis: Quality, Productivity and Competitive Position*. Cambridge: Cambridge University Press.

de Wit, B. and Meyer, R. (1998). *Strategy – Process, Content, Context*. London: Thompson Learning.

Ellram, L. M. (1991). Supply chain management: the industrial organisation perspective. *International Journal of Physical Distribution and Logistics Management*, **21** (1), 13–22.

Ellram, L. M. (1994). A taxonomy of total cost ownership models. *Journal of Business Logistics*, **15** (1), 171–91.

Fisher, M., Obermeyer, W., Hammond, J. and Raman, A. (1994). Making supply meet demand in an uncertain world. *Harvard Business Review*, **72** (3), 83–93.

Ford, D. (1990). *Understanding Business Markets – Interaction, Relationships, Networks*. London: Academic Press.

Ford, I. D. and Farmer, D. (1986). Make or buy – a key strategic issue. *Long Range Planning*, **19** (5), 54–62.

Forrester, J. W. (1961). *Industrial Dynamics*. Boston, MA: MIT Press.

Fransoo, J. C. and Wouters, M. J. F. (2000). Measuring the bullwhip effect in the supply chain. *Supply Chain Management*, **5** (2), 78–89.

Gereffi, G. (1994). The organization of buyer-driven global commodity chains: how US retailers shape overseas production networks. In *Commodity Chains and Global Capitalism* (Gereffi, G. and Korzeniewicz, M., eds). Westport, CT: Greenwood Press, pp. 95–122.

Goodwin, J. S. and Franklin, S. G. (1994). The beer distribution game: using simulation to teach systems thinking. *Journal of Management Development*, **13** (8), 7–15.

Green, K., Morton, B. and New, S. (1998). Green purchasing and supply policies: do they improve companies' environmental performance? *Supply Chain Management*, **3** (2), 89–95.

Hakansson, H., Johanson, J. and Wootz, B. (1976). Influence tactics in buyer–seller processes. *Industrial Marketing Management*, **4** (6), 319–32.

Harland, C. M. (1995). Supply chain management: relationships, chains and networks. *British Academy of Management Proceedings*, Sheffield, pp. 62–79.

Harrison, A. and Storey, J. (1996). New wave manufacturing strategies – operational, organisational and human dimensions. *International Journal of Operations and Production Management*, **16** (2), 63–76.

Harrison, A. and van Hoek, R. (2002). *Logistics Management and Strategy*. London, FT: Prentice-Hall.

Heckert, J. B. and Miner, R. B. (1940). *Distribution Costs*. New York: The Ronald Press.

Heide, J. B. and Miner, A. S. (1992). The shadow of the future: effects of anticipated interaction and frequency of contact on buyer–supplier co-operation. *Academy of Management Journal*, **35** (2), 265–77.

Hines, P. (1994). *Creating World Class Suppliers: Unlocking Mutual and Competitive Advantage*. London: Pitman.

Hines, P. and Rich, N. (1994). Focusing the achievement of continuous improvement within the supply chain: an automotive case study. *3rd International Conference of the International Purchasing and Supply Education and Research Association*, University of Glamorgan, March, pp. 219–33.

Hines, P., Lamming, R., Jones, D., Cousins, P. and Rich, N. (2000). *Value Stream Management – Strategy and Excellence in the Supply Chain*. London: Financial Times/Prentice-Hall.

Hobbs, J. (1996). A transaction cost analysis of quality, traceability and animal welfare issues in UK beef retailing. *British Food Journal*, **98** (6), 16–26.

Hogarth-Scott, S. (1999). Retailer–supplier partnerships: hostages to fortune or the way forward for the millennium? *British Food Journal*, **101** (9), 668–82.

Houlihan, J. (1984). Supply chain management. *Proceedings of the 19th International Technical Conference*, BPICS.

Hunter, N. A. (1990). *Quick Response in Apparel Manufacturing*. Manchester: The Textile Institute.

Hunter, N. A. and Valentino, P. (1995). Quick response – ten years later. *Journal of Clothing Science and Technology*, **7** (4).

Hunter, N. A., King, R. E. and Nuttle, H. L. W. (1992). An apparel supply system for QR retailing. *Journal of the Textile Institute*, **83** (3).

Hunter, N. A., King, R. E., Nuttle, H. L. W. and Wilson, J. R. (1993). The apparel pipeline modelling project at North Carolina State University. *Journal of Clothing Science and Technology*, **5** (3/4).

Iyer, A. V. and Bergen, M. E. (1997). Quick response in manufacturer–retailer channels. *Management Science*, **43** (4), 559–70.

Jones, T. C. and Riley, D. W. (1985). Using inventory for competitive advantage through supply chain management. *International Journal of Physical Distribution and Materials Management*, **15** (5), 16–26.

Kanter, R. M. (1994). Collaborative advantage: the art of alliances. *Harvard Business Review*, **72** (4), July–August. Boston. HBR Publications.

KSA (1987). New technology for quick response: how US apparel manufacturers can capitalize on their proximity to the US market. *Getting Started in Quick Response*. Arlington: Technical Advisory Committee, AAMA.

KSA (1993). *Efficient Consumer Response – Enhancing Consumer Value in the Grocery Industry*. Kurt Salmon Associates, Inc. (KSA), Washington, DC: The Research Department, Food Marketing Institute.

KSA (1997). The ABCs of strategic alliances. *Womens Wear Daily Reprint in WDinfotracs*, New York: Wdinfotracs.

Lamming, R. (1993). *Beyond Partnership Strategies for Innovation and Lean Supply*. Hemel Hempstead: Prentice-Hall.

Leidecker, J. K. and Bruno, A. V. (1984). Identifying and using critical success factors. *Long Range Planning*, **17** (1). Oxford Pergamon Press.

Lowson, B., King, R. and Hunter, A. (1999). *Quick Response – Managing the Supply Chain to Meet Consumer Demand*. Chichester: Wiley.

Macbeth, D. K. and Ferguson, N. (1990). Strategic aspects of supply chain management. *Paper Presented at OMA-UK Conference on Manufacturing Strategy – Theory and Practice*, Warwick, June.

Oliver, R. K. and Webber, M. D. (1982). Supply chain management: logistics catches up with strategy. *Outlook*. USA: Booz, Allen and Hamilton Inc.

Porter, M. E. (1980). *Competitive Strategy – Techniques for Analyzing Industries and Competitors*. New York: Free Press.

Prahalad, C. K. and Hamel, G. (1990). The core competencies of the corporation. *Harvard Business Review*. Boston, MA: HBR Press.

Sako, M. (1990). *Prices, Quality and Trust: Interfirm Relations in Britain and Japan*. Cambridge: Cambridge University Press.

Shapiro, J. F. (2001). *Modeling the Supply Chain*. Pacific Grove, CA: Duxbury Thomson Learning.

Slack, N., Chambers, S. and Johnston, R. (2001). *Operations Management*, 3rd edn. London: FT/Prentice-Hall.

Stalk, G., Jr. (1988). Time – the next source of competitive advantage. *Harvard Business Review*, **4**, 41–51. Boston, MA: HBR Press.

Stalk, G., Evans, P. and Shulman, L. E. (1992). Competing on capabilities: the new rules of corporate strategy. *Harvard Business Review*, **70** (2), 57–69. Boston, MA: HBR Press.

Stevens, G. C. (1989). Integrating the supply chain. *International Journal of Physical Distribution and Materials Management*, **19** (8), 3–8.

Williamson, O. E. (1979). Transaction Cost Economics: the governance of contractual relations. *The Journal of Law and Economics*, **22** (2), 232–62.

Womack, J. P., Jones, D. T. and Roos, D. (1990). *The Machine that Changed the World*. London: Macmillan.

Chapter 4

Market-driven and customer-focused supply chain strategies

LEARNING OUTCOMES

After reading this chapter you should be able to:

- know that supply chain strategies are more effective when they are market-driven and customer-focused;
- know and understand what it means to be customer-focused and what it means to have supply chains that are market-driven rather than supply-side-driven;
- know the importance of product definition in terms of a bundle of goods and services;
- identify and discuss the differences between manufacturing and service industries and implications for supply chain strategies;
- understand that strategic thinking is important for developing appropriate supply chain strategies;
- have knowledge of different supply chain strategies that can be employed in manufacturing and service industries.

This chapter examines a number of important concepts in relation to organizational supply chain strategies being market-driven and customer-focused. It begins by discussing management functions and management integration across functional and organizational boundaries. The distinction between product push and market pull strategies is explained before discussing product and service attributes in the context of being customer-focused in the supply chain. Supply chain strategies are discussed for products and service industries and a number of supply chain levers are discussed building a conceptual framework in which supply chain strategies are conducted. Market-driven supply chain strategies are examined using Ansoff's product/market matrix before finally exploring order-winning supply chain strategies.

Organizational structure in relation to supply chain strategies

Historically organizations were managed functionally to structure and co-ordinate different activities. For example, production was concerned with transforming inputs into outputs and the focus might have been on production efficiency. A consequence of production efficiency might be that unit cost could be lowered being achieved through scale economies. In this approach to managing the business functions there is a risk of *'silo mentality'* inside an organization, which results in different functions working independent of organizational strategic objectives. Organizations become blind to inefficiencies and to opportunities. Production departments would be rewarded for efficiency even though their efficiency might result in *'making for stock'*. The consequences of this could be to increase inventory-holding costs. Thus the actions of the production department impact adversely upon the cost structure in the warehousing and distribution function. There is also an *'opportunity cost'* attached to this decision since capital tied up in inventories could have been applied elsewhere to earn a return rather than incur higher than necessary cost. Functional thinking also encouraged the organization to think in terms of *'supply push'* to move stock on to customers. The question was not one of: 'Does the market demand the product?' but 'Can we sell it?' Figure 4.1 illustrates how supply chains cut across organizational and internal functional boundaries to deliver products and services to customers. A network of supplier organizations provides inputs to the firm that in turn transforms into customer products and services.

An important question is: Where does the process begin and where does it end? It begins with customers signalling demand for specific products and services. It ends with satisfied customers receiving the products and services they demanded. It is the marketplace where demand is created and markets drive business supply chains to fulfil the customer promise by delivering their requirements. Organizations, therefore, need to be customer-focused to create value through their supply chain strategies. Figure 4.2 demonstrates that the starting point in creating value through supply chain strategy is to understand fully the customer needs. Customers drive markets and market demand.

From the customer's point of view products and services have a number of attributes such as price, quality, time, functionality and

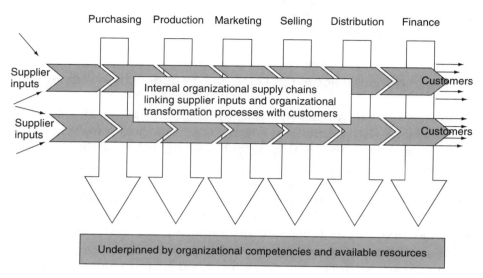

Figure 4.1

fashion. How these attributes are bundled determines the value that customers place upon the products. In addition to the core product and service attributes one could add service, customer relationships, image and reputation.

It has already been noted that market-led supply chain strategies begin and end with the customer. Focusing upon the customer may also mean involving customers at an early stage of product or service design. Figure 4.3 illustrates an input, process and output model for the firm connecting to its supply networks and to its customers. The organizational boundaries are shown by the dotted line illustrating the fact that in many contemporary organizations these boundaries are not as clear-cut as they once might have been. Take the example of the way automobile manufacturers interact with their suppliers and customers often involving both in designing products, specifying product components

Strategic focus begins by being customer-focused
Understanding the customer perspective
What does the customer value?

	Product/service attributes					Relationship	Image
Customer perspective	Price	Quality	Time	Functionality	Fashion	Service relationships	Brand reputation

Figure 4.2

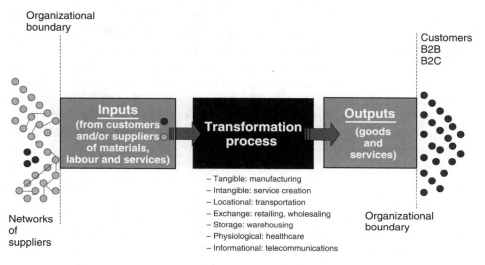

Transformation processes apply equally
to manufacturing and service industries

Figure 4.3

or in the design of manufacturing processes. Alternatively, take the case of service interactions with reality TV programmes where customers design challenges for contestants by e-mailing, texting or phoning the programme makers.

Inputs will come from two main sources: the customers and the suppliers of materials, labour and other services. The transformation processes involved depend upon the particular organizational context. For example, healthcare providers are concerned with improving patient welfare as a strategic objective. In meeting this end they will procure medical supplies from various sources together with the necessary medical expertise and physical assets (buildings, equipment, other resources) to deliver the health services required. The effectiveness of the healthcare provision will be dependent on technical and managerial core competencies and resources at the organization's disposal. The efficiency of the healthcare provision will be dependent upon the organization's capability to transform the combination of resource inputs into effective outputs at lowest cost. Customers in this context are patients. Effectiveness should take priority over efficiency in this context but efficiency cannot be ignored. It is through efficiency that better service and more effective use of resources will lead to improvements in healthcare. Efficiency means that more patients can be treated from the same resource envelope. Supply chain strategies that can achieve high levels of effectiveness and efficiency are desirable.

Products (tangible) or services (intangible)

Supply chain management tools and techniques were developed originally in manufacturing industry. The developments are fully explained in Chapter 3. Engineers, purchasing professionals and production managers concerned with lowering costs of manufacture in automobiles, aerospace and electronic products whilst maintaining or improving quality levels championed operational aspects of supply chain management. Managing supply chains not products became the focus of ways to improve cost structures and efficiency. Managing supply chains as a system in a way that the Japanese automobile manufacturers had practised focusing upon quality improvements and cost efficiency became fashionable in management during the 1990s. In 2000 manufacturing industry in Japan contributed 37 per cent to their GDP whereas for the United Kingdom it was 27 per cent and for the United States only 20 per cent (World Bank Statistics, Year Book). Conversely, service industries in these three countries represented 63, 73 and 80 per cent of GDP, respectively. So the question is: Are supply chain strategies important and appropriate in all sectors of an economy? The answer has to be yes. The example of healthcare has already been given to illustrate how supply chain strategies can improve well-being. Supply chain strategies and the operational tools and techniques developed for manufacturing industries are transferable and adaptable to different contextual settings.

It is recognized in the literature that theoretically businesses range from pure services to pure goods but that it may be very difficult in practice to identify these pure forms (Bateson and Hoffman, 1999, p. 8). Therefore most business will be delivering a mix of services and products. The degree of mix and how to manage the mix is the challenge facing most organizations. In developed economies the importance of services in the mix is increasing. Thus, as competition increases services become more important in that mix and may give rise to what Porter (1980) referred to as advantage through differentiation. In highly competitive environments firms competing on cost grounds alone only have one management lever that of cost control, hence productivity improvement becomes a main focus of attention. Service and focus on service improvement is one way for a single firm to differentiate its competitive offering in the market. Rathmell (1974) and Shostack (1977) recognized the importance of the product/service spectrum. The rise in the importance of services in the UK and US economies has been well documented (Baron and Harris, 2003; Bateson and Hoffman, 1999). It is also important to recognize that even in developing economies the growth of the service sector has been instrumental to development. For example, India's service economy is now approaching 40 per cent GDP from a low base around 10 per cent some 50 years ago. Services are important in economic development at the macrolevel. Service innovations are also a significant component of firm capability and ability to grow at a microlevel. A number of propositions could be developed from these observations two of which are:

P0 = Innovations in customer service lead to improved competitive positioning, higher profitability and higher return on investment.

P1 = Firm growth is dependent on designing appropriate levels of service.

These may or may not be true we are simply hypothesizing here.

Bundles of goods and services

Many organizations offer customers a bundle of goods and services. The idea of what constitutes the bundle offered to a customer is given in Figure 4.4. It shows some combinations of goods and services. In the example a food retailer is bundling 90 per cent goods and 10 per cent service. At the other end of the spectrum a marketing consultancy represents 92 per cent service and 8 per cent goods. The tangible items may be consumed in the final report. These are only meant to be

Bundling goods and services examples

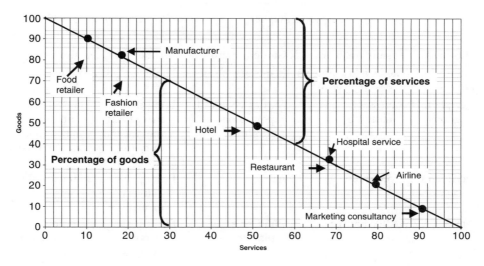

Figure 4.4

indicative and the particular context of the customer proposition would determine the actual bundling. For example, purchasing an airline ticket offers different bundles depending on how much you want to pay and what class of travel is required. More services are bundled with first class travel as opposed to flying economy.

Table 4.1 offers an analysis of the different elements that make up the core goods offer or the core service offer using two examples of each to illustrate what may be involved. Two examples are given for each category: core goods and core service. None of the examples are representative of pure goods or pure service industries; they are combinations or *bundles of goods and services* packaged for their customers. The ideas of elements relate closely to the concept of core products, augmented products developed by Levitt (1988). It has not been unknown for the peripheral goods and services to move to the core offer through trading experience. There are many business transformation examples where this has happened. For example, breweries operating public houses have given up brewing to concentrate on activities once regarded as peripheral to the core brewing activity such as retailing food and providing accommodation. Other examples include retailers offering a peripheral service of store credit to help support sales of their core products. These retailers have found it profitable to become banks or credit card companies, e.g. Co-op, Tesco, Sainsbury. Some Premier League soccer clubs in the UK can generate as much, if not more revenue from the sale of corporate entertainment and hospitality than from match day ticket sales.

Table 4.1

Element	Core goods example		Core service example	
Business	Fashion retailer	Garden centre	Airline	Hairdresser
Core	Men's and women's designer-wear	Plants and shrubs	Flights	Cut, wash, blow dry
Peripheral goods	Accessories, costume jewellery	Garden chemicals, pots, tools, furniture	Inflight magazines, movies and duty-free items	Hair-related products – shampoo, conditioner
Peripheral services	Store credit	Advice	Pick up and delivery to airport	Manicure skin care
Variant	Coffee lounge	Children's play area	Dedicated airport lounges	Internet café/reading lounge

Differences between manufacturing and service industries

Services industries are different from manufacturing industries producing goods. A brief sojourn in the services marketing literature would identify four critical differences between the two sectors and these are highlighted here as follows:

1. Goods are *tangible* whereas services are *intangible*.
2. Goods can be *inventoried* whereas services cannot be inventoried, they are *perishable*.
3. There is usually no interaction between customer and process in manufacture. The process of manufacture is *separate* from the customer, whereas there is always customer interaction between service and process. Service and service processes are *inseparable*.
4. Goods produced in factories are homogeneous (*same*) whereas services are heterogeneous (*different*).

These differences are important to recognize and understand because they determine the nature of supply chain strategies, structures and relationships that can be developed in the different contexts.

The extended marketing mix developed in services marketing literature during the 1980s recognized the shift in developed economies away from industrial products to service-based economies (Zeithaml et al., 1985). Delivering marketing activities based on theories developed for the US and UK economies of the 1950s became less tenable in the economic context of the final decades of the twentieth century. Many marketing academics questioned the appropriateness of the four P approach (Product, Price, Promotion and Place) that had remained the tenet of basic marketing texts since the 1950s. Some academics still have a problem with the P approach to marketing generally including the author. Nevertheless, the services marketing literature added a further three P's, people, process and physical evidence, to address the gap in the ability of marketing theory to deal with service-based industries.

People
People become far more important to service providers because they are in the front line whereas in the supply of goods the majority of people are in the back-office or factory. The interaction between the person delivering services and the customer becomes a critical interaction in many service industries. People unlike machines may not behave consistently for whatever reason, let's call it human nature, personality, attitude or individuality. This lack of consistency has been the major factor in distinguishing good service from poor service. When a company is designing services it can eliminate or design out inconsistencies

in people behaviour, and there is a better chance of the service supply and delivery being consistent. Management intervention through training may also be an important influence on behaviour, the nature of interactions and the customer experience.

Process

Processes are another important component in the service delivery interactions. If service delivery processes can be standardized through carefully designed operating systems and procedures the customer experience should be the same, i.e. consistent for all customers purchasing the service. *Blueprinting* is often used as a technique to carefully analyse existing services and design improved or new services. Essentially this is a process-mapping technique similar to those found in work study. It offers a systems approach to the delivery of services. Carefully designed processes supported with staff training can offer the organization a way of reducing variability in their staff behaviours during customer interactions.

Example of process mapping

By analysing processes an organization may be able to identify non-value-adding activities such as transport, storage, inspection and delay. The process times can be calculated and time wasted identified. Process mapping is the tool used to identify these non-value-adding activities. Process-mapping tools have formed the basis of many industry studies examining supply chains to identify blockages in the supply chain. Both the DAMA Project and the KSA analysis of the US Textile and Apparel Pipeline described in Chapter 3 employed the technique to discover the blockages and delays. An example of how process maps might be used is given below:

		ASME Symbol				
Activity	Description of Element	Operation	Movement	Inspection	Delay	Storage
1	Order goods from supplier	●	➡	■	▶	▼
2	Transmit specification for SKUs	●	➡	■	▶	▼
3	Check prices by e-mail	●	➡	■	▶	▼
4	Arrange shipment	●	➡	■	▶	▼
5	Check expected delivery dates	●	➡	■	▶	▼
6	Notify RDC of expected date of arrival	●	➡	■	▶	▼
7	Goods despatched from supplier to port	●	➡	■	▶	▼
8	Goods shipped by carrier to London	●	➡	■	▶	▼
9	Goods awaiting collection from port	●	➡	■	▶	▼
10	Road transport carrier arranged	●	➡	■	▶	▼

Source: Author.

Activities 1–6 are operations, 7 and 8 are movements, 9 a delay and 10 an operation.

The ASME symbols are used to chart the processes. In this example the business process re-engineering consultant would simply use a pre-prepared sheet with the symbols on it and enter the activities in sequence with a description and draw a line to link each activity step. Times taken might also be recorded for each of the activities.

Planning supply chain operations is a critical activity for the success of any organization. Operational plans may be delayed and that will impact on the strategic plans for the organization. Delays in sourcing or procuring supplies of raw materials, work-in-progress, components, finished goods and merchandise for resale would cause underachievement of revenue budgets and affect period profitability. This in turn has the knock on effect of disrupting the organization's strategic goals. Planning tools such as GANTT charts are useful for keeping plans on track. Microsoft Project part of the Office Suite of Programs is an example of such a tool. It has the advantage in being electronic that it can be quickly updated and plans can be posted to the Microsoft website to be shared by authorized parties who work on the project. For example, suppliers could access data and share the file details to make adjustments and inform supply chain parties including customers of necessary changes. Figure 4.5 illustrates a GANTT chart using Microsoft Project.

Physical evidence
Physical evidence is the final component identified in the services marketing mix. It is probably most easily explained using a hotel as an example of the service encounter. Entering through the front door the customer is greeted, a bellhop takes the customer's luggage and the doorman guides the customer to the check-in desk. On entering the hotel the customer feels a sense of comfort on site of the large luxurious leather seating areas, marble floors and walls, contemporary lighting and spacious entrance foyer with a thick pile red carpet clearly marking a footway to the check-in. The customer also walks past several hotel guests and they appear to be content smiling as they go about their business. One or two say hello as they pass by the guest, as do two members of staff. Arriving at check-in the guest is greeted by name by the Duty Manager and cannot help but be impressed by the hitech computer facilities that deliver a pre-programmed plastic room key and a safety deposit box key. The guest is introduced briefly to the concierge before being led past the large central staircase adjacent to

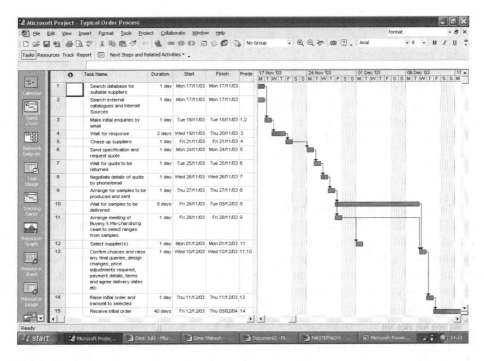

Figure 4.5

Source: Author.

the restaurants, leisure facilities and ballroom towards the lift. The guest arrives at her room and is amazed on entry at how spacious it is. It looks bright, clean and has a large window with views over the city and river below. She is pleased to notice that the cases have already been placed on the luggage rack. The member of staff points out the bathroom facilities and offers brief instructions on how to work the shower and hair dryer before doing the same for the TV, room lighting and electronic curtains. The guest cannot help but feel impressed as he leaves her commenting 'if there is anything you require simply call the front desk on one'.

In the example there are a number of service encounters with different members of the hotel staff and brief interactions with other customers but the overall impression of the customer's experience is clearly shaped by the physical evidence. The hotel decor, design, cleanliness, facilities and technology to support a speedy check-in were all part of the physical evidence in this example.

Lovelock (1992) drew the analogy that many service operations are literally *'factories in the field'* which customers enter when they need a service. One difference between a factory and service has already been noted that the completed service is often consumed as it is produced (*inseparability*), and there may be direct contact between production (operations) and customers. The inseparability between production and consumption means that consumers are exposed to many aspects of a service operation that are kept hidden in manufacturing operations. Lovelock's (1983) categorization questions are as important today as when first asked focusing upon the nature of the service act, the type of customer relationship involved, room for customization on the part of a service provider and how the service is delivered. Much of the early work on service management concerned itself with consumer markets but interestingly the work of Langeard and Eiglier reported in Langeard et al. (1981) developed the 'servuction model' based on a factory production system as a 'metaphor' for service experiences.

The servuction system model developed by Langeard and Eiglier is illustrated in Figure 4.6. It explains that customers receive a bundle of benefits from each service experience, resulting from their interaction with visible elements of the service system. Visible elements may comprise: all contact personnel employed by the service provider, aspects of the inanimate environment (physical evidence referred to earlier) and interactions with other customers. Invisible elements comprise: back-office staff, technological support systems, policies, procedures and organizational infrastructure. The invisible elements are often referred to collectively as the organization's *'technical core'*. The model is useful in that it draws distinction between visible elements and

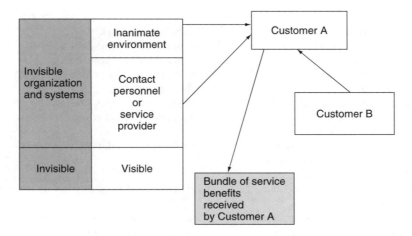

Figure 4.6

invisible components of the system. It acknowledges the customer's role in service production and provides a structural representation of services. It conceptualizes the service as having three overlapping systems:

1. Service operations system (back stage invisible to the customer and front stage contact points visible to the customer);
2. Service delivery system;
3. Service marketing system.

It also draws attention to the interaction between different customers and how that may shape the service experience. It Illustrates integration of marketing, operations, human resources, physical (and or virtual) environments and emphasizes the customer perspective. It is for this latter reason that the 'servuction model' is conceptually useful in strategic thinking applied to supply chain strategies for service industries.

There are some further differences between goods and services that become clearer from the servuction model and they are highlighted in Table 4.2. Earlier the fact that services cannot be inventoried was identified. This is important because it means you can plan for service delivery and you can source, order and purchase the goods elements in advance of delivery but the service itself has to be created at the point

Table 4.2 Further important differences between services and goods

Services	*Goods*
Cannot be inventoried	Can be held in stock
Time-dependent (perishable)	Not necessarily time-dependent
Place-dependent	Not necessarily place-dependent
Consumers are always involved in the factory	Consumers hardly ever involved in the factory
Changes in the service operation always cause a change in consumer behaviour	Changes to factory operations do not necessarily affect consumer behaviour
Everyone and everything coming into contact with the consumer is delivering the service	Only front office staff deliver service
Quality cannot be controlled at factory gate	Quality control at factory before delivery
Contact personnel are like products they are part of the experience	Contact personnel not as important as how the product performs

The Virgin Upper Class Lounge at Heathrow made two noticeable changes to service in an attempt to lower staff costs after 9/11. The first was to change food and beverages from table service to self-service reducing the variety of food and cutting the numbers of staff required. The second was to change the hair salon to first come first served where previously passengers were able to pre-book a timed appointment in advance by telephone or through e-mail. The reaction to these service changes from customers has been generally hostile. Passengers who experienced the higher level of service previously offered when waiting in the lounge often remark on the changes to other passengers and to staff. Some feel so strongly that they enter comments in the suggestion book held in the lounge. So far these reactions have not caused changes to the service at Heathrow but passengers notice the difference and comment on it when they visit similar Virgin lounges that still offer the superior level of service that the London terminal previously did. Staff, customers and physical conditions interact to create the service experience.

of delivery. Supply chains for the service element are short, e.g. from kitchen to restaurant. Food, beverages, cooking utensils, kitchen tools and aprons can all be procured in advance and inventoried until the point of service delivery. Services are usually time-dependent, e.g. a hotel room for the night, a hospital bed, completion of tax returns, a theatre production, a vacation. Services are also place-dependent, e.g. you need to go to a hospital, a theatre, a holiday destination and a hairdresser. Granted some hairdressers may do home visits as do accountants for tax returns but usually many services are place-dependent. This place dependency has coined the phrases *'destination marketing'* or *'place marketing'*. Consumption always takes place at the point of delivery and the consumer is involved in the creation process. The consumer experience is created at point of delivery. Consumers of goods hardly ever visit or become involved in factory production of the items. Changes to service operations will always lead to changes in consumer behaviour in the case of services.

Schmenner (1986, p. 25) developed a conceptual model of viewing services as high or low labour-intense organizations *vis-à-vis* degree of contact and customization involved. This model identified and differentiated four types: service factories, service shops, mass services and professional services. An adaptation of this model is shown in Figure 4.7.

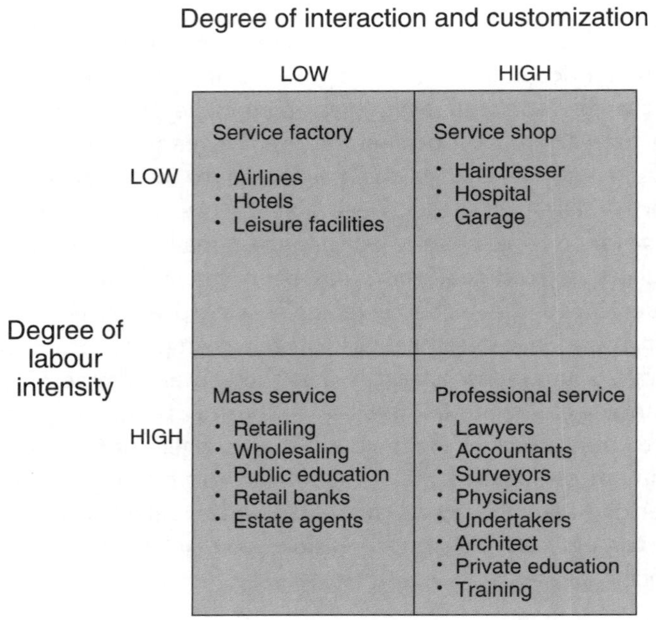

Degree of interaction and customization

	LOW	HIGH
LOW	Service factory • Airlines • Hotels • Leisure facilities	Service shop • Hairdresser • Hospital • Garage
HIGH	Mass service • Retailing • Wholesaling • Public education • Retail banks • Estate agents	Professional service • Lawyers • Accountants • Surveyors • Physicians • Undertakers • Architect • Private education • Training

Degree of
labour
intensity

Figure 4.7

A dimensional perspective is useful to observe. Mass-market suppliers of services require high degrees of labour intensity but offer low customer contact and customization. Services are standard and market price is often a key competitive feature. Professional services too are usually labour-intensive but the degree of contact and customization is high. Professional services usually compete on grounds other than price and they are generally not price-sensitive. Points of difference become a competitive dimension for these types of organization. Service shops also offer a high degree of contact and customization but they are lower in terms of labour intensity. Services classified as factories are low on both dimensions.

Customer focus

This section builds on the ideas developed in services marketing and the analytical frameworks used to identify the different elements of service degrees of customization, contact with customers, labour intensity and more particularly the useful constructs developed from the 'servuction model' and service design using a form of *blueprinting* to examine supply chain strategies. Figure 4.8 re-visits the customer's

The next stage is to determine how the firm can deliver customer value. After having identified what the customer values and wants from the organization

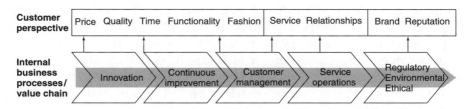

Develop or buy in competencies to improve organizational capabilities to deliver customer value

Figure 4.8

perspective but adds what can be called back-office elements to the perspective. In effect the diagram shows how the organization's invisible elements support the attributes valued by the customer. These invisible elements form the organization's *'technical core'*, i.e. organizational competencies. The quality of these competencies determines organizational capability to deliver customer products and services. In effect these are the business processes behind customer service where the organization is able to create value for the customer and value and/or profit for the organization depending on the context in which the organization operates. It is in effect the organizational value chain in Porter's (1980) terminology.

The elements shown in the business processes reflect what the organization is able to do to support the attributes valued by the customer in broad generic terms. By examining briefly each of the customer attributes the organizational competence needed to support this is identified:

1. *Price* is dependent on the organization's capability to lower cost and hence lower prices for the customer. If price is a key attribute for the customer then the firm will need to find ways to lower cost through productivity improvements. These may be achieved through continuous improvement processes following *Kaizen* philosophy or they may be achieved through innovations (*breakthroughs*) in product/service design, product/service delivery and fulfilment, achieving economies of scale or scope. Another aspect of price may be that it is not simply the lowest price that the customer wants but rather value for money. This has similar implications for the competencies required but the focus is on delivering goods and services to the right value

rather than the lowest price. Price, cost and value are discussed more fully elsewhere in the text.

2. *Quality* from the customer's perspective involves two aspects: (a) product quality and (b) service quality. Both product and service qualities are achieved through innovation and through the adoption of Kaizen, continuous improvement whereby quality of processes in production or service results in improvements to the finished goods or services. The customer focus is upon reliability and reputation when making choices between competitor offerings.

3. *Time* may be critical in some markets and to certain customers. If this is an attribute that is particularly valued then the organization must develop business processes and competence to deliver products or services at the right time. Innovations such as QR using a JiT approach have helped manufacturing organizations to respond quickly to customer needs adopting *agile manufacturing* and flexible manufacturing systems (FMS). Retailers have developed ECR techniques to deliver goods on time to consumer markets. If time is a valued attribute then the focus for back-office must be to build competencies in being *responsive* to the customer.

4. *Functionality* if valued will depend upon the organization's technical competence to meet the demands of customers and to compete within the market against organizations offering similar goods and services (substitutes). Technical competence once again can be improved through continuous improvement or through innovation.

5. *Fashion* is *time-dependent* and *design-dependent*. Organizations competing in fashion markets need to innovate and be responsive. Formal systemic approaches to innovation are often observed in organizations competing within this type of market. New product development or new service development becomes a paramount concern.

6. *Service* if valued by customers requires the organization to develop competencies in *responsiveness* and *customer relationship management* (CRM). CRM is not simply about technology but technology may well support or facilitate the quality of CRM. Competencies in managing the customer interactions are particularly important when organizations compete on this dimension.

7. *Relationships* are important to service operations. It doesn't mean all customers want a 'special' relationship with the organization as we have seen; there are different types of relationship and it is important for an organization to identify the level and intensity of customer contact that is required to meet the customer needs in the context of the market and the value placed upon the attribute by the customer. It is also important to be able to identify circumstances when customers do not require high levels of contact. A matter that some service organizations often fail to recognize is the change from

traditional *'interruption marketing'* to *'permission marketing'* where the marketing organization leverages *permission* from the customer over time to further marketing initiatives. *Services* and *relationship marketing* approaches together with CRM are ways to build competence in this area.

8. *The brand and reputation of the organization* will be an important focus for many customers in making purchase decisions. For the customer brands often guarantee quality through established reputation. Brands communicate differences in the product/service offer. Customers often feel secure selecting a branded product/service *vis-à-vis* an unbranded competitor's offer. A brand creates value for customers and value for the organization. This value is measurable through increases in revenue, profit and higher returns on investment with appropriate economic rewards for the organization and its owners. Organizations must develop competence in communicating their reputation through the brand if this is important to customers.

There are only two ways in which organizations acquire competence to build value for their customers: (a) they either develop it in-house through experience, learning and development some of which may be brought in from outside organizations, or (b) they buy in people with the competencies.

Strategic thinking makes the difference?

Drucker (1956) once commented that there were only two functions of a business: marketing and innovation. In essence this is a strategy statement. It is as relevant today as it was then. Supply chain strategies need to be configured to match customer demand by being customer-facing and customer-focused. This ensures that customer needs are identified and the organization must then assess whether or not it is able to satisfy the need profitably or in the case of public services within budget constraints. The ability to satisfy customer needs will depend on the organization's capabilities (the *visible* front office and *invisible* back-office, *the technical core*) and how managers and/or entrepreneurs are able to configure resources at their disposal to supply bundles of products and services efficiently. Doing so will require creativity and innovation by managers or entrepreneurs. The concept of the entrepreneur has been deliberately introduced at this stage of the argument to demonstrate that entrepreneurial thinking is critical to generate creativity and innovation. The term entrepreneur has been used to describe the founder of an organization, an owner manager and an innovative leader. In this context creativity and innovation are key to the definition. The ways in which the product and service attributes are combined to deliver customer requirements is determined by entrepreneurial thinking. This develops from Schumpeter's (1950, p. 84) original idea that the entrepreneur is not simply someone providing capital or an inventor but rather the person with the business idea. For Schumpeter the entrepreneur's ability to see possible new combinations, do things differently or do new things was the key to their success. It is the notion of *'creative destruction'*. Schumpeter drew attention to the fact that managers focus upon administering existing structures whereas the focus ought to be on how they create or destroy them. In contemporary organizations there is no reason why entrepreneurial thinking cannot be the province of managers. Drucker (1970, p. 10) took this view when he aligned entrepreneurship with management stating it was the entrepreneurial act, risk taking that was central to the business enterprise. In essence this is *strategic thinking*. This is a key factor why some managers improve the firm's performance whereas others faced with the same opportunities and threats and resource base are unable to do so. Strategic thinking makes a difference.

Reminded of this consider the change in fortunes of Ryanair the Irish low budget no frills airline. Michael O'Leary is the 42-year-old CEO and an accountant by management discipline. He pioneered the business strategy to develop Ryanair as a low-cost supplier and identifies cost discipline as central to success. This is, however, only half the story because Ryanair is a marketing success story too. He took over the airline at a time when it had lost £25 million in 4 years and been through five CEOs who had failed to make a go of things. O'Leary was asked if he would take it over when he was Financial Director to which he reportedly replied 'close it f******down it's a basket case, it's never going to make money'. Finally, he did agree to accept the position for 25 per cent of the company profits in return. This was a good deal for the Ryan family when the airline was losing £3 million a year but not when it began to make money. When the airline turned a profit of £10 million the Ryan's had to write O'Leary a cheque for £2.5 million. He swapped the money at that point for a 25 per cent stake in the business. Effectively becoming an entrepreneur by the classic definition of being the risk taker. The company was floated on the Irish stock exchange in 1997 at a valuation of €500 million at current prices. In August 2003 the company was valued at ten times that value €5 billion. In the last financial year ending in 2003 traffic growth was 41 per cent, revenue was up by 35 per cent, profits up by 59 per cent, earnings per share improved by 54 per cent, the load factor was up by four points and the business made 28 per cent profit after tax. So what was it that turned a basket case into a success? It is the ability of the entrepreneur to combine resources differently that makes the difference either through marketing and/or innovation. In Ryanair's case both are evident.

The company transformed itself from a 'me too copycat' type airline losing money because it could never achieve the economies of scale required to turn a profit into a European low-cost no-frills US type supplier based on South West Airlines business model. An activity map of Ryanair's strategy is shown in Figure 4.9.

It is important to note that Ryanair has a customer-focused supply strategy even though service elements are limited. The company has identified a gap in the market for the supply of low-cost no-frills flights from a to b that offer a simple, safe, reliable and lower-price alternative to conventional airlines. It is pursuing a profitable low cost and clearly differentiated strategy from many of its rivals in the airline industry.

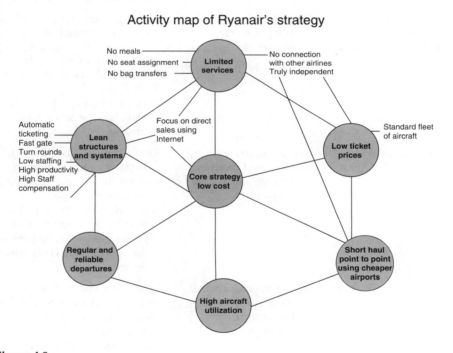

Figure 4.9

Different strategies require different activities to be performed

According to Porter (1980) organizations have two sources of competitive advantage (cost and differentiation) that lead to three main strategies (cost, differentiation and focus). Table 4.3 illustrates four different strategies, their definition and the types of activities that the organization would need to focus upon and develop competencies in order to pursue each strategy. The low-cost strategy has already been examined

Table 4.3

Type of strategy	Strategy defined	Strategic activities
Low cost (mainly compete on low prices)	Producing the lowest cost products in the market	Sourcing and purchasing products/services at lowest cost Efficient operations seeking to improve productivity Achieving scale economies (administration, purchasing, production, distribution and marketing) Achieving economies of scope
Market segmentation (compete on price and/or differences)	Satisfying the needs of a particular market niche	Target particular groups of customers based on characteristics, e.g. age, lifestyle, location, other identified customer attributes Focus marketing activities to match the target customer profile
Market differentiation	Offering customers perceived or actual differences through branding	Promote differences through brand strategy and brand development, e.g. reliability, reputation, service Innovation and creativity in marketing communication Confuse the market and make product/service comparison difficult
Product differentiation	Offering products that differ considerably from competitor offerings	Innovation and creativity Product/service development Time to market – quick response Continuous improvement (Kaizen) Confuse the market and make product/service comparison difficult

in the Ryanair case. Essentially this type of strategy is focused on value proposition customers, customers who buy lowest price items. These customers want a bargain. If the organization can offer bargains the customers keep buying. There is a great deal written on customer loyalty and whether or not customers are loyal. It is often stated that value proposition customers are not loyal but this is not necessarily so. It is argued that these customers migrate when there are bargains to be had from alternative suppliers. This is also partially true. However, most of the literature fails to recognize that the same customers may require the value proposition for some purchases but require a different bundle of attributes for other items for which they will be prepared to pay a premium. Customer loyalty is much more complex than it is often reported to be. It is this complexity that makes it difficult for organizations to identify which buttons to press in designing a market-driven supply chain strategy.

A market segmentation strategy requires the organization to focus upon a particular group of customers. If you consider the metaphor of an orange you are now focusing attention on one part, a segment rather than the whole orange. In marketing segmentation terms the organization must identify groups of customer with similar characteristics such as demographics, psychographics, geographics and lifestyles. An illustrative example might be a niche retailer such as *Agent Provocateur* that targets the young and sexy lingerie market or convenience stores targeting time-poor cash-rich busy professionals. This strategy is what Porter referred to as a focused strategy. A market differentiation strategy creates difference through reputation, reliability, branding and service elements. Note the product or indeed service itself may not be that different from competing offers but the way it is communicated to the marketplace will be. The final strategy is product or service differentiation: a better product, more features, more benefits bundled for the customer to make the product or service more attractive to the customer. Perhaps more peripheral goods and services are included in the offer or the variant is more attractive to the customer. For example, the hairdresser with DVDs and a coffee shop while waiting.

Supply chain strategies are market-driven. For example, signals from the marketplace such as a sharp fall in sales for a particular product may indicate that customers are no longer favourably disposed to the products and services supplied by the organization. This has an impact upon the whole supply chain. Finished goods inventories rise because the goods in question do not sell as quickly, work-in-progress and capacities need to be adjusted swiftly downwards so as to avoid inventory build up elsewhere in the organization. Purchase orders need to be changed to accommodate lower sales volumes and suppliers connected in the chain will mirror these activities. Investigative work will be needed by the organization to determine reasons. Cause and effect diagrams such as the Ishikawa or Fishbone diagram as it is sometimes called may be used for this purpose. There may be other analytical tools at the organizations disposal to identify causes such as focus group analysis with small groups of customers, individual interviews with particular customers to determine why they have stopped buying the organization products. This type of research is in the domain of marketing researchers. Organizations may need to buy in expertise if they do not have the knowledge and skills in-house. Once the reasons for the sharp fall in sales have been established the organization may be able to enhance product/service features to improve the customer offer. In the longer-term the organization may develop a range of new products and new service that will recapture the customers. In the short-term the company may decide to offer a discount against competitor goods to stem the tide and retain customers. This is really a tactic rather than a strategy since it is only a short-term solution to the problem. For example, you may continue to sell old technology (video recorders) by offering lower prices short-term but as DVD technologies improve and products have more features that consumers value it will be difficult to give them away.

Figure 4.10 takes a more optimistic view of market-driven supply chains identifying growth strategies and productivity improvements.

Markets generally drive organizational behaviour. In business this is certainly the case. In the service sector too markets are artificially created where they do not exist, for example, in public services transfer prices are agreed between service providers and customers. In a sense all organizations respond to markets. How much they do is a matter of degree. All markets are regulated either by laws or by government and

Figure 4.10

quasi-governmental policies, e.g. the National Health Service in the UK and Health Authorities under the Department of Health. In business organizations the signals are much clearer because the market determines revenue streams and profitability. Unless businesses generate profits they cannot survive in the longer-term.

The signals from the market drive behaviour in business activity. Entry into new markets, developing new products (NPD) or new service development (NSD) may be planned to increase revenues. In actual performance these strategies carry risk and risk means cost. If the organization decides to enter a new market and it is not a success then resources are effectively wasted. There is an opportunity cost. Laura Ashley, the fashion retailer sold a batch of 11 stores in Belgium, Luxembourg and the Netherlands for €2 in August 2003. The business is expected to lose £6.5 million in the next financial year as it withdraws from Europe. City analysts also questioned the appointment of two CEOs neither of whom have experience of UK fashion retailing where the company stated it now wanted to focus its efforts. This illustrates the consequences of risk. It also demonstrates the doubt over the management competencies to deliver the new strategy.

On the right hand side of Figure 4.10 productivity strategies are highlighted. These improvements are also often market-driven. Pressure is placed on the organization from competitors who are able to deliver goods and services of equivalent or better value at lower prices. Some organizations even signal this to their customers through advertising. For example, Asda, now Asda Wal-Mart in the UK, are part of the largest retailing group in the world with access to their supply chains and economies of scale. Their customer-focused strategy states 'Asda price, rolling prices back'. The technical core of the organization has supply chain competencies to deliver the customer-focused strategies. They lower operating costs through efficient asset utilization and by squeezing supplier margins. They assist their suppliers to search for efficiencies in their own business in this process. Once again the supply chain is market-driven.

Figure 4.11 illustrates a number of possible market-driven supply chain strategies focusing upon product/market improvements using an adaptation of the Ansoff matrix.

Existing products in existing markets

The purpose of this strategy is to protect markets and build markets through existing products and services. It is a strategy that carries least risk for an organization. In effect they need to maintain and improve what they are already doing. Doing things better is the means to grow

Product/market supply strategies based on Ansoff

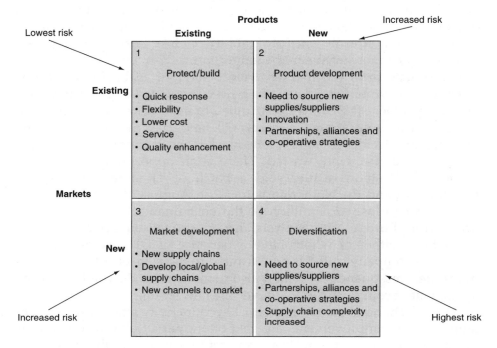

Figure 4.11

the revenue streams. Supply chain strategies to support this business strategy might include:

● quick response (QR);
● flexibility;
● lowering costs;
● quality enhancement;
● service improvements.

Quick response (QR)

Faster response times getting product to market improves the chances of achieving higher revenue streams. One important financial measure of business performance has been stockturn ratio. This particular measure examines the speed at which a business is able to sell goods.

$$\text{Stock-turnover ratio} = \frac{\text{Cost of goods sold}}{\text{Stock at cost on balance sheet}}$$

Consider an example where a manufacturing business supplies customers with memory chips for computers. Examining the profit and loss account for the current financial year indicates that invoiced sales achieved were £600 000. The gross margin achieved on sales is a standard 50 per cent. Therefore, you know that the cost of stock sold is £300 000. Examining the average stock held during the financial year you ascertain from stock records for the category that during the 12-month period average stockholding was £60 000. It is now possible to compute the stock-turn as follows:

$$\frac{£300\ 000}{£60\ 000} = 5 \text{ times in the period}$$

This would indicate that stock is turning over at the rate of five times in a year or alternatively you could translate it to days as follows:

$$\frac{365 \text{ days}}{5 \text{ times}} = 73 \text{ days}$$

Supposing customers had indicated that if the business was able to improve its lead times to fulfil orders they would place double the number of orders. By speeding up its supply chain operations and assuming average inventory holding remained constant at £60 000 the performance would improve as follows:

$$\frac{£600\ 000}{£60\ 000} = 10 \text{ times in the period}, \qquad \frac{365 \text{ days}}{10 \text{ times}} = 36.5 \text{ days}$$

The business is now turning inventories at ten times per annum owing to increased sales caused by the company's improved capability to offer QR to customers.

QR strategies applied not simply to the business but to its suppliers would offer further improvements in performance. For example, assuming the business was able to lower its average inventories to £20 000 and sales remained at £600 000 the business would turnover stocks 30 times per annum, i.e. just over 12 days. Reducing inventory holding in this way enables the business to become more efficient, secure new business and maintain current customers and it reduces cost and risk. Costs incurred in storing and insuring stock can be lowered, and the risks (redundancy, obsolescence) are lowered.

Flexibility
Flexibility is the firm's ability to reorganize internal processes to align them with customer demand requirements. For example, if an automobile company has ten different car configurations in production in a

factory it may forecast in advance of the sales period how many of each type will need to be produced. However, it may postpone purchases of the 'Bill of Materials' making up the cars until closer to the selling period. When actual sales orders are known the manufacturer may confirm orders and operate JiT systems with its suppliers. At this point the manufacturer will reprogramme production schedules and move materials, labour and machinery between different production lines to match actual demand. The capability to realign processes, people, machinery and materials in this way is what gives the organization flexibility. Organizations are able to respond more effectively to customer demand as a consequence. Having standard components that are interchangeable between different products is one way in which FMS are able to respond. The flexibility advantage allows an organization to be more responsive and to gain business from customers competing on time. An organization is able to protect and build market share through developing comepetencies in flexibility. Honeycutt et al. (1993) put the flexibility advantage succinctly when they describe a situation where a manufacturer is asked the question 'what business are you in?' the traditional manufacturer responds by describing products whereas the flexible manufacturer is customer-focused and replies 'whatever business you want us to be in'.

Lowering costs

In highly competitive markets where there is little to distinguish one supplier (product or service) from another the customer may simply make choices by focusing upon cost. In these markets it is important for the supplier to find ways of increasing productivity. The productivity advantage lowers cost and helps the firm compete. This particular strategy is difficult to sustain because there is always someone either in the market or entering the market who is able to achieve a lower cost. A technological breakthrough (innovation) or greater economies of scale (production, purchasing, technical, administrative) are a means of lowering cost.

Quality enhancement

Quality enhancement is appropriate to keep ahead of competitors. This is essentially a continuous improvement approach whereby the organization continuously strive to do things better. The quality advantage is covered more fully in Chapters 8 and 10.

Service improvements

Service improvement is similar in many respects to quality improvement. It is a continuous process. Customer-focused service organizations seek opportunities to improve the level of service offered to customers with a view to gaining a sustainable competitive advantage.

Many of the service improvements discussed in this chapter fall into this category and are illustrative of how, what and why organizations focus attention on improving service operations as part of their supply chain strategies.

Product development

New products in existing markets – this is a difficult strategy to pursue. Developing new products takes time. The strategy may consume resources that could be better applied to different strategies. Product development strategies may require sourcing of new suppliers, innovations or collaboration with partners to deliver timely new products to market. Organizations must evaluate carefully the strategic opportunity costs involved. Statistics have shown that across a number of different industrial sectors the chances of successfully introducing new products to market are slim. Failure rates of 80 per cent are not uncommon (i.e. four out of five products introduced, fail). Conversely an organization may have only a one in five chances of success. It is essential that organizations understand their customers. Understanding customers requires knowledge of their requirements, budgets, buying habits, preference factors and values. For example, in consumer markets understanding customers through their lifestyles has become much more common. Lifestyle data tracked through EpoS systems, RFID, credit card expenditures and other means of electronic data monitoring are now very common. The recent introduction by large retailing groups combining to share data through 'loyalty cards', e.g. Nectar, and through own brand credit cards, e.g. Sainsbury, Tesco, M&S (& More Card) are all means to an end of understanding consumer behaviour better. It is important to understand both rational and emotional drivers of behaviour in order to target the customer better and offer goods and services in different ways through different category channels to enhance sales. It is not simply a case of using data to develop new products but to offer existing products and services in different category channels. That leads to market development.

Market development

Existing products in new markets – this strategy requires the organization to be creative in bringing its existing goods and services to new markets. One way to do this has just been discussed. New supply chains may need to be developed closer to the new markets being served. The organization may need to learn how to manage its supply chain structures and relationships differently to accommodate the new markets being served. New channels to market may need to be developed. Once again these strategic options could involve heavy investment. Options need to be carefully considered before resources are committed. For example, international market development strategies are often viewed as a means of taking existing products into new markets. Once again this has to be carefully researched and the differences between existing market structures, relationships and behaviours need to be considered *vis-à-vis* new markets. Market entry too can be a very risky strategy. Many organizations with good product offers in home markets have tried and failed to penetrate overseas (e.g. Boots in Japan, M&S in the USA and parts of Europe, Laura Ashley in Europe and the USA). Entry modes and business models need to be carefully developed. Franchises, joint ventures, concessions, licensing and distribution arrangements are all ways to enter new markets without the risk of direct investment.

Diversification

New products in new markets – this is the most risky of all strategic developments. Developing completely new products for completely unknown, untried markets is highly risk. Supply chain complexities will be increased in pursuing this option. Complexity may involve sourcing, structures, relationships, lead times, co-ordination and management capabilities.

Supply chain strategies that win orders

The framework developed by Hill (2000) of order qualifiers and order winners is useful to help understand what the customer might value from your firm as supplier. Process mapping tools are often used to help identify the key issues from a supplier perspective. In the figure a number of possible qualifiers and order winners are identified over time. For example, in the 1950s it may have been sufficient for suppliers to compete on the basis of cost alone. However, during each decade there have been different factors that have been the key to order winning strategies for many organizations. In many respects it is simplistic to argue that there are generic order winners that are the same for all products in all market conditions. There are indeed differences between customer requirements even in the same market. However, it is often the case that there are factors that organizations focus on and that in many cases these are time-specific and common across different sectors. In many respects the market is full of paradox and complexity. Spring and Broaden (1997) said that order qualifying and order winning criteria are often linked and it is difficult to say whether it is a qualifier or a winner. Organizations may produce the same or similar types of product for two different markets from a single production process. It is important to understand it is not products or processes that win orders. The market makes choices on the basis of the benefits from the product or service that are valued by customers, for example, value for money in comparison to competitor offerings are judged in terms of different benefits gained from the purchase. Reputation and branding may enter the decision equation also. One doesn't often hear anyone comment that they bought the product because the production process was efficient, better or superior to competitors. However, one does hear buyers drawing comparisons between the benefits a particular supplier, product or service offers them.

The example of order winners and order qualifiers is illustrative and offers a generic temporal perspective. Sustainability of strategy is an important consideration for organizations. Strategies wear out just like assets. However, unlike many assets the finite life of strategy is difficult to predict. In Figure 4.12 a lifecycle proposition is shown whereby for approximately a decade from introduction to maturity the effectiveness of the strategy is gradually reduced as it becomes mature. Maturity in this sense means that the number of competing suppliers in the industrial sector or markets in which the organization operates increases

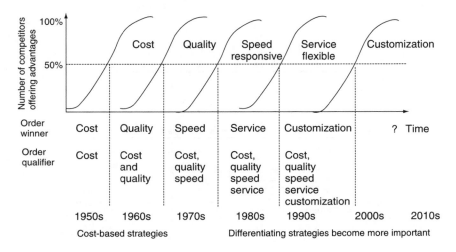

Figure 4.12

over time thus ensuring that the strategy is eroded over time and that a new strategy is needed to compete in the next decade. Each time period into the future the competitive intensity increases. Cost initially won orders and was a qualifier in the 1950s; by the year 2000 maybe customization is the order winner and the qualifiers are a list of previous order winners that have by now become simply order qualifiers.

A further dimension to this competitive environment is the type of operation the organization is engaged in. Figure 4.13 illustrates types of manufacture from project through to continuous flow. Increases in volume lower cost and competitive advantage is achieved through having economies of scale in production. Organizations that operate on projects and jobs require different sources of competitive advantage built on achieving economies of scope. Order winning criteria for firms bidding for projects and jobs would focus on one or more different competitive attributes. The example lists five such attributes: design, innovation, quality, delivery and capability. The higher the complexity of the product or the market, the higher the need for order winning attributes apart from price. In product markets where economies of scale are important to lower cost it is more likely that the order winning criterion is price and one or other attributes simply become qualifiers to get the order. These products are more likely to be 'commodity type' products where differences do not matter so much and competitor substitutes are perceived as equivalent.

Types of production basis of competitive advantage

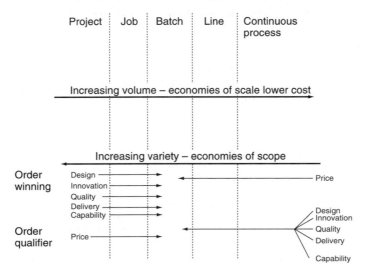

Figure 4.13

In many supply sectors and many markets organizations discount cost at their peril. Cost is always important; the key question for an organization is how important is it to your customer. It is not therefore simply absolute cost but relative cost that is important and suppliers need to know. Lowering cost creates flexibility for suppliers; it may allow them to negotiate on price or it may allow them to negotiate on a range of other issues when price is fixed. A supplier may know precisely its cost and in so doing it creates room for manoeuvre to offer enhanced products or services when a customer is drawing comparisons with a competing supplier.

Summary

This chapter has introduced a number of key concepts involved in developing supply chain strategies that are market-driven and customer-focused. It explained the importance of developing organizational structures to integrate systems and information to serve customer requirements more effectively. The nature of products and services were fully discussed. This has implications for what the customer values from a supplier. Strategic thinking and strategic options were also discussed using theoretical marketing frameworks as the basis of that discussion. In particular the Ansoff matrix was used to consider market-driven supply chain strategies before finally considering what factors are likely to win more business in highly competitive markets and how these factors change through time. The next chapter considers sourcing and procurement decisions and their role in supply chain strategies in more depth.

Discussion Questions

1. Explain the terms 'market-driven' and 'customer focused'.
2. Explain why supply chain strategies need to be customer focused and customer driven and how supply chain strategies can meet market demand.
3. 'Organizational structures may help or impede supply chain strategies.' Discuss.
4. 'Supply chain strategies are not simply for manufactured goods but involve the creation and delivery of services.' Discuss.
5. 'The extended marketing mix is perhaps the most important aspect of developing and managing demand for contemporary organizations in Western Europe and the USA.' Discuss.

6. Identify the key differences between a service and a product and explain how these differences may be accounted for when designing supply chain strategies.
7. 'Applying the "Ansoff Matrix" to organizational supply chain strategies requires managers to focus attention on the customer and in so doing the organization must be sure that it has the necessary competencies to implement the chosen strategy.' Discuss.
8. Select an organization of choice and identify key success factors in relation to their total supply chain and assess how successful the organization has been in choosing and implementing appropriate supply chain strategies over the previous 5-year period.
9. 'The notion of order winners and order qualifiers is important for organizations to understand how they might be able to generate more business and to do so the organization must develop appropriate supply chain strategies to meet customer requirements.' Discuss.
10. Explain why volume, variety, velocity, variability and value need to be thoroughly understood when it comes to developing appropriate supply chain structures and relationships.

References

Baron, S. and Harris, K. (2003). *Services Marketing – Text and Cases*. London: Palgrave.

Bateson, J. E. G. and Hoffman, K. D. (1999). *Managing Services Marketing – Text and Readings*, 4th edn. Orlando, FL: Dryden Press.

Drucker, P. (1956). *The Practice of Management*. Oxford: Butterworth-Heinemann.

Drucker, P. (1970). Entrepreneurship in business enterprise. *Journal of Business Policy*, **1** (1), 3–12.

Hill, T. (2000). *Manufacturing Strategy – Text and Cases*. Maidenhead: McGraw-Hill.

Honeycutt, E. D., Siguaw, J. A. and Harper, S. C. (1993). The impact of flexible manufacturing on competitive strategy. *Industrial Management*, **35** (6) (November–December).

Langeard, E., Bateson, J., Lovelock, C. and Eiglier, P. (1981). *Marketing of Services: New Insights from Consumers and Managers*. Report 81-104. Cambridge, MA: Marketing Sciences Institute.

Levitt, T. (1988). *The Marketing Imagination*. New York: Free Press.

Lovelock, C. H. (1983). Classifying services to gain strategic marketing insights. *Journal of Marketing*, **47**, 9–20.

Lovelock, C. R. (1992). *Managing Services Marketing*. New Jersey: Prentice-Hall.

Porter, M. E. (1980). *Competitive Strategy – Techniques for Analyzing Industries and Competitors*. New York: Free Press.

Rathmell, J. M. (1974). *Marketing in the Services Sector*. Cambridge, MA: Winthrop.

Schmenner, R. W. (1986). How can service businesses survive and prosper. *Sloan Management Review*, **27** (3), 21–32.

Schumpeter, J. A. (1950). *Capitalism, Socialism and Democracy*, 3rd edn. New York: Harper and Brothers.

Shostack, L. G. (1977). Breaking free from product marketing. *Journal of Marketing*, **41**, 73–80.

Spring, M. and Broaden, R. (1997). One more time: how do you win orders? A critical re-appraisal of the hill manufacturing strategy framework. *International Journal of Operations and Production Management*, **17** (8), 757–79.

Zeithaml, V. A., Parasuraman, A. and Berry, L. L. (1985). Problems and strategies in services marketing. *Journal of Marketing*, **49**, 33–46.

Chapter 5

Supplier sourcing, procurement and evaluation

LEARNING OUTCOMES

After studying the chapter you should be able to:

- identify the key issues, concepts and appropriate tools to source and procure supplies;
- select and apply appropriate tools and concepts involved in sourcing, procurement including supplier development and evaluation;
- understand key issues in relation to ethical and environmental responsibilities of suppliers and buyers;
- analyse the key variables and their relative importance to decisions in global and local sourcing;
- evaluate supplier selection and procurement decisions (e.g. single and multiple sourcing).

The aim of this chapter is to introduce you to a number of important concepts involving sourcing and procurement decisions. All organizations face decisions of supplier selection, sourcing, risk evaluation, legal and ethical considerations. Organizations need to source supplies from a variety of different organizations locally, nationally and/or globally. Each type of sourcing has its own merits and they are discussed in the first part of this chapter. The iceberg theory of cost comparisons in sourcing and procurement decisions is then explained and examples are given relating to hidden costs in the decision-making processes. In explaining these hidden costs a number of influencing factors are discussed including the ways in which organizational performance and buyer performance is evaluated and the consequences of the measures on the decision-making processes. The next part of the chapter discusses supplier selection criteria and examines the role of manufacturers, wholesalers and distributors as intermediaries. Also examined are single and multiple sourcing strategies and their relative merits before assessing environmental and ethical issues related to sourcing and procurement. The final part of the chapter focuses on supplier development programmes and their role in supply chain sourcing strategies and the modern trend towards supply base rationalization.

Sourcing and procurement decisions

One of the most important considerations for any organization is where to source product and which suppliers to select. Building an effective supply base is critical to the success of most organizations. The decision to source is often divided into three geographical considerations: local, national and global.

Buying locally

Many supply managers prefer to purchase from local sources when prudent to do so. Local purchasing has a number of advantages that may include:

- Close co-operation through close proximity, e.g. enabling JiT solutions;
- More certain delivery dates since lead times not affected by transport delays;
- Short lead times may eliminate inventory;
- Faster replenishment possible;
- Discrepancies and disputes may be more easily resolved;
- Implied social responsibilities to the local community may be satisfied.

However, local suppliers may lose out to national or global suppliers where:

- Local cost of the items is higher;
- Particular goods cannot be supplied locally to the same standard, specification or price;
- Markets supplied are not local and therefore it makes more sense to source closer to the market;
- Better service is possible from a non-local supplier;
- Restrictions may limit the local supply source, e.g. quota restrictions as is the case in the clothing industry – multi-fibre agreement (MFA).

Buying nationally

May have the following advantages:

- National sources offer better quality and/or;
- Faster delivery and/or;
- Cheaper prices through economies of scale (or scope);
- National companies may provide better technical back-up and support services;
- Greater production flexibility may be achieved through national sourcing;
- Shortages may be less likely because of their size or extensive supply networks.

National supply sources may lose out to international sources for the same reasons local suppliers may lose out to national suppliers listed above.

Global sourcing

Empirical case for global sourcing

Currently 49 per cent of clothing imported into the UK is entering under quota arrangements detailed in the multi-fibre agreement (MFA). In 2005 the quota disappears. China's clothing exports to the UK were valued £10.2 billion in 2002, and forecast at £11 billion in 2003 rising to £12.5 billion in 2005. All this occurring at a time when the real prices of clothing items is falling on the High Street. One in five garments sold on the UK High Street will be sourced out of China by 2005. Increasing imports and prices falling by up to 40 per cent as tariffs and quotas disappear. The cost of a cotton blouse to retailers would fall from £4.25 to £2.46 with raw material costs assumed constant. The main reduction of cost is the abandonment of quotas under the MFA. Price competition on the High Street is expected to intensify and lead times may increase as retailers scramble to get best prices. In order to maintain retail margins sales volumes would need to increase by 60 per cent. According to AT Kearney there are three strategies for success in the post-MFA era for retail organizations:

1. Taking a segmented approach to sourcing;
2. Building global supply chains; and
3. Mitigating the risks of cross-cultural trading.

In layman's language this means sourcing fast fashion from low-risk Near East countries, basics from low-cost countries in the Far East and high-end fashion from Europe, mainly Italy.

Source: Material adapted from a Drapers Record Report (2003), p. 27, 15 November.

Global sourcing may yield large rewards but risks are often higher than when sourcing supplies locally or nationally. The main reasons that organizations decide to source from overseas are as follows.

Superior quality

It may only be possible to achieve the superior quality required by buying goods from global suppliers. Some organizations may only be able to source and procure supplies from certain suppliers who have the necessary expertise or access to resources or quality of goods demanded by the buying organization. For example, purchasing minerals is determined by geographical endowments and organizations that have rights to those deposits are the only organizations a buyer may deal with.

Better timeliness

Order lead times may be better than could be achieved from local or national suppliers. This makes suppliers more dependable. Competitive forces are such that time compression may lead to an organization achieving competitive advantage. In such cases it may be that suppliers located in different parts of the world may be able to meet the time-frames of the purchaser better than a local or national supplier. For example, in seasonal produce local suppliers may be constrained by climate whereas an overseas source may be able to supply the produce because their climatic conditions and seasons are different and favourable to them supplying at different times (e.g. grapefruit for UK retailers from South Africa in December, from the Canary Islands in April and so on).

Lower cost

It may be possible to achieve overall lowering of 'total cost' by sourcing supplies globally (Hines and McGowan, 2002). Nevertheless, there are 'hidden costs' associated with sourcing products overseas. To illustrate this point in the clothing industry Hines (2002) has estimated that for UK retailers to source product from outside the UK they need to ensure that the total cost of purchase is at least 50 per cent lower to account for what he refers to as 'iceberg costs,' i.e. hidden costs associated with the supply. Similarly, Burt et al. (2003) estimate that the same is true for the computer industry where US manufacturers need to be sure that global suppliers are 20 per cent lower to take account of hidden cost.

More advanced technology

Some countries may gain advantage by having access to better technologies that give them a better competitive position. For example, it may only be possible to access a source of supply because the organization in a particular country has developed a unique product or alternatively better technology makes their supplies more efficient or cheaper as a consequence.

Broader supply base

Sourcing globally may allow the purchasing organization to spread risk by widening its supply base. Broadening the supply base does not necessarily mean having more suppliers. It may mean fewer but better quality suppliers. Better collaboration may be achieved by broadening the supply base. In addition, if a problem occurs with one country the purchaser may switch between different suppliers to maintain supplies.

Expanded customer base

Sourcing globally may lead to the identification of new market opportunities where those suppliers are based. However, it is important to recognize that trade barriers may exist.

Problems in global supply

There are also many potential problems associated with global sourcing and these are as follows.

Cultural issues

Many different problems can occur as a consequence of cultural differences. For example, it may be inappropriate to place an order for four units in China where the number four is associated with death. Alternatively, it may be that the country has a culture of *'Countertrade'* whereby it is considered normal to make payments or partial payment in goods rather than money. Foreign governments often impose *countertrade* to gain access to foreign exchange or foreign technology. As a means of overcoming cultural differences large organizations sometimes establish International Procurement Offices (IPOs). Their benefit is to gain knowledge and local/cultural expertise and then to apply it to procurement within a country or region.

Long lead times

Greater variability may result from sourcing globally often due to such things as: shipping schedules, customs practice, strikes, storms at sea all of which require greater co-ordination of the supply chain. Sometimes airfreight is used to offset the problems identified but there is a cost 'trade-off'. Often an organization will purchase additional inventories to lower risk in sourcing globally. For example, if lead times are variable the organization may compensate through inventory to ensure supplies are maintained. Alternatively, these 'buffer stocks' may be kept low where supply managers rely on airfreight to compensate for time delays. Any additional inventory carrying costs incurred as a consequence of global sourcing should be added to the cost of purchase along with freight and administrative costs to evaluate the purchase decision.

Lower quality

This can result in potential rework or scrap costs. Lower quality may be an issue but it is not unique to global sourcing often the problem exists for all types of supply. However, it achieves a greater significance in global sourcing because it may result in further delays and higher risks in not being able to satisfy the final customer.

Social and labour problems

There have been newsworthy cases of supplies being sourced from factories where child labour is prevalent in the apparel industry. When these issues are highlighted ethical sourcing is brought to the forefront. Many large retailers have signed up to ethical trading statements that charge them to uphold labour standards and maintain social conditions. This has been a problem in countries where labour laws are weak or simply not enforced. This is an issue that will probably get more coverage in the next few years especially as China and other developing economies get a greater share of world-manufactured goods.

Higher costs of doing business

There are often communication problems sometimes because of language and sometimes culture. There is a need for translators and visits to ensure compliance. In addition currency costs, banking costs, logistics support and communication systems all require investment and incur additional cost.

Opacity

It has long been known that global sourcing incurs additional risks. Price-Waterhouse Coopers, London, developed something called the 'opacity index'.[1] It addresses the following areas: corruption in government bureaucracy, laws governing property rights and contracts, economic policies, accounting standards and business regulations. China is a country where the opacity index score is high and the US achieves a low score because it has less bureaucracy, fewer government restrictions, more liberal economic policies and very little corruption.

An iceberg theory of cost comparison

How buyers make decisions

When making comparisons between two sources of supply a decision is often taken based upon a straightforward cost comparison. This cost concept will usually be bought-in cost. This type of decision has been articulated in the financial decision-making literature as *'make or buy'* decision-making because it often uses the analogy of making a product in-house or buying it in from an outside supplier. This decision-making concept is similar to that applied to outsourcing discussed in the purchasing and general management literature. The figure for bought-in cost is usually defined as the invoiced price per unit. It is the delivered price (i.e. the price delivered to the buyer's warehouse). For example, in clothing manufacture, a labour-intensive industry, labour costs are often the most significant cost of manufacture. Production units located overseas are often favoured with lower labour costs than similar plants in the UK. Average direct hourly wage rates in a UK plant were around £6 per hour in 2000, whereas India were less than £1 and nearer to home in Morocco under £2. Thus labour wage rates provide non-UK suppliers with an immediate comparative advantage compared with UK rates. The other two major cost elements are materials and overheads. Material costs are often similar because fabrics and trims will be bought from a single source for both a UK or an overseas supplier. There are exceptions to this when remote plants choose local sources for fabric and they may gain a further price advantage. However, where a retailer is purchasing bulk materials to distribute to selected manufacturing units throughout the globe fabric prices do not affect the manufacturing decision. The final cost is overhead and will usually be higher in the UK than offshore. The two significant areas of disadvantage for UK suppliers are labour and overhead costs.

How buyer's own performance measures affect their decisions

Buyer performance is often measured by examining target margins and actual margins achieved. This is a very important determinant of choice. A buyer will want to achieve target margins in order to meet specific price points for the merchandise in-store. Bought-in price and retrospective discounts can help the buyer meet their targets. This will be further explained a little later. The rational choice faced with the visual representation given in Figure 5.1 is simple. The non-UK manufacturing source would be chosen because it appears to give the higher margin (the perceived saving gap).

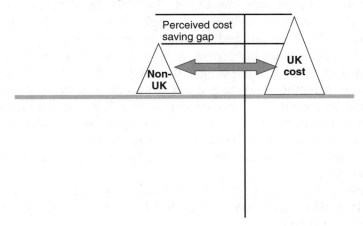

The iceberg theory of cost comparison

Figure 5.1

The iceberg of non-transparent costs

Figure 5.2 illustrates an iceberg where substantial cost is hidden below the waterline. Buying teams may be motivated to procure garments

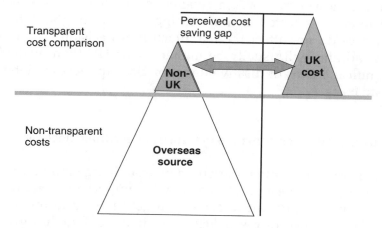

Figure 5.2

from overseas because they are judged by performance measures that are outdated. Gross margin measures are not sufficient because they ignore the 'iceberg' costs, i.e. the hidden cost of procurement. Domestic supply might appear on the face of it more expensive than an alternative source of supply from an overseas source. Nevertheless, in drawing a comparison the buyers may be deciding simply on the basis of direct cost or rather the bought-in price comparison. Their performance will be judged on the basis of target gross margins achieved and this single criterion may be the most important to satisfy the condition. Such a comparison would ignore any additional costs incurred as a result of management time and resources expended in managing an overseas source of supply. Such a decision may not be in the organization's best interests. Managers often articulate other requirements in terms of flexibility and responsiveness but buyers in the final analysis will base their decision on price alone to protect their own interest.

It is assumed in Figure 5.2 that all hidden costs relate only to non-UK supply. In reality there may well be hidden costs associated with some UK sources of supply.

The theory of an iceberg of cost that buyers do not fully appreciate and that may actually help to disguise buying inefficiencies is one possible explanation for the preference given to overseas sources of supply. Nevertheless, it is important to recognize that real costs play a part too. Certainly there is no doubt that growing import penetration in the UK clothing market has been hastened within the past 5 years as a result of increasing overseas sourcing by major UK retail groups. Ignoring the iceberg allows a buyer to:

- compare bought-in prices without recognizing other costs that might make a difference to their decision;
- achieve target margins and price points;
- ignore organizational costs that will never be tracked back to the specific stock-keeping units (SKUs).

However, the iceberg may not be the only explanation. There are of course other reasons why buyers would want to source from outside the UK:

- To offer customers something different;
- To search for lower price merchandise that offer better customer value;
- To acquire different fabrics;
- To obtain different designs;
- To develop new offshore sources to service a growing global distribution network.

The iceberg costs in more detail

This iceberg beneath the waterline contains a number of hidden costs that are often ignored in supplier sourcing and purchasing decisions. The hidden costs identified could be substantial. Furthermore, these costs are often disguised or never traced back to the SKUs. Examples of some of the hidden costs are given in the model illustrated in Figure 5.3. Iceberg costs include: procurement, management, time consumed in pre-acquisition searches, acquisition, monitoring progress, rework or post-acquisition costs including ownership costs. More importantly something that is hardly ever measured in practice are lost sales due to late delivery or incomplete delivery (e.g. wrong size ratios, wrong style mix, wrong colour mix).[2]

Procurement costs

Anecdotal evidence from a number of retail fashion buyers who spend a significant amount of their time travelling abroad searching for new products suggests that the cost is not unimportant. Buyers often spend two or more months travelling to source merchandise during any given year. The cost includes airfares, hotel bills, telephone calls and subsistence payments not to mention the human cost of broken relationships, loneliness and fatigue results that often reflect in inefficiencies and staff turnover measures. Furthermore, if

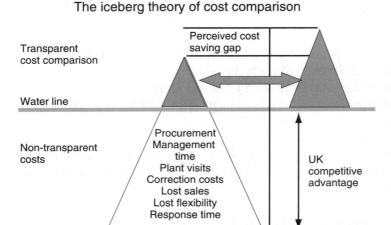

Figure 5.3

one considers the time spent against orders placed there will be times when the cost of procurement is extremely expensive and significantly more than the final invoiced bought-in price which may be the only cost that is measured. Thus procurement costs incurred in sourcing the products and suppliers at the pre-acquisition stage may never be traced back to products. Such costs are more likely to reside in an overhead category. What is more such costs may be allocated or apportioned arbitrarily to products that did not incur the costs when overheads are apportioned.

Management time

Management time is consumed communicating with suppliers before acquisition, during acquisition and post-acquisition. The number of managers involved and the amount of time spent can be significant. One major retailer has a team of managers that co-ordinate activities with offshore suppliers in Morocco. The management teams frequently visit the plants to monitor and plan production, to resolve operational difficulties and to help improve efficiencies. The time spent is not always traced backed to the products that are consuming this resource. Activity-based costing would be a useful tool in these circumstances to gain accurate information.

Opportunity cost of lost sales

By far the greatest cost and perhaps the most significant part of the iceberg could be the opportunity cost of lost sales. If merchandise is not available within a store at the time the consumer wants to buy it the sale is lost. Consumer behaviour theory might suggest substitution.

However, substitution of one product for another may not happen within the same retail store. Substitution may unwittingly help competitors to achieve a sale. This part of the iceberg is where an overseas supplier is at greater disadvantage. A UK supplier is closer to market and a short delay in production will not necessarily result in late delivery or incomplete delivery. Whereas a delay in production from an overseas source would more probably result in missing a shipping date. This may require drastic action to airfreight goods which adds significantly to cost and a cost that has not been built into the retailer's price point. Typically it takes 8–12 weeks to deliver merchandise from a Far Eastern source whereas it may be 4–6 weeks from a UK source and perhaps just 1 week more from Morocco, Portugal, Egypt and Eastern Europe.

Figure 5.3 illustrates the iceberg costs together with potential areas whereby UK suppliers could build competitive advantage. Assuming that the iceberg costs for a UK supplier are less significant than for an overseas supplier would suppose that UK suppliers could build on strengths that an overseas source would find it difficult to achieve.

Sources of competitive advantage for UK suppliers

The iceberg theory identified in this research reveals a number of possibilities that would enable UK suppliers to achieve competitive advantage *vis-à-vis* an overseas supplier, even an overseas supplier located within near reach of Europe. However, it is not simply the iceberg but the size of the iceberg that will determine the relative advantage. In some cases an iceberg may exist but it may not be sufficiently deep to allow the UK supplier to exploit it. The stronger the relationship is between a supplier and a UK retailer, the less likelihood of a large iceberg lurking. Conversely the weaker the relationship is between a UK retailer and a supplier, the more likelihood of a larger iceberg that may be exploited by an alternative supplier. Strength of organizational relationships is therefore a central issue in exploring the iceberg.

Competitive advantage has two sources according to Porter (1980): cost and differentiation. A UK supplier can either compete on cost or differentiate itself in some way from its competitors. The cost disadvantage that seemed so clear-cut when drawing comparisons between a UK supplier and a supplier from overseas (refer to Figure 5.2) where labour cost and overheads are substantially lower may not be so clear-cut if organizations examined more closely their iceberg costs. Caution is the clear message in considering organizational sourcing decisions.

An example of the iceberg effect:

Intake margin	£	
Target selling price	20	
Bought-in cost	10	
Gross margin	10	50.00%

A retail buyer plans to purchase 10 000 units of merchandise at £10 bought-in price or total delivered cost.[3] The proposed target-selling price per unit is £20, which gives the retail buyer a forecast bought-in margin[4] of 50 per cent. The buyer decides to purchase 10 000 units at the price of £10 per unit. A total cash outlay is made of £100 000. The demand pattern turns out to be worse than forecast. Unplanned management time has been consumed in a number of activities associated with the purchase sorting out customs documentation, duties and quality problems with the merchandise. In addition there were substantial sourcing costs incurred before the purchase was made. The retailer is only able to sell 40 per cent at full price and a further 30 per cent are sold at 30 per cent mark-down. The price achieved being £14 per unit. Remaining SKUs have to be written off at cost as they are unsaleable. In addition the retailer has developed a TCO approach and traced a number of additional costs to the particular merchandise. Details are given below in the financial statement.

Demand pattern	*Units*	£	
Sell at full price	4 000	80 000	
Sell at mark-down	3 000	42 000	
Sales revenue achieved		122 000	
Cost of sales	7 000	70 000	
Stock remaining at cost written off	3 000	30 000	
Gross margin		22 000	18.03%
Hidden costs in supply chain	*Cost*		
Inventory holding	1 000		
Procurement	5 000		
Management time	3 000		
Additional administration	500		
Promotional cost	1 000		
Pre-acquisition sourcing	10 000		
Post-acquisition	2 000		
Total hidden cost		22 500	
Net margin		−500	−0.41%

As a consequence of the hidden costs in the supply chain which have now been traced to the SKUs the retailer has made a loss overall. Furthermore the planned intake margin of 50 per cent has turned into an actual gross margin of only 18.03 per cent. A large iceberg indeed.

In summary the post-acquisition margin does not look as good as the target margins forecast by the buyer.

Post-acquisition margin	£	%
Unit sale price achieved	12.20	100.00
Cost of sales	10.00	81.97
Margin on sale	2.20	18.03
Hidden costs in supply chain	2.25	18.44
Loss on product line	−0.05	−0.41

Discussion

Kaplan and Cooper (1998, p. 206) refer to *'choosing low-cost not low-price suppliers'* this is an extremely important lesson for an organization's sourcing and supply chain strategies. The purchase price is only one component that makes up the total cost of acquisition and ownership. A supplier may deliver at the best price but they may not be the lowest cost supplier. There are a number of possible reasons why this can be so, a low-cost supplier may achieve a competitive advantage over their low-price competitor for some or all of the reasons listed below:

- Transparent and timely information flows enable the retail buyer to determine more accurate delivery dates and avoid losing sales by being late to market.
- Suppliers using EDI over virtual private networks (VPNs) or via web-based systems are able to provide better levels of customer service that help retail buyers with their decision-making – e.g. avoid costly stock-outs or overstocking by having early warning information (two way) about demand and supply.
- Zero defects.
- JiT supplies.
- Vendor-managed inventory (VMI).
- Co-ordinated category management from suppliers, e.g. skirts, tops and matching accessories arrive in store simultaneously.
- Collaborative product development may reduce retail and supplier costs.
- Electronic document exchange reduce time in process (purchase orders, invoices, specifications).
- Electronic fund transfer increases cash flow for good suppliers encouraging them to achieve results on the retail buyer's behalf.

Cyert and March in their seminal work in 1963 identified differences between organizational goals and the goals of individual managers as cause for concern. Prior to that economists had assumed that all organizations in business had a single objective – to maximize profit. Whilst maximizing profit may be a sound business objective it is not the only one that is important or practised. Cyert and March (1963) noted that even when the organization's goal is to maximize profit not all the people who work in the organization would be adopting behaviours to achieve this objective. Individuals have their own objectives such as maintaining or improving their own job prospects. In doing so they will act in ways that benefit their own position and this may not necessarily coincide with the objective of maximizing profit. In certain circumstances *satisficing* behaviour will replace maximizing behaviour. An example of this may be found in sourcing and procurement decisions. For example, it was known for many years in the latter part of the twentieth century that organizations purchasing computer equipment chose IBM because *'Big Blue'* was a safe bet. It may not have been the cheapest price, it may not have been the lowest cost supplier as discussed above but as the person responsible for the purchase you were not going to get fired as a consequence of this decision.

Supplier selection

In making decisions where to source supplies it is not simply a question of location. Decisions focus on product, service and capability of the supplier. In addition there may be decisions regarding procurement direct from the manufacturer, through a wholesaler or distributor. Key influencing factors apart from cost include: quality, responsiveness, flexibility and reliability. These influences are discussed thoroughly in Chapter 6. In recent years the environment and ethics have also entered the equation of who to source from. This section focuses on these issues.

Manufacturer, wholesaler, distributor?

Capability, service and access will determine the selection of the supply source. Capability of a supplier to meet the need is of paramount importance. Is the supplier technically competent to achieve the purchase specification? Assuming there are several suppliers equally able to meet the technical specifications of the purchase such that there is no noticeable variation in the product then it comes down to service. Which of the suppliers will offer best service to the customer. It is often service that differentiates a chosen supplier from those who were considered but not chosen. Determinants of supplier choice will be considered more thoroughly below. Finally, it may be access to a supplier that is important. Sometimes organizations may identify capability and service but they may or may not have access to a supplier. Some suppliers do not want to deal directly with a customer because the amount they will supply is insufficient for them to want to engage directly. In such cases they may refer a small customer to a wholesaler or distributor who is able to 'break bulk' on their behalf. In addition sometimes distributors offer specialist services that make it worthwhile for the purchasing organization to deal with them rather than dealing directly with the supplier who may not be able to offer the same services. Often a distributor will also stock competitor products and have a larger range than can a single direct supplier. This may offer the purchaser a considerable advantage in terms of lowering their risk as opposed to dealing directly with a single supplier. In such circumstances it is possible for the purchaser to place a single order with a distributor who is able to supply several different products from several different suppliers. Unit prices may be higher than dealing direct but the total order cost may be lowered when ordering through a distributor and the cost of inventory may also be lowered because the goods are ordered as required rather than for 'buffer' stock.

Single or multiple sourcing strategies?

One question that is often paramount in the mind of the purchaser is should they rely on a single supplier or should they have several? The simple answer is it all depends. So what does it all depend on?

The arguments for having a single supplier include the following:

- Long-term contracts stemming from long-term relationships with that single source.
- The supplier may own a patent or other intellectual property rights (IPRs) that the buyer cannot acquire from anyone else. In other words a unique source of supply.
- The supplier offers better, faster, cheaper sources of supply than anyone else does.
- An order quantity may be too small to split the order.
- A buyer may obtain better prices by purchasing from a single source.
- Purchasing from a single source may lead to economies of scale for the supplier and as a consequence the buyer obtains a discounted price on the product or is able to achieve lower transport costs.
- A single supplier may be more interested in the supply because it represents a substantial proportion of their business.
- It may be easier to establish EDI links with a single supplier.
- It may be easier to implement JiT systems with a single supplier.

- It may be easier to share information with a single supplier.
- Effective supplier relationships require considerable investment in time and effort and it may be that fewer suppliers are easier to integrate into effective supply networks. Single sourcing may lead to effective partnering.

Multiple sourcing is preferred when:

- It is important to spread the risk and when a single supplier may be regarded as a risk.
- It is important to lower cost since the competition may spur a current supplier to become more efficient.
- It may be necessary to ensure supplies are not disrupted through strikes, breakdowns or acts of God beyond the control of any party.
- It is deemed necessary not to rely on a single source for any reason.
- An organization has a historical track record of being able to deal with multiple sources.
- It is necessary to lower the TOC by having multiple sources that are able to offer a bundle of both low cost and service options.
- Strategic reasons are an issue and it is deemed unreasonable to rely on a single source, e.g. military contract supplies.
- The capacity of a single supplier is full.

The trend in sourcing is to have fewer suppliers and to build better relationships with those suppliers. For example, many retailers in the UK have reduced the numbers of suppliers they are prepared to deal with on a regular basis. Bookstores have reduced the numbers of publishers they deal with. The purchasing and stocking policies of larger bookstores have forced smaller publishing houses to use consolidators or wholesalers such as Gardners who purchase stocks at high discounts from the smaller publishers to supply bookstores at a lower discounted rate taking their margin from the difference in purchase and supply prices.

Environmental considerations in the supply chain

'Greening' the supply chain has been considered in a number of ways:

1. Purchasing materials which are recyclable;
2. Liability considerations for disposal of hazardous wastes at any stage in the supply chain;
3. Reducing the distances goods travel to their final destinations.

Many purchase decisions have alternatives or substitutes that can be used to do the same job. For example, wine bottles can be stoppered with cork, plastic or screw tops, which may be metal or plastic. The purchase decision will focus on cost and functionality. However, it may also be influenced by recyclability too. It is often not difficult to obtain supplies that meet cost, technical functionality, aesthetic design considerations and are environmentally friendly through recycling, e.g. biodegradable packaging materials, paper used in book production, plastic goods such as milk cartons, fibres and fabrics used in clothing, glass containers, drinks cans.

Coase (1937) developed an economic theory to deal with a firm's responsibility to manage hazardous waste and pollution it caused in the community. The premise was simple that firms did not pay the full price of production and so they should pay a tax equivalent to the difference between the production cost and the cost of pollution caused by the process it managed. Only in such circumstances is the full cost of production borne by the producer. In recent years governments, policy-makers and pressure groups such as 'Greenpeace' have all shown an interest in Coase's ideas. Responsible suppliers now attempt to meet stringent environmental requirements placed upon them by governments. Environmental consultancies specializing in 'greening' the supply chain have grown in recent years as the demand for their services has grown. Large public corporations employ such agencies to ensure that they comply with appropriate laws relating to hazardous waste and to protect themselves against public liability.

In food retailing one issue that has received a great deal of attention is the concept known as 'food miles'. Suppliers of grocery produce may be located thousands of miles away from their final marketplace. Often there appears to be little logic in the location of a supplier being great distances from market especially when local produce is ignored and a source of supply is chosen that is thousands of miles from the market. For example, potatoes, tomatoes, peas and other fruits and vegetables may travel great distances. The full cost of these journeys is borne neither by the producer nor by the customer. Road traffic congestion and increased pollution from transporting the goods is the burden of a wider community.

Ethical considerations in sourcing and procurement

In recent years organizations have become more aware of the ethical dimensions. Often the ethical consideration is made out of self-interest. For example, bad press can have a major impact on a brand, product or organization. There have been a number of reported incidents that needed careful management to minimize the impact of the bad publicity generated from press reports. For example, Marks and Spencer, GAP and

Nike suppliers were allegedly said to be employing child labour in North Africa and the Far East. Another ethical issue might be animal testing of products by drug companies. More recently in the food industry businesses are reflecting consumer concerns regarding animal welfare by clearly labelling produce from organic farming or welfare approved environments. One consequence of these reports has been for large organizations to enforce compliance measures on their suppliers to ensure that they meet ethical trading standards set by the buying organization.

Mind the GAP – Case

According to a report on the Behind the Label Website it is asserted: 'In factory after factory around the world, GAP workers have described working conditions that harken back to the turn of the last century – physical abuse, sexual harassment, poverty wages and unsafe working conditions. But when GAP workers try to organize unions to defend their rights, they often face severe harassment, are fired and sometimes are even physically threatened.'

If your clothes carry the GAP label (including Banana Republic, Old Navy, and baby GAP), chances are that factories regarded by many as sweatshops in countries like the Dominican Republic, Guatemala, El Salvador, China and southern Africa produced them. GAP says that they are not responsible for the conditions in the thousands of factories around the world that are producing their clothes. They also comment that their suppliers must meet strict codes of conduct. However, it is argued by others that as the largest specialty apparel retailer in the United States, the GAP sets the prices for goods and labour worldwide, creating a global sweatshop system.

Source: Adapted from http://www.behindthelabel.org accessed March 2003.

The above case illustrates some of the difficulties organizations facing when they source materials from suppliers around the globe. There are many pressure groups like 'behind the label' that monitor and report what they see as injustices. Buyers and suppliers can unwittingly become embroiled in these difficulties unless they take care. In order to minimize the negative impact of these episodes buyers need to:

- select suppliers carefully;
- set down and agree appropriate standards;
- monitor compliance with the agreed standards;
- identify areas for supplier improvement.

Suppliers must:

- comply with the agreed standards laid down by the buyer or risk de-listing;
- take responsibility for their own continuous improvement;
- act legally;
- act ethically;
- engage in supplier development programmes.

Child labour is not just a recent phenomenon of course. We have our own industrial heritage in the UK as the first industrial nation and we too are all aware that in the nineteenth century there were many developing industries where the conditions identified in the case study could well have applied.

European pressure groups

In Europe there are a number of organizations concerned with ethical trading. These organizations act as pressure groups exerting influence over organizational behaviours and government. In many ways they moderate the effects of pure commercial transactions by modifying behaviour in favour of wider societal interests. Here is just a small selection.

Transnationale.org
(http://www.transnationale.org/anglais/default.htm)
Transnationale.org is published by Transnationale, a French not-for-profit organization, created in October 1999 in Martigues (France). This website searches and publishes relevant information about large companies, and includes information on brands, political influence, factory locations, working conditions, as well as company policies on the environment, global issues, social and financial strategies.

No Sweat Campaign Against Sweatshops
(http://www.nosweat.org.uk)
The No Sweat Campaign Against Sweatshops website is an interactive online campaign that includes retailer surveys, opinion articles about current labour rights issues, information about upcoming events, and a mailing list, among other things.

Clean Clothes Campaign
(http://www.cleanclothes.org/index.htm)
The Clean Clothes Campaign is an international European network with the goal of improving the working conditions in the garment industry

worldwide. The network is comprised of a wide variety of organizations, such as trade unions, consumer organizations, researchers, solidarity groups, women's organizations, church groups, youth movements and world shops.

Supplier development programmes

In many organizations, suppliers account for well over 80 per cent of overall cost. Efforts to manage these costs are often left to the annual negotiation on price, normally eroding profit margins and increasing other risks to the supplier. How then, can organizations secure cost reductions and still maintain a highly motivated and competitive supply base?

Supplier development programmes are aimed at seeking out areas for improvement in the supply chain and developing mutually beneficial solutions with key suppliers. Key benefits are the elimination of waste, lower total acquisition costs (TACs) and the development of first class suppliers. The aims are to develop commitment throughout the supply chain, to increase co-operation and understanding between companies and their suppliers, to strategically focus manufacturing, engineering, design and purchasing teams to provide a structured approach to improving value.

Among the techniques used in this process are process mapping, value stream analysis, responsiveness matrix, gap analysis, demand amplification maps, quality filters, Kaizen approaches, metaplanning, brainstorming and team presentations. Benefits to organizations engaged in supplier development programmes are:

- Lower TACs.
- Developing world-class suppliers.
- Commitment throughout the supply chain.
- Structured approach to improve value.
- Better cross-functional co-operation within the company and with suppliers.
- Elimination of waste.
- Strategically focused purchasing teams.

The key to supplier development is making sure that the organization wanting to develop suppliers follows some simple criteria:

- Selecting the most appropriate suppliers to develop.
- Identify how well suppliers' capabilities meet business needs.
- Use diagnostic methods to establish cost drivers in the supply chain and thereby develop a value improvement plan.

- Establish key measures of performance and implement effective feed-back systems.
- Generate trust and commitment with suppliers.

Supplier development may involve a detailed examination of some of the following issues with the supplier: value stream mapping, assessing the cost of quality, demand amplification and promotions management, manufacturing and maintenance systems development, efficient consumer response, lean production and supply, and supply chain integration using the supplier association approach.

Some of the outcomes and benefits of the programme included the development of a portfolio of tools for mapping key dimensions of performance and to identify waste down a value stream (e.g. process mapping, responsiveness matrix, quality filter, demand amplification map), the identification of inter-company waste and creation of joint improvement activities on areas with the greatest potential gains and the development of new software programmes to facilitate the use of the value stream mapping toolbox.

In recent years there has been a trend in most organizations to rationalize their supply base. This approach to managing suppliers has a number of benefits:

- Fewer suppliers to deal with require less management time.
- It means that organizations can work more closely with fewer with the management time released.
- Processes in the supplier organizations can be integrated with those of the buying firm.
- Processes and operations can be synchronized to reduce lead times, stock-holding and associated costs.

Supply base rationalization

Many organizations began in the 1990s to reduce the number of supplier accounts they had. Those suppliers who remained were expected to conform and comply with the standards of supply that many larger organizations began to implement. It was recognized by the buying companies that they often had to spend a great deal of time dealing with many supply companies that were either unable or unwilling to respond to the demands the buying organization placed on them. Many smaller organizations often did not understand the need to comply or were unwilling to undertake the investment to be able to comply. Fewer suppliers meant fewer accounts payable and an opportunity to get those who remained to meet the needs of the buyer better.

A bookstore case

W. H. Smith (WHS) in common with many large retailing organizations began to investigate its own supply chain during the 1990s in a search to be more efficient and to be more effective in meeting customer needs. Book publishers were notoriously inefficient in managing their businesses and had been used to some protection from market forces that might have sharpened their management capabilities in the form of the Net Book Agreement (NBA). The NBA effectively allowed publishers to set the selling prices for their books and to operate mainly standard discount terms with booksellers of any size. Large and small booksellers alike received these standard discounts. During the late 1980s a revolution began in this sleepy market sector with the inception and development of Terry Maher's Dillons bookstores. Maher, a trained accountant, was well aware of the importance of gaining economies of scale and using that market power to negotiate better terms including higher discounts. The success of Dillons did not go unnoticed by WHS who were the largest UK bookstore chain and they too began to exert their market muscle. One of the difficulties in this market is the number of suppliers. In the 1980s there were large numbers of publishers in the UK, many of whom were SMEs by any definition and many well-known imprints that readers would know well were actually very small in size. Their reputation being out of all proportion to the size of their business. The abandonment of the NBA in the 1990s led to a number of structural market changes. These changes included: retail consolidation and a number of new entrants to the market from the US like Borders; many small publishing houses merged or were taken over by other publishers and it was generally argued in a series of articles in the Bookseller (the organ of the book trade) that size was important for publishers to have a critical mass in dealing with the large chains of bookstores that had now taken over the high street. In the 1980s there was a plethora of new national chains. Following Dillons' successful strategies to establish a national chain, Waterstones (founded by a former WHS employee Tim Waterstone), Hatchards and Blackwells began to establish larger and national chains of stores. The volumes of books supplied by the biggest booksellers accounted for a substantial proportion of all UK books sold. This retail consolidation in turn led to publishers merging to fight their corner and attempt to maintain their share of the profits.

The pressure applied to all publishers to comply with stringent supply agreements covering deliveries, product compliance (e.g. bar coding), invoicing and payment terms meant that many smaller publishing houses were either unable or unwilling to do so. Electronic ordering systems developed, better information on availability of products was achieved through Whitakers and the Teleordering systems and later through BookTrak. Small bookshops and small publishers found this high street revolution a painful challenge to their conservative industry.

Source: Author.

Summary

A number of important issues relating to the sourcing and procurement of supplies together with their implications for developing appropriate supply chain strategies have been discussed in this chapter. Local supplies *vis-à-vis* national or global sources and influencing factors in those decisions were thoroughly examined. The complexity of the decision-making processes was addressed through the 'iceberg theory of cost comparison' and other influences including ethical and environmental factors. The next chapter will turn attention to supply chain structures and relationships, and their role in influencing supply chain strategies.

ETHICAL CASE
Pennies an Hour, and No Way Up

By Tom Hayden and Charles Kernaghan
Extract from New York Times
July 6, 2002

In last week's meeting in Canada, the group of eight industrial nations grappled with the question of how to better economic conditions in poor nations. One powerful means would be to improve the conditions of workers in sweatshops. Two billion people in the world make less than two American dollars a day. As voters and consumers of sweatshop products, Americans can make a difference in ending the miserable conditions under which these people work.

Some argue that sweatshops are simply a step up a ladder toward the next generation's success: the garment worker at her loom is carrying out some objective law of development, or the young girl making toys for our children is breaking out of male-dominated feudalism. This line of thinking recalls the mythic rise of our immigrant ancestors to the middle class and beyond.

But the real story of those white ethnic ancestors was hardly a smooth ride up the escalator. Life in New York was better than oppression abroad, but people worked 16 hours a day for paltry wages, lived in cellars with raw sewage, died of starvation and fever and were crowded into tenements. Their misery shocked reformers like Jacob Riis and Charles Dickens. They fought their way out 'marched for economic justice, built unions, voted and finally forced the Gilded Age to become the New Deal'.

Today young, mostly female workers in Bangladesh, a Muslim country that is the fourth largest garment producer for the United States market, are paid an average of 1.6 cents for each baseball cap with a Harvard logo that they sew. The caps retail at the Harvard bookstore for $17, which means the garment workers, who often are younger than the Harvard students, are being paid a tenth of 1 per cent of the cap's price in the market. Also in Bangladesh, women receive 5 cents for each $17.99 Disney shirt they sew. Wages like these are not enough to climb the ladder with.

There are similar conditions in China. Three million young Chinese women working for wages as low as 12 cents an hour make 80 per cent of the sporting goods and toys sold in the United States each year. Companies like Mattel spend 30 times more to advertise a toy than they pay the workers in China to make it.

Each year Americans buy 924 million garments and other textile items made in Bangladesh and $23.5 billion worth of toys and sporting goods from China. Don't we have the consumer and political power to pressure our corporations to end sweatshop wages paid to the people who make these goods? These workers are not demanding stock options and Jazzercise studios. Women in Bangladesh say they could care for their children if their wages rose to 34 cents an hour, two-tenths of 1 per cent of the retail price of the Harvard hat.

Some economists argue that even the most exploited and impoverished workers are better off than those who are unemployed or trapped in slave labor. But that argument is not about offering anyone a ladder up, but about which ring of Dante's inferno people in developing nations are consigned to. We don't want Disney, Mattel, Wal-Mart or other major American companies to leave the developing world. We simply want to end the race to the bottom in which companies force countries to compete in offering the lowest wages for their people's labor. There should be a floor beneath which no one has to live.

Our elected officials should end their subservience to corporate donors and begin asking some big questions: Aren't we entitled to know the addresses of corporate sweatshops in developing countries so they can be open to monitoring by local advocates? Why should our tax dollars subsidize government purchases from companies that operate sweatshops? Under our customs laws, we ban imports made with inmate and indentured labor, so why not extend the ban to include those made with sweatshop and child labor? And if we insist on enforcement of laws against pirate labels and CD's, why not protect 16-year-olds who make CD's for American companies? We should be helping these workers elbow and push their way up from squalor just as American progressives once helped our immigrant forebears.

Review Questions

1. What can organizational buyers do to ensure that they are not accused of unwittingly becoming involved in unethical sourcing and procurement?
2. How can suppliers protect their business interests by being both competitive and engaged in ethical trade?
3. What are the risks involved for business organizations who simply choose to ignore ethical considerations in sourcing and procuring goods at the best possible prices from anywhere in the world?

Discussion Questions

1. Identify the main criteria for sourcing goods locally vs. globally.
2. Evaluate the merits of sourcing goods from global suppliers and draw comparisons with the merits of sourcing local suppliers.
3. 'There may be an iceberg of cost involved in purchasing from certain suppliers and supply sources that do not enter the usual criteria for decision-making.' Discuss.
4. 'Sources of supply can be a means of achieving competitive advantage.' Discuss.
5. Identify and evaluate the main sources of competitive advantage involved in supplier sourcing strategies.
6. 'Supplier selection criteria may vary from industry to industry.' Discuss.
7. 'Supplier development programmes can assist suppliers to meet their customer requirements more efficiently and effectively.' Discuss.
8. 'Environmental and ethical considerations sometimes get ignored when sourcing supplies.' Discuss.
9. Explain why buyer performance measures may lead to sourcing decisions that may not be in the best interests of the whole organization.

10. 'The recent trend towards supply base rationalization has caused many organizations to re-evaluate their risk profile.' Explain what you understand this statement to mean and why it is important, if not essential, to consider risk in reducing the number of suppliers.

Notes

1 The opacity index: launching a new measure of the effects of opacity on the cost of availability of capital in countries worldwide. London: PWC, January 2001, pp. 1–13. http://www.opacityindex.com/.
2 The National Textile Center at North Carolina State University together with TC² developed a game 'Sourcing Simulator' that illustrates the effect of lost sales on an apparel/textile pipeline. In practice, however, lost sales data is virtually impossible to capture and measure accurately with current technology and data capture systems. To do so except under experimental conditions would be very expensive.
3 These terms are used by retail buyers and indicate cost incurred.
4 Gross margin.

References

Burt, D. N., Dobler, D. W. and Starling, S. L. (2003). *World Class Supply Management – The Key to Supply Chain Management*, 7th edn. Boston, MA: McGraw-Hill Irwin.

Coase, R. H. (1937). The nature of the firm. *Economica*, **V**, 386–405.

Cyert, R. M. and March, J. G. (1963). *A Behavioural Theory of the Firm*. Englewood Cliffs, NJ: Prentice-Hall.

Hines, T. (2002). Developing an iceberg theory of cost comparison in retail sourcing decisions by UK fashion retailers. *Textile Institute Journal, Supply Chain Special Edition*, Vol. 93, Part 3, ISSN: 0400-0500. Manchester: Textile Institute.

Hines, T. and McGowan, P. (2002). Contemporary supply relationships in UK fashion retailing: developing a research agenda. *Textile Institute Journal, Supply Chain Special Edition*, Vol. 93, Part 3, ISSN: 0400-0500. Manchester: Textile Institute.

Kaplan, R. S. and Cooper, R. (1998). *Cost and Effect – Using Integrated Cost Systems to Drive Profitability and Performance*. Boston, MA: Harvard Business School Press.

Porter, M. E. (1980). *Competitive Strategy – Techniques for Analyzing Industries and Competitors*. New York: Free Press.

Chapter 6

Supply chain structures and relationships

LEARNING OUTCOMES

This chapter introduces a number of key concepts relating to purchasing and supply chain relationships, and structures.

After studying the chapter you should be able to:

■ know the different types of purchasing decision and their characteristics;
■ understand the key processes in the purchase decision;
■ demonstrate understanding of the different types of buyer–supplier relationships and their relative merits;
■ analyse and evaluate the key issues in purchasing and supply management decisions.

Relationships and structures

Relationships and structures within the supply chain are determined by a number of factors: industry structure, characteristics, competitive rivalries, numbers of suppliers and buyers, nature of products and services, industry and organizational cultures. Relationships exist between organizations (inter-organizational), between specific groups of people inside the organizations in business relationships, e.g. buyers and sellers, and inside the organizations themselves (intra-organizational). One way to begin to understand the types of relationships and structures is to examine purchasing and procurement decisions. The chapter begins by defining purchasing and procurement and recognizing different types of purchasing before examining the purchasing decision and different types of supplier relationships moving from adversarial through to partnerships and strategic alliances. Different supply chain strategies require the organization to have different types of relationships and different organizational structures to deal with those relationships. The relative merits of different types of relationships are discussed.

Purchasing and procurement

Purchasing and procurement are often treated as meaning the same thing. However, strictly speaking procurement is wider than purchasing and involves acquisition of goods and services in any way possible. For example, this could include expropriation and other means of acquisition than buying goods and services in exchange for money. Lysons (2000, p. 1) defines purchasing as follows: 'Purchasing is the function responsible for obtaining by purchase, lease or other legal means, equipment, materials, components, suppliers and services required by an undertaking for use in production or resale.' You may be thinking that the definition is remiss in not mentioning services especially when 73 per cent of the UK economy GDP is made up of services. Lysons explains this stating that the term 'production' is used in the economic sense of creating utilities, i.e. goods and services.

Organizational buyers are responsible for purchasing decisions made by companies, local authorities, government offices, charities, partnerships and even sole traders. Organizational buyers have been identified as belonging to buying groups. A typology of organizational buying is given in Table 6.1.

For a typical manufacturing company in the UK the proportion of total manufacturing costs accounted for by purchased materials and components represents over 60 per cent today compared with under 40 per cent 20 years ago. Organizational purchasing decisions are therefore far more significant today and can play a large part in determining company profitability. Purchasing is critical when it represents such a large proportion of the cost. Other reasons when purchasing is important could be due to:

- short run price fluctuations;
- when fashion and innovation are involved good judgement is required;
- when markets for finished goods are highly competitive.

Purchasing will be less important when:

- costs of bought-out items form only a relatively small proportion of total cost;

- when prices are relatively stable;
- when innovation or fashion content is low.

Modern organizations often regard purchasing to be of strategic importance. We have just observed why this may be so.

Table 6.1 Typology of organizational buyers

Types of organization	Characteristics	Examples
Industrial/producer	Purchase of goods and services for some tangible production or significant commercial purpose	Manufacturer, primary extractor – agriculture, forestry, fishing, horticulture, mining
Intermediary	Purchase of goods and services for resale or facilitating resale in industrial or consumer markets	Distributors, dealers, wholesalers, agents, buying offices/groups, retailers, banks, hotels and service trades, e-purchasing auction sites, portals, etc.
Government and public sector	Purchase of goods and services for use by public sector bodies including local and national government. Not always commercially significant	Central, local government and public utilities
Institutional	Purchase of goods and services for use by institutions buying on their own behalf	Universities, colleges, schools, hospitals, voluntary organizations

The purchasing decision

Purchasing activities involve buying decisions to ensure that:

- the right goods;
- are in the right place;
- at the right time;
- at the right price;
- at the right quality; and
- at the right quantity.

These are sometimes referred to as the six R's of purchasing.

The right goods

Acquiring the right goods sounds common sense and it is, but there are many considerations in deciding on the right goods or the right service. It was often stated by buyers of computer hardware in the 1970s and 1980s that 'nobody was ever fired for buying IBM, Big Blue as it was known'. This demonstrates the importance of reliability, another R perhaps. Reliability is often communicated to buyers through the brand identity, and the attributes and perceived benefits that the brand communication conveys to the buyer. In many organizational settings the buyer will specify exactly what the organization requires (based on needs) rather than simply buy from catalogue (what's on offer). Sometimes of course the two may coincide and often when this is the case better prices can be achieved because the supplier does not have to customize the product.

The right place

In making the buying decision it is important to provide detailed instructions on how, when and where deliveries are to be made. For example, many retail organizations will instruct their suppliers to deliver to a central distribution depot (CDD) or directly to store. The advantage of delivering directly to store is it avoids double handling and hence additional transport and storage costs for the retailer. If goods have to go to a depot first they need to be recorded, stored and later transported at the retailer's cost to the store that requires the stock.

The right time

Ensuring that stock arrives when it is needed is fundamental to an efficient supply chain operation. JiT systems are built on the notion that suppliers will supply when the stock is required. This avoids stock-holding costs and lowers working capital requirements since the stock is purchased later in the cycle, cash-outflows happen later and indeed may well coincide with the cash-inflows from the sale if the supply chain operations are synchronized.

The right price

Achieving the right price is important since this will affect the purchaser's cost structure and ultimately the margin achieved (i.e. profitability). Obtaining goods at the right price often involves negotiation and good negotiation skills are pre-requisite for successful buyers. Negotiations will revolve around a number of important buying variables such as delivery dates, time to manufacture, quality, volumes and discounts. However, price is still a very important factor and buyers need to be very careful in making 'trade-off' calculations between price and these other factors.

To illustrate just how important price can be, see Figure 6.1, which demonstrates visually the effect of a simple 5 per cent reduction in cost for materials, labour and overheads, and the impact on profit. As a consequence the profit margin has improved by 10 per cent. This is why the price of materials purchased is important.

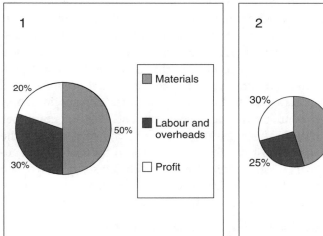 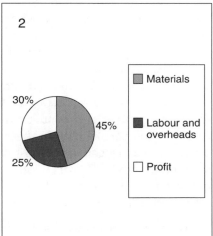

Figure 6.1 The effect of a 5 per cent cost reduction on profit margin

The right quality

The customer either specifies quality or expects the supplier to do so. In either case, for customers to return and re-order, their expectations on quality have to be met. Suppliers must not under – or over – specify quality because either way it will incur unnecessary costs. Quality is explained in more detail in Chapter 10.

The right quantity

The final R of six is having the right quantity supplied. Figure 6.2 identifies key variables in the purchase decision. The six R's identified and discussed in much of the practice and academic literature are depicted on the right-hand side of the figure and these are basic buyer requirements. On the left-hand side of the figure are three more R's attributed

Supply chain management: a job with a long shelf life

Careers in retailing usually conjure up images of bustling store managers and ringing tills but for a growing number of graduates the challenge is how to get the goods from the grower or manufacturer to the shelves. Most shoppers are unaware that getting the right transport, warehousing and distribution is critical to getting perishable goods to a store near them with almost military precision. Getting the right goods onto shelves at the right time is the guiding principle of 'supply chain management'. Supply chain efficiency can make or break a business. Retailers invest large sums of money ensuring stock appears on the shelf at the right time and in the right condition. This is especially important in food retailing where thousands of dairy, chilled or frozen lines are delivered to stores daily. Forecasting demand using sophisticated modelling systems that take account of past weather patterns is commonplace. A Personnel Manager at the Co-op comments that a 'methodical and logical mind is important for the attention to detail and it is vital graduates feel comfortable with computers and technology'. The buzz phrases in supply chain management are: continuous stock replenishment, efficient consumer response and parallel chains. These are simply clever ways of describing the process of getting enough of what the shopper wants into the store. A graduate entrant, now a Primary Distribution Manager, with Sainsbury's says 'one of my jobs is to reduce the food miles that each item travels and to ensure it is handled as little as possible to avoid spoilage or possible contamination'.

Source: Adapted from an article in The Independent, 22 February 2001.

to the supplier in which the buyer will be interested. Reputation includes the brand, product or company reputation which may be communicated in a number of ways to the buyer. For example, reputations are built through word of mouth, through performance, through advertising and through experience of dealing with the supplier.

More R's

Another issue when the organization is buying on specification is responsiveness, another R. Responsiveness will be important to the buying decision when 'time is of the essence' as they often write in the legal purchase document. Responsiveness is the time it will take for the supplier to respond (i.e. to supply/make and deliver the item). When an organization makes a first purchase from a supplying organization it is

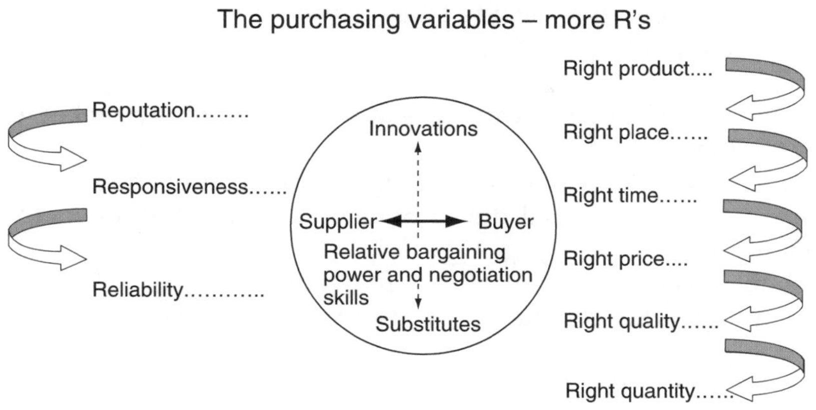

The purchasing variables – more R's

Figure 6.2 The purchasing variables – more R's

always important to check the response times not only on the first order but in the case of replenishing the stock.

Responsiveness covers issues such as how flexible the supplier can be when meeting buyer requirements. For example: Is the supplier able to produce products quickly when required? (speed to market, lead times). Is the supplier able to switch easily between different buyer requirements without too much difficulty? (fast production enables suppliers to delay commitment of resources through postponement until the last possible minute – sometimes referred to under the umbrella term 'quick response'). Responsiveness may be very important to some buyers allowing them to postpone their commitment to production or purchase quantities when they have better customer information regarding volumes. For example, a retailer ordering fashion clothing in season would want to delay a large part of its production until it was able to analyse data on sales quantities, colours, styles that were popular rather than simply base the purchasing decision on forecast data.

Reliability is the final R attributed to the supplier and involves ensuring that the purchased items arrive in full on the date required.

Information is an important resource to purchasing managers. Information is required in relation to:

- price;
- quality;
- specifications;
- terms of business (supplier conditions, payment terms, delivery, after sales service, ownership transfer, insurance, etc.).

Further information will be needed on a number of different aspects of the purchase before a decision is taken.

Purchasing decisions need to take account of the best available information relating to:

- Potential shortages and surpluses of materials and their relative price sensitivities;
- Comparative power of buyers, suppliers and competitors;
- Impact of new material developments, new product developments and obsolescence;
- Technological developments and innovations;
- Changing market conditions – consumer, customer changes in preference;
- New sources of supply;
- Current capacity and competencies of existing suppliers;
- Security of supplies;
- Value analysis of alternatives *vis-à-vis* current purchased items;
- Usage and/or throughput.

Purchase frequency

Purchase frequency has implications for cost, storage and customer service. Purchasing frequency is important because it may mean that more frequent purchasing can be made routine through systematic buying and replenishment buying. It is often the case that with frequent purchases they can be triggered automatically.

Example

The development of Electronic Point of Sale (EPoS) equipment has allowed many retail organizations to link sale data to inventory and automatic order replenishment. When an item is passed through a scanner at the till the bar code is read for price and the item is recorded as a sale to the customer. Simultaneously the bar code reader has recorded a stock movement, i.e. one item moving out of stock. This data is automatically transmitted through the store stock control system to central logistics and purchasing. When the total store stock falls to the specified re-order point an automatic replenishment instruction is transmitted to the CDD who invoke the necessary logistics to get these items to the store. The CDD also has to record movements out so that its automatic replenishment system triggers a new purchase order to the supplier when CDD stock needs replenishment. With frequently ordered SKUs this is fairly simple and replenishment can be automated. In these cases there is seldom a need for human intervention. Soap powders, detergents and certain basic food items would all fit into this category where stock movements are predictable.

It is more difficult to deal with ad hoc purchases or purchases that require careful monitoring such as fashion items. Purchasing decisions and their relative characteristics will vary between different parts of the organization and between different organizations depending upon the types of item being purchased.

Categories of purchasing activity

Purchases may be classified into different types of activity as follows:

1. Ad hoc or one off purchase.
2. Regular or routine supply of purchase items (e.g. automatic replenishment of SKUs).
3. Contract purchases (e.g. goods purchased from sourced and approved suppliers for a particular purpose or to a particular specification).
4. Catalogue purchases (this is a US term for purchases made from an approved supplier from their catalogue of what they have to sell as opposed to purchase to specification).

These categories of purchasing activity are related to frequency of purchase. Ad hoc suggesting irregularity through to routine, regular implying frequent purchases.

It is important for the organization to clearly identify the different types of purchase activity, and design systems and procedures that enable effective execution of purchase orders.

Supplier relationships

Establishing the right kind of supplier relationships is very important. An organization is only able to do this if they know exactly what they want from their suppliers. We have already observed that historically many of the purchasing relationships were 'arms length' and often adversarial in nature. As a professional buyer the aim was often a simple one focused upon getting the best price. It is now recognized that this type of approach may not have always served the needs of the buying organization. Supply base rationalization is a trend in most industrial sectors and some of the main reasons for that trend were discussed earlier in Chapter 3. It is important to re-visit that trend because it impacts upon the ways in which supply chain relationships are established and what the parties in the relationship expect to get from it.

Buyer–supplier relationships

Examining interaction variables provides insights into buyer–supplier relationships; one useful model was provided by Campbell (1985, p. 269). The work takes as its starting point the IMP[1] model illustrated in Figure 6.3 which is mainly concerned with industrial marketing and purchasing, and develops a way of examining the interactions and their impact upon buyer–seller strategies. The interaction variables used in this research are given in Table 6.2. The model could be extended to take account of relationships described as buyer–supplier networks or indeed supply chain networks. The model is fairly self-explanatory and it is a way of examining interactions at different levels – product, industry, company and individual.

The original IMP model is shown in Figure 6.3. The original model assumed that the two organizations operate within an environment that is determined by external factors such as market structure, dynamism and internationalization, social structure and channel position. The term originally used by the IMP model is now referred to and understood as equating with the supply chain. The IMP model referred to a *'manufacturing channel'*. The description given as *'. . . the position of an individual relationship in an extended "channel" stretching from primary producer to final consumer'* (Ford, 1990, p. 17). Atmosphere describes the conditions within which the interactions between the

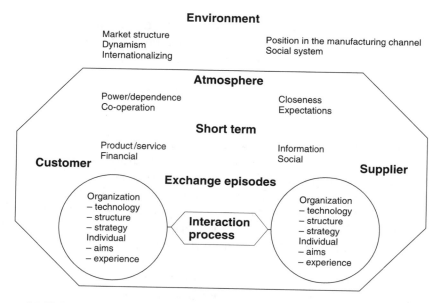

Figure 6.3 IMP interaction model of relationship structures
Source: IMP interaction model (Ford, 1990, p. 20).

Table 6.2 Interaction variables

Buyer	Interaction variable	Supplier
Product	Frequency of purchase Switching costs due to physical and human investment Product complexity	Product
Industry characteristics	Concentration Number of alternative partners Intensity of competition Rate of technical change Traditions and norms	Industry characteristics
Company characteristics	Relative size Preferred interaction style Relative familiarity Centralization of purchasing	Company characteristics
Individual characteristics	Relative familiarity Preferred interaction style Perceived importance of the transaction Risk aversion	Individual characteristics

Source: Campbell (1985).

parties take place. This is dynamic and is affected by episodes of exchange between the parties. Relationships between the parties are shaped by organizational factors: technology, strategy and structures; and by individual factors: aims and experience. Organizational strategy can be affected by both long-term relationships and short-term episodes. Atmosphere maybe described in terms of power dependence relationships, the state of conflict or co-operation, and finally closeness and distance of the relationship. It is in the development of these variables that Campbell's (1985) work is located.

Cooper and Gardner (1993) referred to a continuum of relationships and identified six distinctive types which are:

1. Arm's length;
2. Typical small account;
3. National account selling;
4. Strategic alliance;
5. Joint venture;
6. Vertical integration.

Companies tend to deal with the different types of suppliers differently. It is important to recognize that 'relationship' is often not really the warm and cuddly type but that it may be quite the opposite. All relationships in this context should be based on commercial needs and will revolve inevitably around the needs of the different parties at that point in time.

In arm's length relationships price is the key negotiating point. These relationships are often referred to as 'win–lose' and they often involve adversarial or conflict negotiation techniques. Power is an important issue in this type of relationship. If the buyer is representing a very large organization and the supplier firm is small it may be that there are many alternative suppliers willing and able to meet the large organization's demands. When this is the case the small supplier is at an obvious disadvantage and may often give way on price to get the order.

Small accounts are relatively expensive to conduct and there has to be a unique proposition that the small account supplier is able to provide to the large customer if they are to remain a viable supplier.

National account selling usually involves the supplier firm dealing with one organization that may have multiple sites to supply with their products. These are often handled centrally by the buying organization that may handle distribution to their multiple sites from a centralized depot or through their own supply networks. The detailed arrangements will vary from organization to organization.

Types of supplier relationship

Traditional supplier relationships have been viewed as buyer and seller relationships. The bow tie depicted in Figure 6.4 illustrates the adversarial nature of buyer and supplier relationships that are

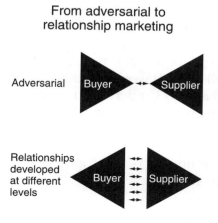

Figure 6.4

common in commodity type markets. It represents a situation where the buyer and seller are locked in negotiation which is focused on price. In this type of relationship there is often a single one-to-one relationship between two organizations, e.g. a sales representative and a buyer. Single-point commercial relationship often involves buyers trying to push costs back along the supply chain and suppliers trying to hold prices firm to secure profit. In this type of relationship neither buyer nor supplier is working together to eliminate unnecessary costs in the supply chain.

In more complex purchasing and supply chain relationships there are a number of different people in each organization who are regularly in contact. Multiple levels of contact are often symptomatic of relationship marketing and supply chain relationships when the products are more complex and the markets served require a co-operative rather than adversarial arrangement.

Supplier networking

There is an extensive literature on networking. Network theory potentially provides a way of explaining business relationships. The reality is that the literature relating to networks is full of ambiguity both in terms of terminology and conceptually (Szarka, 1990, p. 10). Johannison (1987) identified three types of network which are:

  i. Production networks between trading organizations;
 ii. Personal networks based on friendship and trust;
iii. Symbolic networks based on social bonds, community ties and conformity to collective values.

Mitchell (1973) recognized exchange networks, communication networks and social networks which are closely aligned to those categories given by Johannison. Although these typologies may be useful in different contexts to examine the nature of relationships they may in themselves be limited or constraining when examining supplier relationships that could potentially have characteristics of all three types identified.

The language to describe supplier networks more usually refers to partnerships and alliances, whereas networking per se refers to formal and informal networks based upon exchange/production, personal/ social or communication/conformity.

Strategic alliances are usually formed because the two or more parties involved in the alliance have something to gain and each offers something different and something of value to the other parties. The automotive supplies industry has many strategic alliances to share expertise and investment cost. It may also be a way of meeting customer demand requirements better and to enhance service levels.

Joint venture agreements usually involve two organizations that decide to conduct mutually beneficial business. For example, it may be in the commercial interests of a supplying organization to enter into a joint venture with another supplying organization to meet the needs of a common group of customers more effectively. You may be wondering how this type of arrangement is different from a strategic alliance. The answer is that in joint venture both parties invest financially in the venture and agree to share the rewards from the venture in accordance with the agreement. Often the joint venture itself will be a separate entity. A company set up for the specific purpose of the joint venture. Strategic alliances may or may not involve cross-investments. More often than not they will share some markets or some facilities but the parties act as independent organizations. Many airlines have strategic alliances and they are formed to share facilities: booking tickets, engineering maintenance, routes and to facilitate bookings for customers wanting to fly with one of the alliance airlines in specific territories. In this way it is hoped the alliance members benefit by increasing their total and individual market share.

Fully vertically integrated organizations have ownership and control of their routes to market. For example, the Spanish retailer Zara has its own retail stores throughout Europe and has manufacturing facilities in Northern Spain that it owns. These manufacturers supply the retail stores with merchandise. It is argued by many commentators that this is one of their CSFs enabling Zara to produce 'fast fashion'. Lead times of 2 or 3 weeks are often reported from design to store for many of their popular lines.

Figure 6.5 illustrates two different organizations that are vertically integrated. There are four stages in the examples. The first organization owns farms growing cotton for fibre inputs to its owned textile mills who produce fabric for its owned manufacturers of apparel who then

Vertical integration

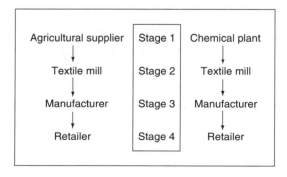

Figure 6.5

in turn supply the organization's own retail stores. In these types of organization the supply chain is both owned and controlled by the organization. It is important to recognize that the benefits of vertical integration may be outweighed by the risks and costs of owning the whole supply chain. One can envisage circumstances when it would be lower cost to buy supplies in the open market rather than incur all the ownership costs and produce goods that are more expensive.

Outsourcing

The trend to demerge businesses has led to a growth in outsourcing. Outsourcing is the term used to describe the buying-in of goods and services deemed to be non-core activities of the firm. This particular trend leads to interdependencies that require relationship management skills. One issue of concern explored by Fitzgerald (1995) and identified by Harland (1995) is the important question of what firms deem to be core or non-core activities. Outsourcing is often pursued to realize a cost advantage and sometimes as a means of protection from being locked into obsolete technologies (Abernathy, 1978; Miles and Snow, 1987). The decision-making approach to outsourcing is also often viewed from the perspective of the traditional 'make or buy decision' (Lui and McGoldrick, 1996; McIvor et al., 1997). Coopers and Lybrand, an international firm of management consultants, lists five major reasons for firms to outsource and these are shown in rank order in Table 6.3. The reasons were drawn from firms across all industries and in a US context. Nevertheless, they provide an indication of reasons why a firm may consider outsourcing in the first place.

The reasons given in 1994 are as relevant today as they were then. Most organization's search for cost savings and efficiencies to be gained from outsourcing non-core activities to specialist providers.

Table 6.3

The top five reasons given for outsourcing	%
Outside providers more efficient	70
Keep focus on own products and growth	45
Save costs	42
Less overhead investment or debt needed	41
Ease regulatory compliance burden	21

Source: Montgommery-Garret (1994).

The spectrum of relationships

The spectrum of relationships examined in the area of supply chains ranges from an integrated hierarchy as in the vertically integrated firms

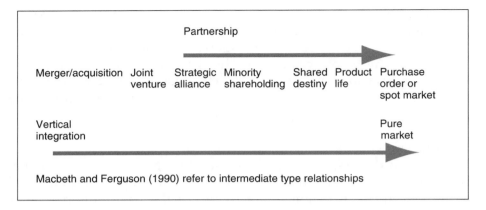

Figure 6.6 Intermediate type relationships

to a pure market view (see Figure 3.10). Both Marshall (1923) and Coase (1937) recognized alternative forms of organization to either market or vertically integrated firms. Ellram (1991) explored relationships in the supply chain from the point of view of obligational contractual relationships or those relying on good relations. So too did MacBeth and Ferguson and their alternatives to vertical integration are depicted in Figure 6.6. Firms adopt acquisition strategies to gain control of a supply chain, take an equity interest or form joint ventures. Long- and short-term contracts form the basis of contractual or relational exchanges. This particular perspective has its origins in an industrial organization and contract view (Aoki et al., 1990). Christopher (1992) has defined supply chain management as an alternative to vertical integration.

Supplier partnerships and alliances

Partnerships and alliances are terms often used in relation to supply chains to gain a thorough understanding of meaning: it is important to examine definitions of the terms.

Definition of terms

A great deal of the more recent literature related to the supply chain has emphasized a partnership approach (Christopher, 1996; Gattorna and Walters, 1996) and referred to the strategic nature of partnerships (Kanter, 1994). Partnerships usually involve a relationship between two or more different types of organization at different stages of the supply chain, e.g. a retailer and a contract clothing supplier. A partnership is distinguished from a strategic alliance which is more usually referred to when two or more organizations at the same part of the chain agree to co-operate. For example, a number of retailers combining to supply a particular market segment, to cover a specific geographical area, or to create a purchasing consortium would be partnership arrangements.

Importance of building supplier partnerships

Wheelright and Clark (1992) recognized that firms are able to get new products to market faster and more efficiently by establishing strategic partnerships with suppliers. Strong relationships between a lead supplier and other outside suppliers nearby play a fundamental role in flexibility according to a number of commentators who have observed the Japanese automobile industry (Fruin, 1992; Imai, 1986). Nishiguchi (1993) referred to this phenomenon as 'clustered control'. Much attention has focused upon strategic alliances in the automotive industry (Lamming, 1993; Smitka, 1991; Womack et al., 1990). 'Co-makership' and lean supply are terms used to characterize customer-driven integrated systems of manufacture and informational relationship systems (Hines, 1994; Lamming, 1993; Womack and Jones, 1994; Womack et al., 1990). Bonaccorsi and Lipparini (1994, p. 135) argued that two dimensions were particularly important in supplier partnerships: the timing of involvement in the product development process and the degree of competition among suppliers. The importance of these two dimensions are further supported by the work of Merli (1991) and Stevens (1989) whose research is discussed in a later section in this chapter.

Strategic alliances

Table 6.4 gives a useful delineation between strategic alliances, operational partnerships and opportunistic partnerships. Many supply chain relationships could be categorized into one of these three types.

Supply chain efficiency and cost reduction are control relationships whereas the other emerging themes would be categorized as co-operating relationships. Co-operating relationships might well lead to cost reduction and efficiency, and therefore could be seen as causal relationships. However, cost reduction or an efficiency gain in the supply chain could be the catalyst to move towards co-operation. It may be a necessary condition that could cause change to happen but in itself may not be sufficient to determine co-operative behaviour. Nevertheless, co-operation is likely to be a necessary and sufficient condition for a firm to achieve both efficiency and cost reduction in any supply chain.

Table 6.5 illustrates what Kanter (1994, p. 100) referred to as 'Eight I's that create successful We's'. The work examined eight variables that characterized strategic alliances. Kanter (1994) argued that all the criteria had to be met if an organization was to achieve what she termed a *collaborative advantage*. In order to be successful in forming a collaborative advantage

Table 6.4

Strategic alliance	*Operational partnership*	*Opportunistic partnerships*
Integrate core competencies of each partner and perform the activities that add most value to the relationship	Partnership based on one partner leveraging another partner's core competence	Based on one party performing activities that the other no longer will
Power is moved towards the consumer and the alliance with equal partners act to serve the consumer	Power equality exists at only one place in the supply chain	Power inequality results in greater demands being placed on one party
Consumer enjoys measurable value from the alliance	Both partners benefit but not always equally	Results in one partner gaining at the other's expense
Information analysis is performed jointly and information is shared	Risk is greater for one of the partners	Risks are always greater for one party
The alliance results in a more efficient supply chain	Consumer receives only some value from the partnership	Consumer does not receive greater value as a result of the agreement
	Information is shared on a selective basis	Information is rarely shared
	Partnership has the effect of shifting costs and efficiencies within the supply chain	Cost reduction or inefficiency in the supply chain is ignored

⇐ Co-operation ⇒ Control

Source: The table is based on KSAs description of different relationships that exist in industry between merchant and vendor (retailer and supplier).

it was necessary that both organizations in the partnership had something of value for each other and that by focusing those combined values it would enable new opportunities for both parties. Both parties needed to have long-term goals where their mutual objectives could be realized and where interdependence was essential as each leveraged complementary assets and skills (competencies) to achieve their objectives. Tangible signs of commitment would be cross-investment, sharing of information, integrated policies, procedures and systems thus 'institutionalizing' the relationship. Mutual trust was seen as a necessary condition for the relationship to survive.

Despite all the discussion and rhetoric relating to managing the supply chain, however addressing issues to do with partnerships, alliances and relationships, the reality is still somewhat different. According

Table 6.5 Eight I's that create successful We's

Individual excellence	Both partners must have something of value to contribute to the relationship. Both partners are strong. Motives for the relationship are positive and focus on opportunities. Reasons for entering the partnership should not be negative to mask a weakness or to escape from a difficult situation
Importance	The relationship must fit-in with each partner's strategic objectives and they must make it work. Each partner must have long-term goals in which relationships play a key role
Interdependence	Each partner needs the other. They have complementary assets and skills. Neither can accomplish alone what both can together
Investment	Partners invest in each other (e.g. through equity swaps, cross-ownership or mutual board service) to demonstrate their respective stakes in the relationship with each other. They show tangible signs of long-term commitment by devoting financial and other resources to the relationship
Information	Communication is reasonably open. Partners share information to make relationships work. This includes: objectives, goals, technical data, knowledge conflicts, trouble spots or changing situations
Integration	Partners develop linkages and shared ways of operating so that they can work together smoothly. They build connections between many people at many organizational levels. Partners become teachers and learners
Institutionalization	Relationships are given formal status, with clear responsibilities and decision processes. It extends beyond the people who formed it, and cannot be broken on a whim
Integrity	Partners behave honourably to each other, which enhances mutual trust. They do not abuse information gained from working together to undermine each other

Source: Adapted from Kanter (1994, p. 100).

to Cox (1999, p. 167), the predominant orthodoxy of supply chain management thinking is devoted to, 'discovering tools and techniques (quick response, lean supply, co-makership, agile manufacturing, value streams) that provide increased operational effectiveness and efficiency throughout the delivery channels that must be created internally and externally to support and supply existing corporate product and service offerings to customers'. Cox goes on to attribute this thinking to studies of the Japanese Automobile industry in the 1970s and 1980s by Womack et al. (1990). These views are in contrast to the views expressed by Fearne (1998), which emphasize the importance of the customer and building relationships – 'a philosophy of doing business'. These two approaches highlight the differences between product push (supply) and market-led (demand) strategies. The first approach is essentially internally focused on efficiencies. Whereas the latter is a market-focused approach taking account of the firm's external environment and simultaneously creating 'strategic fit' between the supply networks and their customers.

To be effective in developing supply chain strategies it is not necessarily collaborative approaches that succeed according to Cox (1997). Cox's view is supported by Cousins (2002). First, partnership relationships do not exist but there is a range of collaborating relationships which are all competitive. Second, organizations do not trust each other, they manage risk based on business objectives they have set themselves. Third and more importantly, the relationship itself is a process not an entity and as such focuses on definable outcomes. If these assertions are correct it is even more important to recognize where power within a supply chain resides.

One interesting way to view power relationships in a buyer–supplier dyad was demonstrated by van Weele and Rozemeijer (2001, p. 92) using a portfolio approach illustrated in Figure 6.7.

Power positions are discussed in terms of strategic positioning using the Boston Consulting Group Matrix. This is a simple four-box model comparing relative market growth *vis-à-vis* relative market share. A supplier assesses the product position and segments the market from their perspective relative to the customer perspective. Suppliers who supply strategic products recognize that these are very difficult for their customers to replace in the short-term. They are in effect high growth and high share supplies critical to their customers needs and would have a high financial impact both on their customer and on themselves. An organization that supplies products in this category is high risk for their customer especially if the supplier became vulnerable to takeover or failure. Business history is littered with examples of such supply firms being purchased by their customer(s) to secure supplies as a last resort. Bottleneck products have a monopoly or oligopolistic market and they are difficult markets to break into because of high barriers to entry. There is

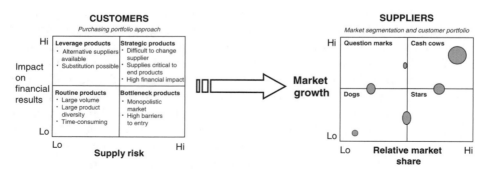

Figure 6.7

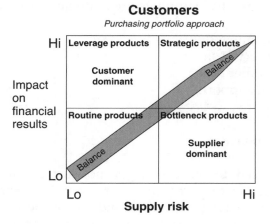

Figure 6.8

little or no alternative supplier and the risks for the customer are extremely high. Market share of the supplier is usually high and growth may be possible in immature markets but limited in mature markets. It is shown between a star and cash cow in this example. Routine products are shown as dogs with low market share, low growth, large volumes, small value and time-consuming. These are category C products in ABC analysis terms. Leverage products are high growth, high value but low market share because there are many competing suppliers and substitution is possible. Figure 6.8 illustrates power strategies when customers are dominant and conversely when suppliers are dominant. The model identifies four categories of product in relation to supply risk and the impact upon financial results. Strategic products carry high risk and have a high impact upon the financial results. These products require strategies that minimize these effects. Partnerships, alliances and collaborative strategies are required for this type of supply. In the case of routine products there is low supply risk and little impact upon the financial results. Routine products are in effect 'commodity products'; there are many suppliers for this type of product and many substitutes. Price is the most important attribute. In customer-dominant and supplier-dominant products there are a number of useful power strategies and they are listed below.

Power strategies when customers are dominant include:

- purchasing co-ordination: combining volumes;
- multiple sourcing;
- competitive bidding;
- cost down programmes;
- 'open cost' or 'open book costing';
- consortium buying.

Power strategies when suppliers are dominant include:

- technological innovation;
- value-added services;
- takeover customer tasks;
- offer technical support.

Make or buy decisions

Organizations need to make strategic not just operational or tactical decisions in relation to purchasing. For example, a simple operational decision to stop making a product and use resources to make other products may lead the organization purchasing the previously made item to reduce its capacity, to close a plant and hence lower its costs. This type of supply chain decision is often referred to as 'make or buy'. If an organization produces goods it incurs the full costs of owning plant and manufacturing capacity. It could choose to buy-in those goods from another supplier and dispose of assets, resources and competencies it owns. The organization will need to carefully evaluate the risks in taking this course of action. Organizations have been known to make the switch from 'make to buy' on cost grounds alone only to realize that in the short-term they still carry the fixed costs (factory, plant, machinery and people) or have disposed of key assets and discarded key competencies needed elsewhere in the business. Make or buy decisions must ensure that the resources and competencies can be better applied elsewhere or disposed of if the organization stops making and buys in products instead.

Purchase portfolio matrix

The purchase portfolio matrix is presented in Figure 6.9. It is based on an earlier model known as Kraljic's[2] sourcing tool. It assumes that customers seek to maximize purchasing power. Key factors affecting the relationship are strength of the buying organization in the buyer–supplier relationship and the number of suppliers able and willing to supply goods in a given time period.

Bottleneck items are those where the buyer has little power and few alternative sources of supply. The best strategy in these circumstances would be to try and reduce dependency on the source of supply and search for alternatives that meet the requirements of the buyer. Searching for alternative sources and substitute products is appropriate in these conditions. The buyers should try and work with design teams more closely to remove the bottlenecks and to ensure that lead times are maintained or reduced. Design is an important competence for the

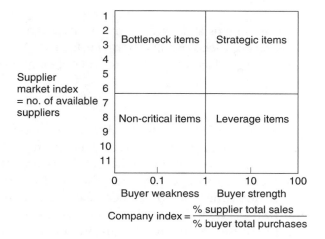

Figure 6.9 Purchase portfolio matrix
Source: Syson (1992).

buying organization to have or to buy-in since a combination of design and value engineering may be useful to ensure that cost is removed from the supply chain and value is added.

Strategic items are those where the buyer has strength but few alternative sources of supply. The best strategy in these circumstances would be to draw the supplier into longer-term contracts to ensure future supplies. Establishing and maintaining successful long-term relationships are critical to the purchasing organization in this context.

Non-critical items are those where there are many suppliers and perhaps in a context of using standardized parts. Competitive tendering may be the way in which these goods are acquired. These types of supply have the following characteristics:

- Not jointly developed;
- Unbranded and standardized items;
- Low investment in specific tooling and equipment;
- Do not affect performance and there is no safety risk involved.

Leverage items
Leverage items present opportunities for the buyer to use market power amongst many suppliers to get a good price and preferential treatment. Larger organizations are often able to exert this type of leveraging because of the volumes of business. For example, a large publishing company such as Elsevier would be able to use its market strength when negotiating with print suppliers to get good prices and to negotiate other benefits like flexibility to schedule in their books before other smaller organizations and to get good production and delivery lead times.

Leverage (non-critical) items and routine items were originally viewed by Kraljic (1983) as tactical decisions and bottlenecks, and strategic items were viewed as strategic decisions critical to the organization's success.

Relationships are dependent on the relative market power relationship between buyer and supplier. In many economic sectors those organizations that have direct contact with final customers often hold the balance of power. For example, in retail the top 10 leading grocery retailers have enormous market power because they have access to a very high proportion of the market. This is known as retail concentration. Because of this these organizations can often dictate the terms on which they will do business with many suppliers. This is particularly the case for non-branded suppliers. In these circumstances it is essential for the supplier to become strategically important to the retailer perhaps forming a partnership, co-operative or collaborative relationship. One example might be for the supplier to offer exceptional service, be responsive or flexible in its dealings with the buyer. Another example might be a transport logistics company offering additional services as part of a contract package (e.g. pre-retail services, quality control, inspection, ticketing, tagging, packing, reviving or reworking small corrections in the case of clothing).

Activity

For an organization of your choice, develop a purchase portfolio matrix and plot the names of the top 10 customers and top 10 suppliers. Suggest strategies that could be adopted to improve the organizational performance.

Supply chain partnering

Partnerships or co-operative relationships have some or all of the following attributes:

- Information sharing;
- Trust;
- Co-ordinated planning arrangements;
- Shared risks;
- Mutual benefits;

- Recognition of independence;
- Shared goals;
- Integrated processes;
- Shared culture, compatibility and understanding;
- Open book accounting.

Collaborative arrangements require the sharing of demand and supply information to reduce the 'bullwhip' effect of holding excess stocks in the system through overamplification of demand. Many key or core suppliers have access to retail or customer data in order to plan and co-ordinate resources for efficient and effective supplies. For example, in a VMI system this type of information is critical to its success. In this context the supplier manages the inventories at the point of sale for the retailing organization who will allow the supplier to manage the retail space attracting customers, maintaining adequate throughput and profitability which is in the interest of both parties. The retailer will therefore want to share EPoS data with the supplier to help that supplier plan the inventories in store and to organize production to co-ordinate supplies with demand. In this situation there is a shared risk and there is mutual benefit. Processes are integrated and probably open book accounting is used since the retailer will only pay the supplier for the goods when sold from the store. Both organizations remain independent but co-operate.

Figure 6.10 demonstrates six broad types of relationship identified in the literature together with the key emphasis and the nature of focus for the relationship clustered into three categories: adversarial, partnership and integrated.

Types of relationship

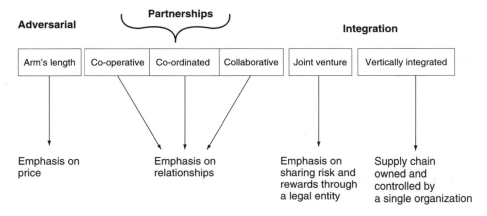

Figure 6.10

Table 6.6 Types of partnership relationships

Partnership type	Activities	Timeframe	Scope
Co-operation	Fewer suppliers Long term contracts	Short-term	Single functional area
Co-ordination	Information links EDI	Long-term	Multiple functional areas

Collaboration	Supply chain
	  integration
	Joint planning
	Shared technologies
	Process and adminis-
	  trative integration
		Long-term	Collaborating firms view
			  each other as extensions
			  of their own organization

Focusing upon the partnership types we are able to identify activities, timeframe and scope of activities in Table 6.6.

Summary

This chapter started by identifying key elements of the purchasing decision developing a conceptual model of the R's in purchasing: right goods, right place, right time, right price, right quality, right quantity. The model also examined factors valued by the purchaser from the supplier organization: reliability, responsiveness and reputation. These variables were examined in a dynamic competitive environment where innovation and substitution were likely to influence decisions as well as the bargaining power of buyers and suppliers. Purchasing frequency and supplier relationships were discussed before examining a number of supply chain strategies involved in purchasing decisions. A range of collaborative strategies was examined from co-operation through to partnerships. These relations are often structural decisions too in that they force organizations to develop new organizational structures in order to deliver the chosen strategy. The next chapter examines further supply chain integration strategies adopting e-business strategies and their implications for organizations.

Discussion Questions

1. Explain why purchasing is not exactly synonymous with procurement.
2. Discuss when purchasing is critical to the organization and illustrate your discussion with specific examples.

3. Explain why purchasing may be considered to be of both operational and strategic importance to an organization of your choice.

4. Purchasing may be critical to the survival and profitability of an organization. Discuss when this might be the case and explain why.

5. Purchasing decisions revolve around the five R's say what these are and discuss their relative importance to the buying decision.

6. This chapter identified another three R's that were required from a supplier. Identify the additional three R's and discuss their relative importance to the buyer.

7. Identify and explain the types of information required before a purchase can be made.

8. 'Supplier relationships may be determined by organizational structures within each of the organizations involved in a supply chain.' Explain why integration is necessary to reduce total supply chain cost and give examples of how integration may be achieved.

9. Explain the difference between different collaborative approaches in developing supply chain strategies.

10. 'Ultimately organizations involved in the supply chain must be competitive.' Explain how co-operative arrangements can be competitive and describe conflicts that might occur through supply chain co-operation.

Notes

1 IMP, The Industrial Marketing and Purchasing Group, has been conducting research into buyer–supplier processes since 1975. David Ford, University of Bath, has been instrumental in bringing together a group of academics and practitioners concerned to know and learn more about interactions, relationships and networks in business markets. Buyer perspectives and relationships mainly in industrial markets which has been the foci for this work.

2 Kraljic was a consultant who worked for McKinsey in the USA and he originally developed a sourcing tool based on Pareto's 80/20 rule, the matrix identified the four types and it was first discussed in the Harvard Business Review in 1983.

References

Abernathy, W. (1978). *The Productivity Dilemma*. Baltimore: Johns Hopkins University Press.

Aoki, M., Gustafsson, B. and Williamson, O. E. (1990). *The Firm as a Nexus of Treaties*. London: Sage.

Bonaccorsi, A. and Lipparini, A. (1994). Strategic partnerships in new product development. *Journal of Production and Innovation Management*, **11**, 134–45.

Campbell, N. C. G. (1985). An interaction approach to organizational buying behaviour. *Journal of Business Research*, **13**, 35–48. Reprinted in: Ford, D. (1990). *Understanding Business Markets – Interaction, Relationships, Networks*. London: Academic Press.

Christopher, M. G. (1992). *Logistics and Supply Chain Management – Strategies for Reducing Costs and Improving Services*. London: Financial Times/Pitman Publishing.

Christopher, M. G. (1996). *Marketing Logistics*. Oxford: Butterworth-Heinemann.

Coase, R. H. (1937). The Nature of the firm. *Economica*, **V**, 386–405.

Cooper, M. and Gardner, J. (1993). Building good business relationships – more than just partnering or strategic alliances? *International Journal of Physical Distribution and Logistics Management*, **23** (6), 14–26.

Cousins, P. D. (2002). A conceptual model for managing long term inter-organizational relationships. *European Journal of Purchasing and Supply Management*, **8** (2), 71–82.

Cox, A. (1997). *Business Success: A Way of Thinking about Strategy, Critical Supply Chain Assets and Operational Best Practice*. Lincolnshire: Earlsgate Press.

Cox, A. (1999). Power, value and supply chain management. *Supply Management: An International Journal*, **4** (4), 167–75.

Ellram, L. M. (1991). Supply chain management: the industrial organisation perspective. *International Journal of Physical Distribution and Logistics Management*, **21** (1), 13–22.

Fearne, A. (1998). *Supply Chain Management*, **3** (1), 4. ISSN 1359-8546. Bradford: MCB University Press.

Fitzgerald, G. (1995). *The Outsourcing of Information Technology: Revenge of the Business Manager or Legitimate Strategic Option?* Unpublished paper. Birkbeck College, University of London.

Ford, D. (1990). *Understanding Business Markets – Interaction, Relationships, Networks*. London: Academic Press.

Fruin, W. M. (1992). *The Japanese Enterprise System*. Oxford: Clarendon Press.

Gattorna, J. L. and Walters, D. W. (1996). *Managing the Supply Chain – A Strategic Perspective*. London: Macmillan.

Harland, C. M. (1995). Supply chain management: relationships, chains and networks. *British Academy of Management Proceedings*, Sheffield, pp. 62–79.

Hines, P. (1994). *Creating World Class Suppliers: Unlocking Mutual and Competitive Advantage*. London: Pitman Publishing.

Imai, K. (1986). *Kaizen*. New York: McGraw-Hill.

Johannison, B. (1987). Beyond process and structure: social exchange networks. *International Studies of Management and Organisation*, **17** (1), 3–23.

Kanter, R. M. (1994). Collaborative advantage: the art of alliances. *Harvard Business Review*, **72** (4), 96–108. Boston, MA: HBR Publications.

Kraljic, P. (1983). Purchasing must become supply management. *Harvard Business Review*, September–October, **61** (5), 109–17.

Lamming, R. (1993). *Beyond Partnership Strategies for Innovation and Lean Supply*. Hemel Hempstead: Prentice-Hall.

Lui, H. and McGoldrick, P. J. (1996). International retail sourcing: trend, nature and process. *Journal of International Marketing*, **4** (4), 9–33.

Lysons, K. (2000). *Purchasing and Supply Chain Management*, 5th edn. London: Financial Times/Prentice-Hall.

Macbeth, D. K. and Ferguson, N. (1990). Strategic aspects of supply chain management. *Paper Presented at OMA-UK Conference on Manufacturing Strategy – Theory and Practice*. Warwick, June.

Marshal, A. (1923). *Industry and Trade*. London: Macmillan.

McIvor, R. T., Humphreys, P. K. and McAleer, W. E. (1997). A strategic model for the formulation of an effective make or buy decision. *Management Decision*, **35** (2), 169–78. ISSN 0025-1747. Bradford: MCB University Press.

Merli, G. (1991). *Co-Makership*. Cambridge, MA: Productivity Press.

Miles, R. and Snow, C. (1987). Network organisations: new concepts for new forms. *California Management Review*, **28** (3), 62–73.

Mitchell (1973). quoted in Johannison, B. (1987). Beyond process and structure: social exchange networks. *International Studies of Management and Organisation*, **17** (1), 3–23.

Montgommery-Garret, E. (1994). Outsourcing to the max. *Small Business Reports (USA)*, **19** (8), August.

Nishiguchi, T. (1993). *Strategic Industrial Sourcing: The Japanese Advantage*. Oxford: Oxford University Press.

Smitka, M. (1991). *Competitive Ties: Subcontracting in the Japanese Automotive Industry*. New York: Columbia University Press.

Stevens, G. C. (1989). Integrating the supply chain. *International Journal of Physical Distribution and Materials Management*, **19** (8), 3–8.

Syson, R. (1992). *Improving Purchase Performance*. London: Pitman.

Szarka, J. (1990). Networking and small firms. *International Small Business Journal*, **8** (2), 10–22.

van Weele, A. and Rozemeijer, F. (2001). The role of power in partnership relationships: an empirical investigation of the current body of knowledge. In *Best Practice Procurement: Public and Private Sector Perspectives*, (Erridge, A., Fee, R. and McIlroy, J., eds.). Aldershot: Gower, pp. 90–100.

Wheelright, S. C. and Clark, K. B. (1992). *Revolutioning Product Development*. New York: Free Press.

Womack, J. P. and Jones, D. T. (1994). From lean production to the lean enterprise. *Harvard Business Review*, March–April, **27** (2), 93–103. Boston, MA: HBR Press.

Womack, J. P., Jones, D. T. and Roos, D. (1990). *The Machine that Changed the World*. London: Macmillan.

Chapter 7

Supply chain integration and e-business strategies

LEARNING OUTCOMES

The purpose of this chapter is to develop your knowledge and understanding of the key business issues relating to supply chain management and e-business. In particular after studying this chapter you should be able to:

- recognize the importance of supply chain integration and how it is enabled through ICT;
- know and understand the opportunities for synchronization, collaboration and joint product developments;
- understand the opportunities and risks involved in electronic supply networks;
- apply integration and e-business concepts to design and plan appropriate supply chain strategies including CRM approaches.

e-Business and supply chain management – an introduction

The biggest impact that the Internet has had on commercial life so far is in restructuring the ways in which organizations communicate both internally and externally. Many organizations have established intranets (in effect a mini-Internet) to share information throughout their own organization which may be established at different geographical locations. For example, most universities have their own intranets that connect a number of different departments and locations. Large commercial organizations have also established their own internal networks (intranets). Organizations link their own intranets to establish extranets and virtual private networks (VPNs) allowing suppliers and customers secure access to their own internal networks. For example, documents such as orders, specifications, despatch notes, invoices, credit and debit notes are just a selection that can be exchanged electronically. This can reduce the time taken to process orders and cash payments.

The standard language used by the computers linked via the Internet is called Internet Protocol (IP). Telecom and cable providers have also invested in IP telephony that allows digitized voice, compressing it, cutting it up into data packets and transmitting it across a data network to be reassembled for reception at the destination. Data transmission now exceeds voice transmission over telephone lines with documents, e-mails, visual images (jpeg, mpeg, TV, video), music on demand and video conferencing changing the balance of traffic. The technical barriers are slowly being removed. The developments in broadband transmission with asymmetric digital subscriber lines (ADSLs) delivery allowing faster and larger volumes of data to travel over the networks has improved data transmission speeds.

Blue tooth technologies

Electrolux has already established a fridge with a bar code scanner and a built-in modem to order replenishment products directly from a supplier over the Internet as householders consume stocks. It is not just businesses that are benefiting. Online grocery sales will rise from £165 million in 1999 to a projected £2.3 billion by 2004. As 'blue tooth' technologies develop and are used by more household gadgets it is not impossible to envisage a world where grocery replenishment can be done automatically. The various electronic sensors fitted in household storage facilities will be co-ordinated by the household master computer which may issue instructions to your local retail stores. In effect an automatic KANBAN controlled by domestic 'blue tooth' equipment.

Business benefits of e-commerce

Cisco Systems (www.cisco.com) state that one in seven smaller- and medium-sized enterprises (SMEs) are currently using the Internet to sell products, deliver services or cut procurement costs. Sixty three per cent of all UK businesses use the Internet. In the US the Boston Consulting Group (www.bcg.com) estimate that companies using e-procurement strategies have cut their material costs by 15 per cent and transaction costs by up to 65 per cent.

Organizations adopt an e-business strategy for one or more of the following reasons:

- To have a corporate presence;
- To have a brand presence;
- To provide information about the organization or its products;
- To create an online market where suppliers and customers can link with the organization either for informational reasons and/or for transactional reasons. One recent statistic from *Forrester Research* stated that 80 per cent of companies in the US have websites but less than 20 per cent were doing any form of e-commerce. You have to be aware that these estimates are exactly that, and that many reports on this topic provide conflicting statistics – so be careful when using them. Also the area is developing and changing daily, so what's true today may not be true tomorrow. This in mind a few Internet sites worth visiting to keep up-to-date are:

    www.emarketer.com
    www.idc.com
    www.bcg.com
    www.kpmg.co.uk
    www.forrester.com

- Marketing and advertising;
- To generate sales;
- To go direct to the consumer avoiding usual distribution channels;
- To provide customer support;
- To allow customer feedback;
- Research;
- Recruitment;
- Internal efficiencies in administration and communication;
- Training;
- To provide sales force support.

Many of the reasons given assume supply chain efficiency exists. Many of the original pure dot.com companies did not succeed because they underestimated the capabilities required by organizations to fulfil the customer promise. This aspect of business is often referred to as the 'back-office' as such the back-office does not get the attention that high visibility front end operations get. Nevertheless, it is important to recognize the critical importance of these supply chain management activities. It is no coincidence that those organizations that have achieved success in B2C markets have been the traditional bricks and mortar retailers who have developed their e-business strategies as part of an integrated and mixed-channel management strategy.

Some retail sites worth viewing if you haven't already are:

www.amazon.com
www.amazon.co.uk
www.barnesandnoble.com
www.jcpenney.com
www.nordstrom.com
www.food.com
www.llbean.com
www.landsend.com
www.wal-mart.com

Figure 7.1 illustrates the possible opportunities that could lead to benefits for organizations employing e-supply chain strategies. The diagram shows an Ishikawa diagram (cause and effect) leading to strategies competing for the future. The context is a retail organization locked in a supply chain with suppliers and manufacturers who supply them with goods and services to satisfy retail customers at some future position. Design and technical considerations can all be influenced by e-supply chain strategies selected by the retail organization. The retailer may require their suppliers to use particular technologies to communicate information with them and other supply chain organizations. Using the

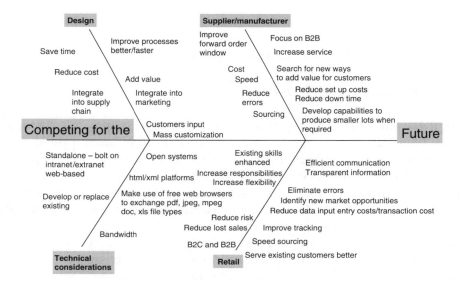

Benefits and opportunities from e-supply chain strategies

Figure 7.1

Internet to transmit design information and specifications can cut time out of the supply system. Technical considerations include choice of technologies, software and platforms to exchange standard data. A retailer may use a large ERP system provider like SAP or i2 and it may expect suppliers to invest in systems and technologies that link with their technology in order to achieve integrated systems. On the other hand it may choose to offer links into the system using open web-based platforms requiring little investment. The biggest opportunities created by e-supply chain strategies are risk reduction through postponement possible through time saved in communications (sourcing, sampling, purchasing and co-ordinating processes between the various supply chain partners).

Nike shoes fly on to the shelves

In February 2001 Nike were experiencing difficulties with their new demand and supply software which they had purchased as part of a $400 million overhaul. The brand was forced to airlift shoes to get the latest designs into store. Revenues in the quarter were expected to be $80–100 million short of forecast with a knock on effect on profitability. The company said it would take 6–9 months to get inventories down to normal levels.

Source: FT, 28 February 2001.

Looking upstream – a consumer perspective

Front end supply chain activities

At the front end of any supply chain is the customer. The customer may be a B2B customer where goods and services are supplied from one business to another business. The customer may also be a consumer of the product. For example, in retail markets people buy goods from high street stores and supermarkets often with the intention of consuming those goods themselves individually or by their family members or in the case of gifts their friends. The consumer of the product is the final link in any supply chain. The terminology used by supply chain professionals is 'upstream' moving away from the consumer to a retailer, onto their supplier, manufacturer, raw material provider until the primary source is reached, e.g. farm, mine, chemical plant.

'Downstream' is the reverse movement from the original source through to final consumer. Consumer issues are examined in relation to e-supply chains in the next section.

Some benefits of e-commerce to the consumer

- Presents an environment in which the descriptions and prices for a range of goods and services can be compared quickly and easily, e.g. books, records, clothing, travel and accommodation. This has been referred to as the 'commodotization' process meaning that such comparisons effectively turn the buying process into commodity purchases.
- May speed up transactions.
- Reduce time spent on shopping important for time-poor but cash-rich consumers
- Reduce delivery times.
- Convenience of home delivery removing the need to visit stores, i.e. virtual shopping rather than physical shopping.
- Creates a more competitive marketplace as information transforms the market allowing consumers to make more informed choices about their purchases by being able to search and find a larger variety of competing products and services.
- Competition in turn creates lower prices.

Secure payment systems

One issue in particular is often put forward as a barrier to the uptake of B2C e-business – the risk of presenting credit card details for payment online. It is interesting to note that Amazon UK reports that fax and phone payments represent 0.75 and 2.5 per cent of transactions, respectively, the remainder being online credit card payments. One explanation for this might be that the customer segment has a broad knowledge of the underlying technology and have reached a conclusion that the risks are no higher than paying with a credit card in a restaurant when the waiter disappears with your card for a few moments or in paying over a telephone when you give your personal details to an unknown telesales person. Perhaps there is no such thing as a perfect security system. Nevertheless, encryption systems protecting consumers have become more sophisticated. Encryption codes scramble the data so that they cannot be read or tampered with by anyone not authorized. Netscape developed the principle of secure socket layering (SSL) which is in effect a private key – your personal digital signature. There are also digital certificates, issued to companies alongside a public key that confirm websites and transactions are valid. These certificates are only issued after scrutiny and are changed regularly to prevent 'hackers' and fraudsters accessing the data. Your browser will recognize and alert you when a site is not secure. In such circumstances the person can make a reasonable judgement whether to proceed or not with the transaction. Digital certificates and signatures form the basis of an emerging standard for VISA and MasterCard known as SET (secure electronic transmission) which they use to verify transaction data.

Safeguarding deals on the net

The British Chambers of Commerce announced an electronic signature system that will authenticate anyone who does business over the Internet. The new security system should allow more than 13 million companies in Britain and Europe to trade safely with each other over the net. It will be possible for a firm to transact business with a customer who has signed documents electronically and be confident that the signature is genuine. The launch coincided with the British government's Electronic Communications Bill which will give electronic signatures the same status in law as handwritten signatures.

The top 10 visited sites in the UK as reported by Connectis, Issue 3, May 2000 published by the Financial Times (see www.ft.com/connectis) (see Table 7.1):

1. www.yahoo.co.uk Internet portal
2. www.msn.co.uk Internet portal
3. www.microsoft.com Software supplier
4. www.freeserve.co.uk ISP
5. www.lycos.co.uk Internet portal
6. www.aol.com ISP
7. www.excite.co.uk Internet portal
8. www.demon.net ISP
9. www.tripod.lycos.com Community
10. www.altavista.com Internet portal

In 1999 B2C e-commerce in the US was estimated to be worth $507 billion. There were 40 million shoppers. $1.1 billion was spent on apparel representing 1 per cent of the total apparel market and it is worth noting that this figure although still small was double that of the previous

Table 7.1 Some facts about Internet usage

	UK	*US*
Corporate		
Per cent of companies with websites	51	54
Per cent of companies selling via the www	9	12
Value of goods sold online in 1999 (£m)	5300	15 300
Per cent of companies with intranets	30	29
Per cent of companies with extranets	5	8
Consumer		
PC penetration at home per cent of population	37.3	51
Online penetration per cent of population	26.6	39
No. of people with Internet access (millions)	9.8	70.1
Mobile phone penetration per cent of consumers	42.9	32
Per cent of Internet users who shop online	34.8	28.4

Source: Connectis, Issue 3, May 2000, pp. 4–5.

year, i.e. 1998. The 35–44-year-old demographic comprises the single-most slice of the online apparel market accounting for 41 per cent of 1999 online sales. In contrast they make up only 25 per cent of total apparel sales (including catalogue and store sales). Twenty-five to thirty-four-year-olds represent 24 per cent of the online market for apparel. More affluent households – those earning over $70 000 – are also disproportionately represented among the online apparel buyers. These households accounted for 61 per cent of the total dollar spend online in comparison to just 38 per cent of total apparel spending for the year 1999. In 2000 US business trade on the net was estimated to reach $250 billion up from $110 billion in 1999. US online revenues doubled from around $20 billion in 1999 to $40 billion in 2000. Currently 57 per cent of all www users speak English. However, the proportion of non-English speakers is set to grow and the balance of English speakers was estimated to have fallen to 43 per cent in 2002. The US currently accounts for 69 per cent of total e-commerce revenues worldwide but the rest of the world is seeing significant growth. Nevertheless, it is expected that the US will remain a dominant force because there are fewer constraints to growth such as prohibitive access cost, insufficient bandwidth and regulatory barriers.

Internet retailing in Britain soared to £2.5 billion over the Christmas period 2003 (November £1.2 billion + December 1.3 billion = £2.52 billion), 70 per cent up on 2002. It represented 7 per cent of all retail sales over the period. The following table lists the top 10 UK sites and the most popular online products sold.

Top UK retail sites 2003 and most popular products

Rank	Name	Domain	Market share %		Most popular products
1	e Bay UK	ebay.co.uk	25.9	1	Digital cameras
2	Amazon	amazon.co.uk	8.2	2	Mobile phones
3	Argos	argos.co.uk	2.3	3	DVD players
4	e Bay Shops UK	ebayshops.co.uk	2.2	4	Standard TVs
5	Kelkoo.UK	uk.kelkoo.com	2.1	5	Camcorders
6	Play.com	play.com	1.6	6	Watches
7	Tesco.com	tesco.com	1.6	7	Flat panel TV
8	Argos Entertainment	argos-entertainment.co.uk	1.0	8	Women's fragrances
9	Comet	comet.co.uk	1.0	9	Lingerie & hosiery
10	Dealtime UK	dealtime.co.uk	1.0	10	MP3 and digital media players

Source: www.hitwise.com – *The Sunday Times* Business, p. 3, 18 January 2004.

One interesting trend is the development of Wireless Internet as Jean Paul Votron, Director of International Consumer Banking at ABN Amro remarked:

> Mobile is the key revolution. This whole perception that e-commerce equals the computer is . . . . . . misguided. The future of e-commerce is the mobile telephony.

Good news for Europe?

According to the European Union statistics it has one of the highest cell phone penetration rates in the world (see Table 7.2).

European B2B is expected to be worth one trillion dollars in 2004 according to Durlacher (see www.emarketer.com/estats). In 1999 this market was worth $33 million. Cumulative average growth rates are forecast at 107 per cent per annum until 2004 reaching $1.3 trillion; Germany ($438 billion), UK ($301 billion), France ($149 billion) and the Netherlands ($78 billion). B2B would then account for 12.7 per cent of GDP in the EU 15 moving it on from its 1999 position at 1 per cent.

Reasons for consumers failing to buy online

Research by the Boston Consulting Group (BCG) found that 28 per cent of consumers' purchase efforts 'failed' when they could not find products

Table 7.2 Cell phone penetration

	%
Finland	64.4
Sweden	60.3
Italy	44.2
Denmark	43.1
Luxembourg	36.9
Austria	35.7
UK	32.2
Portugal	29.9
Greece	29.3
Ireland	28.3
US	25.01

Source: eGlobal Report, March 2000.

they wanted, couldn't finish their transactions or did not complete their purchase to their satisfaction. BCG surveyed 12 000 North American consumers in the fourth quarter of 1999, including 10 000 who had made online purchases. As can be seen in Table 7.3, the most commonly cited problems were:

48 per cent said pages took too long to load;
45 per cent couldn't find what they wanted;
32 per cent product not available or out of stock;
26 per cent system crashed.

Table 7.3 Incidence of online purchasing problems reported by BCG

Per cent of online shoppers experiencing problems sometimes or frequently

Pages took too long to load – I gave up	48
Site was so confusing I couldn't find what I wanted	45
Desired product not available/in stock	32
System crashed got logged off before completion	26
Hard to contact customer service	20
Product took much longer than expected to arrive	15
Returned the product	10
Site would not accept a credit card	9
Tried and failed to contact customer service	8
Site made unauthorized charges to my credit card	5
Ordered product which never arrived	4
Wrong product arrived and couldn't return it	4

Source: BCG.

The study found:

- that consumers expect site homepages to load within 13.2 seconds;
- they expect to find a product or service within 5.8 seconds;
- to complete an online order form within 4.5 seconds;
- and receive shipment within 6.4 days;
- 28 per cent of shoppers who have suffered a failed purchase attempt said they have ceased to shop on the website where they experienced problems;
- 6 per cent said they had stopped shopping from that organization's stores offline;
- 57 per cent of Internet users have shopped online;
- 51 per cent have actually purchased goods or services;
- the typical buyer will spend $460 online over a 1-year period in ten transactions;
- consumers typically have favourite sites and most users visit fewer than ten sites on a regular basis.

BCG consultant David Pecaut cautions that sites must recognize that today's average user may not be very experienced and that Internet shoppers may be amateurs. BCG divides the user population into three types of consumer:

1. 23.2 million who have been online for 3 years or more (pioneers);
2. 39.6 million who have been online between 1 and 3 years (early followers); and
3. the rest who have been online within the last year (first of the masses).

There have also been some dramatic failures in the B2C market that may have dampened some of the early confidence of consumers and suppliers alike. Both Boo.com and Letsbuyit.com exited the market after investing millions to create pure dot.com suppliers direct to consumer markets.

e-Fulfilment

On the supply side the biggest problem for suppliers has been e-fulfilment. This is especially the case for pure 'clicks and clicks' dot.com organizations. Traditional 'bricks and mortar' companies who have established a 'bricks and click' offering have tended to succeed better with their fulfilment. In particular those retail organizations that had experience of catalogue retailing were far more ready than even they realized to compete effectively in the world of e-business because they already had established supply chains.

B2B

Business-to-business (B2B) e-commerce offers many benefits to organizations incorporating the technologies within their supply chain strategies. The technology has evolved rapidly in recent years. Figure 7.2 illustrates the major changes. There have been rapid developments in the marketplace driven by the technological innovations over a short period of time which has created opportunities for organizations to move from simply EDI to e-procurement and to B2B e-markets. New entrants to the market can often avoid the cost of legacy systems by investing in new technologies. Although the technological developments have been evolutionary the opportunities for organizations wanting to develop appropriate e-supply chain strategies can be revolutionary. Technological innovations allow firms to 'breakthrough'. Furthermore, opportunities are not just for large firms as relative cost falls and standard web-based platforms (adopting XML) replace older bespoke technologies B2B opportunities are democratized and available to a wider business community including small firms. The next section discusses some of these opportunities.

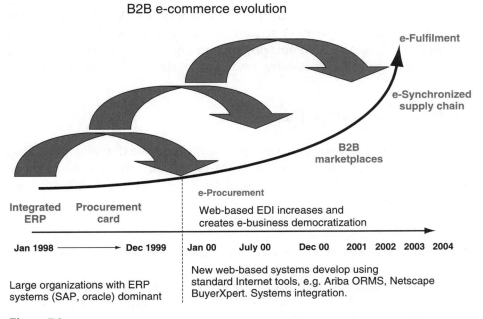

Figure 7.2

e-Supply chain opportunities

A number of areas have been identified where e-business developments have facilitated opportunities for better supply chain management. These areas are:

- Collaborative demand planning between retailers and manufacturers of products;
- Synchronized production planning;
- Joint product development between buyers and sellers;
- Better logistics planning with warehouses and freight carriers;
- e-Procurement;
- Auctions/reverse auctions;
- e-Marketplaces;
- Bar coding and EDI;
- Intranets/extranets and VPNs.

Each opportunity will now be discussed in the context of enterprising supply chain management.

Collaborative demand planning between customers and suppliers

Collaborative demand planning has been made possible in recent years through the development of ICT such as those explained later in this chapter (intranet, extranet and VPNs). Collaborative planning allows the retailer and their suppliers to acquire real-time or forecast demand data and to plan their procurement, production and supply activities in such a way to minimize stock-holding and meet customer demand efficiently.

Synchronized production planning

Synchronization is a similar concept to collaborative demand planning. The idea is to synchronize all aspects of the supply chain to ensure that goods are produced on time. Simultaneously stock-holding can be minimized.

Joint product development between buyers and sellers

One of the biggest opportunities for achieving a more efficient supply chain has been the development of products jointly. This type of co-operation can significantly reduce the time it takes to get a new product to market. It also allows the partners to co-operate to iron out any faults and modify product designs as the product develops.

Better logistics planning with warehouses and freight carriers

Better logistics planning is possible with the development of improving ICT. Carriers are able to plan their activities to maximize efficiency of deliveries and to minimize their costs. Moving goods around supply chains is a very costly business. The principles have to be move it once, don't double handle and make sure the goods get to the right place at the right time.

Planning loads, tracking goods and ensuring compliance with transport, health and safety legislation is essential. Because logistics is quite a specialist activity and can be a substantial cost to any business many organizations have decided to outsource the activity and contract third-party providers. The benefits of contracting third-party suppliers of logistics can include:

- Professional planning with the specialist providers operating the latest software and hardware to help plan and control activities.
- Experience from a number of contracts developed through time provides you with expertise you may find it difficult to buy-in or develop.
- Costs are certain since the contract will specify what the third party will be paid for the service.
- Risks are removed, e.g. cost of owning, insuring, maintaining and managing your own fleet, warehousing and storage are removed along with those costs which could be less predictable than those of third-party contracts.
- Many logistics providers now also offer additional services, e.g. quality control, ticketing, labelling and packaging.
- Specialist logistics firms have the latest technology to track deliveries, e.g. satellite tracking.

e-Procurement

e-Procurement is an important opportunity for businesses to speed up, get what they want and get better value for money. Electronic procurement is conducted in a number of ways. Some e-procurement simply moves the paper-based systems to electronic paperless systems using the Internet to transmit the order documents and the various other documents involved in the purchasing and supply cycle. However, one of the major benefits of e-procurement is that the buyer can search the world for supplies from their desktop or laptop computers. This allows a customer to search supplier catalogues around the globe. It is important that suppliers pay attention to their catalogue data and keep their Internet sites user-friendly and up-to-date.

Some major benefits can accrue from e-procurement which include:

- Direct ordering through the Internet;
- Reduced lead times and reduced delivery times;
- Reduced stock-holding through faster replenishment;
- Remove administrative overheads by allowing direct purchases to be made by authorized personnel;
- Automated approval and workflow;
- Combined purchasing;
- Price transparency.

Typical purchase categories where e-procurement is used:

- IT equipment – computers and peripherals;
- Furniture;
- Office equipment, copiers, stationery;
- Telecomms equipment;
- Electronics components;
- Electrical goods;
- Magazines;
- Flowers;
- Production supply;
- Marketing;
- Canteen supplies;
- Maintenance equipment, components and staff;
- Building equipment;
- Tradesmen (e.g. fitters, electricians, joiners, painters);
- Vehicles;
- Art;
- Giftware;
- Travel (air, sea, rail, automobile) and hotel accommodation;
- Conferences and conference facilities;
- Education;
- Consultants;
- Temporary workers.

Figure 7.3 illustrates new capabilities acquired through e-procurement, benefits and financial impact on buyers using e-procurement strategies.

It is claimed by Accenture management consultants that e-procurement can give rise to benefits through lowering supply costs by between 3 and 20 per cent depending on the maturity of the e-procurement system. As organizations become better at e-procurement more benefits accrue.

However, some of the more interesting purchasing and supply developments in many B2B situations has been the development of auctions and reverse auctions to procure goods and services.

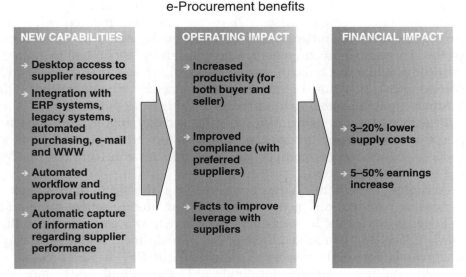

e-Procurement benefits

e-Procurement lowers operating costs by increasing purchasing productivity

Figure 7.3

Auctions

Auctions can take place through electronic networks such as the Internet in a similar way to the way in which they take place in physical space 'auction rooms'. A seller places an item for sale and prospective customers place their bid. The only difference being the bid is made electronically to the seller. This has enabled many sellers to supply goods over the Internet at prices that often exceed what they might have sold the goods for had the seller fixed a price initially. In some situations customers have been able to get a lower price but it really does all depend on supply, demand and error-free or error-prone systems.

Reverse auctions

Reverse auctions are an interesting concept because instead of the buyer bidding a number of sellers bid to supply the customer. In some markets this is very efficient especially when the product required has a particular specification. This makes it easier for a customer to compare supplier offerings and achieve a best price. US company Textilebids.com apply the technique in the apparel sector. Paperexchange.com, Producenet.com are examples from other industries.

Companies spend approximately 60 per cent of revenues on goods and services. Their competitiveness depends on strategically managing procurement. Companies are searching for ways to reduce expenditures and improve sourcing practices. B2B exchanges have emerged with new procurement tools and technologies to meet the needs of these companies. Therefore e-procurement is valuable, but mostly limited to indirect spending, while the bulk of value lies in direct spend (materials and components). Traditional strategic sourcing needs to be enhanced with Internet capabilities in order to maximize value from this tool.

Procurement tools using web-based technology enable true *'dynamic pricing'*. Procurement groups can use this tool to implement *'reverse auctions'*, where sellers compete for procurement contracts bid-out by the buying organization.

Accepting bids online allows buyers to open the bid to more sellers – increasing competition. Increased competition among sellers can result in lower prices for the buyer. Sellers see where they are positioned in the marketplace, and can adjust their prices in real-time. Procurement contracts can be for goods or services, exactly like an RFQ or RFP process.

Online bidding is suitable for goods and services with one or more of the following criteria:

- Well-defined and well-understood specification;
- Relatively standardized product (commodity or near commodity);
- Time-sensitive (producer will be prepared to reduce prices as an expiry date approaches, e.g. airline seats, perishable goods).

Savings on average of 20–30 per cent can be achieved through reverse auctions. The stages involved in the process are to:

- identify the opportunity;
- clearly defined and understood specification;
- recognize that the process is only suitable for standardized products (commodity or near commodity);
- only suitable when the product or service is time-sensitive (producer will be prepared to reduce prices as an expiry date approaches, e.g. airline seats, hotel bookings and perishable goods)

Figure 7.4 illustrates the change in price occurring during a reverse auction over the period of 1 hour. Competing sellers force prices down adding value for the buyer in the process of bidding.

Electronic data interchange

Electronic data interchange (EDI) is simply a generic term for the exchange of different types of information between parties using electronic

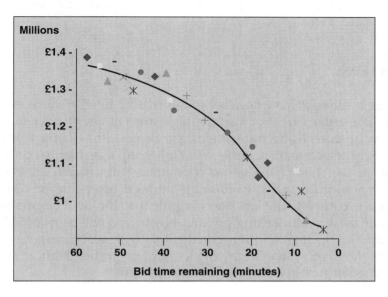

Online auctions deliver value – fast

Figure 7.4
Note: The symbols in figure 7.4 represent different suppliers bidding in the online auction. For example the winning bid entered at £1.3 million and won the bid when the price had fallen to £250 000.

networks. The most common forms of EDI have been exchanges using bar code technologies, e-mails and electronic document exchanges.

Bar coding

Bar codes began to appear on a wide range of products sold through supermarkets in the 1980s. Prior to that it was very difficult to keep track of stock movements from distribution centres to store and onto customers. With the emergence of bar code technology it was possible to track stock movements throughout the retail supply chain. Retailing Management Information Systems (MIS) provide an opportunity for the retailer to:

- gain control over the supply chain;
- utilize in-store space more efficiently by stocking only those lines that are moving quickly;
- identify effective in-store sales locations for particular goods;
- EPoS systems allow low stock-holding;
- EPoS means rapid replenishment of fast moving stock items;
- EPoS allows the identification of slow moving stocks;

- electronic funds transfer at point of sale (EFTPoS) allows the rapid exchange of goods for funds from the customer (e.g. switch cards, smart cards, etc).

EDI and EPoS

Retailing businesses have been revolutionized by EPoS systems. Next time you enter a supermarket or visit the high street stores observe the way in which your purchasing transactions are dealt with. Goods will usually have a bar code on them and the sales assistant passes that bar code over a scanner at the checkout. The bar code holds information on stock item identification, price and store location amongst other things. When your purchase is complete the stock account for the store will be updated, the difference between the selling price and cost price will be recorded to furnish profit on the item and if needs the item will be automatically replenished by the EPoS system triggering a re-order. Further consider the types of information such systems can provide instantly:

- sales by stock item (stock code);
- sales by department;
- sales by store;
- sales by in-store area location;
- fast moving stock items;
- slow moving stock items (items to delete);
- hourly or daily or weekly sales;
- sales by customer;
- sales by staff or till location;
- overs and shorts reports;
- inventory analysis;
- trigger automatic replenishment orders;
- analysis of exception reporting;
- profitability/contribution by stock item;
- transaction type: cash, credit card, switch card, cheque, etc.

Computers allow a company to locate a product in its warehouse, to devise a delivery schedule, which makes the most efficient use of its vehicle fleet, and to track a consignment on its way to its final destination. Managing the supply chain can lead to considerable reductions in the amounts of stock which have to be held. This efficiency enables firms to save money tied up in working capital. Concentrating all of a company's delivery activities in one centre not only reduces the levels of stock, which have to be held, but also means that a wider range of stock is available to customers and allows the distribution centre to add extra services.

Radio frequency identification – power within the supply chain

'Information is power' is a quote attributed to an anonymous Roman General. Supply chain managers are relearning lessons of the past. It is no accident that the power balance within retail supply chains has shifted towards the retailer in the latter part of the twentieth and beginning of the twenty-first century. This has happened because retailers have become prominent in the chain by managing the information for the whole chain. Developments from bar coding and scanners, their increasing capability to gather vast amounts of customer data and use it to target promotional activity, develop new markets and new products and their ability to learn from their retail customers have been contributing factors to their increasing power.

The development of radio frequency identification (RFID) tags has enabled some retailers to experiment with how they can use customer data to generate even more sales. Forrester Research (2003) estimate that there will be 500 billion plus radio frequency chips contained in consumer products and that they will allow suppliers to track products through the supply chain creating visibility for the customer. Payment devices may include watches and mobile phones and they too will have RFID chips that can authorize payment at the checkout or wherever. RFIDs have the capability to revolutionize product and data management. Suppliers, logistics providers and retailers can enter their data via the RFID and they can track progress of the item from start of the supply chain through to the end consumer. RFIDs also have potential to be used by marketers to target particular customer segments and individual customers or micromarkets using the data gathered en route. RFIDs are destined to replace bar code technology and have a number of significant advantages over bar codes which are shown in Table 7.4.

RFIDs currently cost around 20 cents but are expected to fall in the near future as they become more widely used to around 5 cents. In 1994 these tags cost around $1, so you can see how costs have fallen as the technology improves and usage increases.

Drapers Record (2003) reported that Marks and Spencer UK launched a trial of radio frequency identification devices in Menswear at its High Wycombe store in October 2003. If successful they hope to expand the technology to other ranges and stores. In the United States there is a consumer pressure group called CASPIAN (consumers against supermarket privacy, invasion and numbering).

Table 7.4

Bar codes	RFIDs
Identify the SKU only	Identified individual items within a SKU not just the SKU
Can be written to only once	Data can be read from and written to the RFID as many times as you like
Contain only small amount of data 12–15 characters	Can store hundreds of characters of data
Readers use light emitting diodes (LEDs) to scan codes	Readers scan radio signals from the tag
Hand-held and fixed-point scanners have to be close and in line of sight to work properly	Readers can be anywhere; they do not have to be in close proximity but within a specified range and they do not have to be in line of sight
Currently has a cost advantage	Slightly more expensive

Source: Adapted from Forrester Research and author's own research (2003).

Intranets/extranets, VPNs and supply chains

Intranets are internal computer networks. Intranets may link different departments or different functional areas of the business. For example, an intranet might be established to link financial accounting with purchasing and sales departments to exchange data about customers, procurement, payments and receipts.

Extranets are similar networks of computers but they involve external organizations and allow them to access part or all of the company's internal network from remote locations. For example, suppliers and customers may be allowed secure access to an organization's system to check on production, to bid for orders, to check product specifications, to submit tenders, to invoice the company and so on. Extranets usually require the external organizations to have a password and ensuring security by having appropriate 'firewalls'.

Virtual private networks (VPNs) are networks that are restricted between organizations that want to share certain types of information between a number of organizations who are allowed to access the network. VPNs may be more secure than extranets but act in a similar manner sharing electronic data between the parties. VPNs were developed earlier than the extranets, which use Internet technologies and commonly used software based around HTML or XML code.

The purpose of these different networks is to make links between:

- Different parts of the same organization – intranet;
- Different organizations – extranets sometimes regarded as less secure;
- Different organizations – VPNs sometimes regarded as more secure.

These technological networks have enabled organizations to better manage their supply chain. Figure 7.5 illustrates the place of the Internet, intranets, extranets and VPNs in organizational relationships.

Benefits to SME suppliers

These supply chain opportunities are no longer simply available to large organizations. Smaller- and medium-sized enterprises (SMEs) can benefit from being part of an electronic supply chain network especially if they are efficient. Some of the most important benefits that SMEs are able to receive are:

- Acquire customer demand data through the network;
- Tender to supply;
- Bid for orders through reverse auctioning;
- Acquire data regarding specifications a customer makes available;

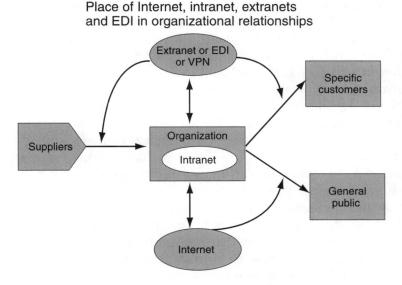

Figure 7.5

- Share information between the customer and themselves to mutual benefit;
- Bill their customers electronically;
- Receive payments electronically;
- Reduce lead times;
- Reduce sampling and development times;
- Reduce production cycle times.

Customer relationship management

The basic premise of CRM is to match a product or service with the needs of the customer. CRM is regarded by many as a natural extension to 'precision marketing'. It is also regarded as a means of creating a single cohesive view of the customer. CRM processes may be managed through specialized software that are in effect building 'data warehouses' and extracting specific information through 'data mining'. The basic concept is that, however, a customer approaches an organization be it by telephone, through the Internet or in person they are recognized by the organization and an intelligent response is made. For example, a customer may visit a retail store to browse or to purchase. If they have previously purchased the organization will have a record of the customer's details and transactions within their data warehouse (i.e. part of their MkIS); as a consequence when the customer makes contact on future occasions the customer's history is known to the different contact points within that organization. The information can be used to develop sales and build a long-term relationship of offering the customer new products and services that become available that are clearly matched to their requirements (stored within the data warehouse). One of the prospective benefits advocated by CRM is that it makes mass customization a reality. An organization is now able to seriously adopt micromarketing to target customers by offering them customized products and services made possible through information.

Organizations have an ever-increasing number of ways of communicating with their customers. These include: direct response mail, call centres, branches in various locations, sales force, help desks, websites, electronic kiosks and digital television. However, each of these systems tells only part of the story. To understand the complete relationship an organization has to link these separate parts. CRM is the concept that synthesizes these individual strands. CRM software companies are attempting to provide the means to link the parts into a total relationship marketing system. Customers are increasingly expecting organizations to recognize who they are, however they might approach the organization. This provides the organization with a single integrated view of the customer, their needs and how they interact with the organization. In summary the back-office is the 'data warehouse' and the front office is CRM systems and procedures.

CRM defined

CRM is a business philosophy, a set of strategies, programmes and enabling systems that focus upon identifying and building customer loyalty with the prime objective being to squeeze additional value from higher spenders – the retailer's most valued customers. It is in effect a simple acknowledgement of the Pareto concept whereby 80 per cent of the lifetime value from customers may be attributable to 20 per cent of your customer base. As an example, traditionally retailers simply encouraged customers to visit their stores, look through catalogues and more recently visit their websites usually with the main objective being to drive footfall into their bricks and mortar stores. Mass media advertising and price promotions were the main marketing weapons in the armoury. Push promotions when sales fall flat, markdown prices rapidly to shift stock and advertise to everybody who could possibly buy from you. 'Exclusively for everyone' perhaps says it all.

Figure 7.6 represents customer interactions with the retail organization. Customers can interact through different communication channels as indicated. The organization has to develop capabilities to present a

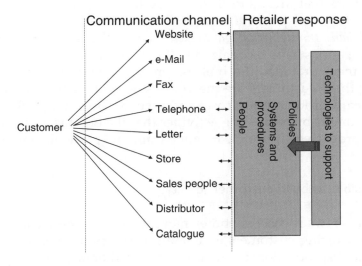

Figure 7.6

consistent response to customers. Policies, systems and procedures need to be consistent across the different channels. Policies, systems and procedures can be supported in this objective by the retail organization having technologies to support each of the channel interactions. For example, when a customer makes an e-mail enquiry it is logged on the system together with the response given. If or when the customer makes a follow up enquiry by telephone, in-store or through the website the information is retrievable by the person handling the enquiry and they know what the previous responses by other personnel in their organization were. CRM is the collective term for this concept of being able to manage customer relationships effectively and efficiently. CRM enables consistency in communicating with customers. The benefit to the supplier in being consistent is that the customer is less likely to receive misinformation and the customer is likely to be dealt with equitably through any channel. Customer attrition rates are likely to be lower as a consequence and it is hoped that the customer will become loyal as a result of consistent standards over time through dealing with the supplier and developing trust. A second major benefit of CRM is for the supplying organization to identify:

(a) How customers interact with the organization;
(b) What they purchase;
(c) How often they purchase;
(d) When they purchase;
(e) How they pay.

Combining these data can enable a supplier to segment customers and target offers that are more likely to be taken up by their customers. *Thus the two most powerful commercial reasons for adopting CRM are to develop loyalty through trust and to identify profitable customer segments.*

Organizations have recognized that in many cases a small proportion of customers provides the bulk of profit. Identifying, collecting and keeping these customers are the very essence of CRM. ABC and ABM are a means of identifying costs and revenue streams attached to specific customers by measuring activities that the organization has to perform in order to generate the revenue from that particular customer.

Is it possible to build customer loyalty?

Research shows it costs six times more to attract a new customer than to retain existing customers and small increases in retention rates can result in disproportionate increases in profitability. Identifying customers who are more profitable is the key to success as is recognizing that it may cost more money to deal with some customers, thus out-weighing the value of their potential revenue stream (Zeithaml et al., 2001). Supposing you can identify profitable customers and encourage them to be loyal it is likely to lead increasing turnover and profitability (Dowling and Uncles, 1997; Foss and Stone, 2001; Johnson, 2002). In theory loyal customers ignore competitor offerings, make repeat visits, are satisfied with their purchase experience and as a consequence spend more with the organization of choice during their lifetime relationship. Loyal customers are not rational consumers in the economic sense looking for the best value bargain. These customers are emotionally bonded with the supplier of choice according to the CRM literature (Foss and Stone, 2001). They feel positive about their experiences with that organization and encourage others to spend there too. The positive effect of 'word-of-mouth' recommendations can be of great benefit.

The CRM process

CRM is data-driven (Rigby et al., 2002). There are five basic steps in developing CRM:

1. Collect customer data.
2. Analyse customer data with the aim of identifying target customers.
3. Design CRM programmes to encourage emotional ties.
4. Implement the CRM programmes.
5. Evaluate the CRM programmes and adjust as appropriate.

Constructing a *customer database* is the first step. The database needs to hold a transaction history (purchase date, price paid, payment mode – cash, credit, visa, SKUs bought and additional data such as whether the purchase was part of a promotional response). It also needs to hold records of interactions that the customer has with the organization including visits to the retailer website, phone calls, inquiries through in-store kiosks, direct mail responses and personal interactions in store and with customer service departments. Customer preferences need to be established and recorded – likes, dislikes, colours, brands, fabrics, sizes, etc. Descriptive data using geo-demographic data (where they live and life-stage) or psychographic profiling (identifying lifestyles) are required too. These data can be used to segment customers differently. These customer data are held in the customer data warehouse. The data warehouse can be mined at different times and cut in different ways to target customers in different ways. For example, knowing the age, sex (29 male) and lifestyle (ski holiday purchase) of a particular customer may be important to target customers with specific categories (ski jackets, boots, skis).

Analysing data to identify profitable segments and target customers is the key. CRM planning activities should focus upon retaining existing customers and acquiring new customers. How often do we hear stories that existing customers are upset by offers only open to new customers? For example, zero rate interest on credit cards for new customers while existing customers are left with higher rates. Is it any wonder that the existing customers do not feel any loyalty to their credit card company? Financial service organizations are notorious for making crass offers that upset their existing customers. However, these same organizations spend a fortune developing CRM systems. So what does this tell us? CRM is a philosophy of doing business. It needs to be embedded in the organization's culture. CRM is not simply about purchasing software systems designed for the purpose; it requires people inside the organization at every level to be focused on the customer. They need to examine ways to enhance customer service levels to increase short- and long-term profitability. They need to ensure consistency and fairness in dealings with the customer that lead to trust and loyalty. They need to target profitable customers by being able to identify them and their particular requirements. Retailers must continuously evaluate how they interact with customers. CRM systems must be calibrated to supply chain strategies and systems.

Consumer power is becoming much stronger in retail marketing. Loyalty cards and retailers own credit cards make it much easier to track and gather customer data to discover spending habits (Mitchell, 2002). In turn these data on spending habits can more easily identify cross-category expenditures, which may be used by the retailers to construct different categories that they may not have realised, were related. For example, young couples purchasing baby products may also spend more on wine because they have to stay at home with the children (Russell and Petersen, 2000). Managing customer data in this way provides an opportunity to marketers to better target their offerings.

Does CRM really mean suppliers can get a bigger share of the customer's purse?

The answer to this question is yes, if and only if organizations buy into the philosophy of CRM. People inside the organization need to be trained to recognize opportunities, to have common sense in dealing with customers, to be empowered to respond effectively as well as consistently and not to rely too heavily on technology alone but use it to support decision-making. Some simple lessons in implementing CRM activities are:

- Target customers and prospects with clearly defined offers.
- Handle enquiries consistently and record interactions as soon as the prospect has shown interest in the offer. Track the interactions through

to purchase completion and after sales, if appropriate. Learn customer likes, dislikes and requirements, so you can satisfy them and increase profitability.

- Welcome new customers and get to know their requirements through data collection about their interactions with your organization.
- Identify profitable customers through clear segmentation.
- Handle complaints effectively, identify the causes and eradicate them as well as thank the complainant for acting as your unpaid consultant and reward them, if appropriate.
- Develop strategies to win back customers who become disaffected especially if they have been identified as belonging to a segment deemed to be profitable.
- Be prepared to lose unprofitable customers but be very sure first – have the information to hand.

Total global revenues generated by consultancy firms in CRM has risen from $2.3 billion in 1998 to $3.7 billion in 1999 and is expected to reach $16.8 billion in 2003 according to AMR Research. Large organizations offering CRM services include: IBM, Andersen, Cap Gemini, Oracle, NCR, Fiserv and SAS Institute.

Summary

This chapter has presented a perspective of e-business developments and their impact upon supply chain strategies. It began by examining the changes in technology and the impact upon B2C markets before turning attention to the implications for B2B markets and supply chain opportunities and potential problems. Fulfilling the customer promise has been a particular issues in e-business transactional models. The final part of the chapter considered specific opportunities for supply chain strategies related to e-business strategy. e-Procurement, collaborative planning, synchronization, auctions, EDI, CRM and RFID developments were all discussed. The next chapter moves on to assess cost, value and measurement in relation to supply chain strategies.

Discussion Questions

1. Explain why it is important for organizations to have in place e-business supply chain strategies.
2. What are the benefits of e-business to organizations designing supply chain strategies?

3. Discuss the consumer benefits of e-business supply chain strategies.
4. 'e-Business supply chain strategies are not always implemented smoothly.' Identify and discuss the reasons for this.
5. 'One major difficulty for pure dot.com organizations operating e-tail businesses was said to be their inability to fulfil the customer promise.' Discuss.
6. 'e-Business strategies present a number of supply chain opportunities for organizations.' Identify three opportunities and explain how organizations can benefit from developing appropriate e-supply chain strategies.
7. Compare and contrast the relative merits of bar codes *vis-à-vis* radio frequency identification tags as a means of controlling inventories.
8. Explain the major benefits that accrue to organizations adopting e-procurement strategies giving due consideration to any risks involved.
9. 'Auctions and reverse auctions are two online innovations that have captured the imagination of buyers and suppliers using e-business strategies.' Explain how each strategy works and the benefits of implementing such a business model for the customer.
10. 'CRM has many benefits for the supplying organization not least of which are reduced costs in doing business and a lifetime value stream.' Discuss.

Glossary of e-business terminology

ADSL   Asymmetric digital subscriber lines; this digital system delivery allows larger volumes of data to travel over the networks at faster transmission speeds.

Browser   Computer software that allows users to surf the Internet – MS Internet Explorer and Netscape are examples of browsers. You cannot easily access the worldwide web without the help of such software.

Domain name   The unique name that identifies an Internet site. Domain names always have two or more parts separated by dots. Examples are: cim.co.uk (co.uk denotes a commercial organization in the UK); y-not-shine.com (com denotes a commercial organization in the US and in other parts of the world); ncsu.edu (educational site in the US); amazon.com; textileinst.org.uk (a non-profit organization

	usually); mmu.ac.uk (a UK academic site); super.net (usually a private network).
DVD	Digital video disks.
Firewall	Computer hardware and/or software that restricts access to a computer network for security purposes.
HTML	Hyper text mark-up language.
Host	Any computer on a network that provides services to other computers on the network
Hyperlink or link	Coloured text or images that allow the user to point and click and by so doing move the user to another part of the same document, to a different document or even a different website. These links are navigational tools that help users find their way round with ease. Although it can be frustrating when the link takes you to an error message stating the document, part or site has moved or is no longer available.
ISP	Internet service provider.
Newsgroup	A discussion group categorized by subject that list 'postings' (messages) from newsgroup subscribers.
Password	A means of protection. Users require their own passwords to enter a system or a protected part of a system. Passwords consist of a mixture of characters and/or numbers and they may be in lower or upper case when the password is said to be case-sensitive.
Portal	A website that is intended to be the first port of call for a surfer when browsing on a particular topic. For example, zoom.co.uk is a portal as is fashionmall.com. Portals have a catalogue of websites, a search engine and a range of other services and content to attract users. Portals are usually careful in whothey include on their site. It is essentially a meansof target marketing if done well and it can encourage and draw surfer traffic to the site. Obviously the more the traffic, the more attractive the site and the higher credibility, and indeed advertisingrevenues that may be generated.
Reverse auction	Sellers bid to supply the customer rather than the traditional auction in which the buyer is the bidder.
Server	A computer providing a specific service to client software running on other networked computers. For example, organizations that have their own intranets require servers.
Spam	Unsolicited commercial messages or e-mails received via a newsgroup or other network communication.

	Sending Spam is usually regarded as a 'naf' activity and frowned upon. For example, I regard unsolicited online questionnaires from students as Spam. The remedy is usually to delete the offending item and to block future access from that source.
SSL	Secure socket layer. A protocol designed to enable encrypted (secure), certificated communications across the Internet. Secure connections are often indicated by a padlock appearing on the web browser in the status bar. Intel state that websites can run up to 50 times faster in SSL mode.
XML	Extendable mark-up language.
URL	Uniform resource locator. This is the standard address format of any resource on the Internet. For example, y-not-shine.com is a URL.
VPN	Virtual Private Network.
WAP	Wireless application protocol – the standard for connecting cell phones and the Internet.
Search engine	This is a retrieval mechanism, which performs the basic retrieval task, by acceptance of a query, and then comparing the query with each of the records in the database, in order to produce a retrieval set as output. Examples are Yahoo.com and Google.com.

References

Dowling, G. R. and Uncles, M. (1997). Do loyalty programmes really work? *Sloan Management Review*, **38** (4), 71–82.

Drapers Record (2003). *Drapers Record and Menswear*, 18 October.

Forrester Research (2003). www.forreseter.com, accessed 23 October.

Foss, B. and Stone, M. (2001). *Successful Customer Relationship Marketing*, London: Kogan Page.

Johnson, L. K. (2002). The real value of customer loyalty: Customer lifetime value is more than a metric; it's a way of thinking and doing business, *Sloan Management Review*, **43**, Winter, 14–16.

Mitchell, A. (2002). Consumer power is on the cards in Tesco plan. *Marketing week*, 2 May, 30–1.

Rigby, D., Reichheld, F. and Schefter, P. (2002). Avoiding the four perils of CRM. *Harvard Business Review*, February, 5–11.

Russell, G. and Petersen, A. (2000). Analysis of cross category dependence in market basket selection. *Journal of Retailing*, **76**, Fall, 367–91.

Zeithaml, V., Rust, R. and Lemon, K. (2001). The customer pyramid: Creating and servicing profitable customers. *California Management Review*, **43**, Summer, 118–43.

Chapter 8

Strategic supply chain cost, value and measurement

LEARNING OUTCOMES

The aim of this chapter is to introduce a number of key measures including financial and non-financial performance concepts. After studying the chapter you will be able to:

- explain the concept of value in relation to managing the supply chain;
- explain the importance of total acquisition cost in relation to supply chain management;
- identify how value is created within the supply chain and the concept of value systems and value streams;
- analyse and evaluate supply chain cost and value;
- know and understand the relative importance of different types of supply chain metric (e.g. financial and non-financial);
- be aware of and able to explain specific terms related to performance measurement including: best practice, world-class, benchmarking and balanced scorecard;
- know and understand the importance of having key performance indicators (KPIs);
- analyse and understand the importance of developing and using appropriate measures in relation to the supply chain, e.g. benchmarking and balanced scorecard approaches.

Introduction to cost and value concepts

It is particularly important for organizations to know and understand in detail their cost and value structures in relation to managing their own supply chains. All organizations form part of a much larger value system that links with other suppliers and other customers locked in a single or multiple supply chain structure. For example, if your organization supplied just five customers and two of those customers accounted for a substantial proportion of business it would be very important to know cost drivers and value creators for the two major customers since following the 'Pareto' concept. It is essential for managers to focus their activities on the areas where there is high risk or high returns.

It is often stated that cost is fact. There is some truth in this statement since many costs incurred are invoiced or determined from exogenous suppliers. These are often regarded as unavoidable costs. Nevertheless, there are a number of costs that are determined by people managing the organization. This second category of costs is avoidable depending upon the decisions taken by managers. We will return to this later.

Value added

Value added is essentially a financial concept. It may be explained by the difference between input cost and output value. For example, if you are familiar with the concept of value-added tax (VAT) you will know that this tax is paid on the difference between sales value taxes added to the invoice of customers and input taxes paid on purchase invoices in a period of time. For example, if during a 3-month financial period a firm incurred £1000 in input taxes and had to charge £3000 in output taxes they would pay over the difference (the VAT element) £2000 to HM Customs and Excise. Figure 8.1 illustrates the value-added concept.

Value is created only when someone is prepared to pay the price that the value represents. This is a very important point to understand. The number of times one hears, reads or observes people discussing value creation when what they really mean is cost incurred is astounding. Value is only realized when someone external to an organization creating value is prepared to pay the price, which equates to the value placed on the item by the producing or supplying organization.

So how do you know value has been created?

The truth is when you receive something of value, e.g. money, in exchange for outputs created. An organization may of course place an internal value on its production based upon input costs but until the product is sold there is no extrinsic value. It is the market that ultimately determines the value of a firm's output. Until goods reach their market and are exchanged for money through selling to organizations and people who

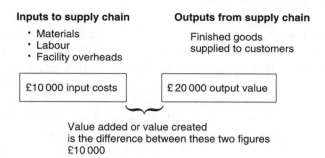

Figure 8.1

demand the product there is only cost. It is a myth to believe otherwise and all organizations whatever their size would do well to reflect on this salutary lesson. Figure 8.2 illustrates this argument using a simple input, process and output model.

Figure 8.2 demonstrates a model of inputs, processes and outputs from an organization's supply chain. The inputs to the firm's supply chain system are categorized in terms of inbound materials, labour and facility, and other costs classified as overheads. These elements are inputs to a manufacturing process or service process. Outputs from the system take the form of tangible goods or intangible services supplied to a customer. In such a model presented in Figure 8.2 inputs and processes are costs and value is only recognized when the customer pays for the outputs. It is important to understand where the value is created inside the organization but it is essential to recognize that value is only created when the customer pays the price and that this price is a figure above the cost incurred.

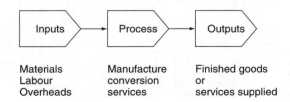

Figure 8.2

Value chains, value systems and their strategic relationship with supply chains

Value in a supply chain is not simply the organizational value but it is the value created across different organizations that combine to create the supply chain. In strategic terms supply chains cross organizational boundaries and are part of a wider value system. This can be illustrated conceptually adopting Porter's (1980) value chain analysis (VCA). Inside an organization Porter (1980) identified nine key areas that need to be examined when examining how value may be created. He divided these nine areas into what he referred to as: primary activities and support activities. The primary activities included: inbound logistics, processes, outbound logistics, marketing and sales, customer service. The support activities included: technological developments, human resource management, procurement and firm infrastructure. Identifying and examining each of the nine key areas would provide the organization with an audit of capabilities. This audit could be compared against competitor profiles and gaps may suggest opportunities or weaknesses in the organization's strategic capabilities. It was further argued by Porter that the firm's individual value chain was part of a larger value system in which the firm participates. This is very similar to an internal supply chain within a single organization and a number of supply chains that are linked together in a value system that is created to satisfy the ultimate customer, the consumer.

Figure 8.3 shows a diagrammatic representation of Porter's (1980) value chain. Figure 8.4 shows a number of value chains locked together in a value system.

The value chain

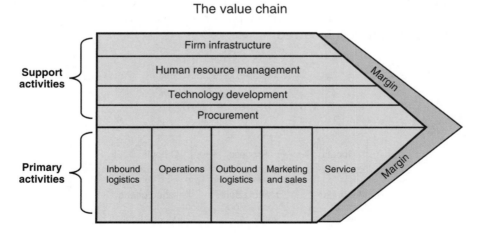

Figure 8.3

The value system

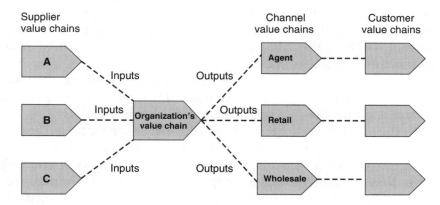

Figure 8.4

In the diagram of the value system the example illustrates an organization with three suppliers: A, B and C. The suppliers have their own value chains which are individual to each separate entity. The organizations they supply in this example have three channels or routes to market: through an agent, through a retailer and wholesale. Each of the channel firms has their own value chain and finally the customers that they supply have their own value chains. All these organizations form part of a value system. In effect organizations locked together in any supply chain form part of the value system for each of the organizations involved. If the suppliers, channels and customers illustrated were the only ones involved with the 'organization' at the heart of this system then this would represent the complete value system for that particular organization.

Supply chain cost and control

Nature and characteristics of supply chain costs

Supply chain costs accrue based either on time or on activity undertaken. For example, storage costs have both a time-based element and an activity-based element. Financial managers regard the time-based cost element as the overhead cost. This cost is often referred to as a 'fixed cost'. It is said to be fixed because the cost of storing goods requires physical space to be rented or purchased and both rental and purchase costs relate to time. If property is rented it has an annual rent. If property is purchased the cost of using the property has to be amortized over its lifetime use. Activity-based costs (ABCs) are often referred to as the variable cost of performing the activity. For example, the higher the throughput in a warehouse facility, the greater is the cost of labour to handle the volumes. It is important for supply chain managers to make the distinction between costs that will be time-based and those that will be activity-based; in essence the identification of annual fixed cost and variable cost elements.

Supposing the cost elements were identified for a particular organizational supply chain activity and separated into two categories labelled fixed and variable, the data might be as indicated in Table 8.1.

From the chart in Figure 8.5 you will be able to see that fixed costs do not vary with changes in volume. In other words those costs remain fixed regardless of changes in output. The variable costs of course do change; they vary according to output quantity. The table may make this distinction clearer for some of you. Fixed cost remains constant at £100 000 from 1000 through to 10 000 units of output. The variable cost changes at each level by £5 per unit of output. For those of you mathematically inclined, you may have noticed that the equation to represent this would take the form of:

$$y = a + b\,(x)$$

where a is the fixed cost, b the variable cost and x the quantity or output.

Notice in the example that the fixed costs were said to remain fixed between an activity level of 1000 and 10 000 units. Supposing that to increase storage beyond 10 000 units the firm had to acquire a further storage facility at an annual cost of a further £100 000 the picture for the volume of output in the range from 1000 to 20 000 units would look as seen in Figure 8.6.

Table 8.1 Fixed and variable costs

Output quantity	Fixed cost	Variable cost	Total cost
1 000	£100 000	£5 000	£105 000
2 000	£100 000	£10 000	£110 000
3 000	£100 000	£15 000	£115 000
4 000	£100 000	£20 000	£120 000
5 000	£100 000	£25 000	£125 000
6 000	£100 000	£30 000	£130 000
7 000	£100 000	£35 000	£135 000
8 000	£100 000	£40 000	£140 000
9 000	£100 000	£45 000	£145 000
10 000	£100 000	£50 000	£150 000

Fixed and variable costs

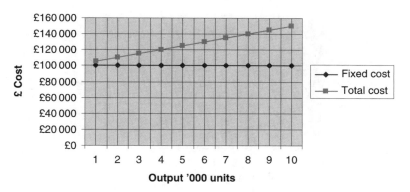

Figure 8.5 **Effect of output volume activity on fixed and variable cost**

This type of cost is often referred to as a 'step cost' because when the firm reaches certain level of activity the only way it can deal with the increase is to incur further fixed costs as in the example an extra storage facility. Figure 8.6 clearly illustrates the step cost at 11 000 units of output. Suddenly cost has increased not simply by the variable element £5 per unit but by a further £100 000 plus the £5000 variable element to a total cost of £255 000. It is very important to understand the effect of this change on total cost and unit cost. At 10 000 units the total cost was £150 000, i.e. £15 per unit. However, increasing storage costs to hold an additional 1000 units at 11 000 units has raised the total storage costs to £255 000 and the unit cost to £255 000/11 000 units = £23.18 per unit. This assumes that the total cost is to be spread over the full range 11 000 units.

Effect of output changes on costs

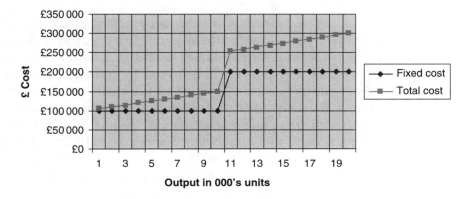

Figure 8.6

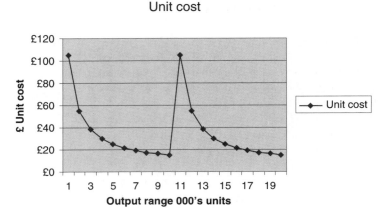

Figure 8.7

However, in essence the incremental element of the cost is £105 000 (the additional storage cost £100 000 and £5000 variable cost) for the first 1000 units which makes these units £105 each to store. The new storage facility does not become efficient until maximum capacity is reached at 22 000 units. This incremental effect is illustrated in Figure 8.7.

Figure 8.8 demonstrates the effect of volume change on unit cost assuming the costs are spread over the full range of output. The data on which the figures are based are given in Table 8.2.

Unit costs fall as volumes increase. You will note that the lowest unit cost of £15 is achieved at 10 000 units and again at 20 000 units.

Forecasts and budgets and the internal supply chain

Some definitions might help you think critically about the important distinction between a forecast and a budget. A forecast is a prediction about future events based on some past and current data. It is essentially an experiential approach. Just consider for a moment a weather forecast reported on TV. The forecaster demonstrates what the likely outcome for the next day or next few days is likely to be based upon recent past data. For example, cloud patterns, wind directions and comparisons with previous seasonal data allow the forecaster to make a prediction about the short-term future. In business too past data about business performance matched to current business and wider environmental conditions allow a forecast to be made. These forecasts are better than guesswork and are based on previous data. The downside is that sometimes businesses past experience may not provide a good indication of the future. Only if the business conditions are continuous rather than discontinuous is the past

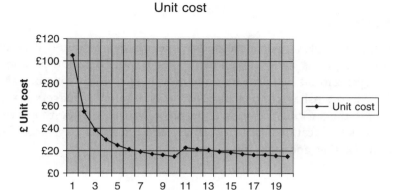

Figure 8.8

data going to be useful. Supposing the business has entered new markets, developed new supply chains and distribution channels and developed many new products? In these circumstances it is unlikely that past data will provide a good indication of future events.

Table 8.2 Data

Output quantity	Fixed cost	Variable cost	Total cost	Unit cost	Incremental unit cost
1 000	£100 000	£5 000	£105 000	£105	£105
2 000	£100 000	£10 000	£110 000	£55	£55
3 000	£100 000	£15 000	£115 000	£38	£38
4 000	£100 000	£20 000	£120 000	£30	£30
5 000	£100 000	£25 000	£125 000	£25	£25
6 000	£100 000	£30 000	£130 000	£22	£22
7 000	£100 000	£35 000	£135 000	£19	£19
8 000	£100 000	£40 000	£140 000	£18	£18
9 000	£100 000	£45 000	£145 000	£16	£16
10 000	£100 000	£50 000	£150 000	£15	£15
11 000	£200 000	£55 000	£255 000	£23	£105
12 000	£200 000	£60 000	£260 000	£22	£55
13 000	£200 000	£65 000	£265 000	£20	£38
14 000	£200 000	£70 000	£270 000	£19	£30
15 000	£200 000	£75 000	£275 000	£18	£25
16 000	£200 000	£80 000	£280 000	£18	£22
17 000	£200 000	£85 000	£285 000	£17	£19
18 000	£200 000	£90 000	£290 000	£16	£18
19 000	£200 000	£95 000	£295 000	£16	£16
20 000	£200 000	£100 000	£300 000	£15	£15

Definition

A budget is a plan in financial and/or quantitative terms. It may show volumes as well as values. It is normally for a specific period of time, e.g. most organizations will prepare an annual budget which will normally be split up into smaller control periods – say 1 month. Budgets are prepared for the various activities undertaken by the firm or they may be for products, locations (sites or SBUs) and functions (e.g. production, sales, marketing, administration, etc.)

Note a budget is not a forecast. Forecasts are used as inputs to a budget which is a plan. For example, sales forecasts establish the likely revenue streams; cost forecasts provide input data with regard to labour, material and overhead costs. Within the supply chain budgets are very important and set performance measures with regard to efficiency (input/output measures) and effectiveness (e.g. comparisons with previous time periods, comparisons with competitors). Establishing budgets and budgetary control are essential supply chain management tools. Benchmarking and performance measurement are discussed more fully elsewhere.

Budgets are needed to establish:

Plans. To help formulate plans for different activities and co-ordinating plans to prepare a budget for the whole organization.

Control. To produce reports that compare performance of actual outcomes against the planned performance. These reports are sometimes presented as variance reports.

Organization. To ensure that the accounting reporting and information system is closely aligned to the organizational structure and organizational goals.

Communication. To ensure plans are communicated and that appropriate feedback mechanisms are in place in the system.

Motivation. To motivate employees to meet performance objectives through the budgeting process.

The budgeting process inside an organization is mapped in Figure 8.9.

Budgetary control

To be effective in achieving any plan there needs to be control. Budgets are controlled by breaking the plan into smaller control periods and measuring variances between the actual results and the plan (budget). Action will need to be taken as appropriate either to adjust the budget or to adjust the actual activities to keep to the plan. Variances may occur for the following reasons.

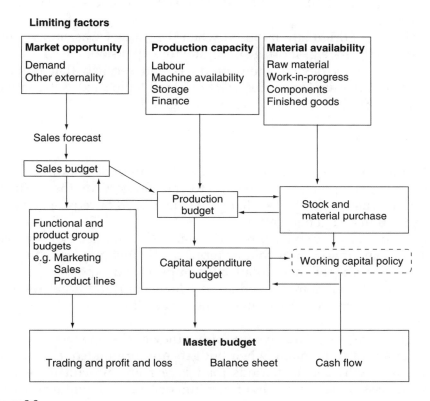

Figure 8.9
Source: Hines (1990).

Internal factors

1. The organization may change in terms of structure and therefore the planned expenditures are not appropriate within the budget headings originally assigned. For example, if previously when a budget was set and agreed sales and marketing was a single departmental function but during the budget period it was re-organized into two separate departments, one for sales and one for marketing then the budgets would need to be adjusted in some way to reflect the change.
2. Productive capacity may change owing to the purchase of new plant and machinery or methods of working.
3. Sales and marketing policy may become more effective thus penetrating new markets or by increasing market share. Opening up new markets may mean that a revised sales budget is needed.

4. Other personnel may become more or less effective in their roles and this may be identified through efficiency variances actual against budget.
5. Constraints originally imposed when the budget was set may have been removed, e.g. shortage of capital for expansion.
6. The firm may develop new products and services that require a switch in the way resources were originally allocated. Alternatively, existing products or services may be deleted.

External factors

1. Market conditions may change causing a shift in demand.
2. Government policy with regard to the industry or the particular type of business may also change, e.g. increased or reduced taxation, legislation and general attitude.
3. Inflation may increase costs and revenues. In monetary terms variances may occur but in volume terms the budget may be achieved.
4. Exchange rate fluctuations affecting imports and exports.
5. Changes in the demand and supply for labour and other resources which give rise to price changes and wage rates.

These lists are not exhaustive but rather they give some measure of the considerations to be made when budgets are formulated, and furthermore show why longer periods than 1 year are difficult to plan for. Nevertheless most businesses of medium or large size will tend to plan strategically for periods of 3–5 years. This is often referred to as the corporate or strategic plan. The annual budget will be only one component in that plan.

Activity-based cost and management systems

Cost systems are designed to perform three primary functions according to Kaplan and Cooper (1998, p. 2):

1. Valuation of inventories and the measurement of cost of sales;
2. Estimation of the costs of activities, products, services and customers;
3. To provide managers with feedback on their performance and operatives about process efficiency.

Activity-based cost (ABC) systems emerged during the 1980s as a response for more accurate information about the cost of resource demands with an emphasis upon products, services, customers and channels. ABC systems support decision making by presenting a clearer picture of costs. Indirect or support costs are driven first to activities and processes, and second to products, services, customers and channels.

The clearer picture obtained from ABC led to the development of ABM. Figure 8.10 divides ABM into operational and strategic issues, which an organization manages. Operational ABM is about doing things right focusing upon efficiency, cost reduction and asset utilization. Resources are released by changing business processes, by eliminating activities that do not yield value in excess of their cost or by increasing the efficient use of assets. Cost reduction programmes may provide better use of existing resources and therefore obviate the need for further capital investment.

Strategic ABM focuses upon doing the right things and in so doing attempts to lower the demand for resources. For example, by designing products or services better it may be possible to lower resource requirements. It is estimated that 80 per cent or more of manufacturing costs are determined during product design and development (Blanchard, 1978; Michaels and Wood, 1989). Unprofitable activities can be identified and eliminated. Effective suppliers and profitable customers can be developed and the ineffective and unprofitable ones can be removed. Information can be used by marketing managers to explore ways of increasing incremental revenues and reducing incremental costs by identifying highly profitable products, services, customers or channels. Similarly low-cost rather than low-price suppliers may be expanded.

Table 8.3 demonstrates the shift in focus away from expense categories towards activity analysis. In the example, four expense categories are re-analysed to yield an activity-based costing.

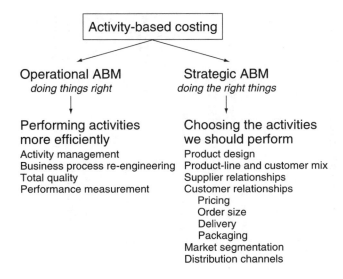

Figure 8.10 How activity-based costing turns into activity-based management

Table 8.3 From traditional to activity-based costing

Traditional costing by function

Salaries	£250 000.00
Occupancy	£100 000.00
Technology	£150 000.00
Materials	£50 000.00
Total	£550 000.00

Activity-based cost analysis

Activity	Salaries	Occupancy	Technology	Materials	Total
Process customer orders	£50 000.00	£12 000.00	£30 000.00	£500.00	£92 500.00
Purchase materials	£37 500.00	£15 000.00	£22 500.00	£600.00	£75 600.00
Schedule production	£45 000.00	£22 000.00	£27 000.00	£250.00	£94 250.00
Move materials	£17 500.00	£5 000.00	£10 500.00	£8 500.00	£41 500.00
Set up machines	£25 000.00	£4 000.00	£15 000.00	£2 500.00	£46 500.00
Introduce new products	£50 000.00	£41 000.00	£30 000.00	£35 000.00	£156 000.00
Resolve quality problems	£25 000.00	£1 000.00	£15 000.00	£2 650.00	£43 650.00
	£250 000.00	£100 000.00	£150 000.00	£50 000.00	£550 000.00

Accounting for customers rather than products

Traditionally accounting methods have identified and analysed product costs. However what may be more relevant particularly when considering customer service is a way of measuring customer profitability or customer account profitability (CAP). ABC is a way of viewing costs differently. It has often been difficult for operational managers to obtain the types of financial data that they require to manage more effectively. For example, there has been a general ignorance of the true cost of servicing different customers, different segments and different channels of distribution. This is because costs have focused upon the product and not the market. In other words inputs to the product rather than outputs to the customers. Conventional accounting systems are functionally oriented rather than output-focused. They have been designed not as a management tool but as a reporting tool of what happened in the past. Even when accounting systems or parts of the system have tried to look forward they have not focused upon market issues but rather the product has been central to the analysis. This is not to say that it is unimportant to identify product costs but rather to recognize that this is only one perspective for cost management. Furthermore, full costing (absorption costing) is based upon a number of key assumptions relating to the ways in which overheads might be recovered.

Essentially ABC is concerned with the identification of activities that cause cost. Such activities might be the order cycle times required by customers, the availability of stock, frequency of delivery, technical support, order status information and visits to customers by sales personnel. There will of course be many other types of activity. ABM involves four key steps:

1. activity analysis;
2. cost reduction;
3. product/service 'offer' profitability;
4. development of an integrated ABC system.

Direct product profitability

This is a concept that has been extensively used in retailing environments. The logic behind the concept is that in many transactions the customer incurs costs other than the agreed purchase price of the goods from a supplier. These hidden costs can be substantial and can in some cases eliminate profit on a particular product line.

Exhibit 1

DPP		£
Sales		100
Less cost of goods sold		25
Gross profit margin		75
Add allowances and discounts		10
Adjusted gross margin		85
Less warehousing costs		
Labour costs	6	
Occupancy cost	5	
Inventory cost	4	
		15
Less transportation costs		5
Less retail costs		
Stocking labour	3	
Occupancy cost	2	
Inventory cost	4	
		9
Direct product profitability		56

From this exhibit you can see that the selling price for a particular item is fixed at £100 and that the invoiced cost of the item from a supplier is £25. The gross margin before any adjustment is 75 per cent. Suppliers may give the retailer a discount for early settlement or an allowance as part of a promotion from the supplier or an allowance in respect of the quantities the retailer is prepared to take or for some other reasons. These allowances or discounts have an effect upon the gross margin the retailer is able to achieve. So in this case we have an adjusted gross margin as a result of the allowances given by the supplier. However, the retailer incurs other costs in relation to warehousing, transportation and the very business of retailing itself. These additional costs have been grouped together and are then deducted from the adjusted gross margin to provide the retailer with DPP. This information will then be used to compare similar products across a particular range. The buyers, buying teams or decision-making units (DMUs) will take decisions regarding which products to stock. These decisions are not purely financial decisions, they are in reality marketing decisions. Marketing managers must be involved in this process. It would be foolish to base the decision regarding which products to stock simply on the basis of this financial information. Nevertheless, it is important to be informed about which products achieve higher profits after all the costs of ownership are taken into account.

Question

You are told that a particular item retails for £25 and that the supplier's invoiced price to you is £5. The supplier has agreed further discounts amounting to 20 per cent off their price if you agree to take a minimum quantity. Warehousing costs based upon average inventories that you expect to hold, the space the items will occupy in the warehouse and labour handling costs are estimated to add a further £4 per item. Additional transport costs moving goods from the regional distribution centre (RDC) to the stores are expected to add a further £2 cost per item and retail costs will add a further £3 per item. You are asked to compute the DPP for this item assuming you will take the minimum order quantity and hence the additional discount.

Answer

DPP	*£*
Sales	25
Less cost of goods sold	5
Gross profit margin	20
Add allowances and discounts	1
Adjusted gross margin	21
Less warehousing costs	4
Less transportation costs	2
Less retail costs	3
Direct product profitability	12

Total cost of ownership

The purchase price of any item is simply one component of cost of material, product or service. The TCO is important to understand because it represents not simply purchase cost but other costs that comprise the TCO. Ownership and post-ownership costs are often ignored in the analysis of cost. For example, a retailer purchasing stock for resale (SKU) may simply decide to make the decision to buy on the basis of cost price and target margin. The target margin or the 'intake margin' as it is often referred to assumes paramount importance but it may be ignoring a raft of other costs that make up the TCO. Manufacturers purchasing materials as inputs to a manufacturing process also are able easily to identify the purchase cost but additional ownership costs may be ignored. In service environments the position is similar organizations may purchase insurance or other services and overlook additional costs and benefits when making decision choice.

Total cost of ownership (TCO) is an important concept. Ownership costs essentially fall into three categories: Acquisition costs, ownership and post-ownership costs. The focus for many purchasing decisions is simply that of the first category acquisition cost. The overemphasis on this category is likely to lead to flawed decision-making. Ellram (1996) reported that the generally accepted purchase cost figure for a capital purchase represents only 30–50 per cent of the TCO. A TCO analysis is time-consuming to perform and generally not worthwhile for low value or low impact items. It is an approach that can bring benefits for larger value or high impact items. Systems and procedures need to be set-up to capture the cost data easily. It is a useful continuous improvement tool and a useful means of strategic cost analysis. TCO is a philosophy to understand supply chain costs. Automobile manufacturers have, for example, identified new ways to reduce TCO for customers by improving their own manufacturing processes (re-design, re-engineering) and have been able to pass these benefits on to car owners in the form of fewer breakdowns, improved warranties, longer service intervals and improved fuel consumption.

TCO applies a number of different concepts to the analytical process from eclectic disciplines, e.g., net present value (finance), product pricing and costing (accounting), reliability and quality measures (operations management), customer measures (marketing), systems integration (IT), material movement (logistics) and minimum average total unit cost of production (economics).

Lowering the cost of goods sold and associated overhead costs (procurement, inventory holding costs and selling) improve the 'bottom line' profitability. Firms will spend much time searching for ways to lower these costs especially when markets are difficult and it is not easy to increase prices or volumes to improve overall profit. As a consequence some large retailing organizations have empowered major suppliers to manage their inventories for them adopting a system known as *vendor-managed inventory* (VMI). VMI allows the supplier to manage the inventories by managing store space allocated by a retailer in return for guaranteed minimum returns and filling it with their merchandise without reference to the retailer. This allows the vendor to replenish stocks quickly to capture sales, avoiding stock-outs and allows the suppliers to manage their capacity planning and manufacturing processes more effectively since they get a forward window on what is and is not moving through store. The advantage to the retailer is that they do not have the headache of managing the inventory nor do they incur procurement and inventory holding costs in advance since the supplier only gets paid when the stock is sold through the store.

TCO analysis will inevitably involve managing a number of trade-off situations to achieve a minimum cost. Those employees working in key areas of the supply chain should identify TCO analysis and the detail may differ between different organizations. The analysis may include:

- Product design (value engineering and value analysis techniques);
- Manufacturing infrastructure costs (machines, equipment, storage and transport facilities);
- Make or buy (outsource or self-manufacture);
- Responsiveness of first-, second- and third-level tiers of suppliers within the supply chain;
- Any taxes, duties, quotas;
- Transport costs and times;
- Legal and regulatory costs;
- Foreign exchange and risk;
- Inventory risk relocation, damage, obsolescence, shrinkage;
- Political and economic stability;
- Quality costs;
- Communication costs (includes language requirements in overseas environments).

Most of these items can be quantified in cost terms but some will inevitably require qualitative judgements to be made.

The three component costs of TCO

1. Acquisition costs;
2. Ownership costs;
3. Post-ownership costs.

Acquisition costs

There are a number of dimensions to this cost which are:

Purchase price paid – This is the invoiced price paid for a material, a product or service. The invoiced cost may include a charge for freight, delivery, site preparation (in the case of capital purchases), training, installation and testing. What is included in the invoiced price will be dependent on the purchase contract and the prior negotiations that agreed the price to be paid. Effective negotiation by purchasing professionals may well reduce the price by agreeing quantity discount, prompt payment discounts or through specifying standard parts or by aligning standard specifications across products such that components are standardized. The key to successful negotiation is not to compromise longer-term ownership costs for a short-term gain.

Planning costs – These are costs incurred in planning an acquisition including development of requirements and specifications, price comparisons, cost analysis, supplier selection and sourcing, contract determination, order processing and monitoring. An increase of spending in these areas may well achieve future benefits by lowering TCO. For example, reconfiguring designs to use standard parts across different product ranges may lower purchasing costs, inventory carrying costs, and future maintenance and repair costs for the customer.

Adopting e-procurement, B2B e-commerce or e-supply networks may further lower acquisition costs. Research time, paperwork, ordering and processing specification approvals, deliveries and payments can all be speeded up.

Quality costs – Often higher initial engineering costs to improve quality at a design stage impact upon future ownership and post-ownership costs. In addition quality costs can be lowered by having established long-term (strategic) relationships with suppliers. Process costs, communication costs, innovation and development costs can all be lowered through effective relationship management.

Taxes – Often represent a hidden cost that provides the purchaser with a sting in the tail. Hours are spent focusing upon the unit price of a purchase and then negotiating a satisfactory price. However, this may all be in vain if the purchaser fails to recognize taxes that have to be incurred. Direct taxes (e.g. duties and processing fees) and indirect taxes (e.g. fuel taxes, tolls, facility fees, etc.) must be identified. Janis (2000) recognized the following examples:

Customs duties and tariffs	Plan to minimize their effect, ensure compliance and avoid penalties
Virtual warehousing	Within the EU information about goods flows through centralized virtual customs clearing houses while the physical goods move unhindered from source to destination
Regional trade agreements and free trade zones	Goods sourced and produced in these areas have the benefit of lowering or removing all duties and tariffs
Income-base shifting	Apply transfer prices to legally avoid tax by shifting the incidence from high to low tax areas

Financing costs – Any cost incurred to finance the particular purchase of material, inventory, facility, acquisition, capital purchase. Mortgages, loans, bonds, lines of credit, capital lease, sale-leaseback, securitization of receivables, equity financing and the associated opportunity cost[1] including straightforward cash purchases.

Ownership costs

These are costs incurred after the initial purchase, e.g. energy use, downtime, maintenance, repairs and financing. In addition there are costs that arise from ease of use (does it save time?), unplanned additional training and ergonomics (to reduce fatigue or increase productivity).

There are also costs related to:

- risk;
- cycle time;
- conversion;
- non-value-added; and
- supply networks.

Risk costs. These are 'trade-off' costs involving management judgements about issues such as maintaining excess inventory to satisfy possible customer demand and avoid a stock-out. Just-in-case (JiC) inventory can be very expensive. It is a form of waste and is treated as such in the literature relating to JiT systems. The costs associated with JiC should be eliminated or at very least minimized. Excess inventory costs include: reduced cash flows, lost interest on cash tied up in inventory, additional storage and associated costs, additional financing cost when borrowed funds are used to make purchases and finally the risks associated with obsolescence, redundancy and shrinkage.

Dependability is an important issue when dealing with a new source of supply and a reason why firms adopt dual or multiple sourcing. Dependability is also referred to as reliability in the literature. This is critical to organizations that operate JiT systems with fewer and fewer suppliers.

Cycle time costs. Faster cycle times and/or increasing throughput reduce the time cost elements. This improves profitability and ROI by lowering total cost. Strategies for reducing cycle time cost include:

- Implementation of JiT inventory flows;
- Forming strategic alliances with key suppliers to reduce cycle times;
- Co-operation or collaboration in the new product development cycle;
- Cross-functional alliances within the organization to speed up cycle times.

Conversion costs. Purchasing inappropriate material, inadequately trained labour, excess inventory, poor design of materials, products and processes can all add to the cost of conversion unnecessarily. As mentioned earlier spending less on planning may result in higher operating costs when manufacturing. Production methods (e.g. assembly lines vs. cellular manufacture, labour intensive vs. automated production) may also alter the nature of cost of conversion. The assignment of overheads to the unit of product or service and the particular accounting methods employed can also influence these costs adversely.

Non-value-added cost. Non-value-added cost has been estimated at as much as 40 per cent of all costs. These costs include:

- Unnecessary materials movement;
- Double handling materials;
- Poor facility layout;
- Poor scheduling;
- Duplication of processes;
- Inefficient processes;
- Random routing of materials, and material and production flows rather than systematically routing to reduce times and distances travelled.

The Japanese Kaizen approaches require the identification of unevenness in production or process flows (mura), difficulty in conducting operations (muri) and waste (muda). The objective being to remove obstacles or blockages that cause the unevenness, improve process design for smoother operations and eliminate waste. In other words Kaizen is a means of striving to achieve continuous improvement (CI) with the aim of lowering or eliminating non-value-added costs. Figure 8.11 illustrates the concept of continuous improvement to remove waste, difficulties and unevenness by configuring people, materials, machines and methods differently to add value for customers. Continuous improvement may require trade-offs

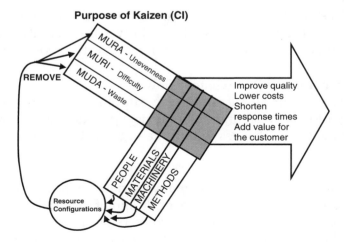

Figure 8.11

between the mix of resources (people, machinery, materials and methods of working) to achieve these aims. Tools that assist managers with these processes are:

- total quality management (TQM);
- activity-based costing (ABC);
- activity-based management (ABM).

An alternative to the CI approaches identified above is business process re-engineering (BPR) which is essentially a form of innovation or breakthrough as it is sometimes called. BPR is revolutionary change whereas CI is evolutionary change.

Process mapping tools are used to identify non-value-added (NVA) times in business processes. Processes are then re-designed to eliminate NVA. When applied to supply chain solutions BPR may have an impact upon all organizations examined within a single supply chain.

Supply network costs. The extended enterprise is effectively how some commentators refer to the single supply chain explained above. Thus efficiencies and cost reductions can be implemented across organizational boundaries in a single supply chain or supply network.[2] Organizations that outsource non-essential or non-core activities may eliminate many NVA costs and improve efficiency by focusing on what they do best. Supply network costs can be lowered in a number of important ways which include:

- Improving forecasting of customer demand, sharing information with supply chain partners to improve scheduling and inventory management.
- Implementing EDI between supply chain partners facilitating more effective communication and removing errors through single source data entry, reducing purchasing time and paperwork.
- Improving transportation possibly through outsourcing to reduce cycle times.
- Improving inventory management by implementing JiT philosophy.
- Improving business processes that are reliable, responsive, improve quality and are efficient.
- Better capital and revenue budgeting.
- Improving levels of customer service by being responsive and efficient. Listen and remove any blockages.
- Improve supplier selection finding appropriate sources of supply that lower TCO.
- Establish better supply chain relationships (transactional, co-operative, collaborative, co-opetitive or strategic partnership and/or alliances).

Need to focus on lowering cost and achieving other objectives such as quality, reliability, dependability and responsiveness.

- Establish global sourcing strategies to lower cost, improve quality and take advantage of low-cost EDI and low-cost transport.

Post-ownership costs

Historically post-ownership cost has been easier to identify in capital purchases. This is because salvage value or disposal costs could be more clearly identified and established markets were available in which price was determined. Today there is less certainty and more risk involved and the world is a more litigious place with armies of 'ambulance chasing lawyers' waiting for the opportunity to scavenge a deal by winning cases for customers based upon environmental disasters, product liability, failed warranties or simply customer dissatisfaction.

Finally, it is possible to provide an equation for determining the TCO as follows:

$$TCO = A + PV \sum_{i=1}^{n} (T_i + O_i + M_i - R_n)$$

where TCO is the total cost of ownership, A the acquisition cost, PV the present value, T_i the training costs in year i, O_i the operating costs in year i, M_i the maintenance cost in year i and R_n the residual value in year i.

This formula can be adapted for different TCO requirements. The formula is very similar to that required for investment appraisal decisions in capital budgeting and adopts the same discounted cash-flow principles.

Finally, it is worth noting that TCO is a philosophy and an analytical tool that organizations may use to support management decisions in the supply chain.

Performance measurement – an introduction

Supply chain metrics

Supply chain metrics are used to establish comparisons between time periods, activities in the same organization or across competing organizations. They will usually involve measures of efficiency such as on-time deliveries, complete orders, throughput times, lead times (production, time to market) and a range of financial measures such as asset utilization, capacity, inventories and inventory turnovers, profitability and ROI.

Measuring performance is critical to the success of organizational strategy. Once an organization has set its course it is important to know how far away it is from meeting its strategic objectives. In measuring strategic supply chain performance there are two critical focal points: the customer and the competition. It is important for the organization to know how it is performing against its competitors in the market-place and how it is performing in the eyes of its customers.

For the purpose of illustration five key performance areas are chosen: cost, speed, quality, reliability and flexibility. Performance objective and some typical measures are listed in Table 8.4.

Table 8.4 Five key performance areas

Performance objective	Measure
Cost	Delivery times (min, max, average)
	Budget variance
	Resource utilization
	Productivity
	Cost per hour
	Efficiency
	Value added
Speed	Enquiry to order lead time
	Throughput time
	Production lead time
	Cycle times
	Actual vs. standard times
	Delivery lead times (min, max, average)
	Time to market (various cycles, e.g. new product, replenishment)
Quality	Per cent of defects per unit
	No. of customer complaints
	Customer satisfaction scores
	Warranty claims
	Average time between failures
	Level of scrap
	Per cent of rework
Reliability	Per cent of orders on time
	Per cent of orders complete
	Per cent of orders on time and complete
	Per cent of stock availability
	Average delivery time vs. promised delivery time
Flexibility	Time it takes to develop new products/services
	Set up/change over times
	Time to change capacity
	Time to change schedules
	Average batch sizes
	Time it takes to increase activity rates
	Range of products/services offered

Performance measures may be measured in terms of historical standards, target standards, competitor standards or absolute standards. Historical standards compare current performance against a previous performance. It is useful to measure performance through time to judge how well an organization performs over time. A target standard is set by the organization based on judgement of what is deemed appropriate or reasonable. Competitor standards are those set by one or more of the organization's immediate competitors. For example, a common customer may declare that a competitor is able to deliver in 2 weeks. This may set the standard for your organization. Absolute standards are those that may be set at the theoretical limit, e.g. zero defects or zero inventory.

A useful strategic improvement tool is the importance–performance matrix (see Figure 8.12). This measures what customers value in terms of what wins business and how the organization shapes up against competition. The customer may consider some aspects essential to do business and these are order qualifiers. However, some factors may strongly influence buying decisions and these are order winners. Table 8.5 lists an example.

A similar table (Table 8.6) can be considered for organizational performance against competition.

The appropriate zone above the lower bound of acceptability is where an organization wants to be situated to satisfy customers and to be achieving appropriate performance in the competitive marketplace. The improvement zone below the lower boundary of acceptability indicates areas for improvement. The urgent action zone indicates that

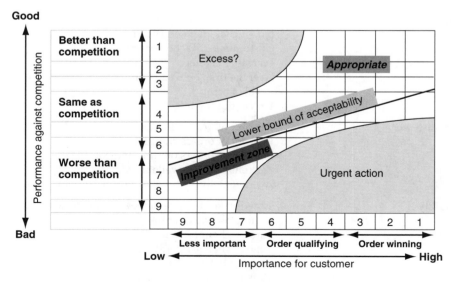

Figure 8.12 Importance–performance matrix

Table 8.5 What the customers value

Order winner	Strong	1	Critical advantage
	Medium	2	Important advantage
	Weak	3	Useful advantage
Order qualifier	Strong	4	High industry standard
	Medium	5	Average industry standard
	Weak	6	Approaching industry standard
Less important	Strong	7	Not usually important but may be in future
	Medium	8	Very rare that customers value this
	Weak	9	Never considered by the customer

these are factors valued by customers and the organization's perform-ance is worse than the competition. The excess area demonstrates that the organization is beating competitors in these areas but that the customer does not value them. The strategic question is whether or not resources should be applied in this area or would they be better used elsewhere where the customer places value.

Figure 8.13 maps five competitive dimensions that the organization has identified are valued by customers: cost, flexibility, speed, respon-siveness and dependability. For each of the dimensions a measure of how well the organization is able to compete is required. In addition a measure of how well competitors do along each dimension is also required. The best way to do this would be to ask your customers although this may not always be appropriate. It may not always be in the customer's interest to reveal this information. Nevertheless, if accur-ate measures could be taken an organization would have a clearer picture about where it is able to compete more effectively and the strategies needed to do so. In the example, a Likert scale has been used to obtain the measures with 5 being the best performance measure.

Table 8.6 Evaluating performance against competition

Better than competition	Strong	1	Much better
	Medium	2	Better
	Weak	3	Marginally better
Same as competition	Strong	4	Sometimes marginally better
	Medium	5	Nearly always the same
	Weak	6	Slightly lower than average
Worse than competition	Strong	7	Usually marginally worse
	Medium	8	Usually worse most times
	Weak	9	Always worse

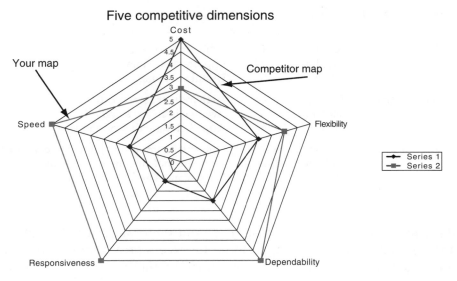

Figure 8.13

Competitors beat the organization on cost but lose on every other dimension. If customers are still buying competitor offerings it means they value cost above all other factors. In these circumstances you are probably supplying in what essentially is a commodity market and more importantly perhaps you should recognize that you are incurring costs unnecessarily in areas your customers do not value since they are not prepared to pay you any more for the services you offer in excess of your competition.

A material example (performance standards vs. actual)

One important financial measure in any supply chain is material cost and material usage. This is often analysed using a budgeted standard cost figure and drawing comparisons between that figure and the actual price paid for materials. Usage variances can also arise in production processes for a variety of reasons. Let's take a look at an example to illustrate how the budgeted standard cost and actual figures are compared.

$$\text{Material price variance} = (\text{Standard price} - \text{actual price}) \times \text{actual quantity}$$
$$= (SP - AP) \times AQ$$

$$\text{Material usage variance} = (\text{Standard quantity} - \text{actual quantity}) \times \text{standard price}$$
$$= (SQ - AQ) \times SP$$

The standard cost information for the production of one unit of product X is as follows:

Direct materials   5 kg of material Y at 60 p per kg

During a certain cost period 4000 units of X were manufactured and the material used in production was 20 200 kg of Y at a total cost of £11 716. If we calculate the material cost variance and separate the results into a price and usage variance we will get the following figures:

	£
STD direct materials	12 000
(4000 × £3)	
Actual cost	11 716
Favourable variance	284

The question is, was it a price or material usage variance?

Price variance = (SP − AP) × AQ
= (£0.60 − £0.58) × 20 200
= £404 (favourable price variance)
Price variance = £404 (F)

Material usage variance,

(SQ − AQ) × SP = (20 000 − 20 200) × £0.60
= £120 (adverse material variance)

Note that the standard quantity was obtained from the original data where it stated that 5 kg of material was required to make one unit of product therefore [4000 units × 5 kg].

Taking the two constituent variances together we have a net favourable material cost volume of £284 (F).

Reasons for material price variance

1. Efficient or inefficient buying of materials.
2. A reduction in production may mean smaller amounts purchased, therefore a loss of quantity discount. The reverse may also be true, i.e. an increase in the amounts of material bought leading to increasing discounts.
3. The need to acquire emergency supplies may lead to higher prices. For example, when your JiT system of stock replenishment fails.

4. Changing quality of the material purchased.
5. The loss of a source of supply which was inexpensive.
6. External factors, e.g. if you buy from abroad, exchange rates. Other factors – inflation.

Reasons for usage variance

1. Inefficiency by an operator using the material (if not watching a machine and a fault occurs, e.g. in printing – operative may fail to turn off machine in time to minimize quantity of paper spoilt).
2. Spoilages due to insufficient maintenance of machinery.
3. Substitution of poor-quality material resulting in lost production.
4. Change in the methods of production which makes the standard being used obsolete.
5. Inadequate storage causing damage.
6. If the actual mix of materials in the product changes then the usage variance would change also.

Having metrics that help identify and establish causes for variances from the plan are important especially when material costs form a high proportion of the total cost for the organization. From the analysis the organization is able to identify management actions to improve the situation.

Benchmarking

The term comes from surveying whereby a mark would be cut into rock as a reference point for land surveys. Xerox was the first company to use the term 'competitive benchmarking' in 1976; since that time benchmarking has been used to describe various aspects of measuring performance and the meaning has been extended considerably. It is no longer restricted to manufacturing but has been extended to include other areas such as marketing and purchasing. It has been used in service organizations such as banks and public sector organizations such as social services, health service, etc. It is no longer the domain of external consultants alone and may involve all staff working in the organization. Competitive benchmarking has been widened in meaning to include not just direct competitors but other organizations regarded as the best in their class.

Macneil et al. (1994) suggest that benchmarking 'is a method for continuous improvement that involves the systematic evaluation and incorporation of external products, services and processes recognized as best practice'. A management method or tool used alongside other performance enhancement tools or philosophies such as TQM or

Figure 8.14

competitive analysis. Continuous improvement is an integral part of benchmarking. It is a systematic search for 'best practice'.

$$\text{Benchmarking} = \text{Evaluation}$$

Benchmarking supply chain activities usually focuses on operational improvements identified in Figure 8.14.

Different types of benchmarking

The focus for benchmarking may be internal or external. Internal benchmarking is used to compare performance between different parts of the same organization, e.g. different car plant efficiencies in the same automobile manufacturer. External benchmarking is used for comparing similar activities in different organizations. Competitive benchmarking is used to achieve a number of outcomes, which are summarized in Table 8.7.

Customer service benchmarks are particularly important in supply chain management. These benchmarks are designed to measure:

- order cycle times;
- delivery reliability;
- frequency of delivery;
- stock availability;
- documentation quality;
- order completeness;
- technical support.

For example, if a supplier delivers on time 95 per cent of the time and the orders are complete 90 per cent of the time combining the two

Table 8.7 Reasons for competitive benchmarking and process steps

Planning	Identify benchmark outputs
	Identify best competitor
	Determine data collection method
Analysis	Determine competitive gap
	Project future performance level
	Establish future goals
Integration	Communication of data and acceptance of analysis
	Develop functional action plans
Action	Implement specifications
	Monitor results/report progress
	Recalibrate benchmarks
Maturity	Leadership position obtained
	Process integrated with practices

measures gives a benchmark for suppliers who are both on time and complete: 95 per cent $\times$ 90 per cent = 85.5 per cent.

Customer service level benchmarking can also provide a series of trade-offs.

Operational *vis-à-vis* strategic measurement

The supply chain council (www.supply-chain.org) identifies four major processes that organizations undertake and they are categorized as: plan, source, make, deliver. In essence this is a useful categorization for in-house manufacturing. However, for many contemporary organizations the dynamics may be somewhat different. For example, they may design, plan, source, collaborate, outsource and deliver. The focus of the SCOR model shown is very much operational and ignores the strategic options available to the organization. Operational benchmarking is conducted against each of the SCOR activity areas. Strategic areas in addition to those already used by SCOR are shown in Table 8.8 and explained.

Design and innovate

This activity is wider than the task of design. It is rather a way of thinking, constructing and implementing design from concepts into practical customer-focused product and service solutions. Innovations in design and design processes enable organizations to compete on a number of

Table 8.8

SCOR activities (operational focus)	Strategic activities (strategic focus)
	Design and innovate
Plan	Plan
Source	Source
Make	Outsource
	Collaborate
	Make
Deliver	Deliver
	Obtain feedback from customers and re-plan

different strategic dimensions (time, cost and difference). It is the step before supply chain planning.

Plan

Any operational plan balancing supply with demand to manage capacity must be aligned with the organization's strategic planning processes. For example, resource planning to acquire plant, machinery, storage and distribution facilities, people with appropriate skills and knowledge, capital to finance operations.

Source

Sourcing is both a strategic and an operational decision. On a day-to-day basis sourcing materials for ongoing production activities may simply be viewed as an operational activity. However, sourcing is also strategic since it impacts upon the strategic capabilities and competitive advantage of the organization. A decision to source materials, components or merchandise from remote parts of the world may indeed bring cost benefits simply because labour costs, material and processing costs may be cheaper and the cost advantage is greater than the additional transport cost incurred. Sourcing further away from the market carries higher risks. Hence there may be possible disruptions to supplies through political instability, legal sanctions, ethical considerations, changes to economic conditions and social unrest. However, although the organization may win on cost grounds it may lose its capability to be responsive. For example, sourcing lower cost products from the Far East may be attractive on cost ground but may reduce the organization's ability to deliver products to market quickly. Organizations must keep their strategic focus on the customer requirements and organize their sources appropriately. This is not simply operational but strategic in nature because sourcing can be a costly activity and once sources are established they may not be easily changed. Furthermore, sourcing in one area may also involve local investment in the area, which cannot easily be switched when the cost/benefit equation variables shift.

Make

Producing the goods within the overall production system by executing operations to achieve the task of making the goods. This is a very 'operations'-driven focus. However, it is not simply about making unless you are the manufacturer. It is about meeting customer demand. Adopting a strategic focus would lead to other alternatives being considered such as outsourcing and collaboration.

Outsourcing

Traditionally this has been viewed from a cost point of view and is often referred to as a 'make or buy' decision. However, outsourcing may bring other strategic benefits apart from simply a cost advantage. For example, an organization may want to outsource part or all of its production or service activities because the customer can be served better by doing so. The organization may not have access to technology, skills and other competencies that it can buy-in through outsourcing. There are arguments that relate to 'core activities' and 'peripheral activities'. It is sometimes argued that organizations should 'stick to the knitting'; in other words do what they do best and outsource everything else (cf. Peters and Waterman).

Collaboration

Organizations strategically do not simply make but they may collaborate with other suppliers of goods and services to produce a superior customer offer than can competitors. Collaboration may bring benefits such as access to better technology, better know-how and better service standards. Collaboration in this context may not be with the customer but rather with other suppliers. Although one could think of some industries where the customer is given the tools to make their own products by the service provider and hence there is customer collaboration without making by the supplier. An example might be digital music that is made available from stock by a copyright owner and the customer enters digital web space and constructs their own unique collection to download to their PC, PDA or digital music disk.

Deliver

Delivery may need to be considered more widely in a strategic context. Traditional delivery modes have been chosen on the basis of time and cost. The key elements are managing demand, orders, storage and distribution. Delivery for some goods and services may be digital and it may be self-delivery. Deciding on how customer fulfilment will be achieved is critical to the success of the organization. In many respects it is the most important but perhaps least understood aspect of managing market demand. Strategically organizations must consider means of fulfilment and organize resources appropriately. This may involve capital investment in facilities, technology and equipment to deliver.

Feedback

The final stage in strategic supply chain management is to obtain feedback from customers to learn and improve operations and to develop more effective strategies (see Table 8.9).

Table 8.9 What to benchmark (SCOR) Supply Chain Council – Supply Chain Operations Reference

Metric type	*Outcome*	*Diagnostic*
Customer satisfaction/ quality	Perfect order fulfilment Customer satisfaction Product quality	Delivery to commit date Warranty costs, returns, allowances Customer inquiry response time
Time	Order fulfilment lead time	Source/make cycle time Supply chain response time Production plan achieved
Costs	Total supply chain costs	Value-added productivity
Assets	Cash to cash cycle time Inventory days of supply Asset performance	Forecast accuracy Inventory obsolescence Capacity utilization

Best practice defined

Best practice is simply that identifying the best practice in the activities performed in the same industry, sector or in the wider definition best practice across all competitive environments. This latter definition is sometimes referred to as 'world-class'. Best practice is about:

- Doing things better, i.e. more effectively;
- Focus on operations – usually inventory management or distribution management;
- Making comparisons with organizations who are acknowledged leaders in the particular area;
- Identifying similarities between your own organization and the 'benchmark' company chosen;
- Staying focused on context.

Companies pursue 'best practice' to:

- achieve targets they set themselves;
- become more effective;
- become the best in their class at what they do;
- become recognized as best in the world at what they do – reputation.

There are four critical elements to achieving 'best practice' which are:

- focus;
- flexibility;
- continuous improvement;
- visibility achieved by effective use of ICT.

Customer focus is central to achieving best practice and requires that these four critical elements receive attention.

World-class organizations

World-class organizations combine these elements into their philosophy and set benchmarks that measure activities along each of these dimensions (see Figure 8.15). In recent years it has become popular in 'management speak' to refer to 'world-class' organizations. This essentially has developed from organizations wanting to achieve 'excellence' or become 'best in class'. Schonberger (1990) developed his world-class organization concept further and referred to building a chain of customers rather

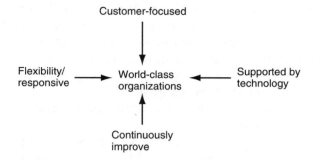

Figure 8.15

than a supply chain. This turned the focus away from supply and towards satisfying demand. It was an important conceptual focus switch.

Balanced scorecard

The balanced scorecard (BSC) is a structured approach to performance measurement and performance management that link the organization's strategic thinking to the activities necessary to achieve desired results. The BSC is a vehicle for communicating an organization's strategic direction and for measuring achievements towards these predetermined objectives. The BSC clearly establishes linkage between strategic objectives, the measures for determining progress, the long-term targets established and the focused initiatives needed to move the organization forward to meet those organizational goals.

The BSC utilizes organization-wide measures plus individually tailored local measures (e.g. SBU or department) to achieve the strategic goals the organization has set itself. Results of BSC measurements provide decision-makers with critical information on:

(1) the efficiency with which resources are transformed into goods and services; and
(2) the effectiveness of organizational activities and operations in terms of their specific contributions to strategic objectives.

It is a means of assigning accountability to individual staff by flowing down the BSC to individuals and teams.

Kaplan and Norton (1996) developed the BSC approach to develop a range of different performance measures to examine and control organizational performance at a strategic level to ensure that the organizational strategies were being controlled. The approach is important because it allows organizations to develop non-financial measures in addition to the traditional financial measures that most organizations adopt. The claimed benefits for the approach may be summarized as follows:

- Gives management strategic control.
- Communicates to everyone in the organization and provides a clear context for their work.
- Discusses how competencies will be developed to meet the challenges, examines customer relationships and how IT will pay off in future.
- Creates an opportunity for learning by more systematically measuring factors important to success and uses the data to involve people in discussions about what the CSFs might be.
- Takes a longer-term perspective by explaining measures that have no immediate effect on 'bottom line profit' or revenue streams.
- Adds to the financial picture already available in the Financial Annual Reports.

Figure 8.16 illustrates the BSC approach with four dimensions centred around the organizational strategy. Financial, customer, internal business processes, and learning and growth are the four dimensions measured. To the left of the BSC you can read the perspectives that are being highlighted yesterday, today and tomorrow. Financial measures tell us what happened yesterday, business processes and customer measures tell us what is happening currently, and the learning and growth measures indicate what could happen tomorrow. These past, present and future perspectives are essential for successful supply chain strategy

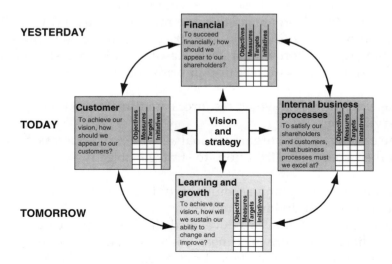

Figure 8.16 The balanced scorecard

development. It also shows how these perspectives are linked to each other reflecting two-way loops between past and present; and present and future all centred on the vision and strategic direction for the organization. How an organization chooses to design, manage and control its supply chain is an important strategic and operational matter.

According to Olve et al. (2000), BSC approaches have gained popularity with many organizations examining their strategic performance using the approach. It can be used to drive strategy forward. The BSC approach shifts focus from purely financial measures towards measurement of how the organization appears to its customers and measuring business processes that deliver or fulfil the customer promise.

Summary

The chapter started by examining the concepts of cost and value in relation to the supply chain. Value added, value chains and the value system were explained before assessing the role of forecasts and budgeting as part of the supply chain planning processes. Different aspects of performance measurement were discussed from simple variance analysis to benchmarking and BSC approaches. The BSC approach was deemed particularly appropriate for measuring supply chain performance because it offered three different perspectives using different types of measure. Financial measures generally examined the past, and current measures focused upon customers and internal business processes while future perspectives addressed the organization's capabilities to improve through continuous learning. Best practice models and the concept of developing world-class organizations were also discussed.

Discussion Questions

1. Present a rationale that carefully explains the importance of having supply chain metrics and identify three important supply chain metrics that your organization of choice is currently using and discuss how each of the measures identified helps to improve the organization's competitive supply chain performance. Examine any potential shortcomings with the measures and evaluate their relative importance to both strategic and operational decision-making. You should provide examples of the measures to illustrate your discussion.
2. For an organization of your choice select one supply chain process or activity, and identify and analyse costs involved in the process or activity in terms of material, labour and overhead or activity costs. Explain how value is created for the customer through the process identified.

3. Explain the terms cost and value in relation to supply chains.
4. There are three cost perspectives that need to be considered in relation to ownership; list them and explain the importance of identifying these costs in relation to managing supply chain costs.
5. Explain the term risk cost.
6. 'Budgeting is important to managing supply chain costs.' Explain why budgeting within organizations needs to be extended to the whole supply chain if supply chain strategies are to be evaluated.
7. Material price variances are just one aspect of managing supply chain costs but why do you think managing material cost might be critical to supply chain efficiency?
8. Explain the term 'benchmarking' and discuss the importance of benchmarking supply chain performance.
9. 'Balanced scorecard approaches have been viewed by many organizations as an essential performance measurement tool.' Discuss.
10. Explain the concept of 'world-class' in relation to organizational supply chains.

Notes

1 'Opportunity cost' is the cost of the alternative foregone a term used in economics.
2 Some of these ideas were articulated by Leroy Zimdars, former director of supply chain management at Harley-Davidson, quoted in John Yuva, 'Reducing costs through the supply chain', Purchasing Today, June 2000.

References

Blanchard, B. S. (1978). *Design and Manage to Life-Cycle Cost*. Portland: M/A Press.

Ellram, L. M. (1996). A structured method for applying purchase cost tools. *International Journal of Purchasing and Materials Management*, Winter.

Hines, T. (1990). *Foundation Accounting*. London: Checkmate Arnold.

Janis, R. (2000). Taxes: The hidden supply chain cost. *Supply Chain Management Review*, Winter, pp. 72–7.

Kaplan, R. S. and Cooper, R. (1998). *Cost and Effect – Using Integrated Cost Systems to Drive Profitability and Performance*. Boston, MA: Harvard Business School Press.

Kaplan, R. S. and Norton, D. P. (1996). *The Balanced Scorecard*. Boston, MA: Harvard Business School Press.

Macneil, J., Testi, J., Cupples, J. and Rimmer, M. (1994). *Benchmarking Global Manufacturing*. Australia: Longman.

Michaels, J. E. and Wood, W. P. (1989). *Design to Cost*. New York: John Wiley & Sons.

Olve, N. G., Roy, J. and Wetter, M. (2000). *Performance Drivers – A Practical Guide to Using the Balanced Scorecard*. London: Wiley.

Porter, M. E. (1980). *Competitive Strategy – Techniques for Analyzing Industries and Competitors*. New York: Free Press.

Schonberger, R. (1990). *Building a Chain of Customers*. London: Hutchinson Books.

Chapter 9

Inventory management

LEARNING OUTCOMES

After reading this chapter you should be able to:

- know why inventory management is important;
- recognize that managing inventories is a strategic as well as an operational issue;
- identify strategies to reduce inventories within organizations and across the supply chain;
- explain the importance of associated tools and techniques used by organizations to plan and control inventories, e.g. ABC/Pareto analysis, EOQ, VMI, collaborative planning, TQM, KANBAN, JiT, LP, MRP and MRPII, DRP, ERP, BRP.

Introduction

> Your best employees are leaving, your warehouse is full of unsold stock and the only person who ever calls is the bank manager.
> *The Sunday Times*, 9 November 2003, p. 15, Business Section 3
> 'Warning signs of a failing business'

Inventory management or stock management are terms that can be used interchangeably. It is an essential part of managing the supply chain activities. The management challenge is to minimize the stock-holding costs whilst simultaneously satisfying customer demand. In other words there is a trade-off between customer service levels achieved and inventories held.

There are a number of tools and techniques that enable managers to manage the trade-offs involved in managing inventories and balancing customer service levels. These include: ABC/EOQ/JiT/MRP/DRP/CRP/ERP each of which will be explained below.

ABC analysis applying Pareto's concept

ABC analysis is a simple but very important technique to identify different categories of stock. It is sometimes referred to as the Pareto concept because it applies Pareto's 80/20 rule. In other words 80 per cent of the value is accounted for by 20 per cent of the volumes. These are in effect the 'A' items of inventory. 'B' items represent 10 per cent of the value and 30 per cent of the volume, while the remaining 'C' items represent the remaining 10 per cent of value but constitute 50 per cent of the volume.

This is a useful concept to apply to any inventory. It will help the managers focus on what is important in terms of allocating their time and effort. A simple example will illustrate the concept. Consider an automobile manufacturer they will need to have many different parts that make up the car. The analysis of the bill of materials (BoM) for the vehicles will reveal a hierarchy of parts. Figure 9.1 demonstrates an abbreviated summary of car parts that make-up the vehicle. Higher value items would be categorized as 'A', medium value as 'B' and low value as 'C'. The rule can be applied to any inventory. The majority of inventory items will always be low-value–high-volume and the smallest category will always be high-value–low-volume. In the example, finished goods items (the vehicle itself, engines and the immediate

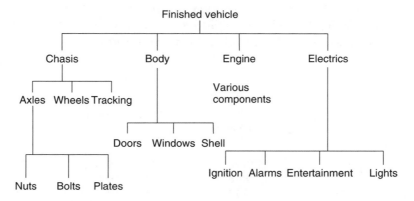

Bill of materials in summary form

Figure 9.1

Table 9.1

Class	Percentage of total items purchased	Percentage of value of total purchases
A	20	80
B	30	10
C	50	10

sub-assemblies) that make the final vehicle would probably constitute the 'A' category. 'B' category items would be those items that feed into the sub-assemblies. The 'C' category would be all the nuts, bolts, rivets, plates, wiring, etc. that there is lots of but the unit cost is relatively low.

Table 9.1 provides a summary for this concept. These values may vary somewhat from organization to organization. The representation is a 'rule of thumb' approximation. Some organizations may decide to use more than three categories but the principle is always the same. It is used to allow managers to concentrate their attention and efforts on those areas that promise the highest 'pay-off'. An example for a manufacturing organization may look as seen in Table 9.2.

The example in Table 9.2 demonstrates how the actual percentage values and volumes may vary in reality. This type of analysis can also be applied to customers and to suppliers. For example, it is highly likely that an organization will earn a high proportion of revenues from a small number of customers. It is also highly likely that an organization will acquire a high proportion of total value for supplies from a relatively small number of suppliers. In any of these situations it will reap rewards for managers who focus their attention and interventions on these high value items A and B categories rather than on C items.

Figure 9.2 illustrates the ABC categories identified by recognizing the percentage of stock value represented by percentage of stock volumes. Data from Table 9.2 has been plotted to produce a cumulative frequency curve to create this graphical representation.

Table 9.2

Class	No. of items	Percentage of items	Annual purchase value	Average value percentage
A	2 325	18.78	£28 500 000	79.61
B	3 232	26.10	£4 100 000	11.45
C	6 825	55.12	£3 200 000	8.94
	12 382	100.00	£35 800 000	100.00

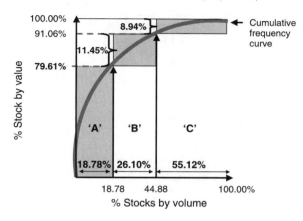

Figure 9.2

Recent trends for many organizations has concentrated their time and effort into managing relationships with fewer suppliers, getting agreements right, working on quality issues, stockless buying agreements or systems contracting and by placing transaction responsibility with the end user. These techniques reduce administration time and effort but maintain high service levels.

Figure 9.3 illustrates a trade-off between customers service and cost. The determining service level is what the organization is aiming to achieve. The qualifying service level is what it must achieve. This illustrates the computation of a trade-off between cost of service and possible increased revenue streams from a service improvement. If the difference between two revenue streams r2−r1 is greater than the incremental cost of service improvement, the difference between c2−c1, it is worth pursuing a higher service level on cost *vis-à-vis* revenue improvement grounds.

Figure 9.4 re-visits the 'Pareto' concept or ABC type analysis which can be applied to a number of different supply chain issues. It is often

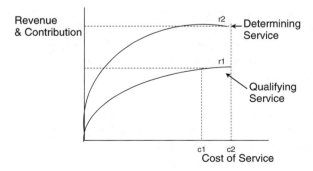

Figure 9.3

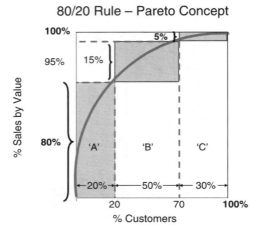

Figure 9.4

perceived as an inventory management tool as in the inventory chapter example in this text. However, it may be applied in different contexts. In this example 80 per cent of sales achieved are attributed to just 20 per cent of customers. These are identified as A items. It also shows that a further 15 per cent of sales are attributed to 50 per cent of customers (B items) and the remainder, 5 per cent, to 30 per cent of customers that are labelled C items. ABC analysis is a means of prioritizing management attention. It is obviously very important for the managers in this scenario to pay particular attention to satisfying the needs of the 20 per cent of customers identified in the A category since they represent such a high proportion of sales value, 80 per cent.

Stockless buying or systems contracting

Sometimes organizations buy large quantities of relatively low value items from a specific supplier, although systems contracting has been extended by some organizations to include higher priced items. The purchaser simply stores the items at the supplier until they are required, thus avoiding costs until there is demand. The arrangement is that goods are replaced using a computer-generated order.
It works as follows:

1. The buyer places the order at firm prices.
2. The supplier delivers a predetermined quantity to the buyer. The supplier may still own items at this point.
3. Buyer inspects items when delivered.

4. Computer system directs storage to designated bin or space.
5. Buyer places purchase order (PO) through computer system which then updates supplier records.
6. Pick sheets are computer-prepared. Buyer physically removes items from supplier's inventory.
7. Supplier submits a single monthly invoice for all items picked.
8. Buyer's accounting department makes a single monthly payment for all items picked.
9. Computer system generates summary reports monthly or when required showing items and quantities used. These records are used for future planning by both buyer and supplier.

Systems contracting is popular because it shortens the time from requisition to delivery and lowers inventory-holding costs. The user is also usually able to give a good forecast to the supplier and that in turn reduces the risk of holding stock nobody wants. Often the purchaser will compensate the supplier for inaccuracy in the forecast but this depends on the initial purchase contract and negotiations. These types of relationship are often more information-rich and less risky than the traditional 'arms length' purchasing approaches.

Outsourcing stockless stores

Many large organizations have entered into outsourcing arrangements with contractors who are responsible for managing this type of operation on their behalf. This is often an efficient means of lowering inventories of large quantities of smaller value items. It allows the organization to focus its management towards the higher value elements of the business. For example, outsourcing consumable stores or the maintenance tools stores may release management time and indeed may remove costs of stores operation for a contractual price that is lower than doing it themselves. If costs are not lower the benefit of allowing managers to focus on parts of the business that require more attention may be important.

Economic order quantities

This particular technique is used to determine economic order quantities (EOQs), lot or batch sizes. The model in Figure 9.5 illustrates the trade-offs that occur between ordering inventories and holding

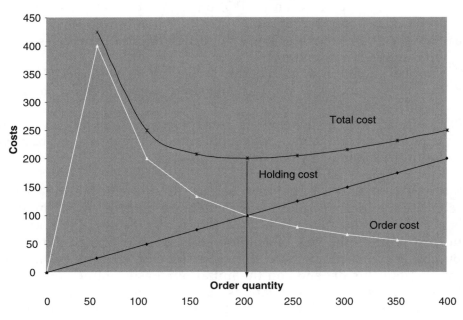

Figure 9.5

inventories. The objective is to order quantities that minimize the cost of ordering and the cost of holding stocks.

The mathematical formula for calculating the EOQ is stated below:

$$EOQ = \sqrt{\frac{2\,Co\,D}{Ch}}$$

where Co is the cost of placing an order, D the demand in a period and Ch the cost of holding one unit of stock.

Table 9.3 provides you with an illustration of the concept in use. The data is available regarding a SKU.

Intuitively what do you think is the EOQ and Why?

Well from the data provided bearing in mind that the EOQ is a point at which total costs for ordering and stock-holding are minimized you might guess that this occurs at an order quantity of 200 from reading Table 9.3. You would be right. This is the point at which all costs are minimized. In mathematical terms it is the turning point. You can compute the same result by applying the formula given above.

Table 9.3 Example of a stock keeping unit

Order quantity (Q)	Holding cost (Ch) (0.5Q × Ch)	+	Order cost (D/Q) × Co)	=	Total cost	
50	25		400		425	
100	50		200		250	
150	75		133		208	
200	100		100		200	min TC
250	125		80		205	
300	150		67		217	
350	175		57		232	
400	200		50		250	

Demand (D) = 1000 units per year; holding costs (Ch) = £1 per item; order cost (Co) = £20 per order.

$$EOQ = \sqrt{\frac{2\ Co\ D}{Ch}}$$

The calculation is as follows:
2 × 20 (cost of order) × 1000 (annual demand) = 40 000/1 (cost of holding stock) and then take the square root of 40 000 = 200 units.

Graphically you can see the trade-off for this data in Figure 9.5. You can see that the turning point for the total cost curve is shown at 200 units. This is the point at which total costs are minimized and where the order cost crosses the holding cost, i.e. the trade-off point.

A number of assumptions apply in the EOQ model, which may be summarized as follows:

(a) Demand is constant;
(b) Re-orders when made can be delivered without any time delay;
(c) Prices do not fluctuate between order periods; and
(d) No small order surcharges apply (or discounts for higher quantities).

These restrictions are quite limiting but the model can be adapted to take account of variations. The simple fixed quantity model can be illustrated as in Figure 9.6. Figure 9.6 shows a situation where 1000 units are ordered regularly. Demand is constant at 250 units per week. There is no lead time and inventories are replaced immediately when required. In this example the average stock-holding in any 4-week period is simply

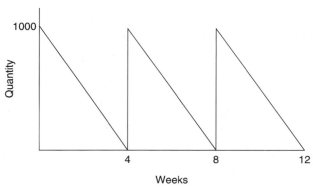

Figure 9.6

$1/2 \times 1000$ units (the total stock for the period). At any point in time the organization will hold average stock of 500 units.

Figure 9.7 shows the average stock-holding graphically. Figure 9.8 shows the effect of introducing a 1-week order lead time into the situation.

The re-order point is therefore at the end of week 3. When this point is reached the organization would need to place an order to replenish the stock. A further complication can be introduced which is 'buffer stock'. Organizations sometimes anticipate the effect of being out of stock (stock-outs). In order to avoid this position and maintain supplies it is essential to hold a 'buffer'. This is stock to cover a stock-out position. Stock-outs occur when demand exceeds forecast, supplies are disrupted by some unforeseen event (e.g. war, strikes, accidents, closure of supplying firm).

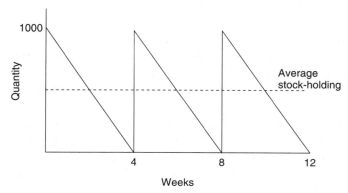

Figure 9.7

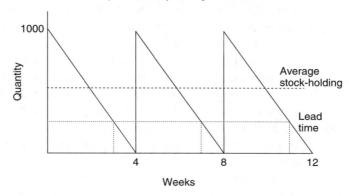

Figure 9.8

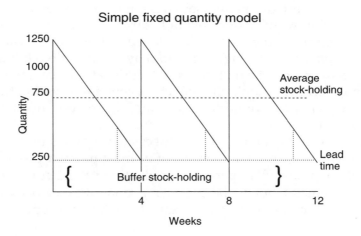

Figure 9.9

Figure 9.9 shows the effect of holding buffer stock equivalent to 1 week's demand. Note how the average stock-holding has increased as a consequence.

Demand-led management

Recent focus on managing the supply chain has switched from simply organizing supplies of materials towards managing customer demand. In order to achieve this *'synchronization'* of materials movement is required throughout the chain triggered by customer demand. Managing demand requires information to be shared across the supply chain in order to achieve synchronization. The accuracy and timeliness of this information is of paramount importance to reduce risks from demand amplification. Demand amplification and its consequences have long been recognized as having a *'bullwhip'* effect on the supply chain. This simply means that distortions can occur causing excess inventories at a number of links in the chain. It is often the retail store that receives signals of demand from customers at the end of a supply chain. This demand then triggers further supplies along the chain. However, if that information is inaccurate it may cause inefficiencies in the rest of the chain by signalling to increase production and order components to make end products in excess of the quantities demanded.

Forrester (1961) was the first to recognize and study the effect of inaccurate demand forecasting upon the supply chain. Forrester examined channel interrelationships to demonstrate how demand forecasting could amplify positions within the channel such that oscillations occurred to correct the pattern of over- and under-demand from the market. The 'bullwhip' is depicted in Figure 9.10 using a retail example. Demand from the end consumer is relayed to the retailer who relays it to their supplier at each stage demand may be amplified. Initially there may be an overenthusiastic forecast which is later re-balanced may be by an underforecast. A bullwhip effect is experienced within the supply chain as it oscillates around 'real demand', i.e. market demand by the end consumer.

Proctor & Gamble explored this effect after a series of erratic shifts up and down a supply chain for one of its most popular products (baby disposable nappies – Pampers). They identified the cause of excessive swings in demand not to be increasing quantities of baby waste at certain times but simply that the retail stores failed to update demand

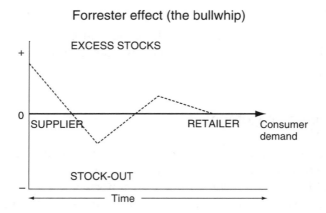

Figure 9.10

forecasts, batched orders, changed prices (causing rationing by the customer). These three elements linked together caused the bullwhip in the supply chain.

The Forrester effect is illustrated in Figure 9.11. In this example, demand from the customer is transmitted to the retailer and then passed upstream to first tier and from first tier to second tier suppliers. At each stage the demand is amplified causing increased inventory to be held at each stage in the supply chain.

Similarities exist in a number of different supply chains. It is a known fact in the grocery trade that promotional activities such as 'buy one get one free' (BOGOF) or three for two or simple discounting may cause problems within the supply chain. Forecasting with accuracy the effect of the promotional offer on likely customer demand then becomes crucial. Forecast accuracy however may be problematical because other conditions outside the forecasting equation may have changed, e.g. environmental conditions (taxes, stability, consumer attitudes to name but three).

With the development of appropriate ICT it has become possible to forecast demand more accurately. Personal computers and forecasting software make this possible. However, inaccurate demand forecasts are still a problem. One major challenge facing supply chain managers is how to work across organizational boundaries effectively to share responsibility for the accuracy of the market demand forecast. Collaboration across functions within the firms involved within a supply chain and

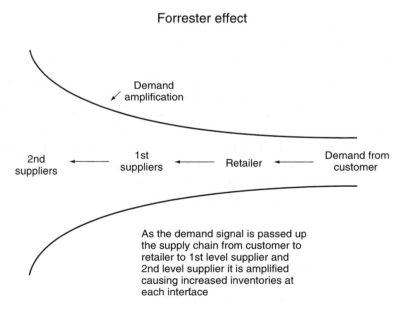

Figure 9.11

collaboration throughout the chain involving both customers and suppliers is needed to achieve this. Large organizations working with large suppliers have been able to respond by employing ERP systems such as SAP and ORACLE.

Collaborative planning

Collaborative supply chain strategies are important for organizations that recognize that to deliver customer-focused products and services the means cannot always be achieved independently by a single organization. To serve customers better may require different types of collaborative strategies: outsourcing, co-makership, co-operation agreements in, for example, technical knowledge transfer, strategic alliances, partnerships of various kinds and joint venture arrangements.

Some firms produce many products, with different customers, suppliers and delivery methods; the challenge for them is how to deal with the complexity of the different supply chains they manage. In the USA Textile and Apparel Supply Chain work was conducted by TC2 a solutions consultancy firm under the lead consultant Jim Lovejoy. The DAMA (demand-activated manufacturing architecture) Project decided to pick a specific product, for example, a man's nylon parka and trace all the steps in the process for the product from raw materials to its final purchase by a retail customer. The team comprised the retailer, an apparel manufacturer, two textile mills and two fibre suppliers involved in the production.

In this supply chain, the total time from the nylon fibre to the retail customer buying the jacket was 45 weeks. Nine weeks was process time but the actual assembly (cutting and sewing) of the parka took only 55 minutes. So why did it take so long for the raw materials to reach the end customer? The primary reason discovered in the project was due to uncertainty in the retail forecast. As Lovejoy stated 'there was a lot of "just in case inventory" in the supply pipeline'. This was because no one wanted to disappoint their immediate customer. In addition, there were 15 inspections, 10 transportation steps and the goods spent 24 days in trucks. The total supply was not synchronized and only a small number of business processes were integrated between organizations making up the supply chain.

Transparency or visibility within the supply chain

Many large retailers have shared information with their large suppliers using state of the art information systems that allows point of sale information to be viewed by the supplier. This releases resources and management time within the retail organization and enables their suppliers to manage demand for their own product supplies with the retailer. This doesn't just happen in retail but it is happening within other industries too. The demand for automobiles and the complexity of managing their supply networks may be achieved better through sharing information to create transparency throughout the supply chain.

Vendor-managed inventory

One approach to the demand management problem has been for organizations to shift the responsibility for inventory management to their supplying organization. Wal-Mart has worked with its major suppliers for several years to allow them access to customer demand information and then organize their own operations to ensure they can meet the customer demand. For example, the VF Corporation is the largest clothing manufacturer in the world and they have major brands such as Wrangler jeans. VF are able to manage and co-ordinate the flows of materials (denim, zips, cotton, buttons, studs) to their production units worldwide to ensure that they supply jeans (finished goods) on time to their retail customer. VF develop ranges and fill the store space and are paid when the products are sold out of store (Hines, 2004). This has a number of benefits for consumers, retail customers and supplier. These may be listed as:

- Consumers get what they want when they require it.
- The retailer does not have to manage the inventory nor do they pay for it until it is sold.
- The supplier only produces what is required (assuming the demands are accurate from the retail information systems and they should at least be more accurate because they are now based on real-time information rather than forecast data).
- The supplier has an added benefit because they are allowed to manage store space, they can introduce new products and try them on customers before committing to large production quantities.
- The benefits to the whole supply chain are to remove waste and inefficiencies.

There are also some potential problems that could occur:

- Unwillingness of the retailer to share data.
- Seasonal products or fashionable products may make it difficult to predict the demand.

- The cost of restructuring systems and the investment required in appropriate information systems.
- The effective 'outsourcing' of supplies to the supplier may make the retail customer vulnerable if the supplier fails to deliver.

Just-in-Time

Just-in-Time is one of the many management principles that have been known for years but prior to the 1970s and 1980s it was simply too difficult to apply consistently and across all categories of stocks. The main reason was the mathematical algorithms involved required many complex calculations to be performed. It was not until the development of high-power business computers in the 1970s that these computations could be easily facilitated. Toyota, the Japanese automobile manufacturer, was keen to pioneer a number of innovative management practices as part of its 'Kaizen' philosophy. JiT became closely associated with this approach.

The basic principle is simple. Order stock items when required. This avoids the need to hold any stock and as a consequence avoids risks of obselescent, redundant or waste in inventories. The practice requires the co-ordination processes to be managed efficiently. It places a great deal of responsibility with suppliers who must be able to respond quickly when supplies are ordered. Components and raw materials must arrive at the production centre exactly when they are needed. This eliminates the need to hold stock and reduces queues in the work-in-process inventory. Effectively peaks and troughs are ironed out of the system. The right goods, in the right place, at the right time.

Think about what would happen to our inventory in a system where this happened. Figure 9.12 illustrates the effect of JiT on traditional purchase ordering approaches represented by the EOQ examples earlier. In this example daily orders of 50 units are placed. Assuming a 5-day week the effect is to deliver 250 units per week at a rate of 50 per day as required. Inventory costs have fallen substantially. In this example at any point in time the organization only hold an average of half a day's stock ((opening stock + closing stock)/2) or 25 units. This is a substantial saving in inventory-holding costs from the previous example. Another very important issue in considering JiT systems is the effect on storage space. In the example where traditional EOQ was applied the average storage space needed to store 500 units ignoring the buffer. Under the JiT system with an average of 25 units this has fallen to 1/20th.

Demand and supply are balanced in a JiT system. Processes need to be designed to co-ordinate the supplies required as customer demand

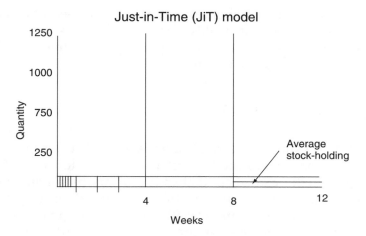

Figure 9.12

triggers orders. This process of balancing inputs to the system, processes and outputs to meet customer demand smoothes production flows and inventories are only held for very short periods of time when production is taking place. JiT treats set-up and order costs as variable rather than fixed costs implied by the EOQ model.

Three key TQM concepts underpin the JiT approach

They are:

1. The maker is responsible for quality or as buyers sometimes say 'quality is a given'.
2. The quality is built-in rather than inspected-in. This means that each production operative is responsible for quality and not simply a quality control inspector.
3. Compliance is required with the quality standards set by the buyer.

These are important principles in the JiT system. The small lot sizes and the reduction in inventory substantially lowers risk for the purchaser. There can be no build up of defective parts or problem parts. Smoothing the inventory flows avoids any 'bullwhip' effect in the system. Manufacturing plants are not stressed by producing large quantities. This allows planned maintenance to occur. Thus future problems are not simply stored but eradicated. Machines and working areas are kept clean. Maintenance, cleaning and tidying areas can take place in a planned working environment. Problem solving too can often take place when problems are identified by quality control checks. Ishikawa (why,

why – cause and effect, fishbone diagrams) can be used as an analytical tool along with statistical quality control techniques. JiT systems are essentially demand-driven. It is a 'pull system' (market-driven) as opposed to a 'push system' (production-driven).

Kanban system

The Kanban is a simple effective control system. It is essential to JiT as a visible tool that makes the JiT system operate effectively. Kanban is simply Japanese for card. The Kanban is most useful for small lot sizes, high volumes and low value items that are regularly used, e.g. C items in ABC terminology. Kanbans are either single or double card systems. In the double card system there are two types of card: conveyance (C) and production (P). In the single card system only the C card is used.

Rules of the double card system are as follows:

1. No parts may be made unless there is a P-kanban authorizing production. Workers may do maintenance, cleaning or work-improvement projects until P-kanban arrives rather than making parts that are not required. Similarly C-kanban controls the transport of parts between departments.
2. Only standard containers are used and they are always filled.
3. Only one P- and one C-kanban per container.

The essence of this visual control system is that it prevents an unwanted inventory build-up.

Inventory build-ups often disguise more serious problems. It is essential to systematically reduce inventory. Not only to reduce cost but to identify problems. For example, an organization may simply be holding a buffer stock to accommodate inefficiencies of a supplying organization.

Implications of JiT systems for supply management

Transport logistics need to be carefully organized to accommodate JiT systems where routing may be critical to the organization of pick-ups and deliveries. Deliveries may also need to be re-organized away from a central depot to the place at which the items are required. This avoids double handling. Many organizations have organized their transportation and warehousing capabilities to operate effectively with JiT. For example, many retailers who operate JiT replenishment systems have organized 'cross-docking'. This is a system whereby the delivery arrives at a transport storage depot not to be stored for any length of time but to be 'cross-docked', i.e. switched between delivery vehicles that take goods to their final destination using standardized containers to facilitate ease of handling. Many of these transportation adjustments are important to manage the system effectively.

McLachin and Piper (1990) identified 11 benefits of JiT systems. They are:

1. Set-up time reduction.
2. Small-lot production possible.
3. Small-lot transportation possible.
4. Multi-process handling through automation.
5. Zero-defect quality control.
6. Equipment maintenance.
7. Smoother and mixing of production flows.
8. Withdrawal by subsequent processes.
9. In-house modification and production of equipment.
10. JiT supply arrangements.
11. Employee involvement in continuous improvement.

Buyer–supplier relationships in JiT systems

One of the biggest adjustments required when adopting JiT systems is the close level of co-operation needed between a buyer and a supplier. Organizations operating JiT systems often have fewer suppliers but they must work very closely with them to co-ordinate the different parts of the supply chain. It was Demming who first suggested that organizations needed to develop closer relationships with fewer suppliers in his list of 14 principles of TQM.

Lean production or the 'Big JiT'

Lean production (LP) is sometimes called the 'Big JiT' and was pioneered by Toyota. It focuses upon Kaizen and in particular the elimination of waste. Lean production systems are flexible and responsive to customer needs. Organizations implementing these LP systems can lower costs in production. These principles were developed in the automobile industry and have since been transferred into a number of manufacturing and service sector organizations. In many of the case studies reported focusing on LP a key principle seems to be for the suppliers to understand the key manufacturing processes in the buying organization. As a consequence these organizations often need to work closely together and the automobile manufacturers often went into supplier companies to explain why they needed supplies presented in a particular way at a particular time. In these exchanges they help suppliers to identify waste and inefficiencies in their own systems that they aim to remove. This type of involvement is often based on another approach known as 'business process re-engineering'. In these exchanges often suppliers engage in 'open book' accounting revealing their cost structures to the buyer. This is essential if costs are to be reduced. This is a radical departure from adversarial purchasing negotiations (win–lose). In the LP approach purchasing behaviour is a win–win situation for all parties. By lowering the whole supply chain cost between the two or more organizations involved in these processes each can gain. For a fuller account of the benefits of LP see Womack and Jones (1994).

Lean and agile strategies

It is not simply lean manufacturing systems that are important but agility is important too and this has been recognized in the phrase 'leagility' coined to denote the concept (Naylor et al., 1999). Suppliers need to be responsive to variable customer demand by being agile enough to deal with shifts in volume while keeping inventories to a minimum. Replenishment lead times and information flows become critical to managing leagility. In lean strategies the emphasis is on manufacturing to a forecast, keeping inventory holding low and seeking economies of scale in production. Agility relies on making to order acting on actual demand signals from the market, postponing production until that demand is known and being capable of adjusting capacity quickly (van Hoek, 1998). Decoupling points become central to the concept of leagility. An organization is able to postpone production if it is able to hold strategic inventories which can be used across different products. For example, generic and modular parts and components that can be interchanged between different finished products would be classified as strategic inventories. In apparel manufacture greige cloth is held for the purpose of postponing colour dying processes until demand is known with greater accuracy than a forecast. Dell computers are manufactured in a similar way using shared components between different model specifications.

Materials requirement planning

Demand for the final finished goods triggers a number of other purchase orders in a hierarchical structure. For example, the order for a single automobile creates demand for all the sub-assemblies and components that comprise the vehicle. Demand for these lower level items is dependent on final demand for the vehicle. A master schedule is needed. These schedules are created in a tree form with the principal item at the head and all the sub-assemblies and branches shown as branches. The BoM shown earlier is similar to a Master Schedule in structure. The difference between the BoM and the Master Schedule is that the BoM is for a single item whereas the Master Schedule would incorporate orders for several different products within the production period. At each subsequent level (and there may be many levels) the required materials are identified. The aim of MRP systems is to minimize cost of inventories and maintain customer service levels. These aims are often in conflict under other systems, e.g. JiT but under an MRP system they are achievable simultaneously. MRP benefits include the ability to rapidly re-plan and re-schedule in response to changes in a dynamic environment. For example, supposing a company wants to change some key components in a computer build, say a P4 processor rather than an equivalent Athlon processor to enhance the build quality. MRP would quickly facilitate this change. When the next order is placed the build specification and hence the BoM can be altered to implement the required change. It is flexible and responsive to the customer needs.

There are three principles of MRP. They are:

1. Dependence of demand on demand for the final product.
2. Netting of inventory with expected deliveries and open orders to give a balance on-hand.
3. Time phasing by using information on lead times and needs.

There are three basic MRP inputs to the system which are:

1. Master production schedule (MPS).
2. The structured BoM for the MPS.
3. Information on inventories, open orders and lead times.

Within the MRP system a number of rules need to be specified. They include:

1. Acceptable lot sizes.
2. Safety stocks.
3. Reject allowances.

MRP II systems and capacity requirements planning

Manufacturing resource planning involves the merger of data sets from the firm's planning systems and the firm's financial systems. When

MRP systems were introduced it was not possible to easily merge these different data sets because each system maintained its own integrity. Furthermore, each system had its own inputs, process routines and outputs. The development of modern computer systems that are more powerful has enabled these data sets to merge and from a single point of entry the data can be manipulated and addressed to answer different sets of questions.

This has led to the development of capacity requirements planning (CRP) which is essentially planning various resources to achieve capacity in rather similar fashion to MRP systems for materials. CRP translates people and machine requirements and creates a match between what is needed and what is available. If there is insufficient capacity the manager must either adjust capacity or the master production schedule. This feedback loop to the MPS allows the organization to produce iterative solutions to the production problem. It is often referred to as 'closed loop MRP'. The CRP module links to MRP and allows managers to manage the whole production process not simply the materials element. These systems are only as good as the quality of information that is input to the system. Consistent, complete, accurate and timely data are required. Many contemporary MRP II systems integrate cost accounting data and are used in conjunction with budgetary control and product costing systems.

These systems provide managers with performance measures, planned order releases and the ability to simulate a master production schedule in response to proposed changes in production. They can be expensive to introduce and require careful management. Training, organizational change, computer hardware and software, and different procedures may all be required to implement these systems successfully. In a large organization the benefits can be immense and far outweigh the cost of introduction, e.g. reduce inventory, shorten lead times, split orders, increase delivery efficiency and allow production flexibility.

Distribution requirements planning

Distribution requirements planning (DRP) and DRP II are applications of time-phasing logic of MRP to the distribution function. DRP forecasts demand by distribution centre and aims to plan deliveries accordingly. Figure 9.13 illustrates DRP with a manufacturer delivering to a central warehouse which moves goods to local depots which move goods onto individual sites as and when required. DRP is an essential part of efficient MRP systems.

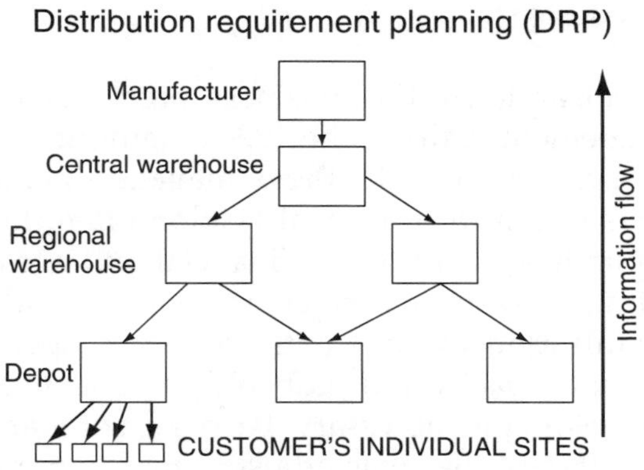

Distribution requirement planning (DRP)

Figure 9.13

Enterprise resource planning systems

Enterprise resource planning (ERP) systems view the whole organization as an information system, different parts of an organization's management information is integrated. The big advantage of such systems is that data should be entered once only and people should be able to access the data to inform any other parts of the system. It is an enabling technology. Large suppliers of these systems include: SAP, Oracle, PeopleSoft and I2 technologies. ERP should allow an organization to develop an integrated management information system that not only links all parts of the internal organization but also links with customer and supplier information systems to share data and improve the quality of management decision-making.

ERP systems are used to integrate business processes throughout the organization. Manufacturing, marketing, finance, human resources and purchasing information may be combined and analysed in different ways depending on the questions the organization wants to answer. For example, when the company receives a sales order it allows purchasing to be aware that the demand has been registered, production to be aware of the capacity needed (materials, manpower, machinery), sales to be aware of lead times involved and finance to address cash flow planning, budgetary control, profitability and other financial commitments involved. Integration is a major benefit of these systems and although expensive they can remove costs through efficiency and standardization of systems and procedures.

Web-enabled systems allow supply chain partners to exchange information (orders, forecasts, production schedules, inventories and fill rates) via the Internet. Real-time accurate, consistent data can be exchanged between buyer and seller.

Business process design

Designing efficient and effective business processes is the essence of operations management. During the 1970s many firms began to introduce computer systems to help them manage operations. Many of these investments began in piecemeal fashion often the computer system would be purchased to process financial and accounting records, followed by sales and order management systems and to pay personnel. As the organization extended its computer operations it would purchase additional capacity and probably had a team of programmers employed to develop the necessary bespoke software or purchased some standard software that was adjusted to accommodate the need. The added modules were often a bad fit with existing systems and often different software worked on different assumptions or in a different programming language and glitches occurred when the organization tried to integrate the different modules. A consequence of this piecemeal approach was a series of 'legacy' systems. Data storage and data processing was very expensive. Developers used complex programming algorithms to reduce data storage and data processing times but in so doing they often designed problems into the systems. One example of this is the *Millennium Bug or Y2K* where to save storage space only the last two digits were used in the year recognition of a date. This along with the falling price of computer technology in the 1990s drove many firms to re-invest in new technology in the 1990s to eradicate the problem that was in store when they hit the year 2000. For example, many organizations invested in ERP systems to achieve consistency, economies of scale and integration. In developing these systems, an organization may have to re-design business processes to achieve consistency in the processes and to ensure effective integration between different areas. Internal integration may only be one aspect within a supply chain context. It may also be important to establish external integration also with supplier's and customer's business processes and systems. Figure 9.14 provides an illustration of how an organization may decide to structure its key processes to interface with external customers and suppliers and to integrate internal systems to support business operations. In effect the internal supply chain and the upstream (supplier) and downstream (customer) networks.

Business process re-engineering

Business process re-engineering was the term assigned by Hammer and Champy (1993, p. 30) to explain 'fundamental re-thinking and radical re-design of business processes to achieve dramatic improvements in

ERP architecture

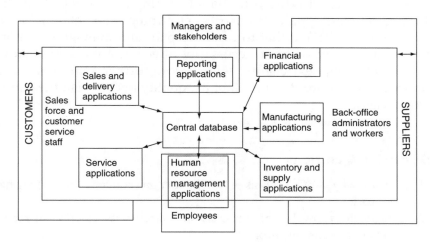

Figure 9.14

Source: Adapted from Davenport (1998).

critical, contemporary measures of performance, such as quality, cost, service and speed'. Hammer and Champy provide seven key principles for re-engineering:

1. Organize around outcomes not tasks;
2. Have those who use the outputs of a process perform the process;
3. Have people who collect information process it;
4. Treat geographically dispersed resources as though they were centralized;
5. Link parallel activities instead of integrating their results;
6. Put the decision point at the point work is performed and build in controls to the process;
7. Capture information once at source.

Summary

A number of key supply chain strategies focus on lowering inventory to minimize cost and simultaneously satisfy customer demand. This chapter has discussed a number of inventory management tools used by organizations to manage inventory. Japanese LP techniques pioneered these approaches in practice during the 1980s and 1990s. Since their development in the automobile industry LP systems have transferred to and been adopted by a number of other industrial sectors.

Principles of lean manufacture have played a part in supply chain management concepts introduced to manufacturing and service industries including: textiles, apparel, aerospace, electronics and retailing sectors in an acknowledgement that to carefully plan and manage inventories is to minimize cost without necessarily affecting adversely customer service levels. The next chapter will explore further some key supply chain levers for improving profitability, quality and re-visit the concept of world-class.

Discussion Questions

1. Explain why ABC analysis is an important concept for managing inventories.
2. Explain the term 'bill of materials' and discuss its function in managing production inventories.
3. 'The "trade-off" concept is important for managers trying to balance customer service and profitability'. Discuss.
4. Explain what is meant by a stockless purchasing system.
5. What is a Kanban and why is it used?
6. Explain the differences between MRP and JiT.
7. Why is continuous improvement critical to JiT systems?
8. For your own organization or any organization with which you are familiar identify categories of stock applying ABC analysis. Explain and evaluate why it is important for the organization to do this and demonstrate how managing inventories can improve overall performance.
9. 'Inventory management is both a strategic planning activity and an operational issue'. Discuss.
10. 'ERP systems are often developed to integrate different organizational subsystems. The big advantage is not simply internal integration but linking externally with customers and suppliers who have similar systems. However, many commentators have said that organizations buying ERP technologies need to be careful that they are not buying legacy systems'. Discuss.

References

DAMA Project (Demand Activated Manufacturing Architecture). www.dama.tc2.com.

Davenport, T. H. (1998). Putting the enterprise into the enterprise system. *Harvard Business Review*, July/August, p. 124.

Forrester, J. W. (1961). *Industrial Dynamics*. Boston, MA: MIT Press.

Hammer, M. and Champy, J. (1993). *Reengineering the Corporation: A Manifesto for Business Revolution*. New York: Harper Business.

Hines, T. (2004). The emergence of supply chain strategy as a critical success factor for retailing organizations. In *International Retail Marketing – A Case Study Approach* (Birtwistle, G., Bruce, M. and Moore, C., eds). Oxford: Butterworth-Heinemann.

McLachin, R. and Piper, C. (1990). Just-in-Time production. *Business Quarterly*, Summer, pp. 36–42.

Naylor, J. B., Naim, M. M. and Berry, D. (1999). Leagility interfacing the lean and agile manufacturing paradigm in the total supply chain. *International Journal of Production Economics*, **62**, 107–18.

van Hoek, R. I. (1998). Reconfiguring the supply chain to implement postponed manufacturing. *International Journal of Logistics Management*, **9** (1), 95–110.

Womack, J. P. and Jones, D. T. (1994). From lean production to lean enterprise. *Harvard Business Review*, **27** (2), 93–103.

Chapter 10

Supply chain profitability, quality and world-class organizations

LEARNING OUTCOMES

The purpose of this chapter is to develop your knowledge and understanding of the key business issues relating to supply chain profitability, quality management and world-class organizations. In particular after studying this chapter you should be able to:

- recognize the importance of supply chain profitability and how it is achieved;
- know and understand the importance of quality management and its impact upon profitability;
- be aware of the different management approaches to quality including the use of statistical process control charts and the development of international standards.

Supply chain management and profitability

Managing the supply chain is a core competence that the organization must possess to deliver profit and return on investment (ROI). It has a major impact on organizational objectives and effectiveness in achieving those objectives. According to Dyer (2000, p. 27) maximizing supply network effectiveness is the key to individual and supply chain profitability. Virtual integration is achieved by firms collaborating in partnership (alliance), which is also referred to in the literature as the extended enterprise, strategic network or virtual corporation. Figure 10.1 illustrates how supply chain strategies can impact upon sales revenues and costs and how total profit is affected as a consequence.

How supply chain management can affect the 'bottom line'

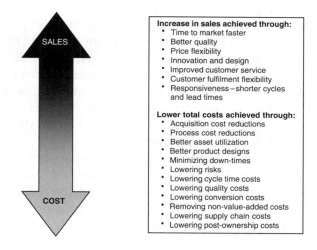

Increase in sales achieved through:
* Time to market faster
* Better quality
* Price flexibility
* Innovation and design
* Improved customer service
* Customer fulfilment flexibility
* Responsiveness – shorter cycles and lead times

Lower total costs achieved through:
* Acquisition cost reductions
* Process cost reductions
* Better asset utilization
* Better product designs
* Minimizing down-times
* Lowering risks
* Lowering cycle time costs
* Lowering quality costs
* Lowering conversion costs
* Removing non-value-added costs
* Lowering supply chain costs
* Lowering post-ownership costs

Bottom line profit = sales revenue – total costs

Figure 10.1 How supply chain management can improve 'bottom line' performance

The principle of 'world-class management' is focused upon maximizing profitability by driving revenue up and lowering cost or eliminating completely non-value-added costs. Schonberger (1986) introduced the notion of world-class manufacturing and principles to achieving world-class performance. The next section explains in more detail how 'world-class' management principles may be applied.

World-class supply chain management principles

Time to market

Time to market has important implications for lifetime profitability (Stalk and Hout, 1990). Research has shown that being faster to market with new products is important and 40 per cent or more of the market may be gained at entry with a new product if it is timely. Conversely being late will definitely cost the firm introducing new products late. Often late entry may result in the loss of a market or it may simply be that the late entrant firm withdraws because it cannot get hold of enough market share to make persistence worthwhile. Buzzell and Gale (1987) demonstrated that being first with a new product could earn profit margins that were twice as high as their competitors.

Developing appropriate partnering strategies is one way to achieve this (Buzzell and Ortmeyer, 1996). Reducing product development cycles has been a prime focus for 'world-class' organizations and many have reduced these cycle times by as much as 30 per cent. Often cross-functional teams are used to examine the different processes and times taken. Time compression is a strategic objective and can enhance competitive advantage (Towill, 1996). One important development has been the introduction of 'concurrent engineering' principles (O'Neal, 1993). Put simply this means that processes that hitherto would have been performed in sequence are now rescheduled and done in parallel thus removing time from the total process.

Developing responsive supply chains has also been important for organizations to respond to peak demand. Responsive organizations are able to shift resources (material, labour and overheads) quickly to manufacture products or provide services that have higher demand than expected. Responsive organizations are able to save cost and achieve additional revenue by 'catching these waves of unexpected demand'.

World-class organizations draw comparisons with the best in the world when it comes to measuring their responsiveness. Measures include various cycle times and costs (e.g. time to market, time from receipt of order to delivery of order). Inevitably such measures translate easily into cost. The more difficult measures that are often overlooked are those that sometimes remain hidden such as 'opportunity cost' measures (e.g. sales that would have been lost if the firm had not been responsive).

Consistent on time deliveries, high fill rates, complete orders and QR are essential for ECR. Striving to improve customer satisfaction is essential in 'world-class' organizations. The customer is the key focal point and the raison d'etre.

Supplier choice is an extremely important aspect of any decision regarding sourcing. Sourcing and purchasing decisions can influence cycle times greatly. In making supplier choices an organization will need to consider the many trade-offs involved in order to achieve the right combination of quality, service and price.

Quality improvements

There are numerous examples of organizations where quality improvements manifest themselves by translating quality into profitability. Doyle (2002) provides an example of the Prism, a Toyota manufactured under license at the GM factory in the USA. This particular product earned 50 per cent more in 'lifetime' profits than its GM near competitor.

The premium price charged was achieved simply through reputation of the brand despite the fact that the car was virtually same as the GM substitute, made with the same components and in the same factory. This provides one episode of consumer confidence being achieved through reputation of Toyota product quality. Interestingly it was not always so, back in the 1950s when Toyota first introduced its cars to the USA it had a disastrous launch with numerous manufacturing faults identified. However, within a short period of time Toyota did decide to withdraw completely from the US market to minimize damage to their reputation. They did not re-enter the US market for 10 years but when they did they spoke the language of quality with 'zero defects'. The damage limitation exercise had paid dividends and Toyota maintained and enhanced its reputation as a quality automobile manufacturer.

It has been estimated that as much as 75 per cent of many manufacturing problems is attributable to defects in purchased materials (Burt et al., 2003). The principle of zero defects and six sigma have been adopted by world-class organizations with the specific aim of eliminating such problems. Collaboration with suppliers during product development cycles is of paramount importance if such costs are to be fully eradicated. The problem has been identified in service environments too and although lower it is still thought to be a significant cost. Japanese automobile manufacturers have been pioneers in working closely with suppliers and their supplier's supplier to identify problems and lower total product cost through quality improvements. Indeed this is the 'Kaizen' principle in practice.

Innovation

Many successful new product innovations have come from technologies, designs and prototypes developed by suppliers. It has been estimated that as much as 35 per cent of all new product innovation may be attributable to supplier firms. Leveraging supplier technology or other specific competencies in design may be an important difference between those organizations with longevity and those with shorter corporate lives. Business history is cluttered with examples of organizations that started out in one industry and moved to another industry not simply once in their corporate lifetime but may be more times. These businesses also provide evidence of being able to work collaboratively with suppliers for mutual benefit. Toyota themselves provide one example; 3 M, Pearson, P&O and Ocean provide other examples of successful re-invention. For the many who did evolve there are equally many who did not. Some of these once household names no longer exist. Collector catalogues and antique showroom sales are littered with examples of this genre of business history, e.g. Dinky, Matchbox, Triang, Raleigh, Sinclair, BSA.

Lowering total ownership costs

The other part of the equation to improve the competitive position of an organization's supply chain is to examine total costs of ownership (TCO). There are only two ways in which financial improvements can be made: one is to raise revenue and the other to reduce costs. This section is about how to lower costs, more specifically TCO. Costs are incurred acquiring, converting, holding and even after ownership (i.e. post-ownership). Acquisition and conversion costs are easily understood. Post-ownership costs may include dealing with hazardous waste materials, manufacturing waste or the cost of lost sales as a consequence of poor product/service quality. The latter may have been a consequence of purchasing defective materials and incorporating them in the manufactured product. It is important that manufacturing organizations engage in effective supply chain management to prevent this happening. It is not only manufacturing companies at risk. Service providers can just as easily damage their reputation by purchasing defective materials consumed in the service. For example, a training provider that provides support materials for a management training course may purchase folders to hold materials and papers that subsequently fall apart. It will not be the company providing the folders but the training provider that will receive the criticism and loss of reputation. Poor catering, poor accommodation and poor organization of a conference could similarly damage reputation and all these activities may have been outsourced to supplier firms whose reputations remain intact while the conference reputation is damaged.

There are four key stages involved in managing supplies:

1. Requirement identification;
2. Sourcing supplies and suppliers;
3. Pricing;
4. Post-award activities.

Generating the initial requirements is critical to the success of any product or service. It requires that materials and services to purchase be optimized. Simultaneously specifications need to be developed and statements of work describing the requirements. Whitney (1988) stated that approximately 85 per cent of cost in terms of materials, services and equipment was 'designed in' during this key stage. It is essential at this stage to examine cost, availability and substitutes carefully and to search for ways that these costs may be lowered without sacrificing quality.

Sourcing supplies and suppliers takes considerable time and may involve hours of research in searching, visiting, negotiating, inspecting and ensuring compliance issues are resolved. Cost, quality, technology, timeliness, dependability, responsiveness and service are all issues that require thorough investigation. It is true that electronic searches using Internet technologies can now save time and cost but they are no substitute for thorough investigation and the thinking processes that must be engaged in to select appropriate products, services and suppliers.

Prices negotiated and conditions and terms attached to the purchase must be fair to the supplier firm if you expect them to deal fairly with you. If the supplier firm receives appropriate and just rewards for their effort they are more likely to search for ways to lower cost that bring benefits to both parties – purchaser and vendor.

Post-award activities refer to ensuring that the product or service ordered is received on time, complete, at the agreed price and agreed quality meeting fully the specifications outlined in the requirements stage.

So how can TCO be lowered?

There are a number of ways in which these costs can be lowered which are as follows:

- Better product design – supplier involvement at an early stage can search for ways to work collaboratively and lower costs.
- Acquisition cost – identification of appropriate suppliers, products, services that meet specifications without sacrificing quality and at lower cost. Negotiating hard but fair deals that provide appropriate rewards.
- Processing cost – meticulous planning and implementation to increase efficiencies.
- Better asset utilization – collaborative and alliance relationships often remove obstacles, enable sharing of knowledge, resources and equipment and provide better scheduling to minimize wastage and idle time. These combined activities result in better asset utilization.
- Quality cost – working with carefully selected suppliers and continuously improving quality can lower costs of quality by removing inspection costs. Statistical process controls can be applied and other conformance measures to ensure that quality enhancement takes place.
- Down-time cost – removing costly down-time through planned maintenance programmes and by re-engineering processes that ensure efficiency without placing undue strain on processes.
- Risk cost – working more closely with chosen suppliers who meet the supply standards set by the purchasing organization may lower

Risk cost. Recent trends have witnessed many firms lowering risk cost by working more effectively with fewer suppliers who meet their requirements.

- Cycle time cost – Shorter cycle times for sourcing and selecting suppliers, bringing new products to market, for production processes all lower cost, as 'time is money'.
- Conversion cost – reducing time, increasing productivity through better asset utilization, better use of labour and materials can all lower the conversion cost. These costs are every bit as real and important as the purchase cost itself.
- Non-value-added cost – Womack and Jones (1994) identified that the average time taken for cola to reach the consumer's refrigerator is 11 months. The actual time taken in conversion processes is 3 hours.
- Supply chain cost – developing and managing the supply chain network requires considerable investment, primarily in people. Proper recruitment, selection, training and education are essential as is the investment in appropriate software systems and the design of appropriate systems, policies and procedures to manage these activities.

Quality management

Quality management is about competitive capability, reputation and profitability. It is widely acknowledged that there are many different pathways to achieving quality. A number of individual pioneers stressed the importance of quality improvements for many years but much of this prescription was ignored by large businesses that failed to see the link between quality and competitive performance. Today this is unthinkable since every aspect of competition depends on quality of product, quality of service and quality reputation in the congested marketplace. It is well documented that many large automobile companies like GM only acknowledged the importance of quality when their very survival was threatened. Those companies like the American Motors Company that did not simply went out of business.

The visionaries whose underlying philosophy of business was built on quality are often referred to as 'Quality Gurus'. In the early days of quality management it was difficult to prove the link between quality and performance, and measures, tools and methods were underdeveloped. The link between performance, cost and quality came much later. The early pioneers like Deming, Crosby and Juran often found it difficult to justify their hunches.

Most of the focus of the quality evolution was focused upon improving internal processes, organizational systems, methods and tools. For today's supply chain managers the focus has shifted to managing across organizational boundaries. In the following sections a brief summary of the contribution of acknowledged quality gurus is given before summarizing the importance of TQM within the context of SCM.

W. Edwards Deming

Deming is widely acknowledged as the original pioneer of quality management in the twentieth century. However, it was not until the 1980s that Deming's work was acknowledged in the US and Europe. He had spent most of his career in Japan as a consultant helping the Japanese rebuild their economy after the Second World War. Deming is best known for his 14-point plan, which is general enough to apply to most organizations and still have relevance for the modern supply chain manager. Perhaps the most important of his fourteen points for the modern supply chain manager is the fourth one which states: 'end the practice of awarding business on the basis of the price tag. Instead minimize total cost. Move towards a single supplier for any one item, on a long-term relationship of loyalty and trust' (Deming, 1982).

Deming was a keen advocate of statistical method in order to identify when a process is becoming unstable or unpredictable with the purpose of preventing defects occurring. The modern manager would recognize this in terms of what we now refer to as statistical process control (SPC). Deming recognized that a major cause of defects in production processes were actually bought-in being directly traceable to poor-quality materials, parts and components.

Philip Crosby

Crosby is another US quality guru who spent his formative years in manufacturing and management consulting. Crosby is best known for championing the concept of 'zero defects' and 'do it right first time' (Crosby, 1983).

Zero defects is about focusing upon the customer's perspective and defining quality from that angle. The product needs to conform to requirements and processes need to be improved to prevent defects occurring and ensure quality. He promoted the idea of costing quality. Unfortunately for Crosby many organizations latched onto the motivational aspects of the slogans without recognizing the importance of the substance that underpinned the approach. As a consequence these organizations became somewhat disenchanted with the approach and eventually gave up the program. Zero defects was meant to be a management performance standard not a motivational program. Deming believes that the strive for perfection caused anxiety in organizations with fear, distrust of management and frustration when the concept was used without the actual performance measurement to support the ideas.

Kaoru Ishikawa

Ishikawa was the first to introduce the concept of quality control circles. Perhaps his most important contribution to the continuous improvement movement is his 'fishbone' cause and effect diagrammatic representation used by consultants and managers worldwide. Ishikawa argued that 90–95 per cent of all quality problems could be addressed by simple statistical techniques that do not require specialist technical knowledge (Ishikawa, 1985).

Masaaki Imai

Imai's trajectory was similar to Deming and Crosby in that he too was a management consultant who introduced the world to continuous improvement through his 'Kaizen' philosophy (Imai, 1986). The Kaizen approach is one of continuous improvement with constant and small incremental change in every process leading to improvements. Processes stretch across supply chains, so in this context it is important for those involved to be able to work together to improve the whole supply chain. Kaizen is perhaps one of the most useful management tools and philosophies in improving supply chain performance. Each improvement is secured by making the improvement level a standard rather like a mountaineer anchors a position before climbing onwards and upwards to reach new heights of achievement. Kaizen is for long-term, longlasting improvements resulting from team efforts focusing upon process improvements. Because it uses internal teams it requires less initial investment but requires great effort to sustain the approach.

Genichi Taguchi

Taguchi served as Director of the Japanese Academy of Quality and has received the Deming Prize for Quality four times. Taguchi defines the quality of a product as the loss imparted by the product to the society from the time the product is shipped. The loss may include customer complaints, additional warranty costs, damage to company reputation, loss of markets and so on (Taguchi, 1986). Statistical techniques in addition to SPC are used to enable engineers and designers to identify those variables, which if uncontrolled can affect product manufacture and performance.

Joseph Juran

Juran is probably best known for his handbook on quality control published in 1951. This book is updated and still has relevance for the modern supply chain manager. Similar to Deming and Crosby, Juran is a management consultant with an international reputation who also worked in post-Second World War Japan. Juran's main contribution is focused upon 'breakthrough' through planning and examining organizational issues and in preventing adverse change through control. He has a four-point plan to achieve his aims.

1. *Establish goals to be reached* – identify what needs to be done, the specific project that needs to be tackled.
2. *Establish plans to reach the goals* – to give structure to the process.
3. *Assign clear responsibility* – make it explicitly clear who is responsible for achieving these goals.
4. *Base the rewards on the results achieved* – feed the results back into the plan to keep it on track – hence control it.

Juran refers to the 'quality trilogy' as quality planning, quality control and quality improvement. Objectives must be clearly set annually to increase performance and reduce costs. Development of these goals, plans and structures are the responsibility of top management. Juran took issue with Crosby's approach claiming it to be simplistic with slogans that do not provide structure, which is important. 'There are no shortcuts to quality' according to Juran (1988). Juran's approach has received wider acceptance than perhaps both Crosby and to some extent Deming probably because he set clear lines of responsibility and the focus was on detailed planning. This is appealing to practical managers who consider some of the alternative approaches to be more vague.

Management approaches to achieving quality

Sigma six, TQM, Kaizen – continuous improvement, zero defects, QMS and JiT are management systems that continue to make large contributions to the improvement, maintenance and performance of quality across supply chains and within individual organizations. Sigma six and statistical process control charts are examined in the next section.

Statistical process control charts (SPC) and six sigma

The most commonly used statistical process control charts are $\overline{X}$ and R for control variables. They are typically used for situations in which the quality variable to be controlled is a dimension, a weight or other measurable characteristic. In practice the two charts are used together with the $\overline{X}$ to monitor absolute value or the location of process average and the R chart to measure dispersion (the range) of the output distribution.

In most applications the $\overline{X}$ control chart limits are set at $\overline{X} \pm 3$ standard deviations of the $\overline{X}$ value (i.e. 3 sigma limits). The frequency distribution of measures used in constructing control charts are distributions of averages, not measures of individual values produced by the process. This fact ensures that the distribution is statistically normal when the process is in control. Sigma six is the range (± 3 sigma limits) of the chart and accounts for 99.9 per cent of the $\overline{X}$ values that result from the process operation as long as only natural random variables occur. An example of such control charts is shown below.

In the example the $\overline{X}$ control chart shows five frequencies with an upper control limit (UCL) = 1004.3 and a lower control limit (LCL) = 995.36. The average around which the measures occur is 1000. The data comprises individual sample measures taken for 32 sub-groups the readings were taken at 15-minute intervals over an 8-hour shift. They measure pipe diameters. The measures for the sub-groups are then summed and the average $\overline{X}$ is computed. It is the average of the averages for each sub-groups sample. An average of the subgroup range values is then taken $\overline{R}$. The $\overline{X}$ value 1000 is used as the process average on the chart. The $\overline{R}$ value represents the mean value of the range of diameter sizes found in each sub-group and is the average range value used on the chart. 99.9 per cent of the data fall within these ranges and are normally distributed. Interpretation of the chart is relatively simple: any points outside the control limits are usually explained as a non-random variation. *If this process was in control it would only happen three times in any sub-group inspection*. The appearance of other non-random patterns may also be observed. An unusually large number of points in sequence on the same side of the average line provide an indication that a process is out of control. Clear-cut trends of points in one direction may indicate an adjustment problem or a problem with wear on a tool. In either of these cases the process should be stopped and the problem investigated (Figure 10.2).

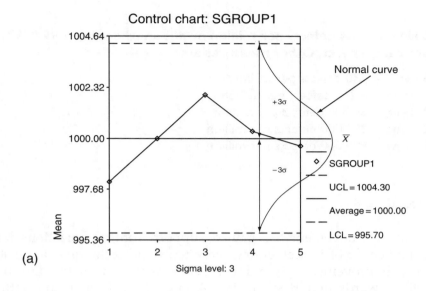

(a)

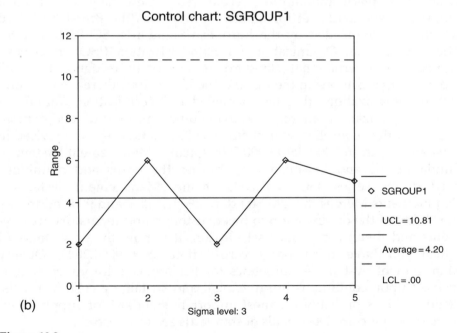

(b)

Figure 10.2

6 sigma = 3.4 defects per million or put another way is 99.99971 per cent perfect. Other measures are:

5 sigma = 230 defects per million
4 sigma = 6 210 defects per million
3 sigma = 66 800 defects per million
2 sigma = 308 000 defects per million
1 sigma = 690 000 defects per million

Standards

The quality movement has gained support from organizations reaping the benefit of implementing these tools and techniques to achieve quality improvements. A number of awards such as the European Quality Awards and Best Practice Awards have been made both of which take place annually. In recent years there have also been a number of standards set for quality. BS5750 was the British Standard which was superseded by the European Standards ISO 9000 in 1987. The International Organization for Standardization (ISO) in Geneva is now the international standard setting body recognized by all member organizations in the EU and the US. In 2002 there were around 400 000 organizations that had achieved ISO certification around the world. Organizations are required to document procedures and demonstrate that they complied with them. The ISO standards were revised in 1994 and again in 2000. ISO 9000:2000 Quality Management Systems – Fundamentals and Vocabulary establishes the terms and definitions used in the series. ISO 9001:2000 Quality Management Systems – Requirements Merges the Old Standards 9001, 9002, and 9003 addresses the ability of the organization to meet customer and regulatory requirements and thereby customer satisfaction. It is now the only standard which can have third party certification. ISO 9004:2000, Quality Management Systems – Guidelines for Performance Improvements, is focused upon continuous improvement and sustaining customer satisfaction. This is probably the most important standard for supply chain managers. For complete details of standards see www.iso.ch.

Quality function deployment (QFD)

QFD is a disciplined approach to problem solving. It is also called House of Quality (HOQ). Japanese shipyard workers at Mitsubishi's Kobe site developed the technique. Many organizations have since used the technique including Toyota, Ford, GM, AT&T, and Procter & Gamble. The strength of approach is its ability to draw together different views (knowledge and experience) from across the organization in addressing the needs of the customer.

House of Quality Example – mobile phones

HOQ measures how well the organization can match customer requirements by building a house of quality. Firstly customer requirements have to be established from market research. The rank importance of each requirement is obtained through survey data using a Likert scale 1–5 or 1–9. In the example 1–5 is used with 1 being low importance and 5 being high importance. Product attributes are identified and then measured against the customer requirements. In the example this has been done using a better, same worse scaling where high relationships = 5 and low relationships = 1. Importance ratings can then be calculated by multiplying the two values for each attribute. The organization may have pre-established target values it wanted to achieve and these are shown too (in the basement of the house). In the example, the keypad and VDU are slightly lower than the target. The correlation matrix in the roof of the house identifies potentially difficult trade-offs. For example, the handset is highly correlated with the keypad and the VDU meaning that changes to the handset will impact on both the keypad and VDU design. Similarly the keypad is correlated with the VDU meaning a change to one will affect the other.

The stages are:

- Identify what the customer wants
- Identify how the goods/service will satisfy customer wants
- Relate customer wants to product hows (in the example, handset, keypad, VDU)
- Identify relationships between the firm's hows
- Develop importance ratings
- Evaluate competing products – this can be done by identifying competitor offerings and adding a column for each one at the right end of the house and scaling them against the criteria set by the customer.

An example is given in Figure 10.3 that defines customer requirements for a mobile telephone. The ratings are developed from an average of all customer survey data. The rank order of importance in this example is:

1. Functionality = 5
2. Convenience = 4

3. Fashionable = 3
4. Easy to use = 2
5. Reliability = 1

Symbols have been used but we could equally have simply used the numbers throughout. Sometimes the roof is used to identify correlation distinguishing between positive and negative correlation using (p) or (n) to do so.

The technique is particularly useful in designing goods and services that meet customer expectations.

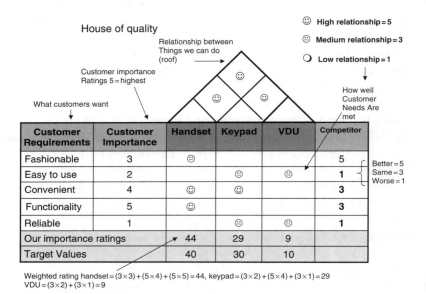

Figure 10.3

Summary

This chapter has introduced a number of important supply chain concepts linked to performance and quality. It began examining how supply chain profitability can be achieved. Time to market, quality and innovation were identified as key influencing factors. These are often major influencers in increasing revenues. Total cost of ownership was then examined to explore the different ways in which organizations can lower their total costs. Quality management is inexorably linked to competitive performance and a number of key practitioners who have made major contributions in the field were identified before explaining management approaches to quality. Finally statistical process control and the concept of sigma six were explained, as was the technique of quality function deployment or house of quality.

Discussion Questions

1. For an organization of choice select a process and discuss issues relating to quality improvements that could be implemented and explain how the quality improvements identified would impact upon supply chain profitability.
2. 'Supply chain profitability is relatively a straightforward matter. Organizations may either lower cost and/or increase revenues.' Discuss.
3. 'World-class organizations focus on time, quality, innovation and cost.' Discuss.
4. How can organizations lower their total cost of ownership?
5. What impact will lowering the TCO have on profitability in
   (a) the supply chain?
   (b) the customer?
   (c) supplier behaviours?
6. 'Quality management is sometimes overengineered.' Discuss.
7. Why is it important to have quality standards and what are the implications of standards for supplying organizations?
8. Explain why statistical process control is an important concept for managing quality.
9. 'Designing quality in and cost out is essential in competitive markets.' Discuss.
10. Explain what you understand by the term 'zero defects'.

References

Burt, D. N., Dobler, D. W. and Starling, S. L. (2003). *World Class Supply Management – The Key to Supply Chain Management*, 7th edn. Boston, MA: McGraw-Hill Irwin.

Buzzell, R. and Ortmeyer, G. (1996). Channel partnerships streamline distribution. *Sloan Management Review*, Spring, pp. 85–96.

Buzzell, R. D. and Gale, B. T. (1987). *The PIMS Principles: Linking Strategy to Performance*. New York: Free Press.

Crosby, P. (1983). *Quality is Free*. Maidenhead: McGraw-Hill.

Deming, W. E. (1982). Quality, Productivity and Competitive Position. Boston, MA: MIT Press.

Doyle, P. (2002). *Marketing Management*. Hemel Hempstead: Prentice-Hall.

Dyer, J. H. (2000). *Collaborative Advantage: Winning through Extended Enterprise Supplier Networks*. Oxford: Oxford University Press.

Imai, M. (1986). *Kaizen: The Key to Japan's Competitive Success*. New York: Random House.

Ishikawa, K. (1985). *What is Total Quality Control? The Japanese Way*. London: Prentice-Hall.

Juran, J. M. (1988). *Quality Control Handbook*. Maidenhead: McGraw-Hill.

O'Neal, C. (1993). Concurrent engineering with early supplier involvement: a cross functional challenge. *International Journal of Purchasing and Materials Management*, Spring, pp. 3–9.

Schonberger, R. J. (1986). *World Class Manufacturing: The Lessons of Simplicity Applied*. New York: Free Press.

Stalk, G. and Hout, T. M. (1990). *Competing Against Time*. New York: Free Press.

Taguchi, G. (1986). *Introduction to Quality Engineering*. New York: Asian Productivity Association.

Towill, D. R. (1996). Time compression and supply chain management: a guided tour. *Supply Chain Management* 1 (1), 15–27.

Whitney, D. (1988). Manufacturing by design. *Harvard Business Review*, July–August, pp. 83–91.

Womack, J. P. and Jones, D. T. (1996). From lean production to lean enterprise. *Harvard Business Review*, March–April, **27** (2), pp. 93–103.

Chapter 11

Logistics and fulfilment strategies

LEARNING OUTCOMES

After reading this chapter you should be able to:

- recognize the importance of logistics and fulfilment in supply chain strategies;
- evaluate the appropriateness of outsourcing in a given context, e.g. use of 'third-party logistics';
- know the competitive advantage that computerized systems and transportation developments can give to organizations, e.g. backhauling, cross-docking;
- recognize the strategic importance of storage and distribution in fulfilling the marketing promise to the customer.

Introduction

From a strategic point of view a number of key decisions need to be taken by organizations when it comes to investment in logistics and fulfilment facilities. There are decisions relating to who should do it (the company or a third party), where to locate facilities in relation to markets and operations, and how to plan for increasing or reducing capacities. Issues relating to stores centralization and decentralization, types of building, layout, storage methods and handling equipment are also important considerations. This is a very important part of the organization's strategic decision-making and an area that can make the difference between satisfied customers or disgruntled customers, affect profit and loss, responsiveness, flexibility, quality of service and capabilities to meet market demand effectively.

Logistics and fulfilment are essential operational activities performed by all organizations delivering customer service. Benefits have occurred through the application of better communication systems including: use of bar codes and RFID tracking together with text messaging and hand held terminals (HHTs). Technology has also significantly improved transport communications through global positioning systems (GPS) providing tracking information. Initially voice and text technology was used to guide pickers in the warehouse to specific locations (Kaplan, 2002). It is now an essential part of the logistics function inside the warehouse and on the road.

An important part of the process is warehousing which has been described as that part of an organization's transport system where goods are travelling at zero miles per hour. It is part of a total logistics system that stores raw materials, work-in-progress and finished goods at and between points of origin and point of consumption (Murphy and Wood, 2004, p. 299). Storage can take place at warehouses or distribution centres, the latter being for rapid movement of inventory to where they are in demand to maximize throughput. Faster throughput times means faster stock-turnover, lowering holding cost for inventories. Warehousing allows regrouping in a supply chain and can take four forms: accumulation (bulk-making), allocation (bulk-breaking), assorting and sorting.

A retail example

Deliveries from several suppliers of clothing arrive at a central warehouse *(accumulation)*, where they are divided into store order quantities for delivery *(allocation)* but first they need to be sorted by style, size and colour *(sorting and assortment)*.

Stock and Lambert (2001, p. 391) comment that warehousing is required for the following reasons:

- To achieve economies of transport;
- To achieve economies of production;
- To take benefit from economies of purchase;
- To maintain supplies;
- To support customer service policies;
- To meet changing market conditions (e.g. disruptions to supplies through war, strikes, natural disasters and accidents; fluctuations in demand, seasonality and competition);
- To overcome time and space differentials existing between consumers and producers;
- To achieve lowest total logistics cost by balancing trade-offs to deliver the agreed level of customer service;
- To support JiT systems.

Third Party Logistics (3PL) – Outsourcing the logistics function

Dragan (2002) estimated that contract warehousing expenditure in the US was worth $20 billion and expected to grow by as much as 25 per cent in the next few years. Knemeyer and Murphy (2004, p. 35) estimate that users of third party logistics services may be spending an average of one-third of their total logistics budget by 2005 compared to one-fifth today on 3PL. This demonstrates just how important outsourcing has become and illustrates the rising trend in practice. However, some commentators have argued that the supply of 3PL warehousing and transportation have become commoditized to some extent and that suppliers need to enhance service provision particularly those associated with mass-customization and postponement (van Hoek, 2000). Security might be an important decision variable for organizations making choices whether or not to outsource warehousing (Morton, 1999; Labetti, 2002). Hazardous waste materials may be another consideration (Graham, 2002).

In recent years there has been a further development referred to as Fourth Party Logistics (4PL) which essentially involves one lead logistics supplier in coordinating a number of 3PL suppliers for the contracting organization. Essentially the 4PL source manages the logistics service on behalf of the contracting customer. The main benefits argued for 3PL and 4PL oustsourcing is similar to that for most outsourcing decisions and includes:

- Cost uncertainty reduced since the contract specifies pre-determined costs;
- Risk lowered;
- Maintenance costs lowered;
- Specialist knowledge and skills bought in from supplier (do not have to develop them yourself associated training and personnel costs lowered);
- Specialist carriers invest in state of the art equipment and supporting technologies from which the customer can benefit without incurring capital costs.

Trade-off concept

The trade-off concept is very important in the effective management of supply chains. No more so than in the area of logistics and fulfilment strategies. It usually involves an algorithm of cost decisions between two or more variables that can be offset against some benefit of achieving an objective. For example, holding inventories (stock) involves the

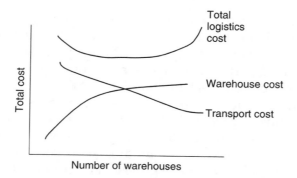

Figure 11.1

organization incurring costs (stock, warehouse and facility costs, labour, insurance and so on). To lower cost the organization may decide to put more resource into carefully planning JiT deliveries. As long as the organization has selected reliable suppliers and agreed service standards then it should be able to remove some of its fixed costs (overheads) in relation to warehousing that it would have previously incurred. You don't need a large warehouse if you can get stock JiT.

The classic trade-off is between the number of warehouse facilities required and transport cost is illustrated in Figure 11.1.

Definition of warehousing

Storage is the physical holding of inventories awaiting transport to customers. There are a number of types of inventory that are held by organizations which include:

- Goods and other assets purchased for resale;
- Consumable stores;
- Raw materials and components purchased for incorporation into products for sale;
- Work-in-progress which includes all sub-assemblies and partly finished goods;
- Long-term contract balances;
- Finished goods.

Storage of these items is an important 'trade-off' decision. Should an organization incur the cost of storing items to deliver customer service levels or should it design systems, policies and procedures that ensure rapid delivery avoiding storage? This is a key question facing supply chain managers. There are no easy answers to this question and it will be a decision that is made considering the effect of various trade-offs.

Size may be an important dimension

Size of an organization may be an important influencing factor in the decision and the bargaining power that an organization is able to apply. Large organizations are often able to exert influence over their smaller supplier organizations to store and supply as and when required operating JiT systems. Smaller suppliers may have little choice but to incur the storage costs and to design their supply facilities and systems to deliver effective customer service to these larger customers. Failure would simply result in the supplier being replaced by another supply source that could meet the requirements.

Storage, inventories, working capital and customer service

Historically the emphasis on storage and warehousing was a means of holding inventories to meet internal and external customer needs and a means of avoiding loss through wastage, deterioration, theft and obsolescence. The current emphasis is on the movement of inventories. According to Lysons (2000, p. 360) there are a number of important issues to be considered:

- Acknowledgement that reducing warehousing and storage costs is essential.
- Automated stores and computerized systems make it possible to better manage these facilities.
- Trade-offs between higher customer service levels, low inventory and low operating costs need to be balanced.
- Changes in business practices through the implementation of JiT and Kanban concepts.
- Better logistics systems.
- 'Time-compression' reducing time consumed in business processes. Elimination of non-value-added time.

Figure 11.2 illustrates the trade-offs involved in achieving conflicting objectives of high customer service levels and low inventories and operating costs. In the operating cycle shown the cycle begins with procurement, inbound logistics and conversion operations, goods are then

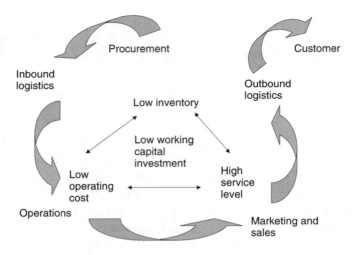

Figure 11.2

sold and distributed to the customer. The organization has a number of conflicting objectives which are:

- Keep inventories low;
- Meet customer demand by being responsive to their needs;
- Minimize operating costs by being efficient;
- Minimize funds tied up in working capital.

The tensions and possible trade-offs between these objectives are indicated by the arrows.

Store operations are an important aspect of all businesses and the processes involved include:

- Receiving goods inwards or from other departments in the same organization.
- Inspection of these inventories.
- Recording the receipts manually or using computer systems.
- Security (avoiding stock-loss, e.g. theft or misplacement).
- Maintenance – protecting the inventories against loss through deterioration (e.g. by fire, water, vermin).
- Stock control – determining ranges, quantity and quality. Dealing with receipt and issues.
- Stock-taking – verification of stock records by reconciling paper/computer record with physical stock. These inventory counts can be done at regular intervals (weekly, monthly, quarterly, six-monthly or annually), i.e. cyclically or they may be done continuously.

- Disposal of surplus stocks (*scrap* – salvageable, re-usable has a value, *redundant* – no value to the organization but may have a value in another organization and is saleable or *obsolete* items which need to be disposed of but have no value to anyone).
- Retail organizations may simply have store stock and stocks held in RDCs that they want to push through their retail organization as quickly as possible to generate cash and to avoid the various costs indicated. In these circumstances they will 'mark-down', i.e. discount the retail price in the hope of moving stock quickly through the system.
- Compliance matters including the implementation of personnel policies in relation to stores staff. Legal compliance issues such as health and safety regulations are also important.

Location of storage facilities

Decisions relating to where to locate facilities to achieve efficiency, economy and customer responsiveness are strategic supply chain decisions in relation to logistics fulfilment. Murphy and Wood (2004, p. 256) identify two commonly used approaches to finding the lowest cost location, which are the 'centre of gravity' and the 'grid system'. The two approaches are illustrated in Figure 11.3. In the illustration of the centre of gravity approach, a map is used to identify a location which minimizes distance between distribution centres, stores and the central warehouse. A grid system could be overlaid on the map to ensure that the distances are optimized. In the illustration of the grid system it shows that the best location for a central warehouse between three stores plotted on the grid is at grid location 20 miles North and 20 miles East. Each store is 10 miles from the facility.

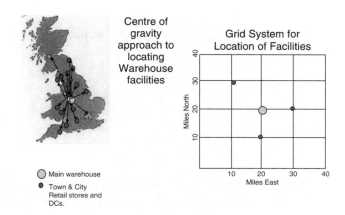

Figure 11.3

Table 11.1

Store	North	East	Monthly volume tonnes	North x volume	East x volume
1	30	10	5	150	50
2	10	20	6	60	120
3	20	30	4	80	120
Totals			15	290	290
Weighted average				19.33	19.33

Supposing additional data such as the monthly delivery volumes were obtained and a table constructed to compute the weighted average centre of gravity for the facility warehouse in the grid system.

The three stores and monthly volumes are used to compute the weighted average centre of gravity as shown in Table 11.1. The result is that the optimum location for the warehouse in the example is 19.33 miles North and 19.33 miles East. Monthly volumes have influenced the small shift in location. The dangers in adopting this approach are obvious. If volumes are accurate and likely to remain stable there is little problem in making the location decision as explained. However, should volumes be volatile then the decision may not be optimum in the longer term. In the example, it would not matter too much because the weighted average centre of gravity has not shifted greatly. However, supposing the store volumes remained the same for stores two and three and doubled for store one. The decision would change to 22 miles North and 17 miles East owing to the higher volumes. This is shown in Table 11.2.

Equations to calculate the centre of gravity location point using grid coordinates on *x* and *y* scales.

$$C_x = \frac{\sum_i d_{ix} W_i}{\sum_i W_i} \qquad C_y = \frac{\sum_i d_{iy} W_i}{\sum_i W_i}$$

where d_{ix} is the *x* coordinate of location *i*, W_i is the volume of goods moved to or from location *i* and d_{iy} is the *y* coordinate of location *i*

n.b. *Examples in the tables have used this method using an Excel spreadsheet*

Table 11.2

Store	North	East	Monthly volume tonnes	North x volume	East x volume
1	30	10	10	300	100
2	10	20	6	60	120
3	20	30	4	80	120
Totals			20	440	340
Weighted average				22.00	17.00

Location decisions applying cost-volume analysis

Another possible analytical tool in deciding location based upon cost and volumes is the break-even tool.

Table 11.3 shows the decision costs of locating a warehouse at three locations. The costs are identified as fixed costs that do not vary with volumes at each location e.g. building costs; and variable costs i.e. costs that are associated with each unit handled at that location and vary with volume. The volume handled in a period is forecast to be 5000 units. It is now possible to compute a total cost of operating the facility for the period. Results are shown in Table 11.4.

Table 11.3

Data

	Liverpool	Manchester	Warrington
Fixed cost	£70 000	£90 000	£50 000
Variable cost	£30	£45	£60
Volume		5000 Units per period	

Table 11.4

Results

Breakeven points	Units	STG Pounds
Liverpool vs. Manchester	−1333.333333	30 000
Liverpool vs. Warrington	666.6666667	90 000
Manchester vs. Warrington	2666.666667	210 000

Volume analysis @5000 units

	Liverpool	Manchester	Warrington
Total cost	£220 000.00	£315 000.00	£350 000.00

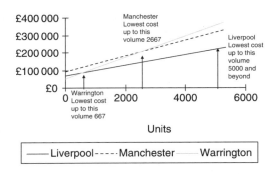

Figure 11.4

The lowest cost location is Liverpool, Manchester is second and Warrington third in the example. A break-even chart for the data showing cross-over points is illustrated in Figure 11.4. The cost volume analysis indicates that Warrington would be the lowest cost for very small volumes up to 667 units, Manchester would then become lowest cost up to volumes of 2667 units and after that Liverpool is lowest cost location.

Geographical information systems (GIS)

GIS systems such as MOZAIC and Microsoft MapPoint use geodemographic data to optimize locational decisions. Combining data from different sources: census, road maps, maps locating rivers, mountains, lakes, forests, utilities, airports, universities, colleges, schools and hospitals; it is possible to optimize locational choices according to different objective criteria. Geographical information systems are used by retail organizations to make location decisions for retail stores. Commercial property organizations may use GIS to site commercial property, entertainment centres, shopping centres, hospitals and other facilities. Businesses may use GIS to determine their head office location taking into account criteria such as quality of life, quality of personnel, transport links, other facilities and costs.

Rating scales and location decisions

Finally, a commonly used method of making locational decisions is to use a rating scale against specific criteria determined to be important to the decision maker. An example is given in Table 11.5. A number of criteria are identified and then weighted in order of importance to the

Table 11.5

Data

	Weight	Chester	Manchester
Labour Availability and Attitude	0.25	6	5
People-to-car Ratio	0.05	5	5
Per Capita Income	0.1	5	7
Housing quality	0.05	7	6
Cost of labour	0.4	7	5
Education and Health	0.15	7	5

Results

Total	1		
Weighted sum		6.45	5.25
Weighted average		6.45	5.25

decision. Each criteria is marked using a scale which, in the example, is 1–10 but 1–100 or another appropriate scale could be chosen. The key is to choose a scale large enough to discriminate between criteria.

Types of storage facility

Storage facilities fall into different categories depending on location, purpose, operation and stock characteristics. Table 11.6 identifies the different categories.

Location

Location may be outdoor (stockyard) as is the case with steel stock-holding, tubes, larger castings, timber, bricks aggregates and some finished goods, e.g. cars. The decision to store these items outdoors is taken because they are items which in general terms will not deteriorate from external exposure to the elements. It is also cheaper to simply store items outdoors. The organization does not need to incur costs of building facilities.

Indoor stores may be single or multistorey buildings that have been specially built for the purpose or they have been adapted from existing premises. Single storey buildings have the following advantages:

- Building costs per cm^3 are lower;
- Extensions are easier and cheaper to build;

Table 11.6 Types of storage facilities

Location	Purpose	Operations	Characteristics of stock
Outdoor – e.g. stockyard Indoor – single storey or multistorey Centralized or decentralized	Quarantine stores – e.g. livestock Bonded stores – e.g. whiskey and other spirits – where customs duties are payable Reserved stocks Hazardous stores – chemicals	Discrete – each operation separately performed Integrated – automated	Raw materials Production supplies Jigs and tools Patterns Lifting equipment Scrap Salvage Work-in-progress Finished goods Consumables Stationery Computer supplies

- Store layouts are flexible;
- Handling costs and handling equipment costs are generally lower (except where upper floors perform the function of a gravity feed, e.g. grain storage silos);
- Fire risks are reduced.

Multistorey buildings have the following advantages:

- Storage capacity on the site 'footprint' is greater;
- Restricted space can be maximized;
- Reduced heat loss as upper floors provide insulation;
- Gravity can be used to deliver goods to lower levels where appropriate.

Centralized stores

One important choice for an organization in designing its storage facilities and systems is to decide how the organization will access stores. This is either done through a centralized store which comprises one large facility that all units of the organization draw their stocks from or stores are decentralized. For example, W. H. Smith has a centralized storage facility that supplies all its retail stores located in Swindon. Local deliveries are also made direct to store from suppliers who are given orders and instructions on how to supply.

Decentralized stores

Many retailers need to have decentralized storage facilities from which to deliver their supplies regularly. For example, regular replenishment

Radio Frequency
Tracking Device
used by warehouse
operatives

Figure 11.5

of food and grocery lines is an important issue for food retailers especially for their perishable lines. Sainsbury and Tesco amongst others have a number of regional distribution centres (RDCs) from which they replenish stores regularly.

Cross-docking terminals

In recent years there has been increasing management attention focused upon improving throughput times in supply systems. Time pressures have forced organizations to improve the way they receive, store and distribute goods; automated handling systems, the use of bar code and RFID tracking systems (illustrated in Figure 11.5) and a reassessment of facilities required. Cross-docking allows deliveries to enter temporary storage until the loads can be married with other loads being sent to the same destination. The aim is to move goods on to their final destination in as short a time as possible. Often in FMCG this is measured in hours rather than days. Cross-docking has been an important logistics development enabling a faster supply chain. Cooke (2000) noted the pressures from virtual sales in a digital economy. Often organizations were able to accept orders but had difficulties in fulfilling them. Figure 11.6 illustrates a cross-docking operation.

From 'push' to 'pull' – the changing face of retail

In the 1950s and 1960s it was usual for manufacturers operating on a nationwide basis to carry out national distribution to retail outlets. Control of these supplies was firmly in the hands of the manufacturers.

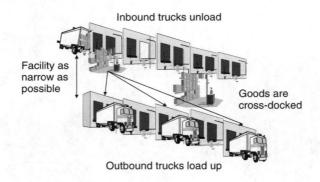

Figure 11.6

Today the control has switched to the retail organizations who aim to respond to their customer demand. Goods are now pulled through the system rather than pushed by the manufacturer.

There is an increasing active involvement by retail organizations and a diminishing involvement of manufacturers in the supply of groceries according to the IGD (2003). Direct to store was the order of the day until the 1970s. In the 1980s suppliers delivered to retail depots which then organized supplies for particular retail outlets. In the 1990s suppliers delivered to a consolidation point where the retailer then took charge delivering to retail depots and on to store from the depots. The next moves may see retailers organize the supplier's supplies and take charge and control of the entire supply chain. This has already happened in some non-food lines. Today only a very small part of the supply chain that between the raw material suppliers and the food manufacturer is outside the direct control of retailers.

The advent of factory gate pricing and increasing 'backhauling' has diminished the suppliers' roles further. Backhauling ensures that trucks are filled both ways to ensure the economies of scale. As more of these operations are done by retail logistics or their third-party suppliers the supplier fleets are left with little to do in this part of the supply chain. As a consequence their economies of scale are reduced.

Automated warehouse facilities

Automated warehouse facilities have become increasingly important reducing handling and speeding up movements through the warehouse. An illustration of an automated retail warehouse facility is given in Figure 11.7.

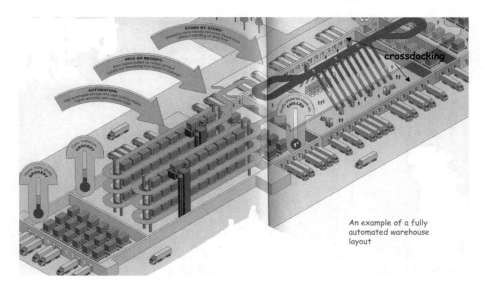

An example of a fully automated warehouse layout

Figure 11.7

Importance of consolidation – a retail example

Some of the largest retail distribution depots operated by large retailing organizations deal with over 2000 suppliers and provide over 14 000 SKUs. Key consolidation sites dotted around the UK will hold and sort goods into full vehicles before they are despatched to the depots. Depots are often operated by third-party logistics providers on behalf of the retailers. Tibbet & Britten, Exel Logistics and Christian Salvesen are some of the largest third-party suppliers operating in the UK. A single depot may handle over 300 000 cases on a single day. A typical depot may supply 100–150 stores in a defined geographic area. Once a delivery is made the trucks will either return to the consolidation point or they will return items to depots from the stores (backhauling – pallets, ex-promotional stock, crates or waste).

Optimization of vehicle fill enables small suppliers to deliver on a daily basis. It reduces the inbound traffic at depots. One of the biggest problems at depots when many different suppliers delivered directly to the depots was delay. Consolidation avoids delays and enables daily replenishment from large numbers of smaller suppliers.

Table 11.7 provides you with some indication of the size and shape of the distribution networks for major UK retail organizations. Table 11.7 shows the number of stores served from a number of distribution centres in the grocery sector. It illustrates the number of cases, how much is centralized *vis-á-vis* direct delivery and where available what percentage is handled by third-party warehousing and transport suppliers.

Table 11.7 Distribution networks of some major UK retailers

Retailers	No of stores	Annual case throughput	No of DCs	Area (ft²)	Percentage of case volumes handled				
					Vols centralized	Vols direct	Warehouse third party	Transport third party	
Asda	256	728 000 000	21	5 543 000	95	5	N/a	N/a	
Co-op	2386	237 100 000	18	2 081 000	90	10	11	11	
Iceland	758	111 000 000	4	815 000	98	2	75	75	
M&S	315	104 500 000	6	691 000	100	0	100	100	
Safeway*	477	561 000 000	20	4 400 000	97	3	55	60	
Sainsburys	468	812 710 000	21	5 400 000	95	5	N/a	N/a	
Tesco	729	1 270 000 000	25	7 327 000	95	5	N/a	N/a	

*2001 profile data
Source: IGD (2003)

TESCO: A CASE IN POINT
Key facts

Tesco has UK sales £ 21 650 000 000 (i.e. £ 21.65 billion) with an operating profit of £ 1 213 000 000. Its stores have 18 000 check-outs that deliver to 12 million customers weekly. It operates 729 stores with total sales space of 18.8 million ft². The average store size is 25 789 ft². It supplies 35 000 SKUs with own lable products accounting for 35 per cent.

During 2001 it opened 55 new stores and Tesco.com now delivers to 95 per cent of the UK population. It won the Queen's award for industry in 2001 for recycling and re-usable packaging and it was e-tailer of the year. Two new RDCs opened in Daventry (Frozen, operated by Wincanton, 200 000 ft²) and Thurrock (FMG, operated by Tibbet & Britten, 500 000 ft²). Paperless picking has been implemented.

Tesco	
Annual case throughout	1 270 000 000
Product range (SKUs)	35 000
Fasy moving goods (FMGs)	28%
Slow moving goods (SMGs)	15%
Frozen	6%
Non-food	5%
Beers, wines and spirits (BWS)	6%
Produce	17%
Chilled and fresh fruit	23%
	100%

Tesco have the following breakdown of categories throughout their network of 729 stores.

The largest National Distribution Centre is 550 000 ft² employing 1382 staff based in Milton Keynes. 12 097 live lines are dealt with servicing all 729 stores.

Tesco has line picking, store picking, cross-docking and some 361 000 pallet locations in their distribution network. Line picks are made in produce (80 per cent), chilled foods and fresh meats (100 per cent). Store picking represents 95 per cent FMG, 100 per cent SMG and frozen, and 85 per cent in non-food categories. Cross-docking accounts for 5 per cent of FMG, non-food and produce. Their vehicle fleet consists of 1386 tractors and a total of 4116 trailers. The trailers are comprised of 1396 that are temperature-controlled, 1520 standard and 1200 composite. These vehicles travel 224 million kilometres in a year making some 1.15 million journeys.

Stock-holding is between 8 and 9 days for FMG, SMG and frozen food categories. Between 11–12 days for beers, wines and spirits and 22 days for non-food items. Produce, chilled and fresh food are replenished daily. They generally perform better across most categories than their major competitors in relation to inventory management.

The typical number of store deliveries in a week across all categories apart from SMGs and frozen foods is 21 with 7 and 14 being the respective figures for the other two categories. Only ASDA with 35 FMG deliveries and M&S with 28 FMG have higher numbers of deliveries on some categories. Sainsbury have 21 FMG deliveries but have lower deliveries across all other categories. Essentially Tesco is receiving deliveries to most stores three times a day across most categories. Their closest rivals are receiving one or two deliveries across produce, chilled and fresh food categories.

Order lead times into stores are generally faster across most categories than their competitors. It takes 18 hours on average for FMG lines, 12–24 hours on chilled, produce and fresh foods and 48 hours for non-food. In general these lead times are between 25 and 50 per cent better than their closest competitors. Lead times into depots for FMG lines are 48 hours. Beers, wines and spirits have some of the slowest lead times reported. This is similar to their competitors.

e-Shopping and home deliveries have become an important part of the business. Tesco is the only store to offer all categories to this type of customer. Other retailers offer limited ranges. They have been able to do this because they use local stores to pick items for the customer in-store for home deliver, store pick-up or delivery to work. They operate 900 deliveries and employ some 1700 drivers and promise to deliver within 24 hours. Tesco is by far the biggest and the most successful home delivery service currently in operation. Some 50–60 per cent of this business activity takes place between Thursday and Saturday. This pattern is similar to traditional in-store shopping where 53 per cent is done between Thursday and Saturday with Sunday and Monday being relatively light volume days.

Sales volumes are fairly constant throughout the year with not much seasonal variation. Tesco has the largest number of automated depots. It uses 24 consolidation centres (three less than Sainsbury) mainly across food categories (grocery FMG, fresh meat, chilled, produce and frozen foods). Large volumes of returnable plastic crates are used in produce, chilled food and fresh food categories. Tesco is the largest packaging recycler in the retail sector handling 196 000 tonnes annually (182 000 cardboard and 14 000 plastic) at a separate recycling plant. Tesco undertakes more recycling than any of their competitors.

Product handling is done mainly using roll cages, standard UK pallets, plastic crates and totes or dolly's (wheeled merchandising units).

Case questions

1. Why have Tesco been so successful in the e-shopping home delivery sector?
2. Explain why numbers of deliveries and store delivery lead times are important to store profitability.
3. 'Re-cycling packaging and storage materials is likely to become a bigger issue with consumers in future'. Do you agree?
4. Explain why Tesco has such a large number of consolidation centres.
5. Explain why Tesco is able to deliver good service to customers when its stock-holding is relatively low.
6. Discuss the wider role of warehousing and distribution within overall company strategy.
7. Explain how warehousing and distribution operations enables Tesco to become more competitive.

Factory gate pricing (FGP)

It is important to know the term 'factory gate pricing' (FGP). It is the point at which the buyer takes control. It will vary according to circumstances and the details of the contract negotiated by parties agreeing the contract (buyer–seller). As it implies the factory gate is the point at which the finished goods are in a complete state for the buyer. No further finishing, packaging or assembly is expected. Depending on what the contract says in practice the factory gate can be:

- port of entry into UK;
- manufacturer's site;
- manufacturer's warehouse or consolidation point.

It is a point in the supply chain when ownership (and risks) for goods pass from supplier (seller) to the buyer (or their third-party agent, e.g. hauliers).

Transport decisions

When goods are purchased there will be a number of complex transport decisions that will need to be taken. These decisions will be dependent on:

- Where the consignment is, e.g. supplier location, factory gate in UK or abroad.
- Volumes and dimensions will determine cost and modes of transport.

- Special considerations, e.g. value, fragility and temperatures.
- Modes of transport depend on lead times, delivery dates required and costs.
- Geographical coverage will determine selection of carrier as will the service levels required. Specialist product knowledge/experience may mean specialist carriers are needed with specialist equipment.
- Required receipt date will impact upon the choices available and there may be trade-offs between fill and cost efficiency and indeed the service level expected by the customer.

Transparency and FGP

One important benefit of FGP is that the buyer knows the cost of the product and the transport cost is separated. Under the alternative of delivered price the cost of the product is not separated from the transport cost element. Knowing the transport cost element allows the buyer to make choices based on the issues listed under transport decisions with the aim of lowering total acquisition costs (TACs). This transparency is very important for buying organizations. It allows the purchaser to make valid comparisons between different suppliers of products and between different suppliers of transportation.

Storage and material handling equipment

Storage equipment is required to store, handle and pick inventoried items.

Storage methods

Storage methods include the following:

Method	Type of goods and equipment
Free stacking	Bulk materials, stacks of units, bulk containers
Shelving and bins	Non-adjustable, semi-adjustable and cantilever
Pallet racking	Adjustable beam, tubular, cantilever
Drive in or drive through racking	Lorries, forklift trucks, cranes may be able to drive through the storage areas
Mobile racking	Mechanical, manual or power operated mobile racks
Live racking	Gravity fed belts, hoppers, inclines or horizontal power-operated conveyors
Automatic retrieval systems	Stacker crane, trucks
Automatic flow through racks	Power-driven with elevators and robot platform

Forms in which materials are moved and stored include the following:

Type	Storage
Bulk materials	Liquids (tanks and containers), solids (tanks and containers) pastes (tanks and containers)
Piece parts	Castings, forgings, components (shelving, bins, racking)
Package	Bag/sack (flour, powder), drum (oil, liquids), carton, cask, cylinder
Unit load supported	Pallets, stillages, post pallets, box pallets
Unit loads without support	Built-in units, shrink wrapped, stretch wrapped and strapped (books, boxes)
Intermediate bulk container	Metal, plastic, other materials
Containers	End loading, side loading, top loading (mixed goods of various types)

Two important types of storage equipment

Pallets and racks are two of the most common types of storage equipment. Pallets are defined by BS2629 (BSISO6780) as 'A load board with two decks separated by bearers, blocks or feet or a single deck supported by bearers, blocks or feet constructed with a view to transport and stacking, and with overall height reduced to a minimum compatible with handling by fork-lift trucks or pallet trucks'.

Pallets are categorized by:

- form of entry (i.e. one-way, two-way or four-way entry).
- construction material (e.g. wood, corrugated metal, wire mesh, aluminium, expandable fibre board).
- shape – basket, box.

BS2629 specifies the standard sizes. The principal benefits of using pallets are as follows:

- Standardization of loads moved by standardized equipment in standardized vehicles;
- Optimizes use of storage space;
- Save time loading and unloading trucks;
- Reduces possibility of damage in transit;
- Minimizes handling allowing pallets to go straight into store;
- Promotes good housekeeping and clean areas by keeping goods off the floor.

Racks are frameworks designed to store loads in upright columns diagonally braced for strength. Racking is very flexible and can be used to store pallets, drums, containers, plates, sheets, bars, tubes, tyres, crates, etc.

Materials handling has three main aspects:

1. Physical movement, handling and storage through the enterprise.
2. Management through effective planning and control.
3. Technology – techniques to move, handle and store linked to information systems.

Manual systems are used for light loads and powered systems are used for heavy loads. Semi-automated systems will be part mechanical and require some human intervention. Fully automated systems are computer-controlled.

Mechanical handling equipment includes hand trucks and fork-lift trucks with or without power. Loads in excess of 23 kg require mechanical handling, when two or more people are needed, when travel time is greater than lifting or handling time and space above floor level can be used.

Assessing storage requirements

Over assessing storage will result in unnecessary cost, e.g. rent, rates, light, heat, water maintenance, labour and so on. Building and building service cost alone can be as high as 40 per cent of the annual cost of storage. An underassessment will result in cramped, inefficient and possibly dangerous conditions.

The objectives are to:

(a) utilize space efficiently within the building cube;
(b) create rapid and easy access to stock and stock movements;
(c) achieve efficient and balanced traffic flows;
(d) mechanize and automate stores operations;
(e) minimize distances and stock movement (e.g. avoid double handling);
(f) clearly identify stocks;
(g) group products with similar storage characteristics and according to frequency of receipts and issues;
(h) maintain adequate security.

Organizational factors to consider include:

(a) Space required and costs for each category of stock.
(b) Whether to centralize or decentralize the stores.
(c) Physical characteristics of the stores at each location, e.g. size, weight, shape, perishable, hazardous.

(d) Flows of materials and handling equipment required.
(e) Goods received into store: quantities, volumes, frequencies, packing, delivery vehicles, handling requirements, documentation, inspection.
(f) Goods outwards – quantities, volumes, frequencies, packing, delivery vehicles, handling requirements, documentation, packaging.
(g) Inventory policies, e.g. JiT, buffer stocks, stockpiling.
(h) Security and safety.
(i) Administrative systems and personnel.

Figure 11.8 illustrates the key reasons for fluctuating warehousing space requirements.

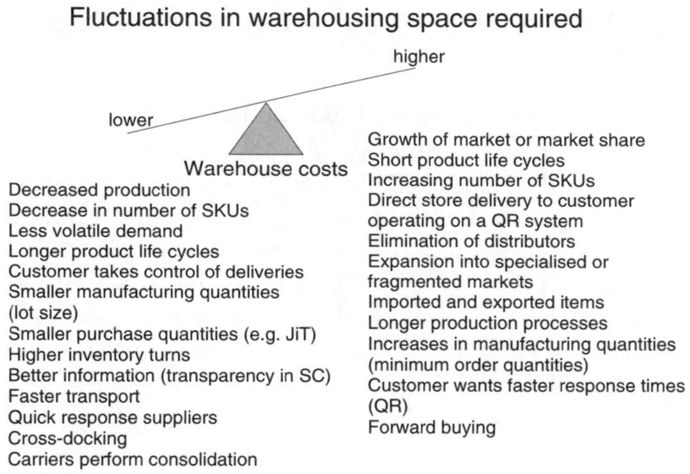

Fluctuations in warehousing space required

lower	higher
Warehouse costs	Growth of market or market share
Decreased production	Short product life cycles
Decrease in number of SKUs	Increasing number of SKUs
Less volatile demand	Direct store delivery to customer operating on a QR system
Longer product life cycles	Elimination of distributors
Customer takes control of deliveries	Expansion into specialised or fragmented markets
Smaller manufacturing quantities (lot size)	Imported and exported items
Smaller purchase quantities (e.g. JiT)	Longer production processes
Higher inventory turns	Increases in manufacturing quantities (minimum order quantities)
Better information (transparency in SC)	Customer wants faster response times (QR)
Faster transport	Forward buying
Quick response suppliers	
Cross-docking	
Carriers perform consolidation	

Figure 11.8

Stores layout

Stores need to be laid out in an orderly fashion to achieve the objectives of (a) efficient materials flows, (b) clear identification and location of inventories and (c) efficient space utilization.

Four principal types of stores layout have been identified by the Chartered Institute of Transport and Logistics:

1. The inverted 'T' warehouse flow;
2. The crossflow warehouse;
3. The corner warehouse flow;
4. The throughflow warehouse.

Essentially these different designs have different benefits (Figures 11.9–11.12).

Goods inwards and outwards are located on the same side of the building. There are designated areas for a bulk store and for low, medium and high usage items to minimize handling. This is achieved by placing low usage furthest away from the exit point and the high usage stocks near to the exit. This also saves time and minimizes the distances travelled for fast moving stocks. Unified bay operations with goods inwards and outwards next to each other provides better security and surveillance. It is also easy to extend these facilities on one of three sides subject to site constraints. The main disadvantage is the central aisle may become congested in periods of high throughput.

The 'crossflow' warehouse is a one-way system with goods inwards flowing to the left on entry and then into one of the three designated storage areas depending on high, medium or low storage items being

The inverted T warehouse flow

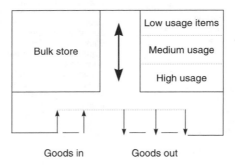

Figure 11.9

The 'crossflow' warehouse flow

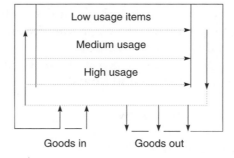

Figure 11.10

The 'corner' warehouse flow

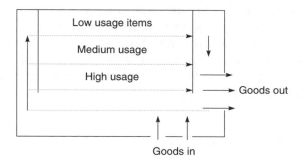

Figure 11.11

The 'throughflow' warehouse flow

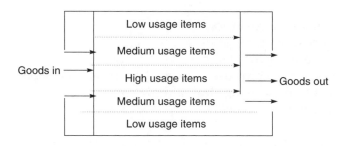

Figure 11.12

identified. This design retains the main advantages of the T system with a unified goods inwards and goods outwards system side by side, but removes the central aisle congestion problem. It is essentially a one-way system. Bulk storage and picking stocks are stored alongside each other. The main disadvantage of this system would be the situation where a high proportion of the stock was bulk may lead to the design being impractical.

The 'corner' warehouse has the goods inwards and outwards areas adjacent on two sides at the corner. This layout reduces aisle congestion in times of high throughput activity. One possible disadvantage is that any expansion can only be developed on two sides. There may also be potential security and surveillance problems with having to monitor two corner positions.

The final layout is the 'throughput' design. This has the advantage of being a flow system with entry and exit points on two opposite sides of the building. It also achieves good aisle areas. There are three main disadvantages to this layout which are: all stocks will have to travel the full length of the building between receipt and despatch; goods in and goods out are on two different sides of the building increasing the security risks and surveillance; third, if the warehouse is to be extended it can only happen on two sides unless bays are moved. This layout may be particularly useful in situations where bays inwards and outwards have different handling requirements, e.g. bay height differences.

Importance of stock codes

A code is a symbol or system of symbols used to easily identify and accurately classify stocks. The advantage of having codes may be remembered using the mnemonic SUPPLIER.

S implicity
U nique
P romotion of standardization
P ricing and costing made simpler
L ocation is made easier in store
I mplementation of computerized stock records is possible
E asier requisitioning using short simple codes
R e-ordering made simpler

Codes can be of three main types: alphabetical, numerical or alpha-numeric.

Transport decisions and supply chain strategies

The choice of appropriate transport modes is critical to determining performance. Table 11.8 provides an indication of how decision choices can affect a number of different aspects of supply chain performance.

In order to make appropriate transport choices a number of issues need to be considered that include:

● Customer requirements;
● Time taken in transportation;
● Cost (and benefits) of different transport modes;
● Security;
● Other risk factors;
● Storage requirements;

Table 11.8 Supply chain areas affected by transportation decisions

Planning	Procurement	Operations	Distribution	Customers
Network and asset rationalization	Landed cost	Inter and intraorganizational movements of inventory	Load plans	Availability and dependability – will goods be available when required?
Lead times	Inbound in-transit inventory management	JiT systems	Pick lists	Responsiveness – How responive is the supplier to customer requests?
Vendor sourcing	Ability to lower inventories	Handling equipment required	Packaging and labelling	Cost – affects total cost incurred
EOQ/JiT inventories	Time	Inventory holding policies	Shipping documentation preparation	Lead times – effect on customer lead times
Facility locations	People – competencies required	People – competencies required	Dock scheduling	
Levels of Technical support and management information systems	Levels of Technical support and management information systems	Levels of Technical support and management information systems	Outbound shipment management	Levels of Technical support and management information systems
			Mode/carrier selection	

- Packing requirements (containers, pallets, crates, etc.);
- Labelling;
- Documentation including shipping, billing, export duties, etc.

Choosing an appropriate transport supplier or partner involves a number of key stages which are illustrated in Figure 11.13.

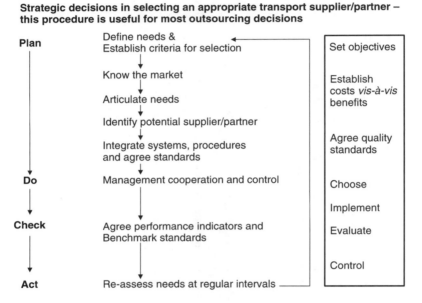

Figure 11.13

Summary

This chapter has demonstrated the importance of organizational capabilities in fulfilling the customer promise. In order to achieve customer order fulfilment organizations must make strategic decisions in relation to supply chain logistics. Decisions on whether or not to own or outsource logistics facilities are of strategic importance. Choices in relation to where to locate warehouses, how many and how big they should be are critical to successful fulfilment operations and strategies. Issues in relation to inventory holding policies and customer service are amongst the important trade-offs that have been considered. Types of storage facilities needed to satisfy customer demand and how they are laid out demonstrate the fine line between operational and strategic decisions. This chapter has recognized the linkages between operational and strategic supply chain issues and how they are interrelated to serve customers more efficiently and effectively.

Discussion Questions

1. Discuss the main general and specific factors to be considered by organizations reviewing their storage and transportation requirements. Explain how efficient management of these operations improves organizational profitability.
2. Discuss trade-offs that may occur as a result of changing space requirements for warehouse and distribution facilities.
3. Discuss the use of 3PL suppliers and their relative merits.
4. Explain the arguments in favour of decentralizing stores.
5. Explain the concept of factory gate pricing.
6. Discuss the strategic importance of consolidation in relation to storage and distribution.
7. Explain why materials handling is more than simply an operational concept and why it may be of strategic importance to organizational choices.
8. Assessing storage requirements is both an operational concern and of strategic importance. Discuss.
9. The location and layout of storage facilities is of strategic importance. Discuss.
10. Stock codes need to be designed following key principles. Discuss.

References

Cooke, J. A. (2000). The physical challenges of the virtual sale, *Logistics Management & Distribution*, Oct., pp. 67–73.

Dragan, C. (2002). The rise of the 3PW. *Transporting and Distribution*, June, pp. 61–64.

Graham, P. (2002). Taking the hazards out of Hazmat storage. *Occupational Hazards*, pp. 43–46.

IGD (2003). *Retail Logistics*, London: IGD.

Kaplan, A. (2002). Putting your warehouse on speaking terms. *Food Logistics*, March 15, pp. 48–49.

Knemeyer, A. M. and Murphy, P. R. (2004). Evaluating the performance of third-party logistics arrangements: a relationship marketing perspective. *Journal of Supply Chain Management*, **40** (1), 35–51.

Labetti, K. (2002). Designing for security. *Frozen Food Age*, June, pp. 38–39.

Lysons, K. (2000). *Purchasing and Supply Chain Management*, 5th edn, London: FT Prentice-Hall.

Morton, R. (1999). Keep products from wandering off. *Transportation and Distribution*, June, pp. 84–87.

Murphy, P. R. and Wood, D. F. (2004). *Contemporary Logistics*, 8th edn. Upper Sadle River, New Jersey Pearson Prentice-Hall.

Stock, J. R. and Lambert, D. M. (2001). *Strategic Logistics Management*, 4th edn. London: McGraw-Hill.

van Hoek, R. I. (2000). The purchasing and control of supplementary third-party logistics services. *Journal of Supply Chain Management*, **36** (4), 14–26.

Chapter 12

The supply chain challenges – strategies for the future

LEARNING OUTCOMES

After reading this chapter you should be able to:

- recognize and know the key challenges facing organizational supply chain strategies;
- know key drivers of these challenges and be able to explain them;
- evaluate the importance of the challenges in developing appropriate supply chain strategies.

A study by Accenture Management Consultants (Accenture, 2000) revealed six different but equally successful supply chain strategies which were:

1. Market-saturation-driven: high profit margins delivered through strong branding and ubiquitous marketing and distribution.
2. Operationally agile: configuring assets and operations to respond quickly and fleet of foot to emerging consumer trends through product categories or geographical region.
3. Freshness-oriented: earning a premium by delivering products to the consumer that are fresher than competitor offerings.
4. Consumer customizer: adopt mass customization to build and maintain close relationships with consumers through direct sales.
5. Logistics optimizer: emphasize balance of supply chain efficiency and effectiveness.
6. Trade-focused: priority on low price, best value for the consumer.

It is important to recognize that there are different paths to future successful supply chain strategies. The path chosen by an organization will depend on a number of factors that influence their decision – environmental conditions, organizational capabilities and customer requirements are just three of those issues. This book began by stating that supply chain strategies are customer-driven and need to be customer-focused and the strategies listed above reinforce that proposition.

A number of key supply chain challenges have emerged in recent times. These challenges are business-, consumer- and government-driven. Many issues, concepts and strategies have been discussed in the text but it is worth reflecting on some of the major challenges facing organizations going forward. Supply chain strategies need to address these challenges. A major challenge for organizations is how to create value for individual customers without cost exceeding the value created. In many different markets, consumer markets, business markets and service industries including health and education, creating supply chain strategies that can add value for the customer is essential. Globalization and the changing nature of conditions in world markets and the impact upon local supply present another major challenge. This is particularly the case in a world becoming more environmentally aware of the damage caused to local and global environments through industrial activities. In addition to environmental concerns a parallel concern is the ethics of local and global supply and the impact on the local and global communities involved. These issues present major challenges to governments, policymakers and to organizations and their management teams. Designing green, ethical, customized value-added and efficient supply chain strategies is the management challenge for decades to come. The chapter begins by re-examining mass customization before considering global challenges, ICT, environmental, ethical challenges and the implications for supply chains. The chapter concludes with a research agenda.

Mass customization – the supply chain challenge

Mass customization is a self-contradiction of terms. The concept refers to focusing upon individual customer requirements and the challenge is how to meet customer demand economically.

> All to one cannot be made to work, and the company trying to make it work cannot succeed, unless the whole of that organization has been restructured to focus on the 'All to One ideal.
>
> Luengo-Jones, 2001, p. 6

From mass market to mass customization

As a producer, supplier or retailer the objective is to attract as many customers as possible to ensure profitability. The trade-off is one of value *vis-à-vis* volume. Value can be extracted through offering customers what they want (customization, lower volumes, higher prices, higher margins) or through offering standard products to many (standard items, high volumes, lower production costs, lower prices, lower unit margin but reasonable total margin owing to sales volumes). Customers have become more demanding in terms of requiring special features or adaptations to a standard product and a bundle of services that are perceived desirable. The trick for suppliers is to fulfil the individual customer demand profitably by integrating the supply chain processes to satisfy the demand. This requires focus on customer demand planning and synchronization throughout a supply chain that is enabled to do whatever is needed to develop, produce, market and deliver economical customized services and products. The problem for retailers and suppliers is how to design, configure, calibrate, integrate and synchronize supply chain processes to deliver the customer-focused marketing strategy we recognize as 'mass-customization' without incurring higher costs in inventories or in 'make-to-order' production processes.

Computers

Dell Computers are often quoted when commentators search for examples to explain the 'mass customization' concept. Dell delays the final configuration of their product until a customer specifies the components that they require. The company makes a standard offer at a standard price and then allows upgrades of additional components and services to be configured by the customer at additional price increments. This allows the organization's flexibility to minimize inventory owing to the limited choices available from the standard product. Assembly then takes place with variations to the key components making up the required personal computer (PC). Limiting consumer choice within acceptable ranges is the key to effective inventory control. The variety of inventory held is then minimized and replenishment is relatively simple. As advances in technology or changes to design occur it is possible to re-configure possible choices without too much trouble. New parts can replace older components and sub-assemblies as and when they become available. Since minimum inventories are held there is no major problem with obsolescent or redundant stock items.

Shoes

Christopher (1998, p. 210) refers to the example of Custom Foot, a small shoe company in the USA. These stores carry no shoe stocks except for examples of styles, types of leather and colour possibilities. In effect the store only holds samples of the products possible. Using electronic scanners it is possible to obtain accurate measures of the customers foot and data is then transmitted electronically to an Italian supplier who is able to build and deliver the finished shoes to the customer in the USA within 3 weeks. Prices are very competitive and the important benefit for the customer is that the shoe was built to fit their foot exactly. There is nothing tremendously new in this since it has always been possible to acquire handcrafted shoes built to your own exact specification. However, what is new here is the concept of a shoe shop without readymade shoes. Furthermore, the accuracy of electronic scanning measures, which lower the processing cost whilst ensuring accuracy and the most important point is that the shoes are made quickly at an affordable price because of the 'digital supply chain' processes.

Clothes

Similarly, from the 1950s to the 1980s Burton Tailoring brought customized products to the high street mass market. It was possible to walk into a Burton Store get measured with a tape measure leg, waist, arms, chest and shoulder to waist. Then the customer was able to choose from a wide range of fabrics and colours available in sample swatches. The result is: a customized suit in 3 or 4 weeks delivered to the high street store having been made at Burton's own manufacturing and assembly units near Leeds. All this for a price little more than a ready-to-wear product available 'off-the-peg' that may need to incur alteration charges before fitting. Today some Saville Row tailors have managed to stay profitable by taking customer measurements in-store and transmitting them to tailors in lower labour cost countries who make up the product in standard stock cloths and ship to London for the customer who receives a customized suit within a week. The customer is happy because the price is lower than normal Saville Row tailoring and the Tailor is happy because he retained business and turned a profit better than if the suit had been made on the premises given high UK labour costs by comparison to the offshore tailoring. This customization is made possible by electronic means of communication (e-mail, telephone, fax) and airfreight at costs that are affordable to the customer.

Music

The changes that have occurred in other traditional markets are sobering too. When it comes to the notion of mass customization there is no better example than the growth of personalized digital recordings. Thirty years ago or less people visited their local music store sifted through racks of Vinyl LP's and selected one or two to listen to in a sound booth or later through headphones in store. Today CDs, MP3 players and other digital systems allow consumers to configure their own selections of music and to download them from Internet websites often without any payment. Shawn Fanning founded 'Napster' the free music exchange service as a 20-year-old student writing file-swapping software at Northeastern University in the USA. When payment is made it is often a fraction of the price that would be paid for in store music (CDs, DVDs, cassette tapes, etc.). Music has become an almost free good. Disintermediation has taken place in this market. Music and media companies involved in publishing have built their asset base by developing or purchasing back catalogues often for vast sums of money. The back catalogues guaranteed licensing agreements with other suppliers to publish their material elsewhere for payment of a fee. Many music suppliers are rightly concerned that their long-established catalogues are no longer worth the sums of money invested in them. Without entering into the legality or the ethical aspects of this customization it is easy to conceive how other markets could change significantly in future. Figure 12.1 illustrates the differently configured supply chain options. There are different channels to market that music can take with different costs and prices. What is salutary is that the digital route with its highly customized concept is probably lowest cost and lowest price.

Conditions give rise to change

The rise of the global economy and the impact of macroenvironmental change have consequences for consumer behaviour. People travel more

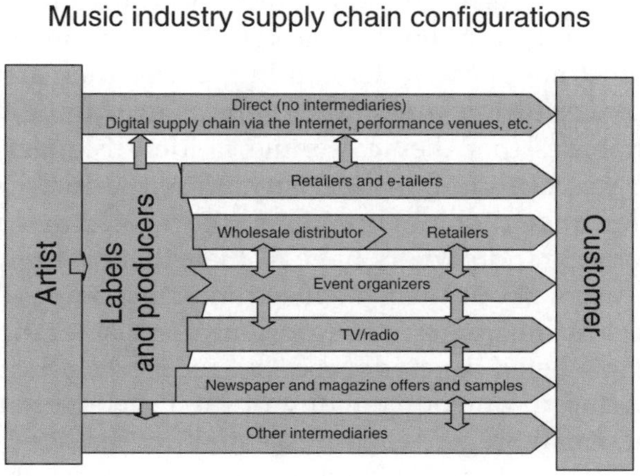

Music industry supply chain configurations

Figure 12.1

and have greater expectations than their parent's generation. Socio-cultural shifts and demographic change have given rise to new market opportunities whilst simultaneously hastening the decline of long-established mature industries and products. Product life-cycles are becoming much shorter in many markets (Handfield and Nichols, 1999, p. 8). The rate of change in technology, markets and products has led to the need for managers to make decisions rapidly, with partial information and with uncertain financial consequences. The levels of risk have increased generally. According to Pine (1993) only those organizations capable of mass customization will survive in many market segments. Schmenner (1988, p. 11) has drawn a comparison between global markets and the fashion industry, in which products go in and out of style with season.

The rise in consumerism has brought with it more fickle buying behaviour. Consumers expect more for less after all they have witnessed a long-term trend of falling prices in real terms and increasing improvements in technology, design and other features that have brought benefits without necessarily increasing the prices paid. They want instant or near-instant availability. It is often said that today's working consumer is time-poor and cash-rich whilst the reverse is true of those who find themselves out of work. Demographic change brings with it shifts in consumer behaviour, for example, it is estimated that 50 per cent of the UK population will be over the age of 50 by the year 2020 (Hines, 2001). This has implications for demand, service, products, place and shifts in specific consumer requirements. They also have more choice, are likely to be less loyal, are not prepared to accept second best and have become more sophisticated in their tastes and their approach to buying goods and services.

Global companies who want to achieve market dominance through developing their powerful brands in order to transcend local domestic markets are shaping competitive markets. These organizations need to satisfy their customers by understanding better their needs. They are developing powerful information systems that provide their owner(s) with vast databases that they can mine to identify market trends and utilize for targeted promotional activity. New product innovation and creativity to leverage both the brand and the vast arrays of information that these global brand owners have at their disposal requires them to think in new ways about their business and the competition they face. Owning assets is no longer as important a consideration as owning customers. This belief is evidenced by recent trends to restructure organizations and to outsource many of the functional and traditional activities previously regarded as essential to the well-being of the organization. Efficient and effective supply chains are required to manage customer demand and brand operations.

Customer relationship management and customization

Customer relationship management (CRM) is supported through e-commerce. Back-office support activities are more focused on satisfying customers and fulfilment of the marketing promise is critical to the organization's future. Organizations are focused on value creation rather than merely short-term profitability. Creating value streams is important as markets, marketing processes; supplier networks and operations throughout the globe become integrated through e-linkages in a complex chain moving parts, products and information around the network in order to meet customer demand. Different strategies are required to pursue this goal as time and distance shrink (Cairncross, 1998). Internet strategies present opportunities to integrate complex supply chains from concept design to store to consumer. Markets and market opportunity may be both local and global. Organizations will be managing networks to leverage brand values and this can be achieved using global communication systems from anywhere in the world.

From mass market to micromarket

Organizations have also recognized the opportunities that micro-marketing can offer. This is essentially identifying small but profitable target market segments that nobody is serving particularly well or with a substantive coherent offer. Such markets if identified properly can generate high profits because they are relatively low cost to reach and assuming the needs are well met customers in such micromarkets tend to stay loyal. Leadbeater (1999, p. 25) referred to the demarcation line between production and consumption becoming blurred. The terms 'buyer' or 'seller' are not so definite in the contemporary supply network but rather there is mutual exchange of products, services, money, information and emotion. These exchanges have become collaborative in nature in many market contexts. Suppliers listen to customers and make adjustments to products and services that deliver value. In some instances customers collaborate through participation in product design or specification.

Standard products with limited variation

One important aspect is to consider customization as a bundle of standard product variables together with a bundle of services that can be offered to enhance customer value. In this respect many of the issues discussed in Chapter 3 relating to market-driven supply chains need to be considered to leverage value for the customer and the supply network. Usually firms offer product choice from a standard menu with limited variability. Limited variability ensures that costs are kept lower than otherwise would be the case. For example, limiting choice of shirts to six collar sizes, three colours and two styles means holding inventories for 36 possible combinations of choice. If the offer was extended to ten collar sizes, six colours and six styles the inventory combinations increase to 360, ten times the previous example. These decisions become critical to achieving customer satisfaction and profitability. In the example supposing the firm went for the full offer, they would incur higher inventory-holding costs and higher purchasing costs in the hope of achieving higher turnover by being able to satisfy more customers. However, according to market research supposing the majority of shirts purchased fell within a limited range of collar sizes (14, 14.5, 15, 15.5, 16, 16.5) and 50 per cent of sales attributable to white, 20 per cent blue, 10 per cent brown and 20 per cent other mixed colours with classic styles being most popular. In order to satisfy the majority of customers in this market the firm could decide to hold six size variations, three main colours and perhaps only one style. This limits the offer to 18 possible combinations. However, these combinations have been identified, as the best selling lines, which should limit risk, prove profitable and limit the cash tied up in inventories. Although the product is limited the range of services could be infinitely more variable and more personal in nature. For example, a measuring and alteration service to make adjustments to the shirt to customize fit. Customized embellishments, prints, patterns, motifs, buttons added at the point of sale. Such services might add significant value for the customer and generate additional profit for the retailer. In such circumstances the degree of customized service would attract customers to the store more so than the baseline product.

Essentially customization is a way of adding value for the customer and by so doing achieves higher revenue streams and improves total profit. Traditionally the capability of the firm to do things better, faster and cheaper has often been a function of size. Size being important to generate economies of scale for the supplier. Size enabling the firm to achieve purchasing economies with their suppliers by offering large purchase order quantities, production economies by producing large volumes in a given time exploiting their production capacities and through a capability to distribute large volumes at lower unit cost. This traditional business model also depended on large volumes being ordered by the firm's customers. It often meant that the purchaser would get a lower unit price from the supplier but would need to order and store inventory until required by their customer and incur costs in storage and re-distribution through their market channels. Some firms in some industries historically made their living by simply *'breaking-bulk'*. For example, take sugar, wheat or rice, suppliers in these sectors often bought in bulk to get a good price, stored the product in a silo or warehouse, possibly washed and/or refined the product, re-packaged it in very small quantities and sold it onto a wholesaler or retailer at a healthy margin. Today many organizations do not want to hold large inventories because of the high risks associated with doing so (obsolescence, redundant stocks, damage, deterioration in store, changes in demand patterns). Although unit costs for the buyer could be lowered through taking such risks they are reluctant to do so because their total holding cost could be substantially higher if stock becomes obsolete, unusable or unsaleable through deterioration or owing to a shift in demand conditions. It is possible for organizations to generate value in different ways. A greater focus on the needs of the target market and on particular customer needs may be achieved by identifying profitable markets through market research and within the market conducting marketing research to establish particular customer patterns of behaviour that can be translated into information to help focus products and services to address their needs. Speed to reduce development times, production and replenishment cycles and in getting products to market faster are also important elements of achieving higher profits and beating competitors. Figure 12.2 illustrates a value chain for the firm wanting to move to customizing products.

When it comes to explaining mass customization it is important to consider a spectrum of market opportunities with which both supplier and buyer are presented. In effect there is a continuum from a market of one with many suppliers at one extreme and a mass market with many buyers and many sellers at the other extreme. Figure 12.3 depicts such a spectrum of market opportunity.

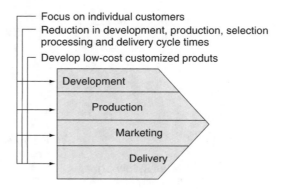

Figure 12.2 Mass customization value chain adapted from Pine (1993)

Market of one   Mass market
Make-to-order   *Standard product*
customization   *mass production*

Figure 12.3 Spectrum of market opportunity

This spectrum of market opportunity can be considered against other dimensions, e.g. price and supply chain structure. Figure 12.4 demonstrates how the two ends of the continuum might cause relative prices to respond and how the supply chain is structured. Quadrant 1 illustrates a situation where the product offering at its extreme would be considered unique. Because the product is considered unique the price is relatively high following simple economic laws of supply and demand. The lower the quantity supplied when the quantity demanded is high determines a higher price. Therefore in market segments where products are scarce and/or relatively unique the price will be higher. For example, in fashion markets haute couture is unique *vis-à-vis* high street fashion and prices are high. Quadrant 2 demonstrates that branded products also realize higher prices than non-branded products for what may be a relatively standard product. For example, Levi jeans sell at higher prices than a

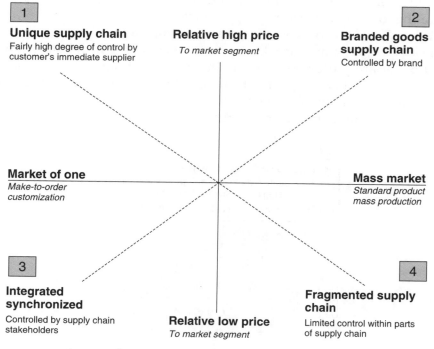

1		2
Unique supply chain	**Relative high price**	**Branded goods supply chain**
Fairly high degree of control by customer's immediate supplier	*To market segment*	Controlled by brand

Market of one		**Mass market**
Make-to-order		*Standard product*
customization		*mass production*

3		4
Integrated synchronized	**Relative low price**	**Fragmented supply chain**
Controlled by supply chain stakeholders	*To market segment*	Limited control within parts of supply chain

Figure 12.4

supermarket own label or a non-label pair. Branded products are differentiated from competitor offerings but they are not unique or scarce nor are they produced necessarily for markets of one like haute couture fashion. Levi amongst others has attempted to customize their products by offering customers limited variations to the standard product using scanning cameras that take various body measurements to adjust the fit to the person's individual size. It was hoped that such customization would secure the market and allow the business to maintain competitiveness and earn a premium over and above standard products by charging higher prices for the service. Essentially it is still a standard product with some variation that effectively would shift the position from right to left in quadrant 2 and move it up the vertical axis to achieve a higher price. However it would not necessarily shift quadrants into 1. It is more likely to move the position of the offer towards quadrant 3 in the longer term. This quadrant suggests that customization is possible and at lower prices if supply chains can be co-ordinated and integrated effectively to generate efficiencies that lower overall cost. For example, in recent years it has been possible to purchase cars at retail garages and to specify a list of variations to the standard product specifications, e.g. types of CD/radio, navigation equipment, seating fabrics/colours, dash board specification, lights, paintwork and more. The variations are recorded at the retailer and transmitted to the automobile maker who co-ordinates the *'bill of materials'* from various retail outlets and orders the various components required to make the cars ordered. A delivery date is given to the customer by the retail garage at the date of order. This is possible because the systems are integrated between the retailer, the manufacturer and their suppliers allowing them to interrogate different supply and production lead time data to create transparency in the supply chain. The benefit to the customer is clear; a degree of customization at lower prices than might be expected.

Figure 12.5 illustrates how organizations may decide to reposition their offerings along these different dimensions and demonstrates implications for managing the supply chain. The circle at the centre shows how the cycle of offers can position in one quadrant along two dimensions: price and degree of customization and how it may move around the quadrants only if the supply chain and the market are configured to deliver and demand, respectively.

If we were to examine these relationships more closely we might find a range of market offers that illustrate each of the different dimensions using shoes as an example of product. Figure 12.6 illustrates a perceptual map using these dimensions.

Figure 12.7 demonstrates the impact of the dimensions further taking clothing and in particular women's dresses as an example to illustrate relationships.

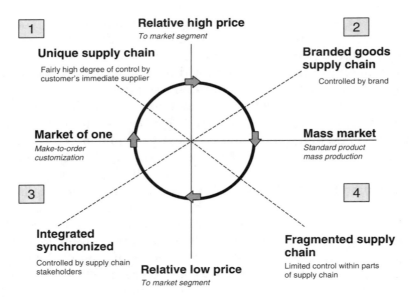

Figure 12.5

Taking two dimensions, price and market volume, it is possible to envisage a number of possibilities within the quadrants illustrated. Highly customized products such as made to order haute couture may lead to high prices whereas involving the customer in the process to

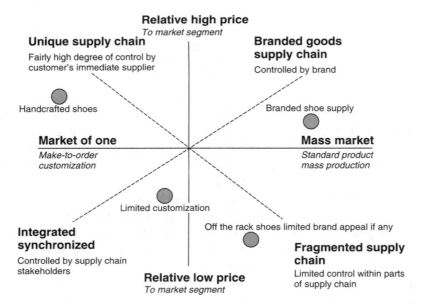

Figure 12.6

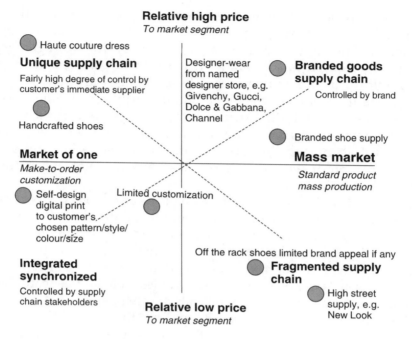

Figure 12.7

self-design, digitally print and customize products enables lower price points but provides higher value for the customer. In the mass market for clothes high street clothes may be sold cheaply because they are standard products. Branded fashion sells for more because it is able to differentiate itself from the standard offer.

Globalization – the supply chain challenge

Many of the challenges are interrelated and none more so than globalization. The impact of globalization is felt everywhere. Mass customization is both a consequence of and a contributing factor to global change. Living at the speed of Internet communications means that many issues can be communicated quickly worldwide. A website publishing communications can be viewed or e-mails sent to people in any parts of the globe where computers with connections to the Internet are available. Mobile telephony too has changed the ways in which people communicate and transmit thoughts across digital networks. Less than 10 years ago it would have been unthinkable to have large numbers of people not only talking on their mobile telephones but sending text messages in shorthand form that in just a few years has become an accepted way of rapid communication and information for many people. This shorthand is also having an impact on language and spelling particularly for younger generations who thing it is acceptable to write shorthand text when they communicate in other mediums. These changes are not unique to any geographical area of the globe but are visible everywhere. Travel to Australasia, Asia, India, Africa, Europe and the Americas, you will see the effects of digital communication. Dealing with your bank, your travel agent, booking hotels, cars, accommodation and a myriad of other products and services has become a normal feature of digital communications.

Instant and rapid communications have affected every aspect of the way we live and interact socially, culturally, politically and economically. Influences from different parts of the globe are assimilated quickly into societies geographically dispersed and discernible patterns of behaviour observed. Social change is endemic. The pace of change too is rapid. It is just over 50 years ago that cables were laid beneath the sea to transmit international telephone calls and telephone ownership was for the wealthier members of society and not the norm. The first satellite launch 'Telstar' took place in 1956 and people were excited by the possibilities to communicate with planets far away from our own galaxy. Now we take for granted satellite transmissions to communicate, distribute and receive information from remote parts of our own world. As a consequence we know the world is a smaller place than it was in 1956.

The economic impact of global change is far reaching. Whether or not you accept the view that global change is evolutionary or revolutionary one thing is indisputable and that is change is more rapid. People communicate more widely, travel further and have access to resources that were science fiction less than 50 years ago. Today's global realities offer both opportunities to organizations and conversely pose threats. Supply chain strategies are both local and global for many commercial organizations. Retail stores now have food on the shelves in Western Europe and the United States all year round. There are seldom shortages because the planning and supply systems ensure continuity. Tomatoes are on our supermarket shelves winter and summer; apples, pears, grapes, bananas too. Seasons do not exist in my local store anymore. Children and young adults in the UK would find it hard to accept that they could not buy a tomato at any time of year. Food now travels around the world to be in a store near you and at a price you can afford. This is at a time when many people in the world population (1 billion people) live on less than a US$1 a day. There are many paradoxes and there is a wide division between rich and poor.

Global supply chains give access to products and services that may not be available locally at the times we want them. Global suppliers also provide goods not available at all locally. Nevertheless, many goods and services that are, and could be, acquired locally are often not because the prices from remote parts of the globe are lower than those locally. This is even the case after factoring in transport cost, insurance, duties and taxes.

Local in Ludlow

Ludlow in the county of Shropshire in the UK has become noted as the gourmet food capital of the UK. There are five local butchers shops in this small market town in the Marches. They have co-operated together in establishing an e-business website to promote their own businesses and to take orders for produce which is delivered by post anywhere in the UK. Owing to the nature of the products the supply has remained local to the UK. This type of arrangement is often referred to as co-opetition. It is co-operative in part (the website) and each of the butchers is in competition for business attracted to the site. Business for all parties has increased substantially and taken them beyond their geographical area. Restaurateurs in the area are quoted as saying they owe their success to the fact that produce is local, and high quality and fresh. The area is also the 'real ale capital' of the UK with around 65 local microbreweries in the county. Once again they identify success as having locally grown hops that move from field to brewery fermentation in a matter of hours.

Source: Author – information gleaned from BBC Radio 4, The Food Programme, 17 November 2003.

Greening the supply chain

Green pressure groups have risen in prominence in the past few years. These groups are generally concerned with protecting the integrity of the environment. They have drawn attention to the fact that many aspects of daily life impact adversely. Many energy sources (e.g. fossil fuels) are not renewable and consumption is damaging the ozone layers in the atmosphere. Increasing distances travelled by goods reaching their market destination consume energy and damage the environment (Green et al., 1998). Many commentators have discussed this particular issue in reference to 'food miles'.

Case: Food miles, local stores and local supply

A survey of London shopkeepers in 2001 found that one-third were intending to retire or close within 5 years. It is claimed that the increasing dominance of supermarkets has been particularly harmful to local economies. The supermarket takeover reduces choices. It forces people to travel to buy standard goods, produced far away from the local communities who buy them, often at higher prices. Small local retail outlets can have a huge beneficial impact on an area. Local shops provide essential community glue without which you get social isolation and a rise in crime and vandalism. One solution is to establish European procurement rules to encourage public bodies to purchase goods and services locally wherever possible. Big food retailers must reduce food miles by sourcing products locally.

Source: Adapted from an article appearing in Regeneration and Renewal. London: 22 August 2003, p. 11.

There was also the issue of genetically modified foods (GMFs) referred to elsewhere in this book. The jury is still out on this issue. However, one thing is clear that large supermarket chains have adopted a consumer-focused and customer-driven approach to their policy towards GM foods so far and many are keen to highlight the fact that they do not stock them. Kerr (1999) examined the issue of genetically modified organisms, consumer scepticism and trade law and the implications for the organization of international supply chains.

In addition to energy consumption within supply chains and issues surrounding the disposal of waste materials there are issues relating to the design of products and supply chain delivery mechanisms. Purjari et al. (2003) examine competitive implications for new product development in relation to environmental performance. Products and services could be better designed to remove waste using reusable energy sources, reusable or recyclable materials and parts. Procurement policies particularly those of public organizations where they serve the needs of local communities through democratic processes should look after the wider interests of the community.

Case: Green procurement policies won't cost the earth

Richmond, British Columbia, Canada, was the first municipality in the Greater Vancouver Regional District to develop green procurement policies supported by a detailed guide to help city staff identify and purchase the most environmental-friendly products on the market. It is only one of 21 local authorities being encouraged to do so. The city identifies environmentally preferred products (EPPs) as those that is: efficient, reduces waste, is reusable or contains reusable parts, is recyclable or uses recyclable materials. The guide includes everything from landscaping, vehicles, office equipment, construction materials, lighting and janitorial necessities. Tips for avoiding paints or carpets that emit volatile organic compounds and buying non-toxic, biodegradable cleaners to selecting power savers and salvaging materials are included in the guide. Through the power of their dollar communities can influence the ways in which products are manufactured and supplier environmental performance. For example, communities with set targets for reductions in greenhouse gas emissions can buy vehicles that are 20 per cent more efficient using biofuels and electricity than traditional diesel or petrol engine vehicles. Critics argue it costs more to be green but this is a short-term view according to the municipality who argue that over the lifecycle it is cost-effective and more importantly improves the quality of life for the local community and the world at large.

Source: Adapted from Summit, September 2003, Vol. 6, No. 4.

Ethical supply chains

Case: Green mountain coffee – profitable fair trade

The coffee business has expanded like few others over the past 25 years. Since 1979, US spending on high-range beans-like French roast and hazelnut has increased nearly fourfold, while the number of specialty-coffee retailers has grown 900 per cent, to 2500. Yet even in that context, the growth of Green Mountain Coffee Roasters has been impressive: It is one of just four companies to make Fortune's Fastest-Growing list for the third consecutive year. By the mid-1990s the company had opened a dozen retail coffee shops, mostly in the Northeast US, they faced stiff competition from other chains. The owner decided to switch out of retail and focused instead on selling beans wholesale to convenience stores and company offices. Revenue has gone up 79 per cent since then. That rapid expansion has forced the company to make some technological changes. Green Mountain had only $38 million in sales. Working with PeopleSoft the company's human resources, financial, supply chain and other systems are now so well integrated that it didn't need to take a physical inventory of its six warehouses this year for the first time ever. The technology saves time and great ability to pack orders efficiently. It also saves money because the business no longer has to manage multiple streams of incompatible data.

About 5 per cent of operating profits are given to charities and non-profit organizations, many of which help coffee farmers. One of the company's fastest-growing product categories is called Fair Trade coffee, a designation guaranteeing that farmers received fair compensation for their beans rather than the rock-bottom prices that often prevail in world markets.

Source: Adapted from FSB-Fortune Small Business. New York: July/August 2003, Vol. 13, Iss. 6, p. 69.

Information, integration and intelligent systems

Chapter 7 examined e-business strategies and implications for the supply chain. Recent technological innovations were discussed and the ability to integrate systems and information to gain better control over supply chain activities through collaboration, co-ordination and synchronization were discussed. Intelligent systems take many forms from intelligent fridges with blue tooth technology, manufacturing systems, logistics and retailing organizations using RFID technology. The availability of and access to these new technologies has allowed organizations to capture vast amounts of data that can be analysed and used to understand better customer requirements. ICT systems have created the opportunities to develop new ways of approaching customers to attract business, new ways of making sure customers do not migrate and stay loyal to provide lifetime value for the organization and new ways to deliver products to market. Some of the latter have been discussed in this chapter, e.g. Napster. The IESA case below is a further illustration of the benefits of having intelligent, integrated information systems.

IESA dispensing supply chain aspirins for blue chip clients

IESA is a supply chain solutions company based in Warrington, UK. The company has developed a ground breaking way of managing and monitoring the dispensing of tools and components with their automated tool dispenser (ATD). It combines proven vending technology, mobile telephony and Internet-based management systems to deliver operational benefits including cost efficiencies. The ATD has a touch screen for user authentication and product selection, which presents users with product images and technical information to enable accurate selection. The ATD records information on each item dispensed (who requested it and when), as well as monitoring the inventory level for each product line and triggering automatic replenishment orders when appropriate. Transaction data is linked to existing ERP systems for consolidated monthly invoicing. The integrated GSM engine provides 24 hours remote access to the ATD product information database allowing changes to product images and descriptions from central control offices. Remote access to inventory data means that 'out of stock' is a thing of the past. Usage trends and tracking data keep close control of inventory. The ATD presents an optimum solution to maintenance, repair and operating (MRO) goods. The system only requires 240 V of power and can be located anywhere convenient where there is a socket.

Source: Author.

Implications for managers, organizations and policymakers

Consumer challenges presented to suppliers in the twenty-first century will be many. Consumers want to buy products and services when they want them, at an affordable price, representing value for money, from sources that are reliable and this might mean that the supplier is ethical, environmentally conscientious and engaged with local communities being served by its products and services. There are a number of important policy implications for governments, organizations and managers engaged in supply chain strategies. Governments will need to establish regulatory frameworks that acknowledge consumer interests and the interests of the wider communities they serve. They cannot afford to continue to simply put these concerns lower down the priority list than business interests. Businesses need to recognize the realities of this situation and take steps to ensure that they can meet the challenges presented by designing green, lean and ethical supply chain strategies that deliver products and services efficiently and effectively adding value for customers. Balanced supply chain strategies must take account of markets served and sources of supply.

It is unacceptable ethically to source lowest cost supplies to serve high value markets if it causes environmental damage or causes social injustice to the indigenous source country and population. Organizations have a social responsibility in designing supply chain strategies that minimize environmental costs and cannot simply ignore them. Globalization throws up many challenges and many paradoxical situations. For example, how do you explain to families who consume products in England that they lost their jobs manufacturing goods locally because it was cheaper to buy them from overseas sources so they could buy them in their local retail store cheaper? It is unsustainable for governments and organizations to allow local sources of supply to completely evaporate. It is 'short-termism' and a high-risk strategy in the longer term for many industrial and commercial sectors. For example, QR strategies need to have reliable, responsive and reputable suppliers to be effective in meeting customer demand. For governments the impact of local organizations moving their manufacturing and sourcing operations overseas upon the balance of payments and employment will give cause for concern.

Implications for a research agenda

A number of important themes have been examined in this book. The themes selected are my interpretation of important developments that have brought us to where we are today. From roots firmly located in purchasing, supply and operations the concept of 'supply chain management' as we now understand owes much to developments in other disciplines: strategy, economics, marketing, organizational behaviour and information technology. It is the integration of these disciplines in terms of thinking and applications in terms of practice throughout the management process that is important in helping to understand the current issues and the future directions that research can take.

Integration is the key to managing these complex processes both internally and externally between firms that co-exist in the numerous supply chains that each organization has. For example, the delivery of a single garment to a retail store may have a network of suppliers stretching around the globe. It is important to recognize that it is only one supply chain configuration that the retailer has to manage. The retailer has numerous supply chains specific to categories (e.g. food – frozen, fresh) and within a range, within a store, within all its stores. The variety of contact points and the number of different relationships that exist in this business to fulfil customer needs are highly complex. An important point to remember is that they are business arrangements and business relationships driven by the motive for profit through exchange. In businesses where profit is not the main motive there are still value exchanges taking place. Therefore, examining the exchange processes and how they are managed has much to offer to gain a better knowledge and understanding of how these processes work and change through time.

Globalization has many facets. The impact of sourcing and purchasing strategies on both the supplying country and their population and the purchasing country population adds an important new dimension considering ethics and green issues.

The study of organizational supply chains can be conducted using a range of appropriate research methods adopting different methodological stances and choices should be made on the basis of the research questions being addressed. Longitudinal studies, quantitative research, ethnography, phenomenology and social interactionism are all methods that could be employed effectively in this context.

Comparisons drawn between different types of supply chain are always interesting. In this respect comparative case study research has much to offer. Why have Benetton chosen to take greater control of their supply chain by vertically integrating operations and expanding the number of production centres overseas. This is not simply a cost reduction exercise although that may be an important outcome. They have taken this decision to gain control over the supply chain to minimize risks as much as anything and to establish centres close to where they think their markets may expand. Fashion and fads in retail strategy could be explored to examine if the decisions taken are influenced by patterns of development elsewhere in the sector. For example, were the owners of Benetton influenced by Zara's success in establishing new markets in Europe outside of Spain quickly and effectively because they were a vertically integrated company applying 'fast fashion' concepts (never repeating) and adopting QR tools. Have other retailers copied or are they copying aspects of the ways in which these companies manage their supply chains or do they do things differently and if so what? It may not simply be knowledge transfer between organizations within a sector that is important but rather knowledge transfer across sectors, e.g. automobiles to textiles.

We already know from the literature that many of the ideas and supply chain concepts were developed originally in manufacturing and in particular in automobile manufacture. Is managing the supply chain in the retail sector different to managing an automotive plant or an electronics plant? Is customization more or less important in fashion retail supply chains than it is in the computer industry? Companies like Dell have pioneered customization and involved customers in the design process, making choices to build their own machine configuration. They supply directly using the Internet and telephone sales. What is different and what is similar about these organizations, their supply chains, their business operations, their marketing and their supply chain strategies? These are all interesting questions that when answered we would all learn something from that would help explain different aspects of supply chain management. Comparative research and research conducted that is interdisciplinary would offer some useful insights in this context.

Whatever aspects of supply chain management researchers examine it is evident from the discussions within this chapter that supply chain strategies are critical to the successful business management of organizations. Researchers from different disciplines have much to offer in contributing to these debates.

Discussion Questions

1. What emphasis should organizations place on ethical practice within the supply chain?
2. Explain why greening the supply chain is viewed as important and what it means to have green supply chains.
3. One aspect of globalization is it has helped many countries have access to uninterrupted supplies of fresh food all year round but what is the impact of this on local suppliers?
4. Local farmers complain that supermarkets will not take their produce because it does not conform to their quality standards (size, shape, colour). They say supermarkets would rather source standard tasteless goods from halfway round the world and local people are being denied local produce. Discuss.
5. Global supply chains are complex to manage and owing to geographical distance they are costly and risky too. Discuss.
6. Local communities losing manufacturing jobs may rightly ask questions about the moral–ethical dimension of the decision to source overseas supplies. How do organizations ensure that the backlash from consumers does not threaten their market offering?
7. Intelligent information systems offer organizations new ways of developing supply chain strategies that improve customer service. Discuss.
8. 'Mass – customization is an oxymoron.' Discuss how organizations that need to produce large quantities to keep costs low offer customized products.
9. Discuss the challenges facing government policymakers when it comes to ensuring organizations develop environmentally friendly supply chain strategies.
10. Choose and discuss one possible research topic and explain how you might tackle the project to deliver the research objectives you have set yourself.

References

Accenture (2000). *Supply Chain Management Review*, March/April, p. 29.

Cairncross, F. (1998). *The Death of Distance*. London: Orion Business Books.

Christopher, M. G. (1998). *Logistics and Supply Chain Management – Strategies for Reducing Costs and Improving Services*, 2nd edn. London: Financial Times/Pitman Publishing.

Green, K., Morton, B. and New, S. (1998). Green purchasing and supply policies: do they improve companies' environmental performance? *Supply Chain Management*, **3** (2), 89–95.

Handfield, R. B. and Nichols, E. L. (1999). *Introduction to Supply Chain Management*. Upper Saddle River, NJ: Prentice-Hall.

Hines, T. (2001). Globalization – An introduction to fashion markets and fashion marketing. In *Fashion Marketing – Contemporary Issues*, (Hines, T. and Bruce, M., eds). Oxford: Butterworth-Heinemann, pp. 1–31.

Kerr, W. (1999). Genetically modified organisms, consumer scepticism and trade law: implications for the organisation of international supply chains, *Supply Chain Management*, **4** (2), 67–74.

Leadbeater, C. (1999). *Living on Thin Air*. London: Viking.

Luengo-Jones, S. (2001). *All to One – The Winning Model for Marketing in the Post Internet Economy*. Maidenhead: McGraw-Hill.

Pine, J. B. (1993). *Mass Customization: The New Frontier in Business Competition*. Boston, MA: Harvard Business School Press.

Purjari, D., Wright, G. and Peattie, K. (2003). Green and competitive influences on environmental new product development performance. *Journal of Business Research*, **56** (10), 657–71.

Schmenner, R. W. (1988). The merit of making things fast. *Sloan Management Review*, Fall, pp. 11–17.

Afterword

Challenges come from the external environment in which organizations operate and from continuous (incremental change) and discontinuous change (breakthrough-innovation). Globalization and its impact upon markets, organizations, individuals, industrial change and innovation influence the strategies that managers are able to select, structure and implement. Changes in attitudes, however influenced, shape the ways in which organizations structure their supply chains and the ways in which they develop relationships underpinned, for example, by information communication technologies, and attitudes towards environmental, ethical, ecological and equitable considerations. These influences are illustrated in Figure 1.

The major business challenges for organizations developing supply chain strategies raised throughout this text have identified a number of critical factors that may be summarized and themed around the following capabilities to manage: **value, volume volatility, velocity, variety, variability, visibility** and **virtuality.** In order to develop strategic capabilities in these areas, organizations need to look at the ways in which they interact with customers at every level and view these challenges from a customer perspective. Customers expect value and suppliers need to anticipate and identify what customers value in order to supply a bundle of goods and services that equate with value in order to exchange money for products. Value in exchange, use and over time may be important to the customer. This is the value challenge. Customers nowadays are seldom prepared to purchase quantities suppliers would like to supply, at a time determined by the supplier,

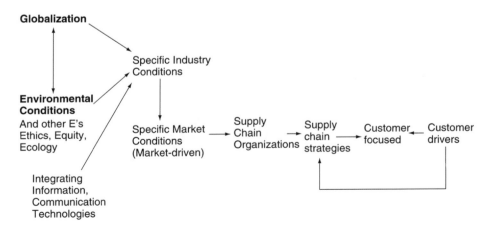

Figure 1

in standard form, with non-standard performance a highly probable outcome. This perhaps best describes a hitherto mass-production era. Today's customer is more demanding in every sense. Meeting the demands of customers when required by ensuring that capacity can be increased when demand is high and lowered when demand is lower without incurring excessive or unnecessary cost is the volume volatility challenge. Velocity is recognition that speed of response has become an important competitive advantage in many commercial contexts. Variety is a recognition that customer requirements vary and suppliers need to be capable of customizing products and services as a consequence. Variety is also what drives customers by introducing new products and services, by being able to anticipate customer demand. Variability is the challenge of management control in ensuring that goods and services satisfy quality criteria and deliver the required standard for customer satisfaction. Visibility is a core capability for managing the total supply chain from source to consumer. Visibility or transparency ensures that parties within the total supply chain know what the current pipeline looks like. Information and Communication Technology has allowed organizations to view frequently status reports on sourcing, procurement, production, logistics and customer demand, ensuring that there are no blockages, unnecessary inventories or unplanned cost build-up. Integration of systems, policies and procedures across organizational boundaries between organizations working together within a supply chain to satisfy the customer has been the catalyst for visibility whilst technology provided the means. 'Virtuality' has allowed organizations to replace inventory with information through the creation of digital supply chains supported by ICT. Organizations need to focus their attention on customers by creating capabilities that deliver market-driven supply chain strategies.

Supply chain strategies must be responsive to customer requirements and in that sense organizations need to develop sustainable strategies, offering service to the customer, with speedy responses, suited to the customer, at a standard quality supported by systems, structures and relationships that deliver customer satisfaction. This is a useful conceptual framework from which organizations can examine their own potential to meet the complex challenges of developing appropriate supply chain strategies.

Table 1 summarizes the main themes developed in this work using a 7V framework and explains the business challenge and customer need. From the identification of challenges it is possible to identify the 7Ss that provide a focus for developing organizational strategies to manage the supply chain.

At a supply chain and organizational level of analysis these frameworks offer a lens through which to focus investigations. These frameworks also offer managers, researchers and academics a different

Table 1

From: Business Challenges – 7Vs that customers want	*To: Supply Chain Strategies – 7Ss that deliver customer-focused organizational strategies*
Value – Offer customers value for money based on their preferences. Value not simply in exchange but through time and use.	**Sustainability** – Must offer customers' consistent value. For example, based on their preferences for time, place, cost, flexibility, dependability and quality. Must identify order qualifiers and order winners and compete managing complexity.
Volume volatility – Customers want to postpone their own supplies until they have a 'best forecast' of demand or accurate demand based on actual sales data. This may mean adjusting order quantities on a regular basis. They are no longer prepared to place standard order volumes in many sectors because their own market demand is volatile.	**Service** – The ability to deliver different quantities of goods through managing capacity not simply operationally but strategically (no longer sufficient to rely on economies of scale). Develop capabilities to manage capacity flexibly to deliver products and services to customers when they are required in the quantities demanded, e.g. from mass production to mass customization (from *n to 1*).
Velocity – Speed of change and speed of response (demand conditions, market structures, production technology, supplier capabilities).	**Speedy response** – Develop responsive capabilities to deliver goods and services when they are required, e.g. efficient consumer response, quick response.
Variety – Ability to customize the product/service offer (move from economies of scale to economies of scope or to 'economies of value to customer').	**Suited to customer requirements** – Develop flexibility capabilities, e.g. agile, lean supply chains, innovations and new product developments.
Variability – Ability to reduce variability and offer standard quality.	**Standards** – Develop supply chain strategies to assure customer quality standards are met effectively and co-operate within supply chains to compete across supply chains.
Visibility – Enabling all parts of a supply chain to be transparent and avoid blockages, 'iceberg' inventories and hidden costs; keeping the customer informed.	**Systems focused on customer satisfaction** – Re-design business processes and develop enabling strategies for all relevant parties including customers to view supply chain information relevant to them (e.g. collaborative, co-operative rather than competitive strategies).
'Virtuality' – An ability to coordinate intangible and tangible assets within the supply chain facilitated by information communication technologies gives customers confidence and ensures dependability.	**Structures and Relationships** – For example, develop digital supply chain strategies to replace unnecessary inventory movements by moving and exchanging information instead of goods.

perspective from which to observe, quantify and qualify organizational behaviours. For the practising manager it is a way to make sense of organizational policies and practices and to identify areas that require attention to acquire capabilities and competence in designing and managing supply chain strategies. For researchers and academics it maps the supply chain landscape from a customer perspective to view topography of the terrain and through a lens from which to focus research activities.

Figure 2 illustrates both the customer focus and the organizational strategic focus required to respond to the challenges. The dotted lines indicate the cross relationships that may occur and in essence the trade-offs that may need to be managed.

The final link in any supply chain is the end customer, the consumer of the products and services. The product has to be of the **right quality** (i.e. acceptable quality standards). It has to be the **right product** (i.e. an acceptable bundle of goods and services) and it has to be delivered in the **right quantity** demanded by the customer. Consumption has to occur at the **right time** (e.g. a service – cash from a bank, a haircut, a theatre performance, vehicle maintenance), at the **right place** (e.g. where it is demanded – home delivery from a supermarket, Internet usage, restaurant), at the **right price** (a price acceptable to the final customer). If and only if these 6Rs are satisfied can it be said that the organization has the **right customer focus**.

Supply chain strategies that are customer focused and customer driven have to fulfil all the criteria represented by the statement:

$$7Vs + 7Ss = 7Rs$$

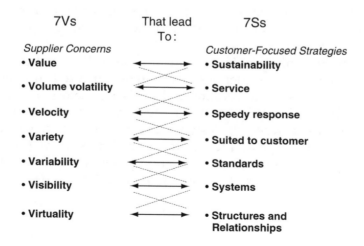

Figure 2

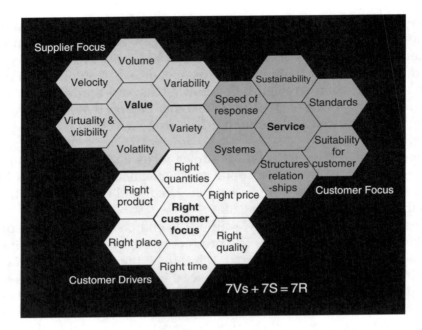

Figure 3 Customer Driven and Customer Focused Supply Chain Strategies

Figure 3 illustrates the customer-focused and customer-driven supply chain. Supply chain strategies must be developed around these themes. The 7Rs indicate factors that influence the customer in making purchasing decisions. The 7Vs are factors that influence supplier choices that need to be balanced when creating appropriate supply chain strategies. The 7Ss demonstrate how supply concerns have to be translated into customer-focused strategies to deliver customer satisfaction. The chapters within this text have suggested many ways that organizations develop appropriate supply chain strategies and the key concepts and considerations that influence choices.

This is an appropriate point at which to conclude by reminding managers, researchers and academics that there is much to learn about supply chain strategies from examining these issues across organizational supply chains and within bounded organizations. Different research methodologies and research designs have much to offer the development of our knowledge and understanding of how, why, where, when and what supply chain strategies are appropriate to satisfying customer needs and simultaneously by satisfying organizational goals.

Glossary

ABC Analysis or Pareto Analysis	This is a technique used to identify the percentage of highest value items by priority. For example, A items may be worth 80 per cent of the value but only 20 per cent of the volume, B items 10 per cent value, 30 per cent volume and C items 50 per cent value from 50 per cent volume. Note the percentages vary from organizational context to context.
Activity Based Cost (ABC)	This is a costing system based on identifying activities that cause cost. It differs significantly from traditional product costing by focusing on the activities causing cost. For example, it may be customer activities and therefore customer account profitability may be determined. It is not simply a different way to cost products as is sometimes suggested by commentators.
Activity Based Management (ABM)	ABM develops from Activity Based Costing and is a tool for managers to intervene based on the activities under-taken. Activity cost and revenue streams will be identified in ABM systems and ways sought to do things better (more efficiently) and to do better things (change processes to be more effective).
Average Cost (AVCO)	A system of valuing inventories based on the average cost of bought in and distributed inventories. Sometimes the term WAVCO is used to indicate that the average is a weighted average.
B2B	Business-to-Business commercial activities such as buyer supplier dealings. It is usually used to define E-business activities through the Internet.
B2B2C	A combination of business-to-business and business to consumer activities. For example, a retailer may conduct business with suppliers through a virtual private network (VPN) using the Internet. Simultaneously it

	may conduct sales transactions directly with consumers through its retail website.
B2C	Business to consumer communications, which may be informational and/or transactional. Usually meant to convey Internet commerce.
Back Hauling	This is a return load taken after a delivery has been made. It ensures that wagons do not return empty and that resources are utilized effectively. For example, a delivery to a depot may be dropped and the truck loaded with goods to move on to a different depot.
Back Order	Orders that cannot be fulfilled at the time most of the order is shipped. Orders are recorded and filled for shipment when available.
Bill of Lading	A contract stating a carrier has received goods and has taken responsibility for delivery.
Bill of Material	A detailed schedule for materials required in manufacturing operations.
Bonded Store	A secure warehouse facility. Most commonly used for imported or exported goods involving the collection of customs duties and excise taxes where taxes are only paid on exit from the storage facility.
Business Process Re-engineering (BPR)	Re-design processes to be more effective and/or more efficient to add value for the customer.
Business Processes	These are activities performed in sequence or parallel by an organization. Business processes will comprise a value chain for the customer. If business processes do not add value they incur cost. In such circumstances they should be identified and analysed to see if they can be removed or redesigned to be more efficient or more effective.
Buying Groups	Independent organizations that may be wholesalers or retailers who join together to obtain better terms of trade from suppliers form these. For example, a buying group may be able to buy in bulk for its members and therefore obtain substantial discounts from prices they would pay individually. Buying groups are not the same as

	symbol groups since members retain their independence in trading names, etc.
Category Management	Categories are identifiable, measurable groups of products/services which are categorized to fit particular customer segment requirements. Traditionally products/services may have been identified by the nature of a product or service e.g. soap powder, cosmetics, clothing and so on. Categories, however, may for example be clustered as disposable nappies and carry out beer in six packs to reflect a particular customer demand pattern. They are grouped by category in the ways in which customers interrelate or substitute products/services. Category management teams may be organized as multi-functional personnel managing across traditional product areas for the benefit of the customer and to deliver better profits for the organization. Category managers will have responsibility for the strategy, operations tactics and performance for their categories.
Category Optimization	Systems designed to balance performance of all lines within a given product category thus reducing cannibalization resulting from price promotions on full margin lines.
Central Distribution Centres and Depots	Centralized distribution depots or centres may be used by an organization to bring all products to a specific location with a view to moving them on to their final sale destinations. The benefit of doing this is control and availability of stock. For example, the distribution depot can hold sufficient stock for stores it serves without delivering all items to specific stores and finding that they sell out in two and remain in the rest. CDCs can replenish stock to where the demand is.
CIF	Cost, Insurance and Freight included in purchase price.
Composite Distribution Centres	A multi-temperature store facility where goods can be stored or distributed in combination (ambient, chilled and frozen products).

Consolidation	May occur when groups of stock are delivered to a single distribution point to wait the arrival of other mixed items for delivery onwards to internal or external customers. Loads are consolidated until they become economic to deliver. For example, airfreight or sea containers are often filled by disparate goods and sometimes by different organizations until the container is full when it is shipped or air freighted to its destination.
Consumer	A person who consumes products and/or services who may or may not be a customer. Often consumers are regarded as the end customer or the final customer in a supply chain.
Continuous Replenishment Programme (CRP)	Essentially the same as Vendor Managed Inventory (VMI). The vendor who shares sales information with the seller and thus knows when stock needs to be replenished replenishes inventories. Suppliers have a forward window on demand usually through sharing EDI. CRP or VMI systems have the benefits of lowering supply chain inventories through better demand planning and hence lowering costs.
Cross-Docking	This is a time reduction technique. It involves processes that marry products received in a facility from different suppliers or destinations with other products being distributed to the same onward destination. Goods are shipped at the earliest opportunity without going into long-term storage. Time in storage at a facility should be minimized as a consequence of cross-docking. Cross-docking terminals are often designed in rectangular shapes where trucks unload on one side and are loaded on the opposite side of the rectangle. Pallets or standardized containers are required if cross-docking is to be efficient.
Customer	A person or organization that purchases products and/or services from a supplier.
Cycle Time	Time it takes to complete one operational cycle. For example in production operations if the cycle time for all operations can be

	reduced to equal *takt* time, products can be made in single flow.
Demand Management	Is a system of developing a customer focused strategy rather than a supply strategy. For example, balancing promotions to optimize supply chain performance and thus avoiding the bullwhip effect caused by uncoordinated promotional activities within the supply chain.
Demurrage	A charge assessed by a carrier for delays by a purchaser in failing to unload and return vehicles, vessels or containers promptly.
Direct Product Profitability (DPP)	DPP is an accounting technique to track those fixed costs attributable to specific products. This technique has the benefit of identifying all costs associated with the product when arriving at a profit figure. It can be difficult to do in practice. Costs *vis-à-vis* benefits need to be care-fully assessed before implementing DPP.
Dovetailing	Occurs when suppliers locate plants close to customer delivery points. JiT systems have encouraged this to occur.
E-business	Any form of electronic business conducted between business partners.
E-commerce	Any form of commercial transaction undertaken electronically. It has come to mean the conduct of commerce over he Internet. However, there are many form of e-commerce (e.g. phone, fax, Internet).
Efficient Consumer Response (ECR)	Developed by KSA who also developed Quick Response for the Apparel Sector. ECR was developed for FMCG products in the USA grocery supply chain. It takes a total supply chain view from a customer perspective and develops capabilities across the organization and the network of organizations working together within a supply chain to deliver products efficiently to the customer when they are demanded. The aim is to deliver superior customer value in faster times at lower cost. Better, faster, cheaper. ECR requires collaborative strategies supported by appropriate technologies.

Electronic Data Interchange (EDI)	It is the exchange of electronic information between parties who trade within a supply chain. EDI usually requires specific standards and formats for the ease of transmission and validation of data.
Electronic Funds Transfer at Point of Sale (EFTPoS)	Customer funds are transferred between parties at point of sale. For example, a consumer pays by Switch, Delta or Credit Card at a check out in a store and the funds are transferred at the point of sale from the purchaser to the vendor account using supporting financial technology (magnetic strips, chip and pin through electronic readers that record the transaction), software that exchanges funds is supplied from technology support organizations like GE Capital. Finally, the banking community manages funds and fund transfers on behalf of the trading parties.
Electronic Point of Sale (EPoS)	A system that records sales by keying in data, scanning bar codes or using radio frequency tags at the till point to record a sale.
E-markets	Any form of electronic market place. For example, the trade in stocks in and shares is an e-market. The traditional definition of a market is a place where buyers and sellers meet. An e-market is simply a space where buyers and sellers meet. It is used in contemporary language to mean digital space through the Internet.
Enabling Technologies	These are technologies that support supply chain activities. For example, EDI, RFT, Bar Codes, EFTPoS, EPoS, SAP, Databases.
ERP	Enterprise Resource Planning. These are enterprise wide systems such as SAP, Oracle, and I2 that attempt to integrate business-wide systems and processes allowing different parts of the organization to access a common database.
FMS	Flexible Manufacturing Systems.
FOB	Free on Board – Purchase price does not cover freight or insurance after goods are placed on board a vessel for delivery. Originated as a shipping term.

First In First Out (FIFO)

A type of Inventory (stock) system that operates on a first in first out basis, Cost accounting systems often adopt this basis for inventory (stock) valuations.

Five S Japanese Model

Five terms beginning with S in Japanese that indicate a workplace suited for visual control and lean production. Seiri = separate tools, parts and instructions are arranged and removed from unneeded ones. Seiton = identify each tool, part, etc. for use. Seiso = clean up the environment, Seiketsu = conduct seiri, seitin and seiso at frequent intervals to keep the workplace in perfect condition (usually daily). Shitsuke = means to make it a habit to do the other four Ss.

Five Whys

Ohno said that you should ask why five times when you encounter a problem in order to get to the root cause. Managers in organizations practising TQM often use five whys to generate Ishikawa diagrams to identify the root cause of problems.

Food Miles

The distance that food travels from source to consumer.

Global Positioning Systems (GPS)

GPS systems have helped transport and logistics management track deliveries and identify the location of vehicles carrying out the deliveries. For example, UPS and FedEx use satellite tracking to identify the precise location of parcels and vehicles. GPS systems can help planners to change routings, timings and other variables that make up the transport management system.

Hollow Corporation

This term was coined in the 1980s to describe organizations that did not desire to own assets but instead built dynamic networks to respond quickly to demand. Flexibility and responsiveness required these organizations to adopt extensive outsourcing of suppliers to meet customer demand. The practice of pure brokering reflects the title 'hollow corporation'.

Horizontal Integration

Acquisition of other organizations at the same stage in the chain of distribution as the acquirer. For example, a retailer purchasing another retail organization, a wholesaler buying another wholesaler, a producer buying other producers.

INCOTERMS
International Commercial Terms define the duties of buyer and seller at each stage in the movement of goods. The terms define who does what (transport, export clearance, import clearance and who absorbs cost and takes the risk. Commonly used terms include: Ex Works (a named place of delivery usually the seller's dockside, Free Carrier (FCA) a named place where goods are cleared for export and lodged with a carrier specified by the buyer, Free Alongside Ship (FAS) goods cleared for export are delivered to named port and carrier when all risks are taken over by the buyer, Free on Board (FOB) risks and costs are passed to buyer when the goods are on board a named vessel at a named port, Carriage Paid to (CPT) named place and cleared for export at which point the buyer assumes responsibility for all risks and costs, Carriage Insurance Paid (CIP) similar to CPT but cargo insurance must be paid by the seller, Cost and Freight (CFR) seller agrees to pay transport costs but not insurance, Cost, Insurance and Freight (CIF) seller agrees to pay transport cost and insurance, Delivered at Frontier (DAF) to named place, Delivered Ex-ship (DES) goods made available to buyer on board ship, Delivered Ex Quay (DEQ) as above but at the quayside, Delivered Duty Unpaid (DDU), Delivered Duty Paid (DDP).

Just-in-Time (JiT)
JiT systems move inventories to the next stage in a supply chain to meet demand. Delivery is made when the inventory is required and not before, hence just in time to perform operations or to be used by the final consumer. The major benefits of JiT are lower inventory cost in a supply chain, increased quality through waste avoidance, obsolescence or deterioration, reduced lead times and greater efficiency in operations.

Kaizen	Continuous improvement to add value and remove cost by removing waste (Muda), smoothing flows by removing unevenness (Mura) and (Muri) removing difficulties.
Kanban	Kanban is a visual card system of inventory control that operates a pull system of production so that inventories are only supplied when they are required. See the text for a full explanation of use in practice.
Kieretsu	A network of Japanese firms with historical and/or equity linkages in a vertical or horizontal chain.
Last In First Out (LIFO)	A type of inventory system based on last in first out. Accounting systems sometimes adopt this system for valuing inventories.
Lean Production and Lean thinking	Lean production systems search for ways to lower cost and add value to production processes. Lean production systems developed in the Japanese automobile industry at Toyota. The concept is simple based upon kaizen philosophy removing waste (muda), smooth flows (mura) and removing difficulties (muri). Lean thinking is the antidote to muda developed by Ohno who identified seven types of waste. J. P. Womack and D. T. Jones (1996, *Lean Thinking*, London: Simon & Schuster) added an eighth 'goods and services that don't meet the needs of the customer'. The key to lean thinking is 'specify value, to line up all value-creating activities for a product along a value stream and to make flow smoothly at the pull of the customer in pursuit of perfection'.
Logistics	Movement, lodging and supplying goods.
Manufacturing Requirements Planning (MRPII)	Expands MRP into a capacity-planning tool with financial interfaces that translate operational plans into cost with a simulation tool to facilitate 'what if' decisions.
Markdown Optimization	Software systems designed to balance real-time supply and demand data in order to select poorer performing lines that can be discounted to clear inventory. Better performing lines remain at full price.

Materials Requirement Planning (MRP)	A computerized system of determining the quantity and timing requirements of materials used in production.
Milk Runs	A routing of supplies or delivery vehicles that make multiple pick-ups and drop offs. Often these are short journeys between stores or places nearby stores without holding stock that can be delivered quickly to satisfy interim customer demand.
MRO	Maintenance, Repairs and Operations.
OEM	Original Equipment Manufacturer.
Open Book Accounting	Financial information is shared between supply chain partners that is relevant to what they do.
Outsourcing	The trend to move operations outside the supplier organization to take advantage of lower cost and/or better quality or efficiency offered by another supplier. Outsourcing as a concept can be traced back to 'make or buy' decisions. Is it better to make an item yourself or buy it in from outside? Many organizations outsource operations. For example, publishers outsource typesetting and printing of books. In effect they can be hollow corporations with capabilities to manage sourcing, production, marketing and distribution. The capabilities may be bought in from outside and simply co-ordinated by the organization's management team. There are debates about which activities ought to be outsourced and many commentators say that non-core activities should be outsourced. However, there is a growing trend to outsource even core activities. One significant issue is that organizations need to know what is core and non-core before making decisions.
Perfection	A term used in lean production to indicate complete elimination of muda so that the value stream creates value and not cost.
PESTEEL	Sometimes referred to as PEST or SLEPT. This enlarged form of the term reflects that analysis of the business environment should encompass, political, economic,

socio-cultural, technological, ethical, ecological and legal issues. These influencing factors will give rise to opportunities or threatsfrom the wider environment.

Plan Do Check Act (PDCA)	An operational improvement tool applied to each activity in a production cycle.
poka yoke	A mistake proofing device or procedure to prevent defects during manufacture. For example, if any assembly is missing a component it cannot proceed to the next stage.
Price Optimization	Software systems designed to test the elasticity of demand discriminating between goods that are price sensitive and non-price sensitive to improve total turnover and earn higher margins on non-price sensitive goods.
Promotion Optimization	Software designed to select lines for price promotion using algorithms that balance consumer demand patterns, stock availability and sales forecasts.
Pull Inventory Systems	An inventory system that responds to 'actual' customer demand rather than forecast demand.
Purchase Order (P.O.)	A firm commitment to buy.
Push Inventory System	An inventory system that supplies to forecast demand rather than actual customer demand.
Quick Response (QR)	It is a form of time-based competition. Organizations need to be responsive to the customer and fast in producing and delivering. QR was a technique developed by KSA for the US Apparel and Textile Supply Chain in the mid 1980s its purpose was to develop competitive capabilities to deliver faster to hold off lower priced foreign imports threatening the industry. QR is now practised in many sectors and by many nations including low cost competitors. QR is about getting the right product to the right place at the right time.
Relationships in the Supply Chain	Relationships within a supply chain may be categorized by type from arms length through to strategic alliances and partnerships. At each progressive stage of relationship the parties work more closely together

and at the final stages may compete through collaborative strategies that integrate systems, policies, processes and procedures. Relationship approaches are often claimed to be 'win–win' strategies for supply chain management, which have benefits of lowering cost or improving revenue streams for parties within a supply chain compared to transactional approaches, which tend to focus on 'win–lose'. 'Relationship contract theory' recognizes that relationships are interdependent across supply chain organizations.

Replenishment Optimization	Software designed to maximize sales and minimize inventories taking account of real time sales data, inventory holding and replenishment lead times.
Retail Distribution Centre (RDC)	A central distribution centre servicing a number of stores in geographically defined area.
Revenue Optimization	Software systems designed to maximize sales and profit through balancing price, promotions and mark-downs.
Reverse Logistics	This is a term used to describe the process of moving products from customers back up the supply chain. (e.g. returning goods for credit, returns for repair or re-works, warranty returns, re-usable containers, a trade-in, consignment agreed returns, product recall, recalibrations, and not-fit-for-purpose supplies).
RFP	Request for proposal. Buying firms issue a document detailing what work is required and request suppliers to make a proposal. Proposals will be evaluated according to predetermined decision criteria and selected suppliers will be chosen after interview or further representations that clearly demonstrate their capabilities to supply.
RFQ	Request for quotation. Similar to RFP processes but in this case a supplier is asked to quote for supplying goods and/or services. A quote is a firm price unlike proposals which are tentative and negotiable.

Sales Based Ordering (SBO)	A system of store replenishment using EPoS sales data to re-stock the store. The data is used to forecast future demand patterns at the store.
Shrinkage	Inventory losses that are difficult to explain and account for. For example, shrinkage may be a consequence of theft.
Sigma Six	A statistical term used in 'world-class organizations' to represent zero defects. Statistically any processes in control (99.99 per cent) is said to have zero defects, which is defined as 0.01 per cent. Sigma six means that all processes fall within ±3 standard deviations of the mean. Organizations who pursue world-class status have 'black belts' who are champions of sigma six. See text for further explanation. 6 sigma = 3.4 defects per million or put another way is 99.999 71 per cent perfect. Other measures are: −5 sigma = 230 defects per million 4 sigma = 6 210 defects per million 3 sigma = 66 800 defects per million 2 sigma = 308 000 defects per million 1 sigma = 690 000 defects per million.
Social Network Theory	This has been used to explain the nature of supply chain relationships and to move the discussion from a previously economic exchange focus towards a relationship explanation of supply networks. See Relationships in the supply chain above.
Space Optimization	Systems designed to match available selling space with appropriate product lines to maximize returns (profits and sales) given consumer demand patterns
Standard Costing	Standard costing systems are developed to set cost around the planned cost for completing a task. Standard costs are planned costs usually set in advance of the budget period as the standard against which actual costs can be measured. Variances obtained by comparing actual and standard costs are then used as performance measures from which to take appropriate management actions to control budgets.

Stock Keeping Units (SKUs)

An identifiable line held in store. For example, 500 ml own brand detergent. SKUs are identified by a unique stock keeping code, e.g. a unique bar code that identifies the items.

Strategic Alliance

Strategic alliances are formed to compete through cooperating. Co-operation might be at any stage of operation within a value chain, purchasing, production, distribution, marketing and sales. Airlines, for example, have strategic alliances to try and cover complementary routes in order to attract customers to purchase an air ticket. The nature of a strategic alliance is cooperative to compete against other airlines not in the alliance. Thus taking customers from them. Without such strategic alliances the individual supplier airlines would be at a significant disadvantage against a competitor who could cover the routes themselves without cooperating.

Supply Chain

Covers all activities associated in acquiring and moving products/services from source to end user. Extraction (mining, quarrying, drilling for minerals), growing, producing through manufacture raw materials, components, work in progress through to finished goods to be distributed and delivered to the customer and lastly to the consumer. Source, plan, make and deliver are often used to describe supply chain activities.

Supply Chain Management (SCM)

SCM coordinates and integrates supply chain activities to deliver customer value. Efficiency and effectiveness are keys to managing supply chain processes. Integration is required to remove functional and organizational barriers that prevent better customer value being delivered.

Supply Chain Strategy

Supply chain strategies need to focus on customer demand patterns to ensure capacity to plan, source, make and deliver superior performance compared with competitors. SC strategies may be designed to do existing things better (through more

	efficiency in current operations) and/or to do better things (through designing more effective systems, processes, policies, facilities and modus operandi).
Symbol Group	These are voluntary associations formed when wholesale organizations reach agreement with independent small retail chains. For example, Spa, Londis. The retailer receives a group identity, better discounts technological support, national and local advertising/promotion in exchange for guaranteeing to purchase agreed volumes of goods.
Takt time	Available production time divided by the rate of customer demand e.g. demand is 60 per day of a sku and the time allowed to produce is 120 minutes the takt time is 2 minutes.
Target Cost	The design, development and production cost that cannot be exceeded.
Third Party Logistics (3PL)	Outsourcing logistics functions to a third party supplier of services. Often specialist carriers such as Excel Logistics, DTP, Salvessen, Tibbet & Britten.
Throughput Time	Time taken from concept launch through to the end customer. It includes waiting or queuing times. A measure of time taken in a system.
Total Cost of Ownership	TCO recognizes that costs are incurred pre-purchase, during the purchase transaction and post purchase. TCO is important because it involves costs other than simple transaction cost.
Total Quality Management (TQM)	A system designed to continuously improve products and processes to deliver customer benefits.
Toyota Seven (muda) Wastes Defined by Ohno	Overproduction, waiting, unnecessary transport of materials, overprocessing, inventories, unnecessary movements, and producing defective products.
Transaction Cost	Transaction cost is 'friction in the physical exchange process' according to economists. Transaction cost economics recognizes all costs involved with a transaction, which

may include: drafting a contract, negotiating costs, cost of any risks and social costs. Transaction costs do not include all pre-acquisition costs, relationship costs or post-acquisition costs. The theory of transaction cost economics, does however recognize that many transaction costs have been reduced through collaboration.

Value Added

A measure of difference in a system between input cost and output cost. Value added is usually measured in monetary terms e.g. the cost of raw materials, labour and overhead incurred in a process = $100 and the sales invoice for the finished item is $150, therefore value added would be ($150 − $100) = $50.

Value Stream

Specific activities needed to design, order and provide a specific product from concept launch into the customer's hands.

Vendor Managed Inventory (VMI)

VMI systems are managed by the supplier. For example, Wrangler's parent corporation VF has an arrangement with Wal-Mart to supply clothes to stores. Wal-Mart EPoS sales data is shared with VF and they forecast forward demand and replenish in-store stock accordingly. Inventories are not paid for by the retailer until sold. Ownership of the goods does not transfer from vendor to buyer until the point of sale. The benefits to the retailer are clear: reduces risk of holding unwanted inventories, lowers stock-holding cost and improves cash flows. For the supplier the benefits are that they can see a forward demand window and build their capacities and production operations to meet demand. They avoid missed sales through not having inventory available in stores and they lower operating costs through better production planning and inventory control. The downside might be an initial worsening of cash flow when establishing a VMI system.

Vertical Integration

Vertical integration is a growth strategy based on acquiring organizations at different points in a distribution chain. For example, a retailer takes over a supplier, who has perhaps in turn already bought into farms or factories to ensure supplies. A fully vertically integrated organization would own raw material suppliers, manufacturers, wholesalers and retail stores.

Warehouse	Storage facility where goods remain for extended time periods.
WAVCO	A weighted average cost valuation of inventory.
Win–lose	This is a strategy based on adversarial negotiations with one winner and one loser.
Win–win	This is a strategy based on collaboration to improve both parties position. Both win–lose and win–win were terms used in the development of 'Game Theory'.
Zero Based Budgets	These are budgets developed without reference to prior budgets. In other words you begin from a zero base and build the budget needed to achieve the result.
Zero Defects	See sigma six. Organizations that are striving to be considered 'world class' pursues a continuous improvement programme in their processes so that the possibility of defective production is eliminated. Crosby introduced the notion of zero defects and his mantra was 'right first time'.

Author Index

Index